# *Ben Jordan's*
# AUTOMOTIVE JARGON

## FOR THE CAR OWNER

### FROM THE

## SHADE TREE MECHANIC'S
# AUTOMOBILE
# DICTIONARY
## WITH
# LAGNIAPPE

NOTE  I: Unrestricted permission is granted in advance to
         any reader of of this book to copy, to quote from,
         or to reproduce all or any part of the **AUTOMOBILE
         DICTIONARY**.  The rationale: to encourage widespread
         dissemination of greater automotive literacy.

NOTE II: All profits from the sale of this **AUTOMOBILE
         DICTIONARY** will be donated to selected SAE
         (Society of Automotive Engineers) Student Groups
         at selected engineering schools and universities.
         The rationale: to promote this worthwhile program
         of the SAE that produces better automotive leaders
         and insures better automobiles and products.

Proudly printed in the United States of America by:
Clements Printing, 795 South Jason Street, Denver, CO  80223


Illustrations by: Bill Ballas, automobile artist _extraordinaire_


Library of Congress Catalog Card Number: 95-90447

ISBN 0-9647392-0-8

If you have any comments, corrections, questions, or suggestions
regarding this **AUTOMOBILE DICTIONARY**, please write the publisher

**PUBLISHED BY:**

WINDMILL JOUSTER BOOKS

1621 SOUTH GLENCOE STREET, DENVER, CO  80222-3915

# A Doctoral Dedication Nonpareil
## to
## Barbara

Barbara, my wife, in 1987, got my engine revved up and accelerated me in the direction of writing this dictionary. Her insistence and persistence augmented by the spectre of a bread-and-water diet raised my inspiration level and motivational temperature until the pen began to write--and define--automobile words. Her frustration with my lexicon mix of shade-tree patois convoluted with stoichiometric stuff and "Bucky" Fuller's Dymaxion dictionographer dictums peaked--and then stalled at top-dead-center--when she approached her college library and resident librarians for assistance.

All wore Ph.D. mantles and a few Phi Beta Kappa keys, but none could define, pronounce, spell, or understand "automobile words". Their reading room housed not a single automobile dictionary (but had volumes about such obscurities as: International Dictionary of Obscenities; General Dictionary of Heraldry; Dictionary of Skin-Diving, a 262 page paperback @ $110.00; Dictionary of Polygraphy, for $125.00; Dictionary of Animal Names; and Dictionary of Cosmetics and Toiletries--it's only $175.00. The best in-house pedestal dictionary defined "automobile" with two lines and spent a quarter-page defining "aardvark", barely mentioned Henry Ford but failed to alphabetize Carlo Abarth, Andre Citroen, Augie and Fred Duesenberg, Bucky Knudsen, Ferruccio Lamborghini, Sir Henry Royce, or "Engine Charlie" Wilson. But their same big book of words expounded extensively about an obscure Cuban Communist revolutionary.

What took so long? Barbara's encouragement and expertise spearheaded the research on 5,016 different marques and the collecting of tons of bits and pieces of automobile lore and trivia.

But the inevitable nemesis of work--the automobile itself--personified by a 1924 Model T Ford depot hack (turbocharged and 100% hydrogen-fueled + burning ten other fuels), a couple of world landspeed record-holding race cars, car clubs, car shows, and swap meets, 2 or 3 go-to-work and fun cars that demanded attention (driving, drooling over, lying about, and petting), and periodic grease jobs, oil-changes, and tune-ups--occupied work time and became prime time.

Possibly the greatest roadblock confronting this "dictionary" was my "windmill jousting" against the hordes of Barnumesque bastards, bumbling bureaucrats, and political panderers whose avarice and criminality in aggrandizing, subsidizing, and selling the technically illiterate American public "air" and "water" vehicle fuels and gimcracks claiming to make our automobiles operate pollution-free for pennies-a-day while burning their "snake oil". A minor pot-hole along the road to this book was an overworked word processor (from screening out my vituperation against the crooks and inserting "politically correct" phrases in hundreds of pages of letters-to-the-Editor and magazine articles rebutting the "air" and "water" fuel advertising lies).

Barbara was ably aided and abetted by her brother--a Brother WP-80.

1621 SOUTH GLENCOE STREET, DENVER, CO  80222-3915

Upper-right
Front Cover

1959 Abarth Zagato
"Double-Bubble"

AUTObiography on
following page
p. V

## ABOUT THE COVER CARS

Bottom Front Cover
Landspeed Record-holding Lakester, "BOCKSCAR"
(Named to Commemorate the B-29 That Ended World War II)

Reprint from BONNEVILLE RACING NEWS
pp. VI, VII, VIII

Bottom Rear Cover

Hydrogen-fueled and Turbocharged
1924 Model T Ford Depot Hack

Handout Flyer used at Automobile Shows
to keep the
Handcrankers, the Lookee-Louies, and Tire-kickers
at a respectable distance
p. IX

# THE 1959 ABARTH ZAGATO "DOUBLE-BUBBLE" COUPE

First purchased in Honolulu and raced in SCCA events in Hawaii until returned to the United States in 1964. This car broke the U.S. Army's long-standing I-GT record of 92+ mph with a speed of 117.896 mph (burning gasoline) at Speed Week 1979. This record was boosted to 120.872 mph in 1980 and remained in the record book until broken in 1992 (121.779 mph). It became the first (at Speed Week 1981) and for the next ten years, the only car to run at the Salt Flats burning 100% hydrogen fuel. Built, driven, and owned by Ben Jordan, Denver, CO, and always wearing Air Force markings, Clemson University decals, a Tau Beta Pi "bent", and a driver topped off by a racing helmet sprinkled with Clemson athletic team's "Tiger Paws". Rah! Rah! Rah!

Converted to 100% hydrogen-fueled and turbocharged for a total out-of-pocket cost of $12.32 plus off-the-shelfstuff (to shame our Solar Energy Research Institute for spending millions of my tax dollars on a "Hydrogen Car" that wasn't and is now rusting away, 1995, at the Colorado School of Mines as a "monument to government waste"), the Zagato was first driven by Ben Jordan at Speed Week 1981 and then driven by M/Sgt. John G. Gowetski of our USAF B-52 hydrogen bomb wing at Blytheville AFB, AR. The USAF newsreel camera crew photographed the Bonneville runs and their documentary film was shown on the October 1981 "Commander's Call" to every unit in the world-wide US Air Force.

The car competed annually at the Bonneville Nationals Speed Trials from 1964 through 1981. It is now competing in Vintage Car races--last race was at Steamboat Springs, CO, Labor Day 1994, driven by Charles M. ("Pete") Kittridge, III, to whom it was given in 1985.

The Abarth has run at the "Flats" with 750cc, 1000cc, and 1500cc displacement engines. It ran with a one-of-a-kind "porcelain" (chromium oxide) crankshaft in 1968 and with an internally-thermally-insulated engine (plasma-sprayed zirconium oxide) in 1969.

First at Bonneville? Documented!

# BONNEVILLE

## RACING NEWS

VOLUME IV, VII                                1994

# SILENT SECOR TALKS part II

pg. 19

The Bockscar lakester, a record setter was named after the B-29 that bombed Nagasaki at the end of World War II. (page 10)

Jack Kelly is kept shaded by his 'pseudo crew chief' and wife, Jerry as they push forward to the starting line at El Mirage. (page 14)

#777, the Kenz and Leslie Streamliner was America's Fastest Hot Rod into the late 1950's. The car is completely restored and is now shown at events across the nation. (page 6)

Bob George (left) signs over his motorcycle streamliner to the new owner, Jack Dolan. This could be the year of the BIG motorcycles. (page 18)

# BOCKSCAR, LAKESTER OR
# WWII BOMBER

Lest the world forget (or never knew) 'twas the B-29 named 'Bockscar' that dropped the Fat Man atomic bomb on Nagasaki, ending World War II. For Speed Week 1985, Mountain States Automation of Denver, Colorado, named their lakester, 'Bockscar' to commemorate the memorable feat of its namesake and to heighten public awareness of its historical significance.

The one-liter lakester has been at the Salt Flats for 20?? consecutive years with a crew dedicated to furthering automotive technology and to promoting honor and respect for the American military establishment. Bockscar and crew are aiming at the big 200 mph.

Bill 'Stainless' Steele, a Boeing Aircraft B-52 Technical Representative with the USAF San Antonio Air Depot for the past several years, is the Bockscar crew chief. He fit this role because he is the biggest of the motley crew. At about 6'6" and weighing an eighth of a ton, Bill is too big to fit into the car. M/Sgt. John Gowetski, USAF retired, is the usual driver. The littlest crew member is Travis Sutton. He has attended Speed Week six years, ever since his first Pit Pass was pinned to his diapers. He is 'Chief Anvil Disassembler' and assistant

to his brother Nicky, age 11, the crew's 'Chief Go-fer'. Martyn and Kevin Sutton provide the high-tech home for the race car in Denver and a lot of go-fast to the car at Bonneville.

This race car first ran in 1974 as a 500 cc Streamliner named 'Dymaxion II'. It was originally built so Jimmy Sack, a paraplegic Navy veteran, could satisfy his dream of driving on the salt. Jimmy never drove however because he was unable to move clear of the car in the event of a crash.

Power was changed to a 750 cc Honda 4-cylinder engine and the wheels were brought outside the body making it a lakester. Car # 1000 was renamed Bockscar in 1985 and driven by Martyn Sutton at 132.316 mph for a new J/Gas Lakester record--having qualified on its first run over the flying mile. Requalifying in the fuel class, a new methanol/nitomethane record of 133.311 mph was established that same year.

Bockscar set a succession of land speed records on both gasoline and fuel in the 750 cc lakester class. It returned to Bonneville in 1986 and raising its gas record to 141.011 mph. In 1988 its J/Fuel Lakester record was boosted to 148.647 mph, taking another trophy home.

Seeking more speed, the Denver crew stuffed a big 60 cubic inch engine under the hood and at Speed Week '89 estab-

lished a new one-liter gas record of 176.911 mph, a quantum jump from the previous mark of 149.672 mph.

Back for the '90 Speed Trials, Bockscar boosted the 'I' class fuel record from 147.605 mph to 182.997 mph . Fittingly, this record run was cheered on by Major Fred Bock, USAF Retired, and his World War II B-29 crew. They were attending their reunion at Wendover where the B-29 atomic bomb crews trained during the war. The lakester again saluted the crew of its namesake B-29 with a subsequent one-way speed of 208.177 mph.

When Bockscar visits the Salt again the car crew will be trying to boost both of their records (gas and fuel) over the magic 200 mph barrier. Bockscar currently owns the I/FL record at 182.997 mph and the I/GL mark at 194.340 mph (1992).

Car # 1000 should be named Bockscar IV. In 1922 Fred Bock raced his one boy-power Stutz bearcat pedal car on the sidewalks of Greenville, Michigan and called it Bockscar (I). Fred became a life-long automobile aficionado from sharing a dentist with Fred Duesenberg and listening to his car lore. He flew Bockscar (II) from Wendover in June 1945 to Tinian and the Nagasaki atomic bomb mission that convinced Hirohito to

capitulate unconditionally thus ending World War II.

Fred's B-29 navigator, Lt. Leonard Godfrey, and Lt. Ira Weatherly, co-pilot on the B-29 'Straight Flush' owned the only private automobile on the Island of Tinian in 1945. Five bottles of whiskey purchased the car which was a Japanese warplane belly-tank powered by a 5 horsepower waterpump engine. This often chauffeured William Laurence, the New York Time's Pulitzer Prize winning war correspondent who covered our atomic program. This car qualifies as a Lakester and Bockscar III.

For those who drive Toyotas you may have Bockscar II to thank. Eiji Toyoda, Chairman, Toyota Motor Company, indicated in his autobiography, Toyota Fifty Years in Motion (1987), the possibility that Bockscar II may have fathered your present car. Quoting: "The last bombing raid (on Koromo) came on August 14, in the afternoon. Three B-29's each dropped a large bomb, either a 500-kilo or one-tonners, I don't know which."

Fred Bock recently informed Mr. Toyoda, now 79, that his Bockscar dropped the one 10,000 pound 'Pumpkin' a high-explosive twin of the atomic 'Fat Man' that destroyed Nagasaki five days earlier. The bomb virtually obliterated the Toyota factory.

Mr. Toyoda verified that there was not one casualty or injury because he had evacuated everyone when he was warned by leaflets dropped from a B-29 on August 13 that Koromo would be destroyed the next day. Koromo has been rebuilt and renamed Toyota City. World War II officially ended while Bockscar was still winging its way home to its nesting place on Tinian.

Bockscar (II) is permanently enshrined in the USAF Museum in Dayton, Ohio. The lakester Bockscar (IV) rekindles patriotism and continues to attack records at the Bonneville Salt Flats.

continued next page

The Bockscar and crew left to right; Kevin Sutton, John Gowetski, Martyn Sutton and Bill Steele.

# Bockscar continued

Before the B-29 or the lakester, there was the original Bockscar, a Stutz Bearcat driven by the one boy-power of Fred Bock.

Fred Bock, Major USAF retired posed by the Bockscar lakester after its record run. The B-29 World War II crew was at Wendover for their reunion while the meet was running.

## AUTObiography
(Ghost written by: the shades of Henry Ford and Henry Cavendish)

I'm recycled from junked Rolls Royce and Duesenberg automobiles with some armor-plate scrap added from the WWI battleships that Henry bought to make Model "Tees" tough. I'm about as "factory original" as any "Tin Lizzie" that Henry's 5-dollar-a-day hired hands ever rolled off his production line--except for my fuel tanks and delivery systems.

My owner has taught me to eat damn near anything that he eats. I run happily on eleven different fuels. My preference is 100% Hydrogen, although it spices up anything it's sprinkled on. Hershey bars are a close second among my dietary choices.

Today, I'm operating interchangeably on Hydrogen or natural gas. Either fuel can be selected, while driving, in any desired ratio from 100% natural gas/0% Hydrogen to 100% Hydrogen/0% natural gas. Either fuel or any mix can be supplied to the engine reasonably close to stoichiometry (equivalence ratio=1.0). Both fuels are stored at an initial tank gauge pressure of 3000psi. Hydrogen pressure is reduced at the tank valve to 20psi and natural gas is reduced to 100psi.

Natural gas enters the engine intake system through an off-the-shelf IMPCO "mixer". Hydrogen is fed by a home-built port-injection timed-pulse system. The entire Hydrogen system was "bolted-on", without change, from my world landspeed (gasoline-fueled) record-holding IGT one-liter Coupe just as it ran at the Bonneville Salt Flats burning 100% Hydrogen at our National Speed Week in 1981.

My turbocharger is **NOT** for power. Any Model "T" would resent that. **VIGOROUSLY!** The turbo does serve a necessary functional purpose. It's waste-gated to compensate for our altitude and for the inherent 15% loss with natural gas and for the 20-25% loss with Hydrogen. Because the incoming gaseous fuels displace so much of the engine's breathing.

**HYDROGEN IS THE FUEL OF SPACE SHIP EARTH'S FUTURE!** The only one! Hydrogen is the most plentiful (it's 93% of our universe--by atom count), zero-polluting (its exhaust is nothing but the purest of water), instantly recyclable ($H_2$ to $H_2O$ to $H_2$), the most energy-dense (60,000 BTUs/#), safe(er) (than any other fuel), cheap(er) (right now, if our environment has any value--in the near future as all other fuels are depleted and their price rises exponentially). Hydrogen's full potential will arrive as soon as we get clean electricity from nuclear (preferably fusion) or high-efficiency photovoltaics. Then all heat users will burn it and all electrics will fuel-cell it.

Recognizing Webster's infallibility, how can any reasonable mind--technically literate--support any "alternative", which Webster defined as "what we use when we can't get what is most desirable or best, an inferior substitute, ersatz"? Opt for the **BEST!**

Our political pollution pimps and those with vested interests, irrationally tout their "most favored" "alternatives" as being less-polluting, cheaper, better, more powerful, more plentiful, safer, and the best. When they **Ain't!** They price-compare fuels that are heavily-taxed (gasoline/diesel at 40+¢/gallon) with fuels that are highly-subsidized such as electricity, Hydrogen, and natural gas that are virtually un-taxed! And claim their's is cheaper. Phony as a three-dollar-bill! Many short-change our technically illiterate society by claiming better mileage and performance for their unequivalent "equivalent gallon" but not delivering equivalent measures of energy (BTUs).

IX

# LAGNIAPPE

Best defined as a Cajun word cobbled together from pidgin French and pidgin Spanish by the same New Orleans chef who first ladled up a cup of that aromatic melange concocted with bay leaves, crawdads, lobster, and shrimp--pronounceable from the chef's patois only as "gumbo", with a musical lilt.

P.T. Barnum, with his cynical bent, defined lagniappe as his "something for nothing" syndrome. European bakers/pastry-makers gave us the "baker's dozen"--with the thirteenth roll that was always added--not from goodness from the heart, but because of harsh laws that were marked with penalties like "sneezing in the bag" (the guillotine) against anyone who shortchanged a purchaser, many of whom were unable to count.

The Cajuns truly put a halo on the word "lagniappe". To them it attained benigness by meaning: a small heartfelt gift to every customer at the time of purchase, as a token of sincere appreciation; something given gratuituously and to insure good measure--never hinting of the crassness of an honorarium, a tip, or vigorish.

So, what's "lagniappe" doing in an automobile dictionary? At the end of every letter--from A through Z--you get lagniappe, some freebie words--for free! And the opportunity to "Add your own words"--also for free--to the next edition of this dictionary, using the address of the publisher included in this book--but no further lagniappe--<u>you</u> buy the postage stamp from Uncle Sugar.

For those with Barnumesque leanings, the cynical, the perceptive, and of <u>un</u>reasonable mind who view all automobile aficionados, with jaundiced eye--as "used-car salesmen" descended directly from Arabian horse-traders and rug merchants--you are right! Your lagniappe is tainted. You are getting <u>this</u> lagniappe not as a benign freebie, but because the book printer demanded large lagniappe largesse to re-alphabetize, insert, and repaginate the automobile words that some vicarious proof-reader thought had to be added. So it was done the easy way--the cheapo way--by the author. Maybe, too, just because he thinks no one dared do it this way until now.

One final request, my plea to you to use the address of the publisher to send your word(s) and definitions as <u>your</u> lagniappe to automobiliana. Comments, corrections, and pertinent potpourri are welcomed and invited for inclusion in the next edition of this dictionary--anything that can be defined as lagniappe toward better communications between automotive engineers/mechanics, shadetrees, and automobile aficionados/owners. Between man and machine. Selah. <u>M'aidez</u>!

## PERMISSION TO COPY, QUOTE, OR REPRODUCE
(your first lagniappe)

Unrestricted permission to copy, to quote, or reproduce any part of this dictionary is granted to any reader. Such should further the author's goal of better communications/relationships among the producers/

sellers, the buyers/users, and the maintainers/regulators of automobiles. There is urgent need for a closer kinship within the nuclear family that genuflects to our common incomparable icon--the automobile.

So why was this book even copyrighted? Maybe because it's "politically correct", knowing that "Uncle Sugar's" Copyright Office is another toothless paper tiger like his other automotive watch dogs: DOE, DOT, EPA, FTC, and U.S. Patent Office--all presenting detours, headwinds, roadblocks, potholes, and washouts copyrighted and intended to impede automotive progress.

The author's goal is (possibly naively) to convert more evangelists who will practice and preach the Scriptures of Science--while willingly obeying Society's Statutes with the same fervor that Nature enforces her laws upon Automobiliana. Spread the word!

## THE AUTHOR'S PHILOSOPHY
(as if you couldn't guess)

Conservative. Built upon a foundation of shade-tree country logic, six years of college undergraduate/graduate engineering studies, military graduation from the Army/Navy Aircraft Engine Design School on the Pratt-Whitney R-4360 ("corncob") engine (1942) and the Allison V-1710 Engine Overhaul School (1943), and an in-born devotion and respect for our great friend--the automobile.

The author's acknowledged anger and bias against the automobile's enemies are strong, deep-seated, and worn as a badge of honor. High on his "hate list": the simple political solutions to complex automotive problems--ALWAYS WRONG!; the phony Ph.Ds. (calling themselves "Doctor" when they **Ain't**) and charlatans among our government agencies, our industry, and our entrepreneurs who promote, support, sell, and subsidize fraudulent automotive devices and fuels claiming to enhance performance, improve economy, and reduce emissions; the U.S. Patent Office that puts its approval number on every damn one of the gimcracks--none of which works as claimed; our national newsmedia that publicizes and praises their arcane "discoveries and inventions" while engendering distrust and disdain of our automotive industry and scientific community--because of the Fourth Estate's technical illiteracy and anti-science stance; our foot-dragging "big bark-no bite" government "watch dogs"--DOE, DOT, EPA, and FTC--whose feeble efforts try to solve problems by throwing money at 'em (flushing our tax dollars into their cesspool of incompetence and inefficiency).

The automobile's very survival in a climate of Uncle Sugar's mandated "friends" (regulators)--who needs enemies?--attests to its true greatness.

The pip-squeak pruriency of the automobile's "Nader enemies" is but a ripple when compared to the tidal wave emanating from our mandated obstructionist "friends" that surround us.

# PREFACE

Cross my heart and the shades of Daniel Webster! And of Willie Shakespeare! The author was just benighted as a "Certified Fool"--by a Federal Judge.

Remember the legalese cliche "He who represents himself before the bar has a fool for an attorney?" The author went pro se before the United States District Court in Denver (that means that he stood naked and quaking with ignorance before that dreaded federal bench).

Can you imagine being surrounded by a gaggle of born-again cultist holy rollers "speaking in tongues" as they genuflected to the Almighty Bench? Amid the babble one could distinguish an occasional "whereas" and "wherefore", a cacophony of "alleged's", the changing beat of "tort, tort, tort", the low but unmistakable rhythm section humming "contingency" and "retainer", until the jaundiced judge spake "overruled". Dead quiet reigned. And nobody knew who had said what, let alone what anybody had meant.

After escaping from the sinister shadow of the Bench, the author's dentist's emergency network summoned with a "Stat . . . Stat, come with lights and siren". The dentist, a wannabe do-it-yourselfer automobile mechanic, needed help installing a new ring-gear in his VW Bug. Working on the crankshaft end-float, the author listened in wonderment while dentist-friend talked on his Cellular phone to patients about periodontics, temporal-mandibular-joints, ondodontics, and root-canals.

Talk about confusion! The across-the-street neighbor, a medical doctor, sauntered over to kibitz. Doctor and dentist spoke in some foreign language that sounded like Latin . . . but 'twas Greek to me. When the author said, "Gimmie a dial indicator under here, "the dentist said, "Duh!" and the doctor wondered, "Whazzat?"

Every prestigious professional discipline genuflects to a proprietary jingoistic jargon, clearly conceived and structured to keep all non-members always on the outside of their inner sanctum. And to camouflage the vigorish that bloats their invoice for "professional services".

If you are an attorney or a medical doctor, forget your Latin phrases, and try a few "automobile" words on your favorite automobile mechanic. Listen and watch for the new rapport. Your automobile maintenance costs will be less, your car will get better fuel mileage, and you can brag at your club about the genius that you have found to take care of your car.

So, did 'ya ever wonder why we ordinary folk can't talk to each other? We've had no definitive dictionary of our jargon.

# FOREWORD

## (Ghost written by Real Ghosts)

Who needs an "automobile dictionary"? You do! The world does. All of us old time automobile aficionados needed one. Every day of our lives. But never had one!

Now you have one.

In the good old days before we became ghosts, when we started the world's "era of the motor car", we had it easy. The rank and file mule-skinner and the elitist carriage trade accepted everything we said and eagerly bought everything we built. For the first two decades of the twentieth century automobile technology muddled along somewhat aimlessly.

Our first big war lit the match that made things hum through the twenties and the thirties. Henry captured the attention of the working man with his mass of Tin Lizzies and his $5/hour produc- tion line pay rate. Many of automobiliana's greatest cars were built then but most of the companies that produced them fell victim to the Great Depression.

Most significantly, automobiliana's icons began to develop feet of clay. Too long imbued with the aura of mysticism around the new-fangled motor car, the general public gradually became aware that its racy car-toys had become utilitarian workhorses. The auto- mobile had arrived, and the world was ready. But couldn't speak the language.

"Boss Ket" arrived with the automobile (he literally pushed a jalopy on stage and let the spotlight of his genius transform it into a thoroughbred). About 1920, the Boss tired of the 37 days it took to hand-paint a car so he did the same job in hours. This one breakthrough, combined with his earlier Nirvana (the electric starter), may have sounded the death knell for Henry's all black "T"-Model in 1927. That had to be hand-cranked.

Remember, Henry had told the Boss that his Model T would never carry a self-starter as long as men had strong right arms? The Boss correctly retorted that broken arms, weak women, and not Mr. Ford would decide that issue. While the on-board starter and the fast multicolored paint jobs were doing in the "T", the Boss may have given birth to the "A" for Henry. Inadvertently.

Boss Ket gave birth to Ethyl after discovering that lead alone was very bad for exhaust valves. Adding bromine (maybe because it sounded like iodine, which also worked) the potion solved the lead problem. The General Motors development let the T's compression ratio of 3.6:1 jump to the A's 4.25:1, saving the Ford marque and Henry's millions.

Augie's Duesey, Benz's 540K, Bugatti's Royale, Pierce's V-12, Amos' Reo Royale, and Maybach's Zeppelin didn't fare so well. These all-time greatest of the species became extinct. Depression's depreciation "deep sixed 'em". Those great gas-guzzlers couldn't be given away by the time they were four years old. But look at what's happened to their price tags since we departed the scene.

Bugatti would never believe that a pizza delivery football fan paid over ten million $$$ for his big one (ex-Harrah's Bugatti Royale). Domino Pizza's Tom Monaghan was the cook.

Another war, our second big one, cast its shadow upon the reawakened automobile giants. Ford's River Rouge converted to bombers, Boss Ket's Allison and Packard to aircraft engines, and every shade-tree shop built tanks and guns. The cars of the forties were drowned out by the noise of World War II with only a few warmed-over 30's models rolling off the post-war production lines before 1950.

The Boss's swan song sounded as the '49 Caddy with the over-head valve V-8 hit the dealer show rooms, sporting tail-fins.

We're kinda glad we weren't around to see the Armenian rug-merchants and Arabian horse-traders reincarnated as new/used car dealers. We never knew that our great automobile legacy would become so convoluted. Our society saved to buy cars, paying in full before delivery. When we ruled the roost cars were made by men who spoke their language and cars could be fixed by the barefoot farm boy because he also lived and spoke automobiles. Fluently!

Where did we go wrong? Foreign-speaking bosses are now running things--the lawyer/financiers only speak "whereas" and "debentures", the scientists speak "stoichiometric", and the filling station mechanics drop "monkey wrenches" and "dikes". What the Hell are they saying? Grease Monkey. Mr. Goodwrench. Lemon Law. Power Brakes. Tape Deck. Tilt Wheel. Does anyone speak "auto-mobile" any more? Can you still buy: a Hand Crank? Buggy-Whip Holster? Lap-Robe? Cut-Glass Vase? Side Curtains? Wind Wings? Whazzat?

That's why we/you need an "automobile dictionary". This dictionary!


Channeled down through that great tailpipe in the sky by the shades of:

|  |  |
|---|---|
| Karl Benz | Floyd Clymer |
| Ettore Bugatti | Henry Ford |
| Walter P. Chrysler | Augie Duesenberg |
| Andre Citroen | Charles "Boss" Kettering |

All of whom spoke "automobile" without an accent.

## INDEX to the ALPHABET
### (If You Don't Know Your Automobile ABCs)

**A**    Obvious, as is the Auburn with pipes

**B**    Bentley, Bugatti, Buick--three Bs

**C**    Cord with a horizontal convex C and GO

**D**    Duesenberg with a "D".  What a Duesy dame

**E**    Easy--it's an Edsel--Going or Coming

**F**    Ford Flathead--with feminine fingernails

**G**    Graham Sharknose, not a Hollywood

**H**    Hudson Hornet, happy helmet, Honda/Hog?

**I**    Isetta, Italy's gift to itsy-bitsy people

**J**    Jordan, by Ned, Somewhere West of Laramie

**K**    Kissel--Amelia Earhart's Gold Bug legacy

**L**    Lincoln Mk I, the Continental Classic

**M**    Merc, to go cruisin' to the drive-in in

**N**    Nash, with a bed--and breakfast?

**O**    Opel's RAK 2, world's first rocket car

**P**    Packard's hood roof-line is a giveway

**Q**    See what a "Denver Boot" does to a Queen

**R**    A paper boy's Rolls-Royce--with Ribbs

**S**    How about a Starlight--it's a Studebaker

**T**    A 1959 Two-by-Two T-Bird, atop a Tee

**U**    A UniPower?  Who sez?  A "Limey"?

**V**    Herbie, the Vee, from "Love Bug"

**W**    Willys dragster goes a draggin'

**X**    Xenia, a memorial "X" to a road-kill

**Y**    Yenko "Stinger" Corvair climbs the "Peak"

**Z**    Zagato "Double-Bubble", a '59 Abarth <u>goer</u>

1

**Automobile:** The first word in the English language; the cornerstone of Americana and the first sound uttered by every newborn man-child. The most used word; the most revered word; the word that best describes modern man's machismo and ego--at the same time <u>auto</u>mobile is the most cussed word; the most discussed word; the most maligned word and the most antithetical and ill-defined of words. It's never spelled correctly: Bucky Fuller revealed its true lexicography--it's <u>ego</u>- mobile. It ain't <u>auto</u>mobile--did you ever see one automobiling along the San Diego Freeway? Sans driver? Selected synonyms: beetle, bucket-of-bolts, bug, cabriolet, caddy, car, classic, coach, coupe, deuce, dual-cowl, Edsel, fast-back, four-banger, grand am, hatch-back, high-boy, low-rider, pot, rag top, rattle-trap, tin lizzie, turtle-back, under-slung, wheels, et. al. Origin: In August 1449, Chief Pierce Arrow of the Goshute Indian Tribe at Wendover, Utah, sent the following smoke-signal message to Chief Izzy Edsel of the Shivwitz Indian Tribe down south of St. George, Utah: "Just lassoed a quarter horse Mustang with a Shibe paint job and a one-horsepower Pinto stallion . . . they really "ought to mobile" it out across our Bonneville Salt Flats". Hence, forevermore, <u>automobile</u>.

**A-Cars:** Of 392 worldwide "A-marqued" automobiles forty-two wore the American "marque" but none are worth remembering. The great Auburn (1900-1937) saved our national pride as one of Space Ship Earth's most memorable automobiles. After installing various odd-ball engines, e.g., Continental, Rutenber, Teetor, and Weidely, E. L. Cord bought the company in 1924 and built their own 4, 6, and Straight-Eight engines. In 1932 came the Auburn with a 6.4 litre V-12 engine complemented by a Columbia dual-ratio rear axle, sleek styling and fantastic performance--all for less than $1,000.00! Unbelievable, but true. One would be remiss not to chronicle Austrian Carlo Abarth who left Cisitalia to launch his own speed marque--"The Scorpion". Breathing speed and style into rather prosaic models of Fiat, Porsche, and Simca became Abarth's forte from 1950 through 1971. Wherever there was automobile racing on the world circuits a Carlo creation, carrying the Abarth name--like "Abou Ben Adhem's--led all the rest". In 1957 a 750cc Abarth averaged 111.92 mph for 72 hours--that's 8,058.24 miles in three days. The marque won the Nurburgring 1,000 kilometer sports car race five years in succession (1960-1964), and finished second in 1965. In 1967 an Abarth took fourth place in the European Hill-climb Championship and a 1-2-3 victory in the 1968 Nurburgring 500-Kilometers. A 2-litre Abarth team ran another 1-2-3 finish in the 1970 Circuit of Mugello. In 1979 a 1959 Abarth Zagato powered by a 1,000cc OTR engine broke the World Landspeed Record for the 1-liter GT Coupe Class at 120.872 mph--a record that stood firm until 1992. In 1981 the record-holding Abarth became the first race car timed through the Bonneville, Utah's, famous "flying mile"--burning 100% hydrogen as its fuel. Always prepared and driven by Ben Jordan --that's me.

**A:** generously applied throughout automobile history to designate all kinds of things, e.g., "A"-model Ford; Model "A" Duesenberg; "A"-frame; "A"-arm.

**AA:** designation of 1928-1931 Ford trucks, usually the one-ton and 1½-ton versions with dual rear wheels.

**AAA:** American Automobile Association. (1) A club originally just for motorists, now evolving as an insurance company, travel agency, and lobbyist powerhouse. (2) The marque of a German car (1919-1922) that is the first car of them all, when listed alphabetically.

**aaahoooga horn:** an early day mechanical vehicle warning device creating sound when the driver pushed hard on a toothed-plunger, causing it to impart ratcheting action against a flat spring strip. Bulb horn, a hand-powered air-horn.

**A-arm:** a suspension-locating beam, sometimes used singly per wheel or often as upper and lower supports with the base of the "A" hinged from the chassis. Most often to locate the front wheels but not uncommon at the rear corners. Also known as "wishbone", from the shape. The ball joints were located at the apex of the "A".

**Abarth:** internationally recognized performance version of several factory marques, e.g., Fiat, Porsche, Simca, et al. Abarths excelled in the smaller displacement classes for many years. Abarth relates to Fiat as Shelby relates to Ford, Gurney to Chrysler, and Yenko to Chevrolet.

**Abarth, Carlo:** the Austrian-born designer who breathed style and go-fast into prosaic factory stock vehicles that proudly accepted his name.

**A-belt:** popular-sized (about one-half inch in width) accessory-drive v-belt.

**ABS:** abbreviation for: (1) Anti-lock brake system that automatically senses vehicle-wheel lock-up and momentarily releases the braking force to stop tire-skidding and repetitively pulses pressure to the brakes. (2) Acrylonitrile-butadiene-styrene, a tough rigid synthetic plastic used for vehicle body panels. See anti-lock brake system.

**absolute humidity:** the mass of water vapor in a specified volume air. Weight of water per cubic volume of air. It can be expressed in any convenient units: usually as pounds per cubic foot or grams per cubic meter.

**absolute pressure:** true pressure of a substance or system.

**absolute temperature:** the degree (Centigrade or Fahrenheit) of heat intensity above absolute zero.

**absolute zero:** minus 273.16 degrees (-273.16°) Centigrade, minus 459.69 degrees (-459.69°) Fahrenheit, or 0 degrees Kelvin.

**A/C:** the universal designation for "air conditioning" and/or alternating current electricity. DC (direct current).

**accelerate:** (1) To cause to move faster. (2) To move faster. (3) To gain speed.

**acceleration:** the act or process of increasing speed or velocity. The state of being accelerated. The rate of change of speed or velocity.

**acceleration lane:** an extra roadway lane at freeway entrances to provide space for entering vehicles to get up to speed and to merge safely into traffic.

**accelerator:** the driver-operated foot pedal, hand lever, or automatic control that increases engine/vehicle speed. Foot feed. Foot throttle. Hand throttle.

**accelerator pump:** a mechanical device within the carburation system to provide extra fuel during increases in throttle opening thus maintaining optimum fuel/air ratios for effective combustion until a steady state operation of the engine (cruising) is resumed.

**accelerometer:** a meter that indicates the rate of increase in speed or movement usually in "G's" or in "feet-per-second-per-second". The gravity units are measures of the acceleration force.

**accessory:** an object, device or gimmick not essential in itself but adding to the beauty, convenience, or effectiveness of the vehicle. Bolt-on. Add-on.

**accessory "pack":** a package-grouping of accessories to enhance vehicle functioning or sometimes to encourage or induce the purchase of less desirable components in order to get something special.

**A/C compressor:** the mechanical pump that pressure-liquefies the refrigerant (usually Freon-12). The Freons are now (1995) being discontinued because of damage to our atmosphere.

**A/C condenser:** a radiator segment (usually in front of the automobile engine radiator) that cools the compressed refrigerant in the air conditioner system until it becomes a homogeneous liquid.

**accordion pleat:** a duct or a flat panel with pleats to allow easy adjustment to varying length or size requirements.

**accumulator:**  a container (device) for collecting and storing, as a battery for electricity or a pressure/vacuum tank for fluids.  Combined hydro-pneumatic tanks are used extensively in vehicle braking, suspension, and steering systems.

**ACD:**  the Auburn-Cord-Dusenberg club composed of members who are owners/admirers of those great cars.

**AC/DC converter:**  a mechanical or electronic device for changing alternating current electricity to direct current electricity.  The device for reversing this process is logically named "inverter".

**A/C dryer:**  a water separator/dehydrator to remove moisture from the air conditioner refrigerant to prevent freezing at/of the expansion valve.

**acetylene:**  a colorless gaseous hydrocarbon fuel ($C_2H_2$) with 1455 BTUs per cubic foot, used extensively in soldering, welding, and in antique gas lights, and that is highly explosive over a wide range (3% to 80%) when mixed with air but safe when dissolved in liquid acetone.

**acetylene bottle:**  the conventional cylinder for storing welding gas with the acetylene in solution in acetone (300 volumes of acetylene in one volume of acetone at 12 atmospheres pressure).

**acetylene generator:**  the container system for chemically producing acetylene by mixing water with calcium carbide pellets.

**acetylene lights:**  antique automobile lights fueled with acetylene gas.

**acetylene regulator:**  a pressure-dropping device for reducing storage pressure to the desired value for welding or lights.

**acetylene tank:**  a container for the gas, usually running board mounted, to supply vehicle lights, or the more common bottle (tank) storing the gas for oxy-acetylene torch welding.

**acetylene torch:**  a controllable burner nozzle for mixing the fuel and an oxidizer (air or oxygen) for effective heating, soldering, or welding.

**acetylene welder:**  (1) One who welds with acetylene.  (2) The equipment necessary to do such welding, including a welding/cutting torch, hoses, pressure regulators, and pressure-storage tanks.

**A/C evaporator:**  a radiator unit where the air conditioner refrigerant is vaporized and a fan blows the cooled air (from vaporization) as desired.

**A/C expansion valve:** a spray valve for vaporizing the liquid refrigerant to cool the evaporator-radiator surface.

**acid:** typically water-soluble and sour-tasting chemical compounds that are capable of reacting with a base to form a salt, that reddens litmus, that are hydrogen-containing molecules or ions able to give up a proton to a base or that are substances able to accept an unshared pair of electrons from a base. Battery (sulfuric) acid --$H_2SO_4$--is most common in automobiles.

**acid core solder:** a soft low-melting-point metallic wire with a center core of acid that melts when heated and cleans the metals to be soldered--insuring a stronger bond.

**acid resistant:** material or paint coating that is not readily consumed by acids.

**Ackermann steering:** a system with steering geometry designed to cause the outside wheel in a turn to turn fewer degrees than the inside wheel to compensate for the larger circular path of the outside wheel.

**acorn nut:** a machine nut with a blanked end of rounded shape (like an acorn) covering the threaded bolt-end.

**acrylic:** relating to acrylic acid or its derivatives. A common synthetic plastic.

**acrylic paint:** a glossy thermoplastic made by polymerizing acrylic or methacrylic acid. Sometimes cast as acrylic sheets and shapes.

**active safety:** accident avoidance (handling, stopping and response) designed into a car that allow a driver to avoid a crash, as opposed to passive safety devices such as air bags and seat/shoulder belts. Must be complemented by capable drivers.

**ad agency:** a promotion group producing aural, print and visual enticements to lure product purchasers to buy--or to create a favorable product image.

**adjustable shocks:** vehicle suspension dampers that can be modified to absorb varying load intensities and rates. Accomplished by changing pre-load, flow orifices, or hydropneumatic pressures.

**adjust brakes:** to manually change the static clearance between the friction pad/shoes and the energy absorber discs/drums. Some brakes adjust automatically.

**adult toys:** the reality of the automobile's versatility to be utilitarian, aesthetically pleasing, and fun--all at the same time--bringing back to adults memories of childhood playthings.

**advance:** moving the relationship of the camshaft or the distributor to the crankshaft ahead so that valve opening or spark firing occurs earlier in the engine cycle.

**aerodynamic drag:** the resistance of air to movement of a body through it. The resistance results primarily from the size hole (flat-plate area) made in the air, from the shape of the body, from the friction of the air scrubbing against the skin of the body, and from the air flowing through the body for cooling/ventilation. Resistance is generally stated in pounds and increases as the square of the vehicle velocity.

**aerodynamic drag coefficient:** a fractional multiplier applied to the flat-plate (frontal) area of the vehicle. Square, boxy cars have large coefficients (Cd) of about 0.75 down to 0.35. Sleek shapes may have Cd's from 0.35 down to 0.15. Notably low-drag cars pre-World War II were Dr. Kamm's BMW and Bucky Fuller's Dymaxion-- post-World War II leaders: the Citroen SM and the contemporary Ford Probe.

**aerodynameic drag horsepower:** the horsepower required to overcome air resistance increases as the cube of the vehicle velocity emphasizing the irrevocable penalty that must be paid to enjoy going faster. As terminal vehicle speed is approached the fuel-use curve rise becomes nearly vertical.

**A-frame:** the standard "A" structural shape. Two "A's" with a beam across the apex (the traditional "saw horse") is the workhorse of the small shop--the poor man's overhead crane--used to R-and-R engines and for generic heavy lifting. See A-arm.

**after-fire:** the phenomenon of an engine continuing to run after the engine is turned off. A red-hot flake of carbon, a sharp-edged valve head, too-fast idle, a hot engine, or detonation-prone fuel may cause this condition.

**after-market:** parts and accessories manufactured by non-major companies, other than "original equipment manufacturers" (OEM parts), for sale as replacements are so classified. Often dubbed "cheapo parts" and sometimes of inferior quality.

**after running:** see after fire.

**aggressive car:** how the French describe the "safety car" that is made so strong that it inflicts excessive damage when colliding with a pedestrian or another car.

**aggressive driver:** the road hog who rudely takes the right away, frequently changes lanes, and gives you the obscene gesture.

**air bag:** an impact-triggered inflatable cushion that provides vehicle occupants protection from the shock of a hard collision stop.

**air bearing:** a usually small very fast-rotating bearing that literally spins free of friction contact between surfaces or with a lubricant film, supported totally by air.

**air bleed:** a small orifice that adds controlled amounts of air where and when needed.

**air bleed jet:** an accurately-sized jet to enhance carburation performance.

**air box:** a large-volume container to concentrate, control and direct intake air to the engine or air-dependent components.

**air brake:** a system (usually on large vehicles) using compressed air to apply braking forces to the brake shoes. Also an extendible panel to add air drag to a race car.

**air car:** a vehicle suspended above the terrain on a cushion of air. Propeller driven. Hovercraft.

**air cleaner:** a porous-paper or oil-bath filter to remove particulates from engine intake air.

**air cooled:** using air as a heat transfer medium with finned surfaces on the items to be cooled to increase the heat-transfer radiation area.

**air-cooled brakes:** drums with fins or ventilated discs to multiply the cooling effect of passing air.

**air-cooled engine:** an internal combustion engine that cools itself with air flow over finned cylinders and heads rather than with liquid flow through casting passages. Air flow derives from vehicle movement or ducted air from an engine-driven fan.

**air cushioned:** a vehicle (usually large such as a furniture van) that is supported on air bags rather than metal springs. Ride quality is air-pressure controlled.

**aircraft cable:** a multiple-stranded flexible stainless steel wire cable of great strength and utility for operating and controlling vehicle components.

**aircraft hose clamp:** a high-quality flat-band circular clamp tightened by a worm screw.

**air dam:** a deflector shroud at the vehicle front to block excessive on-coming air from flowing beneath the chassis.

**air drag:** See aerodynamic drag.

**air duct:** a closed conduit to direct air flow to perform required functions.

**air filter:** See air cleaner.

**Air Flow:** model designation of Chrysler and DeSoto cars of the mid-1930s that were aerodynamically shaped in the style of Bucky Fuller's Dymaxion car.

**airfoil:** a shape configured to minimize air drag on a moving vehicle or to generate up, down, or side forces from the moving air.

**air/fuel ratio:** the amount, by weight, of air used in burning one pound of fuel. The perfect chemical combination is called the stoichiometric ratio. The reciprocal of the fuel/air ratio.

**air horn:** warning horn powered by air pressure, usually from an on-board compressor. Also the shaped air inlet to a carburetor. See velocity stack.

**air horsepower:** the work effort required to propel a vehicle through the air at a given speed.

**air hose:** a flexible rubber or synthetic hose usually reinforced with fabric or wire to withstand the air pressure.

**air impact wrench:** a tool that converts air pressure into a hammer-operated twisting force. Can exert considerable torque and speed when tightening nuts and bolts. Rattle wrench (from its characteristic sound when operating).

**air injection:** the addition of excess combustion air into the exhaust system to further reduce unburned hydrocarbons and carbon monoxide to carbon dioxide.

**air inlet:** any opening designed to admit air into a vehicle.

**air jack:** pneumatic cylinder/pistons or inflatable bags used for lifting weight.

**air line:** rigid or flexible conduits to distribute air for functional use.

**air lock:** term that inaccurately describes "vapor lock". Air in a hydraulic-actuated system is disastrous.

**air needle:** many uses. In carburetors that idle with fully closed throttles the air needle meters idle air thus determining engine idle speed.

**air/oil shock absorber:** a cylinder/piston or diaphram system that cushions and damps road surface imperfections. Supplements and augments a vehicle's metal springs. Rebound rate can be controlled by varying the air pressure pre-load.

**air/oil suspension:** similar to air/oil shocks but functions sans springs, both supporting and damping the total vehicle weight. Examples: Citroen cars; aircraft strut landing gear; some motorcycles.

**airporter:** class of minibuses/vans of about 10-15 passenger capacity to provide pick-up/delivery of airline passengers, supplementing small-group taxi and large-group bus requirements.

**airport roadster:** sport roadster of the twenties-thirties era favored by the daring pilots for their flowing-scarf dash down the flight line to their open cockpit biplanes. The cars came with a golf bag compartment and a retractable jump seat over each rear fender. The pilot's seat-pack 'chutes were form-fitted to the jump seats. A pristine example of these distinctive cars is Amelia Earhart's Kissel "Gold Bug" which she left at the airport before her last flight. (The car is now on permanent display at the Forney Transportation Museum, Denver, Colorado.)

**air pump:** applied to the infamous "smog pump", usually a vane-pump supplying air to the exhaust system to reduce noxious combustion emissions.

**air resistance:** See air drag.

**air ride:** using an air suspension system.

**air scoop:** an opening designed to improve functional air flow into a vehicle. See NACA and NASA scoops.

**air shock:** a device for providing a controllable damping of road shock/vibration.

**air suspension:** a vehicle suspension system using pressurized bladders/pistons in lieu of springs to support the vehicle weight and to damp road shock with controllable-flow orifices/valves.

**air throttled:** the controlling of a vehicle engine's power/speed by the amount of charge-air admitted into the induction system with a butterfly/damper valve, usually in the carburetor assembly.

**alclad:** any of various shapes, especially flat sheets and wire, with a surface coating of pure aluminum or an alloy for protection against weathering. Formerly trademarked.

**Allen wrench:** a tradenamed mechanic's tool with a six-sided (hex) plug end and an appropriate turning handle for loosening/tightening bolts or screws with recessed-hex-heads.

**alloy:** (1) A metal mixed with a more valuable metal to give durability or some other desired quality. (2) To mix so as to form an alloy.

**all-season oil:** a vehicle engine lubricating oil that is termed "multi-grade" because it flows freely when cold (winter) while retaining bearing-protecting viscosity when hot (summer). 10-30. 20-50.

**all season tire:** a vehicle pneumatic tire whose tread represents a compromise, with a deeper thread for better traction in snow and mud but with a pattern and compound that insure quiet rolling and long wear.

**Alpine rally:** a competitive automobile contest involving navigation, controlled speed, and planning to match specified travel times, by segment, over a race course through mountainous terrain with the winner determined by how close each segment time came to the specified time.

**also-ran:** each contestant in a vehicle race that fails to win or to finish in second or third place. From horse racing: win, place, show, and also-ran.

**alternating current:** an electric current that reverses its direction at regularly recurring intervals: AC.

**alternative fuel:** any of various substitute fuels touted as replacement for petroleum (fossil) fuel for vehicles in an attempt to reduce atmospheric pollution and dependence upon imported oil. Although heavily tax-subsidized and politically promoted all have proven to be inferior replacements, leaving hydrogen as the fuel of Space Ship Earth's future--the only one! But only when we get nuclear-fusion or high-efficiency photovoltaic electricity to electrolyze water.

**alternator:** an electric generator that produces alternating current.

**alumina:** a natural or synthetic aluminum oxide ($Al_2O_3$) occurring naturally as corundum and in hydrated forms as in bauxite. Used as a very hard abrasive (hardness 9).

**aluminize:** to apply a protective coating of aluminum or aluminum alloy to prevent weathering.

**aluminum:** a bluish silver-white malleable, ductile light trivalent metallic element with good electrical and thermal conductivity, high reflectivity, and resistance to oxidation and that is the most abundant metal in the earth's crust, occurring always in combination with other elements.

**aluminum block:** denoting a vehicle whose engine uses a cast-aluminum cylinder block (for its great weight-saving, compared to cast iron) and usually having steel or other wear-resistant material cylinder-bore liners.

**aluminum oxide:** alumina ($Al_2O_3$), when fused and then cooled forms a very hard glass ("alundum"), with hardness 9-Mohs-scale, widely used as an abrasive and for heat refractory material.

**aluminum paint:** any of various protective coatings using aluminum powder suspended in a liquid carrier and used for both undercoating and as a final finish (top) coat with excellent resistance against sunlight (U-V rays) deterioration.

**AM:** a radio broadcasting system using amplitude modulation called the "standard" system in contrast to frequency modulation (FM). Standard Broadcast Band.

**ambient:** completely surrounding or encompassing as the atmosphere around a vehicle.

**ambulance:** a vehicle specially configured and equipped for transporting the injured and sick to a hospital, or between hospitals, and operated by technicians trained in the care of patients during transport or at accident/disaster scenes.

**ambulance chaser:** usually a lawyer or lawyer's agent who incites accident victims to sue for damages, often at the same time the victims are undergoing medical treatment. Generally considered a disparaging and unethical practice.

**ammeter:** an instrument for measuring electric current in amperes. The direct current (DC) ammeter, common to vehicles, is of the moving-coil type similar to the d'Arsonval galvanometer in which a coil carrying the current to be measured turns between the poles of a permanent magnet, acting against the torque of a hairspring to cause a pointer to move over its dial in proportion to the current strength (number of amperes).

**amp:** abbreviation for (1) ampere and for (2) amplifier.

**amperage:** the strength of a current of electricity expressed in amperes.

**ampere:** the practical mks (meter, kilogram, second) unit of electric current that is equivalent to a flow of one coulomb per second or to the current produced by one volt applied across a resistance of one ohm.

**ampere-hour:** a unit quantity of electricity equal to the quantity carried past any point of a circuit in one hour by a steady current of one ampere. Used to express the comparative life/strength of a vehicle battery.

**ampere-turn:** the mks unit of magnetomotive force equal to the magnetomotive force around a path that links with one turn of wire carrying an electric current of one ampere.

**amphibian:** a vehicle usually propelled by endless tracks (although sometimes by wheels plus a use-as-needed water-propeller) traversing land or water.

**amplidyne:** a direct-current generator that, by the use of compensating coils, and a short-circuit across two of its brushes precisely controls a large power output whenever a small power input is varied in the field-winding of the generator.

**amplifier:** an electrical/electronic device usually employing electron tubes or solid-state transistors to obtain amplification of current, power, or voltage.

**amplitude:** the extent of a vibratory movement (as of a pendulum or a spring) measured from a mean (center) position to an extreme. The maximum departure of the value of an alternating current or wave from the average value.

**amtrack:** a tracked amphibious vehicle. (Not Amtrak, the railroad.)

**amyl alcohol:** any of eight isomeric alcohols ($C_5H_{12}O$) used especially in solvents and as a petrochemical feedstock in making esters.

**analog:** being or relating to a mechanism in which data are represented by continuously variable physical quantities. The best mechanic's example: the "telling of time" by the positions of the "little hand and the big hand". As contrasted to a digital display.

**anchor:** the point of attachment (and the hardware fittings) of a non-structural stress-carrying component such as passenger seats, safety restraints (lap/seat/shoulder belts) and roll-bar/roll-cage, so essential to user-friendly vehicles.

**Anco:** trademarked line of windshield washer/wiper components and parts.

**aneroid:** of or pertaining to an evacuated container whose walls flex (physically move) in response to changes in atmospheric pressure with the movement transposed to an indicator pointer-hand on a calibrated instrument. Aneroid movement is used in vehicles to correct fuel/air ratios as the atmospheric pressure (altitude) changes.

**angle:** the plane figure formed by two lines extending from a common point.

**angle iron:** (1) A length of structural steel rolled with an L-shaped cross-section. (2) An iron cleat (bracket) for joining parts of a structure at an angle.

**angle of attack:** the acute angle between the direction of motion of a vehicle and the impingement angle of the air through which the vehicle moves.

**angstrom:** a unit of length equal to one ten-billionth of a meter.

**angular velocity:** the time rate of change of angular displacement.

**anhydrous:** classification of a substance as being free of water especially water of crystallization.

**anion:** the ion in an electrolyzed solution that migrates (is attracted to) to the anode (positive). A negatively charged ion.

**anneal:** to heat and then cool under controlled conditions a metal or glass to soften and to make less brittle.

**annulus:** (1) Any of various ring-shaped components. (2) The internally-toothed gear-wheel of epicyclic gears or planetary transmission. Ring gear.

**annulus gear:** a usually large-diameter spur gear with internal or external teeth. Ring gear.

**anode:** (1) The positive terminal of an electrolytic cell. (2) The electron-collecting electrode of an electron tube. (3) The negative terminal of a primary cell or of a storage battery that is delivering current.

**anodize:** to use an object/metal as the anode in order to apply an electrolytic coating for protective or decorative purposes. Electroplate.

**antechamber:** a prechamber or cell into which fuel is injected and ignited before the burning mixture enters the main combustion area of the cylinder/head.

**antenna:** a vehicle-mounted wire or rod, usually vertical, and often retractable or telescoping, whose purpose is to receive or transmit radio signals.

**antibackfire valve:** a valve that supplies air fom a pressure source during deceleration to prevent backfiring.

**anti-dive:** suspension system geometry designed to resist the nose-down pitching during hard braking.

**anti-fouling:** (1) Spark plugs with electrodes configured to minimize combustion by-product adhesion usually by material composition, gap, location, or shape. (2) Additives in fuels and lubricants, usually detergents, to eliminate residue deposition.

**antifreeze:** a substance added to a liquid (as the coolant water of a vehicle engine or windshield-washer fluid) to lower its freezing temperature below the expected ambient temperature.

**anti-lock brake system:** a braking system that senses wheel lock-up and releases braking force momentarily, followed by intermittent pulsed application of brake force to insure against extended lock-up that could cause skidding. See ABS.

**antiknock additives:** during the refining of gasoline and after it reaches the vehicle, the adding of various octane-raising chemical compounds to improve a fuel's resistance to detonation caused by whatever combustion conditions.

**Antiknock Index:** the Octane Number (rating) derived from averaging the Motor Octane Number and the Research Octane Number of a fuel.

**antimony:** a trivalent and pentavalent metalloid commonly silvery white, crystalline, and brittle element used especially in alloys.

**antipercolator:** an orifice, passage, tube, or valve incorporated in a vehicle carburetor through which fuel vapor can escape, often through a collector/condenser, for return to the fuel supply.

**antique:** an arbitrary vehicle classification derived from its age but without any authoritative specifications or inclusive date limitations.

**anti-rattle spring:** a spring that applies force to vehicle mating parts that must have enough looseness to allow free movement to stop unwanted noise-causing motion.

**anti-roll bar:** a torsion bar that couples the vertical displacement of a vehicle's left and right paired-wheels to the body structure in a manner designed to minimize vertical displacement to just one side of the sprung weight that would cause "body roll".

**anti-sail device:** a restraining bar or weight to prevent the mud/spray flap behind the wheels of large trucks from being blown backward by air pressure from high vehicle speeds.

**anti-seize:** a coating compound for machine threads or fittings that allows later loosening/removal of high-torque applications in dissimilar metals, particularly when subject to repeated cooling/heating (as steel spark plug threads in an aluminum cylinder head).

**anti-skid:** (1) A vehicle tire with tread pattern that minimizes loss of surface adhesion. (2) See ABS (anti-lock brake system).

**anti-spin device:** a device as a no-slip differential or anti-lock brake system (ABS) that controls or prevents wheel-spin of one or more vehicle wheels.

**anti-spray flap:** a usually hanging deflector plate behind the wheels of large vehicles to prevent rearward spray of road debris or water.

**anti-squeal shims:** sheet shims of vibration-absorbing material placed between disc brake pad backing-plate and brake actuating piston to dampen noise.

**anti-sway bar:** a transverse link between the vehicle axle and the body that limits lateral movement (sway) of the body.

**anti-vibration mount:** any of various materials as springs, liquid cushions, or absorbent materials used to separate vibration-generating components from a vehicle's main structure for occupant or structural protection, e.g., engine mounts, body mounts, or radiator mounts.

**apex seal:** the combustion, compression, intake vacuum seal between the three apexes of the tri-lobed rotor and the trochoidal chamber wall of a Wankel engine--analogous to the piston rings of a reciprocating engine.

**appraiser:** a trained, experienced, and usually licensed authority who sets the value of vehicles, especially collectible cars and dealer new car "trade-ins".

**apprentice:** one who is learning from hands-on practical experience any of the various skills associated with vehicle maintenance, repair, and service, and who is often called a hostler, shag-boy, go-fer, parts-chaser, et al.

**apron:** applied to various sheet metal panels underneath a vehicle that control air-flow and reduce aerodynamic drag, but most usually to downward-sloping shapes at the vehicle front that initiate smooth flow of entering air below the vehicle. Air dam. Belly pan.

**aquaplane:** the tendency of a vehicle tire tread to become water-buoyed under certain conditions of speed and road-water depth and that is capable of producing a total loss of tire contact/traction with the road surface. Modern tread design has virtually eliminated this problem.

**aquafuel:** any of the various fraudulent fuels whose perpetrators claim can power a vehicle on nothing but--or a high percentage of--water. Air and water "fuels" and gadgets/gimcracks that guarantee to cause a vehicle to "burn" air or water--all "U.S. Patented"--remain the bane of every honest vehicle mechanic and the legendary scourge that scams the technically illiterate vehicle owner.

**aqueous vapor:** the water vapor that comprises from 0.01% to 3.0% of our total earthatmosphere depending on the temperature, source, and history of the air mass in question. Increased humidity makes us think that a vehicle engine "runs like a sewing machine" but, in reality, causes a measurable decrease in engine horsepower due to the fuel energy (non-recoverable) expended to heat the water to combustion-chamber temperature.

**arbor:** a shaft or stud, usually threaded and conical or cylindrical, on which a cutting tool, a tool holder, or a workpiece to be machined is mounted or held.

**arc:** an electrical discharge that is usually continuously visible to the eye as a fiery line or streak that represents significant energy/power flow. In contrast to the fleeting spark that involves infinitesimal energy.

**arc-over:** the flow of electrical current between two conductors at different voltage potentials when there is insufficient dielectric (insulation) between them or there is unwanted conductive contaminant in the gap space.

**Archimedes spiral:** a scientifically proven concept with various applications in the design of fluid pumps.

**arctic oil:** vehicle jargon for a low-viscosity winter-weight engine oil that allows easier starting when cold.

**arc welding:** a method of joining by means of fusion using the heat generated by an electric arc, either AC or DC, to fuse (melt) the metals together often with additional metal from a compatible rod added for additional strength while shielding the weld area from oxidative contaminants by an envelope of inert gas such as argon or helium. Heli-arc.

**area:** the surface included within a closed set of boundary lines as with the outside perimeter (edges) of a sheet or panel. Many vehicle areas are important, e.g., the flat-plate frontal area of the vehicle (the size hole it makes through the air when moving forward) used to determine aerodynamic drag, the brake pad/shoe area, the tire footprint area, the radiator cooling fin area, the combustion chamber wall area, the squish area, et al.

**"Arizona car":** a sometimes descriptive term used when advertising a for-sale vehicle used to indicate the likelihood of freedom from rusting. Rust-free car.

**argon:** a colorless odorless inert gaseous element found in the air and in volcanic gases and used as a filler for electric light bulbs but now being used to shield the weld area in arc welding from contaminants/oxidants.

**arm:** an extended structural or operating beam or rod, e.g., Pitman arm, rocker arm, crane boom, lever arm, et al.

**armature:** one of the two essential parts of a dynamo electric machine. In a generator, the armature is the winding in which electromotive force (e.m.f.) is produced by magnetic induction (cutting the flux lines of the field magnets). In a motor armature, conductors carry the input current which, in the presence of the magnetic field, produces the torque that converts electrical energy into mechanical (rotational) energy.

**aromatics:** Benzenoid hydrocarbons, usually the derivatives toluene, xylene, et al., used in compounding motor vehicle fuels.

**articulated bus:** on heavy passenger city transit routes, a bus so elongated to carry the passenger demand it must be hinged (articulated) near the mid-length to facilitate handling in congested traffic and negotiating city corners.

**articulated truck:** a two-or-more unit (as a tractor + a semi- + a full-trailer) that is hinged for turn-maneuvering and slightly for up-and-down road irregularities.

**artillery wheel:** a sturdy heavy-duty vehicle wheel derived from its likeness to the wheels used to support artillery field pieces.

**Ascot:** (1) British race track. (2) A racing car/class originated in California during the pre-World War II heyday of hot rodding.

**as is:** a condition statement applied to auction-offered vehicles and used cars to indicate that the for-sale item is to be sold with no warranty or guarantee of serviceability. "Buyer beware". Caveat emptor.

**aspect ratio:** a measure of narrowness of a shape, e.g., a square has equal length and width (aspect ratio of 1 to 1) whereas a narrow structural beam 40 feet long and 1 foot wide has an aspect ratio of 40 to 1.

**asphalt:** a black to brown bituminous material found naturally and as a residue from petrochemical refining of crude petroleum that is compounded with other ingredients and used to surface roadways and airport runways and as a waterproofing and roofing cement.  Road tar.  Roofing tar.  Black top.

**aspiration:**  the inhalation or induction of air into a machine or human engine, utilizing suction, and called natural or naturally aspiration or aspirated.  When the charge-air is pushed or pressurized in it is termed supercharging.  Unblown.  Blown. Turbocharged.

**assembled car:**  an automobile assembled from major components purchased from outside companies as was true of many marques that failed because of the higher cost of  assembling compared to in-house manufacturing.  In the good old days--a number of different marqued cars were fitted with Continental Red Seal, Franklin, or Lycoming engines, Borg-Warner transmissions, various differentials, and wheels and axles.

**assembly line:**  an arrangement of equipment, machines and workers in which work passes from operation to operation in/on a moving line, rail, or track until the final completed product exits for shipment at the end of the line.

**asymmetrical beam:**  a vehicle headlight beam that is focused off-center as to provide more light to the right (curb-side) of the road.

**atmosphere:**  commonly used in many world countries as a unit of pressure equal to the pressure of the air at sea level (approximately 14.7 pounds-per-square-inch) and used to mark instruments and state various vehicle pressures, e.g., fuel pressure, manifold pressure, oil pressure.

**atmospheric pollution:**  important to vehicle design and use because of its impact upon all living things and because vehicles are a major contributor of pollution contaminants.

**atomize:**  to convert a liquid (as a fuel) to a minute particle-size (droplet) by pressurized flow through a discharge spray-nozzle.  Fuel-injector nozzle spray.

**ATV:**  abbreviation for an All-Terrain Vehicle, usually a half- or full-tracked or specially suspended vehicle for driving across roadless country.

**Auburn:**  one of the most auspicious of American-marqued cars (1900-1937) and unquestionably the leader of the parade of cars having names starting with the letter "A".  See A-Cars.

**autobahn**  a high-speed German vehicle expressway, analogous to a U.S. Interstate Highway.

**autobus:**  a high-passenger-capacity public conveyance (bus). Omnibus.  Motorbus.

**autocade:** a procession of automobiles traveling together in an organized group for a common purpose to a common destination. Motorcade.

**Autocar:** a large cargo truck marque built in the U.S. continuously since 1907.

**autocross:** a timed contest for automobiles featuring a series of events designed to test the skill of the driver and the maneuverability/performance of the vehicle. Gymkhana.

**autocycle:** a motorized bicycle that requires pedal assistance when starting and operating uphill. Now commonly called Moped.

**Autogas:** European trade name for liquefied natural gas (LPG).

**autoignition:** the early initiation of combustion (before spark occurrence) in a spark-ignition engine caused by internal hot spots, too-high compression, or too low octane fuel.

**automaker:** a manufacturer of automobiles. Car factory.

**automate:** (1) To operate by automation. (2) To convert to largely automatic operation.

**automatic choke:** a carburetor air restriction valve that increases the fuel/air ratio when cold/starting and thermostatically reduces the restriction of air-flow as the engine warms up.

**automatic ignition advance:** a speed-sensitive centrifugal/ vacuum mechanical or electronic computerized spark timing control that coordinates spark-timing with engine load/speed demands.

**automatic leveling suspension:** a hydropneumatic vehicle suspension height-control system that senses height changes caused by front and rear weight imbalances and automatically levels the vehicle. Usually the driver (as in the Citroen) can select various heights to be maintained automatically.

**automatic speed control:** an engine control system programmed to maintain a pre-set vehicle speed by changing power as road conditions (grade, wind, et al.) change.

**automatic transmission:** a vehicle transmission in which gear ratios are selected and engaged automatically with the driver retaining the option of overriding the automatic selections.

**automatic wear adjuster:** a compensating device that automatically corrects for wear in some brake and clutch systems.

**automobile:** a usually four-wheeled automotive vehicle designed for passenger transportation and commonly propelled by

an internal combustion engine.  See "Automobile" as the first
"A" word.

**automobile aficionado(a):**  a man/woman vehicle enthusiast with
obvious devotion/love to/for/of all automobiles and usually
possessing significant automobile literacy.  Car buff.  See
automobile buff.

**automobile buff:**  See automobile aficionado(a).

**automobile music:**  (1) Any of the many and varied musical
scores/lyrics using automobiles as the theme--for whatever
reason, with one of the earliest and possibly best-known being
"The Merry Oldsmobile". (2) The sound of any automobile engine,
that can be inspiring, melodious, soothing ("music to the
ears")--or cacophonous, discordant, too-loud (ear-splitting),
depending upon the receptive ear.  How do you suppose the term
"tune-up" originated?  A properly tuned automobile is a living
symphony.

**autopilot:**  car jargon for automatic speed controls of a  vehicle.  Cruise control.

**auxiliary driving light:**  a forward-aimed extra light complementing the lighted area of the vehicle headlights.  Called
also a fog light when the light frequency (usually an orange
hue) penetrates fog.

**auxiliary transmission:**  an extra ratio(s) of gearing acting
upon the transmission output (drive shaft) to change the engine
rpm-to-wheel-rpm relationship by a multiplier factor.  Two-
speed differential.  Over-drive.  Dual range.

**average piston speed:**  the distance traveled by a vehicle piston per increment of time as feet per minute.  Often stated as
feet-per-mile of vehicle travel.  Piston speed changes from
zero at each dead center position to a maximum when the crankshaft throw is at 90°.

**avgas:**  aviation gasoline that has lower vapor pressure (volatility) than ground-vehicle fuel to reduce evaporation and
vapor lock at higher altitudes.

**avoidance radar:**  a collision warning system already in use
to alert the proximity and closing-rate of nearby aircraft and
now being incorporated in some ground vehicles for collision
avoidance.

**awl:**  a pointed hand tool for marking surfaces and making pin
point points for layout and machining.

**awning:**  a rooflike flexible usually roll-up fabric cover attached to camping trailers/motor homes as extra shade/shelter.

**axis:** one of three straight lines about which a vehicle rotates: lateral, longitudinal, vertical.

**axle:** a pin or shaft on which a wheel or pair of wheels revolves.

**axle strap:** a loop usually of heavy webbing or cable attached to the chassis/frame and loosely circling an axle to limit its downward movement away from the chassis structure.

**axle weight:** the total gross weight transmitted to the roadway by one vehicle axle  and often a design factor in determining the load-carrying parameters of highways.


## LAGNIAPPE

**abampere:** ten amperes.  The cgs electromagnetic unit of current which, when flowing in straight parallel wires 1cm apart produces 2 dynes of force per cm length of each wire.


## "ACCIDENTS" that aren't ACCIDENTS

Traffic "accidents"?  Bullstuff!  Our depraved and illiterate society of apologists and revisionists has been calling 'em "accidents" since that "gas buggy" murdered its first victim in 1902.  When they weren't accidents.  They were caused by the driver!

Oxymorons they are.  Why question Noah Webster's wisdom--that has guided every reasonable mind since 1783--that the word "accident" has a very specific meaning (definition) that bears no relationship to two demoniacal drivers bashing two magnificent machines head-on into a junk pile, to the 200 **speeding criminals** who banged heads on a California foggy freeway, or to the little-old-lady-leadfoot (one of dozens, this morning) who rolled the 4x4 while zipping off the off-ramp at high speed.  Any reason to call 'em "accidents"?

**None!**  Those were/are crimes--not **"accidents"**.  Those who died weren't "accident" victims--they were murdered.  By criminals, that's anyone and everyone who violates **speed limits** (or any traffic law).  Damn near 100% of all highway deaths are **caused**--knowingly and willfully by **speeders**--therefore not accidents and preventable.

"Accident" is best defined as "fortuitous"--occurring by chance--not amenable to planning or prediction--connoting entire absence of cause--lack of real or apparent premeditation or intent. Therefore extrinsic--an unexpected happening, not due to any fault or misconduct on the part of any person involved.  Every competent car buff **knows and believes** two things:  "that" bumper sticker that screams "Accidents Happen", and P.T. Barnum's First Law, **"SPEED KILLS!"**  But forgets that accidents cannot be caused!

Prove to yourself that traffic accidents aren't accidental. Look again at the guy who shaved in your mirror this morning. You'll see the culprit who **speeds** at every opportunity. You, the <u>criminal</u>! Who <u>chooses</u> to **speed**. Who <u>planned</u> to **speed** as a premeditated <u>crime</u> when he bought his radar detector. Who <u>intended</u> to **speed** when he bragged "I'll meet you at the Cheyenne Bar (80 miles distant) in one hour." Whose criminality is unquestionably defined, documented, predictable--and preventable. That's <u>murder in the first degree</u> beyond any doubt. That is <u>not</u> an "accident"! No way!

Was the first "murder-by-vehicle" plea-bargained down to "traffic accident" to salve the conscience of our new-born hedonism? The alibi-addicted? The anti-authority, reject-responsibility generation? Have our feckless political pimps and bureaucratic bunglers--Hell-bent-for-election--caved-in to an apathetic and depraved society? **Speeding** is fun. You can't abrogate my pleasure. Isn't that what you saw in your mirror this morning? But refuse to recognize? The **speeder** who won't admit his <u>criminality</u>?

'Tis a sad commentary. Admitting that Webster knew the meaning of the word "accident", and then reading the annual statistical compilations published by our government, especially by the National Safety Council, will surely confuse even a rocket scientist. Headed "Improper Driving Reported in Vehicle Accidents (1992)", of 40,300 deaths, 55.5% were reported due to "Improper Driving", but 14 of Uncle Sugar's states report driving under the influence of alcohol or drugs under the heading due to "<u>No</u> Improper Driving". <u>Only 16.5%</u> of deaths were due to "**Speed** too Fast or Unsafe". Who the Hell believes that? Then you'll find 13.8% died due to "<u>Other</u> Improper Driving" and a few single-digit percentages attributed to "Failed to Yield . . . . Passed Stop Sign . . . . Disregarded Signal . . . . Improper Overtaking . . . . Followed too Closely". However you define those Alexander Haig "isms", you must still spell 'em **S-P-E-E-D.**

Every reasonable mind knows the cliche "**Speed** Kills!", honors this truism, and recognizes the American driver's infatuation with **speed.** And has known why "**Speed** Kills" since the day Isaac Newton dropped the apple and invented Gravity (g-force).

Jimmy-the-Greek will betcha' my nickel that the figure "Only 16.5%" of traffic deaths are due to "**Speed** too Fast or Unsafe" is as phony as a three-dollar-bill. Have you driven a freeway lately? Then you know, as this curmudgeon claims, that at least 90% of all vehicles in service at any moment <u>are</u> **speeding.** Any airborne "Spy in the Sky" traffic reporter will tell you that every "roll-over" that he saw today <u>was</u> **speeding.** Every racecar driver, every automotive engineer, and every shade-tree mechanic will tell you--and prove it--that no vehicle can be "rolled" unless you exceed posted **speed** limits or maximum safe **speeds**--either is **speeding.** By law, by common sense, by God!

Want more proof? Since accidents happen by chance, are not predictable, are unexpected happenings not due to any fault or misconduct on the part of the person involved--"accidents" are not preventable nor can their frequency or severity be controlled or modified. There is no way the 56,663 "accidental" vehicle deaths in 1970 could drop to 40,300 "accidental" vehicle deaths in 1992 (that's a decrease of almost 30% in the "accidental" deaths), when the miles driven increased about 80%. Even the dum-dums within our D.C. Beltway should recognize that the 40,300 body-bags were filled with victims of first-degree murder--beyond a shadow of doubt! Because the third-grader next-door can understand the infallibility of such mathematical proof by inductive/deductive reasoning from the shade-tree expertise of his country-curmudgeon neighbor.

Misplaced priorities: Hell, that's a gross misstatement. We've got 'em inverted. Former Surgeon General C. Everett Koop, Chairman of the National Safe Kids Campaign, led a gaggle of do-gooders and 102 "accident" victim children to tell a Senate Labor and Human Resources subcommittee on children and family (5/10/94), and most media news-viewers, heart-rending stories about their "accidents". Koop elicited crocodile tears (mine too) with a graphic show-and-tell of their injuries and how they coulda' been prevented. More of the same old coulda', shoulda', woulda' rhetoric. Throw more tax dollars at the problem. Not a single viable solution was proposed!

The political pimping overflowed the Senate chambers and flooded the nation's living room TV's and commuter car radios with mega-millions of sound bytes. Koop's chorus about the nearly 8,000 "accident" deaths of children each year led subcommittee chairman, Senator Christopher Dodd, D-Conn., to proclaim that "preventing accidents should be a key component in any health reform bill." More Motherhood-and-apple-pie!

Nary a word about the nearly 8,000 vehicle "accident" deaths of children nor the 32,300 grown-ups who, too, were vehicle murder victims. Can "Slick Willie's" Hillary-health reform bill insure Koop's 8,000 plus automobiliana's 40,300 and not raise taxes? More pie-in-the-sky!

No amount of federal tax dollars can reduce Koop's 8,000 "accidents". Not ever. Not even a smidgen. Because "accidents", by definition, are not amenable to intentional manipulation--not UP, not DOWN, nor sideways. True accidents cannot be prevented!

The bottom line. The 40,300 vehicle murders can be reduced. Drastically. Call 'em what they are-murder--not "accident", which they aren't! Don't call 'em "accidents", report 'em as "accidents", treat 'em as "accidents", think of 'em as "accidents", or punish 'em as "accidents" (rename 'em and forget 'em). Stop **speeding**! It's doable now. There's an available off-the-shelf, no-cost, high-tech system that'll do it now (already in use in several countries that don't need it). Those same countries already had in place the ultimate solution to vehicle "accidents"/murders--a law-abiding citizenry with respect for the rights of others, leaders leading by example, a justice system that <u>punishes</u> swiftly, surely, and with hurt--but fairly and equitably--with no plea-bargains. Where no one owns, uses, or condones radar detectors. Many drive fast, and well, on Gran Prix courses, auto-crosses, or authorized autobahns--few try it any faster than legally posted.

The American Way and the way Americans do it. Laws were never intended to be enforced--but to be obeyed. Our forefathers viewed laws as of and for the people--not imposed upon the people from above. Once legislated and signed into law, any law becomes community property for the benefit of the community. A civilized moral community then obeys willingly and totally. Only a depraved society (ours) disobeys or obeys selectively. Americans **speed**. **Speeding** is a <u>crime</u>. American **speed** limits are rarely enforced--never aggressively, effectively, or economically. So American **speeders** are willing, self-motivated, pre-meditated <u>criminals</u>--every damn one of 'em. With a political leadership that condones, aids, abets, and aggrandizes this abhorrent abrogation of legal authority. Fellow-traveling <u>criminals</u>--all!

Face reality. Ban radar detectors. They are accessories, before, during, and after a <u>crime</u>--**speeding.** They can claim no other function. Some states and many countries long ago banned these criminals effectively and totally. Why won't we? My recent survey found over 90% of prominent attorneys (many in highly-placed prosecutorial positions) owned and used radar detectors. Why? To violate the very laws they are sworn to <u>enforce</u>--<u>and</u> <u>to</u> <u>obey</u>. Neither the Bar Association nor law enforcement seemed concerned--or even responded to my survey. Bar 'em or impeach 'em!

Every driver knows that **"Speed Kills"**. Every driver who **speeds** does so by conscious choice, premeditated, willing commission of the <u>crime</u> of **speeding**--of the <u>crime</u> <u>of</u> <u>murder</u> in the first degree when someone dies as the result. The driver who presses the foot on the accelerator is pulling the trigger of a weapon far more lethal than any assault weapon. Our 103rd Congress has just committed mega-millions to gutless anti-assault-weapon legislation and not even lip-service or personal commitment to stopping the **speed**-trigger. The total reduction in numbers of murders by banning assault weapons is unlikely to equal <u>even</u> <u>1%</u> of those who will be <u>murdered</u> by **speeding** drivers. Over 40,000 of 'em this year. With no government intervention, "Detroit's" better people-packaged vehicles are solely responsible for the fantastic saving of life from 1970 to 1992. Doing the doable--curbing our rampant pandemic **speeding**--is guaranteed to equal or better this significant progress toward saving lives. Stop **speeding** for a no-cost Nirvana!

Lagniappe: The country logic of stopping **speeding** murders is selfevident as well as further enhanced by concomitant gains. "Small" crimes like **speeding**, shop-lifting, or tax avoidance (be honest, it's tax evasion), when committed with impunity, always lead to bigger crimes by those most susceptible. Like the addictive syndrome grows from cigarettes and pot to cocaine and heroin. Like Denver Bronco's quarterback Craig Morton's shop-lifting of a few drill bits, the _Denver Post_ editor Chuck Green's shop-lifting an over-the-counter antihistamine, a Denver Asst. District Attorney's shop-lifting a blowdryer, a Neil Bush's pilfering a few bucks as phony loans and evading several thousand in gift taxes, and a Colorado Senator/Bahrain Ambassador, Sam Zakhem's plea-bargaining of several flagrant **speeding** charges down to a no-points and no-fine "driving with a dirty windshield" and having their "little" crimes forgiven. When none of them were punished--their peccadilloes escalated into the "big time" crimes of bankruptcy fraud, S&L fraud, and embezzlement of donated funds.

A convincing scenario points in many directions from **speeding** with impunity--maybe straight at "Slick Willie's" White Watergate, Hillary's Bull Futures, the Keating Five, Silverado, and Nanny Gates. Many in high places in government have almost become folk heroes while stealing Post Office pennies, floating worthless checks, evading federal taxes, draft-dodging, and abusing women--while flippantly justifying (irrationalizing) "But I've done nothing wrong!" That's the truth as they see it--myopically, through the miasma of their long-standing personal brand of mythomania.

Pshaw, the pseuds, the psychos, and the psychics now dominate our society and--scariest of all--our government. Dictating a depraved populace's choices in behavior, ethics, morality, and lifestyle. Any wonder that our children are saying Bang! Bang! with real Uzis instead of Pow! Pow! with cap pistols? Because their parents have consigned parenting to the politicians? Because parents and pols--and preachers--think, practice, and teach that "little" crimes are OK as long as there's no punishment? As they **speed** down the road to depravity?

Vicariously watching (about 8 hours of TV-viewing a day) and aping the antisocial antics of the pseudo "role models" who are bellwethering our youth--and infantile grown-ups--away from family values, loyalty to country, regard for law and order, ethical behavior, and morality--are **speeding** them toward the chaos of depravity.

Enter the Fourth Estate. The masthead of those who mouth the news with mike or pen, that once piously proclaimed such lofty credos as "All the News That's Fit to Print", now seems rooted in a cesspool of disinformation, determined to aggrandize the awful and glorify the unlawful. They parrot the prurient pap of the image-makers who aggrandize the antics of those who strut the show-biz stage (misnamed athletic games, entertainment, and music), pound the political podium, or thump the evangelistic pulpit.

If there's any societal community **speeding** faster down the road to depravity than the Fourth Estaters it has to be the Third Estate, trying to upstage the Fourth. Colorado's U.S. Senator Ben Campbell's front-page picture, racing his Harley "Hog" (helmetless) west of Durango and leading a gang of anti-helmet "Hell's Angels" said it all. And then some! His flowing pony-tail made it difficult to see if God (riding the buddy-seat) sported His halo! 'Nuff said!

**B-Cars:** Working backward through the ABCs of Bs most car buffs can name Buick, Bugatti, BMW, and Bentley--then Bam! as the other 182 Bs fade into oblivion.


**babbitt:** a metal alloy containing antimony, copper, lead, and tin and some recently discovered additives and used as a lining for various vehicle bearings.

**back axle:** a vehicle's rearmost axle usually of a two-axle unit. Rear axle.

**back fire:** an unplanned explosion in a vehicle's engine intake or exhaust system.

**back-flush:** the preferred system for cleaning sediment and deposits from vehicle fluid systems as the radiator/block coolant with a high-pressure reverse flow of water or solvent.

**backing plate:** the fixed anchor plate carrying the shoes of a drum brake. The metal portion to which the friction material of a disc brake pad is attached.

**backlash:** the clearance between the input and output elements of a mechanical system allowing the input to begin motion in advance of the output. Freeplay. Play.

**back pressure:** resistance to the flow of a gas in a pipe or manifold usually the result of a previous event as in a vehicle exhaust system.

**back rest:** the rear vertical part of a vehicle seat.

**backstretch:** the side of an automobile racecourse opposite to the homestretch.

**back-to-back:** vehicle seating with a common dividing backrest requiring some occupants to face to the front and some to face to the rear. Common to early day automobiles. Do-si-Do.

**back-up alarm:** a warning bell, beeper, or buzzer usually on commercial vehicles engaged by the reverse gear selector prior to any backward movement.

**back-up light:** a rearward-aimed illumination light that is engaged whenever the gear selector is in "reverse" to provide lighting for a rearward moving vehicle and as a warning to others.

**badge:** an attachable logo or identification of automobile-related associations or clubs to express owner-ego and impress the proletariat. Yesteryear's bumper/window sticker syndrome.

**badge bar:** a horizontal mounting bracket across the front/rear of early prestige cars designed to display owner's array of ego-badges.

**baffle:** a device usually a platform to control, deflect, or impede the flow of gas, liquid, heat, or light. Baffle plate.

**baggage rack:** on early cars a running board or exterior rear platform enclosure to accommodate travel luggage/packages. Today the roof-mounted rack is usually found on station wagons formed by platform/railings to transport accompanying accouterments. Bike rack. Ski rack.

**Bailey bridge:** an emergency roadway surface as for detours consisting of inter-connecting latticed metal panels edge-joined by metal pins providing immediate vehicle passage over rough or soft terrain. A World War II combat innovation by British Sir Donald Bailey. Aluminum or steel. Landing plank.

**bait-and-switch:** an underhanded sales tactic overly prevalent in vehicle transactions in which a customer is enticed by the advertisement of a low-priced item but is then coerced into buying a higher-priced one.

**Baja Bug:** a Volkswagen modified extensively for off-road driving and racing. Originally named for the Baja (Mexico) Road Race. Now generic.

**baking oven:** a high-temperature enclosure where vehicles and components have newly-painted or treated surfaces dried by heating. Baked-on finish.

**balance:** equipoise between contrasting, interacting, or opposing dynamic or static forces. Essential to efficiency and longevity of any mechanical system.

**balance beam:** a walking (pivoted) beam support that couples the suspension of the two axles of a rear tandem axle arrangement of a heavy vehicle making the suspension reactive.

**balanced crankshaft:** an engine crankshaft with integral or bolt-on weights that counteract the out-of-balance effects of the crank throw and the reciprocating components attached thereto.

**balance shaft:** a rotating shaft usually paralleling the crankshaft of a four-cylinder in-line engine incorporating a harmonic balancer or vibration damper.

**balance tube:** a tube or pipe joining two or more cooperating flow/pressure devices as carburetor venturis to maintain equalized pressure.

**bald tire:** a vehicle tire whose tread has been worn smooth through use.

**balk ring:** a rotating component in a synchromesh transmission that prevents or blocks (balks) premature engagement of gears before a synchronized speed is reached.

**ball and socket:** a mechanical joint in which a spherical end (the ball) moves easily within a matching recess (the socket). Useful in transmitting push-pull motions or forces as in suspension, steering and control systems. Ball joint.

**ballast resistor:** an electrical resistor that increases resistance as it warms up providing higher current for a short period during start-up (as for an ignition coil) and regulating the output of the coil after it reaches operating temperature.

**ball bearing:** a bearing virtually without sliding friction utilizing hardened steel balls rolling between inner and outer hardened races.

**ball detent:** the use of a spring-loaded hardened ball fitted into a cupped receptacle to hold or position one moving part in relation to another while allowing forcible movement by an operator. Frequently used in vehicles to hold gears in mesh until shifted.

**ball mill:** a rotating cylinder containing hardened balls that roll against each other and the cylinder walls to crush and pulverize softer materials introduced into the working area.

**balloon note:** an agreement to pay monthly payments on a debt with amounts less than the mathematical amortization with the stipulation that the final payment (balloon) be the total remainder of the debt at the end of the contract period.

**balloon tire:** a pneumatic vehicle tire with a flexible carcass and large bulbous cross-section using very low air pressure to provide soft cushioning to the ride.

**ball peen hammer:** a mechanic's hammer with one flat face on the head opposed by a hemispherical face (peen) designed to make indentations in a metal surface for aesthetic effect or forge-hardening.

**ball socket:** the hemispherical cavity that fits over a ball to form a movable joint as for a control rod or a vehicle trailer connector (hitch).

**banana seat:** a motorcycle seat (saddle) that is decidedly elongated even to the extent that two riders can occupy it in tandem.

**band brake:** an external clamping band with internal friction lining used as vehicle parking devices usually with the drum mounted on the drive-shaft. Also used for speed-change braking in planetary-geared transmissions. The Model "T" Ford with its 3 foot-operated planetary band brakes pioneered this technology.

**band saw:** a shop saw usually powered with a continuous blade running over pulleys.

**band wagon:** originally horse-drawn the truck vehicle evolved with the capacity to transport circus/other musical groups while participating in vehicle parades.

**banjo:** a hose-end fitting for connecting at right angles using a drilled bolt through its circular end-piece whose banjo-shape resulted in the name. Many multiple-carburetor systems used banjos to attach their fuel lines directly to the float-bowl castings.

**Bantam:** two American and one British Bantams were built. The American Bantam Car Company, Butler, Pennsylvania, built slightly larger cars featuring 2- and 4-seater convertibles and roadsters with styling by Alexis de Sakhnoffski. In 1940 ABCC produced the first successful Jeep prototype accepted by the U.S. Army.

**barbed fitting:** a male hose fitting with serrations over which a hose may be pushed but make the hose removal difficult and providing leak-resistant sealing with or without external clamping.

**bar code:** a group of printed and variously patterned bars and spaces that can be read by computer scanners for locating, identifying, pricing, and inventorying vehicles and components to which the codes are affixed. Moving vehicles with codes visible can be checked while non-stop drive-through of stations such as toll booths. One of the great contributions from the Computer Age.

**barometric pressure:** the standard reference for most vehicle operating gas and liquid pressures: 29.92 inches of mercury or 14.7 pounds per square inch. Vacuum depression (pressure) is reflected by values below this standard.

**Bar's Leaks:** a widely-used and effective trade-named additive sealant for radiator/hose/cylinder-head/block coolant systems compatible with water and most commercial antifreezes.

**basket case:** mechanic slang for a vehicle or component that is so badly damaged or worn as to be beyond practical economic repair. Alluding that it's only fit to be hauled away as in a basket.

**batt:**  a clumping usually flattened of a resilient fiber such as cotton, kapok, mohair, or wool formerly used as vehicle upholstery or top padding.  Largely superseded by molded contoured foam.

**batten:**  narrow-wood spaced lath-like strips used to support vehicle roofs/tops.

**battery:**  generically, there are infinite definitions but in the vehicle vocabulary the lead/sulfuric acid electrolyte storage battery must be recognized for its essentiality.  The battery converts and stores electrical energy as chemical energy then reverses the process, returning the electrical energy upon demand.  Without moving parts, the battery still "wears out", requires predictable intervals for replacement.  Actuarially, about ten vehicle batteries are replaced for each seven generator/starter replacements.  The production pollution, disposal pollution, as well as the weight, inefficiency, and limited energy-storage capacity severely constrain electric cars' future.  Newer batteries show some promise but fuel-cell technology (fuel direct to electricity) may be the bellwether toward a successful electric vehicle.

**battery acid:**  the mixture of sulfuric acid and relatively pure water that forms the battery electrolyte (the conducting solution that allows the internal transfer of ions).

**battery blanket:**  a protective and insulating covering for the vehicle battery sometimes containing internal resistance heating units connected to an exterior electrical source to pre-warm or maintain battery temperature of vehicles parked or stored in an extremely cold environment.

**battery hold-down:**  a usually non-conductive frame fitted to the top of the battery case, and with anchoring fittings as j-bolts with wing-nuts for securing the unit to the vehicle structure.

**battery ignition:**  a vehicle engine system utilizing the battery voltage to generate the spark for initial starting and the combined alternator or generator/battery for continued operation.

**battery jumper:**  a usually paired and coded heavy-gauge stranded electrical conductor for emergency interconnecting vehicle batteries for starting when one battery is discharged (low) or to power external electric loads.

**battery strap:**  a temporary handle usually of strap-like material to facilitate lifting and carrying the heavy and awkward vehicle battery.

**battery terminal:**  the external electrical connection to the positive or negative side of a vehicle battery usually with a heavy current carrying mass of lead as a post to which vehicle or external electrical cables are clamped or bolted. Battery post. Terminal post.

**battery tester:** the hydrometer by sampling the electrolyte gives the relative chemical strength. The sophisticated electronic tester can provide accurate electrical values and compute diagnostic conclusions from either a static or dynamic operating vehicle system.

**bay:** any of various compartments, divisions, or sections of vehicular repair shops usually designated and equipped as for specialized operations: alignment, lubrication and oil change, tire and battery, engine and transmission overhaul, electrical, tuneups, et al. Small shops usually have one-vehicle bays with easy entry/egress. Large bus and truck fleet shops usually have a long drive-through configuration where vehicles move through a production-line maintenance sequence of operations.

**BDC:** bottom dead center, the position of a reciprocating engine piston at its farthest point from the crankshaft and cylinder head upon the completion of any down-stroke.

**beach buggy:** a motor vehicle with large fat tires usually for a fun machine on sand/soft beaches.

**bead:** the circular structural part as the inner-diameter seating and retention member of a vehicle pneumatic tire. The bead anchors the casing sidewall cords in a solid rubber fillet shaped to fit the wheel retaining rim.

**bead blaster:** a parts cleaning device utilizing a pressurized stream of air mixed with various material beads, sand, shot, or other degrees of abrasive particles sprayed on the surfaces to be cleaned. The abrasive stream loosens surface soil and deposits it into the collector where it is reprocessed for further use.

**beaded edge:** any formed edge as a continuous angle or curved usually rolled bead that adds rigidity or stiffness.

**bead flange:** the fixed lip around the outer periphery of a vehicle wheel that retains the pneumatic tire. On heavy duty vehicles using less-flexible tires than can be "drop-center" stretched over the fixed lip a spring steel retainer (sometimes split) fits into wheel rim recesses for tire retention on shallow-rim or flat-rim wheels.

**beam axle:** a rigid solid axle usually extruded, forged, or welded unitary members with free-rolling wheels at each end.

**beam deflector switch:** synonymous with headlight dimmer switch.

**beam indicator:** the high beam warning light on the vehicle dash/instrument panel that is "off" during low beam operation.

**bearing:** a machine component, device, or assembly in which another part (as a journal, pin, or shaft) rotates, slides, or is supported.

**bearing blue:** a surface film painted, sprayed, or wiped on a bearing surface that shows contact areas between the fixed element and the moving element to indicate the need for further machining, grinding, or scraping to obtain a more perfect fit.

**bearing lock:** bearing shells (half-bearings) are usually prevented from rotating by tabs at the joint that mate with tab recesses in the bearing cap and matching upper end. Chemical lock/sealants.

**bearing scraper:** a hardened usually three-sided file-like hand tool for removing small amounts of bearing surface metal to obtain a better fit with its rotating element (journal).

**bearing shim:** various very thin sheets of material/metal used between mating surfaces of bearings to obtain the desired fit, location, or locking. Shims that provide proper clearance between bearing and journal are usually removable in layers to correct for increasing bearing wear with use thus extending the time before total bearing replacement.

**beater:** car slang for the obviously abused and ill-cared for vehicle, implying a "beaten-up" appearance.

**beat frequency:** the combination of two frequencies that are usually super/ultrasonic that form an audible frequency (the range in which humans hear and feel the vibrations). A common phenomenon in motor vehicles/airplanes because of the many different vibration producers and rotational speeds.

**bed:** a surface/material in which a device or machine is mounted (embedded). Usually by adhesive contact. Pot/potted.

**beep:** the audible tone still in use as a vehicle warning device (although voice warnings are rapidly replacing non-verbal devices) to alert operators/occupants of unfastened seat belts, unlatched doors, turn signals operating (supplemented by visuals) lights left-on, et al.

**bejesus:** another irreverant expletive often expressed by a vehicle mechanic who has just dropped another of the minute "Jesus Clips"/retainers.

**beaver tail:** hinged ramps or full-width tail-gate for low-bed trailers that facilitate cargo loading from the rear.

**bell-crank:** a lever bent at some angle less that 180° usually shaft mounted/rotated angularly to transmit push-pull motion to connecting linkage. Varying lengths and lever-arms provide for a wide selection of motional multiplication and/or directional changes.

**Belleville washer:** a tradenamed washer usually heavier than normal with conical surface(s) to facilitate location and locking of shapes onto or by shafts, studs, or bolts.

**bell housing:** a conical or bell-shaped extension of an engine block and crankcase pan or bolt-ons of such shape to contain and protect the flywheel and clutch.

**belly pan:** a covering usually of sheet metal used to contain the many protruding/ hanging accessories below a vehicle's chassis to streamline underbody airflow and reduce aerodynamic drag to save vehicle fuel.

**belt:** any flat, contoured (Vee or round), toothed endless belt for transmitting power between matching pulleys. Vehicle occupant restraint system (seat/shoulder). The reinforcing ply of woven strands of steel/fiber radial or bias around the periphery of a vehicle pneumatic tire. Belted.

**belt drive:** any power transmission through a belt from and to pulleys. From the simple accessory (alternator/fan/water pump) to the complex (variable-speed transmission with automatic ratio changes using expanding Vee-pulleys).

**beltline:** arbitrarily named division around the periphery of a vehicle's outer body usually at the bottom of the windshield/ window level which usually is about the same height as the top of the fenders, hood, and trunk. Various visual perceptions are part of the usual desire to make a vehicle appear lower and longer than its actuality. People-packagers (fashion designers) camouflage and distort the human appearance by tinkering with genus sapiens' waist line. Ain't that the belt location? In fairness, Raymond Loewy did some fashionable packaging on the Studebaker, Avanti and others And Bill Blas, Cartier, Givinchy, Gucci, et al., had a hand in draping a few designer Lincolns.

**belt slip:** resulting from insufficient tension, lack of surface friction, or excessive loading resulting in loss of transmitted power, heating, excessive wear and usually total failure of the belt or the system.

**beltway:** a freeway or superhighway that generally circles a major urban area reducing downtown traffic congestion and promoting major cross-country use of interstate routes.

**bench seat:** a vehicle seat cushion that is continuous (no division even when the seat back is divided and/or hinged) for its full side-to-side width.

**bench test:** the testing of components or complete engines outside the vehicle and mounted on special stands or benches usually complete with measuring devices, displayed information, recorders and special tools and drive machinery for static and/ or functional (dynamic) operation, evaluation, and trouble-shooting.

**Bendix:** trade named device widely used on vehicle electric starter motors to engage the starter pinion with the engine flywheel ring gear teeth to rotate the engine for starting and then retract the small pinion gear from engine engagement allowing the starter motor to stop rotating and the engine to continue to run alone. The Bendix technology involves the spirally grooved/toothed/splined shaft and the matching internal shape of the pinion gear.

**benzene:** a hydrocarbon fuel/solvent used in many countries as a vehicle fuel. Quite similar to gasoline with essentially identical energy content to gasoline but far more polluting because of its higher carbon/BTU ratio to hydrogen/BTU (the determinant factor in evaluating the pollution potential of any fuel).

**bevel gear:** a principal gear system element making possible angular changes in the transmission of power by rotating shafts. Best known application (there are many) is the vehicle differential where power from the engine is directed at a 90° angle from the engine's drive-shaft to the wheel-axle using a bevel-pinion and a bevel-ring gear with sophisticated gear-tooth configurations (helical/hypoid/spiral) providing quiet-er, faster, and more power-handling potential.

**bezel:** typically a rim-like retainer used to secure cover glasses over instruments or lights. Often decorative or cosmetic as well as functional.

**BHP:** brake horsepower is the unit of work (33,000 foot-pounds per minute) used in the U.S. for measuring a vehicle engine's power as measured on a dynamometer (prony brake). May be specified as a bare engine (running without certain parasitic accessories) or running with normal vehicle accessories such as alternator/generator, cooling far, water pump, et al.

**bias-ply tire:** a vehicle pneumatic tire having crossed layers of reinforcing ply-cord set diagonally to the center line of the tread. Radial-ply. Belted bias-ply.

**big bore:** hot rod slang for an engine of large displacement (big cylinder diameter). Oversquare.

**"Big Daddy":** Don Garlitz, one of our top drag race drivers.

**big-end:** the larger end of a piston/crankshaft connecting rod that connects to the crank journal. Crankpin end.

**big-end bearing:** the two bearing halves (shells) that are clamped around the crankshaft crank journal by the piston rod big end and cap.

**bi-metallic spring:** a spring usually of two laminated flat strips of dissimilar spring metals having different temperature-coefficients-of-expansion. Any heating/cooling causes a predictable bending of the spring that is used to operate the display needle of temperature gauges, to operate electrical switches for controls or warning lights, and to supply power to open/close shutters, dampers, or valves using mechanical linkage.

**bike rack:** a roof-top or trunk-mount framework attachment for passenger vehicles to transport occupants' bicycles to biking trails and competitions usually padded with quick-release clamps or straps. The typical bike (or ski) rack is likely to remain mounted on the vehicle year-around and always increases aerodynamic drag, often as much as doubling the vehicle coefficient ($C_d$). The largely ego-expression appurtenance significantly increases vehicle fuel use and pollution production, maybe as much as the lawn mowers and gasoline-fueled home gardening tools. There must be a better way!

**billboard:** a large panel designed to display outdoor advertising usually in prominent view of vehicle roadways.

**billet:** a relatively bulky mass of metal used as feedstock for further processing into useful machine parts.

**biodegradable:** capable of being broken down especially from harmful/toxic substances into innocuous/benign products friendly to the environment and reusable to man by the action of living things such as microorganisms.

**bioenergetics:** the biology of energy transformations and energy exchanges within and between living things and their environments. Bioengineering.

**biofuel:** a fuel produced by biological action of living and/or formerly living organisms. Likely the vehicle fuel(s) of the future just as are those of the present and the past. Availability and quantity of our future fuels will depend upon man's success in improving Mother Nature's technology--a speeding up of the fossil factory.

**biomass:** various plant material, animal, industrial, or societal waste products (man's garbage) useful as the feedstock for biofuel production.

**bitstock:** a crank-like device for turning a drill bit using hand power. Brace and bit.

**black:** Henry Ford's contribution to vehicle styling and merchandizing. The only color available on about 15,000,000 Model T Fords, probably the worst possible choice for a vehicle outer color because of poor visibility with low light and high heat absorption/radiation.

**Black-and-White:** like today's "wildebunch" hotrodders, our early lead-foots with Thunder Road rumrunner heritage may have coined the first pejorative--but descriptive--colloquial nickname for the police officer and his patrol cruiser. Because of the striking stripes or checkerboard pattern of black and white. Fuzz. Smokey.

**blackbody:** an ideal body or surface that completely absorbs all radiant energy impinging upon it with no radiation in return.

**blackbox:** a usually complicated electronic device normally encased in a non-removable sealed cover box that is installed/removed as an intact unit. Not intended for individual parts repair.

**black flag:** the automobile race track signal flag used to order race drivers to get off the track and return to the pits immediately.

**black gold:** oil-patch slang for the crude petroleum particularly the massive flow from a new gusher.

**black light:** the invisible ultraviolet (UV) and the infrared (IR) frequencies just beyond the two visible light extremities that excite certain paints (as instrument markings) to emit fluorescent light for nighttime vehicle instrument displays.

**Black Maria:** street name for the police vehicle used to transport prisoners to jail. Paddy Wagon.

**blackout:** a phenomenon caused by lack of blood to the brain from excessive G-forces sometimes encountered in high speed racing. A brief temporary loss of vision.

**blacksmith:** a metalworker name assigned to early motor vehicle mechanics from their predecessor horseshoer/wagonsmith.

**black top:** the bituminous (asphaltic) black coating used as a surface finish for various types of vehicle roadways.

**blade connector:** a flat tongue-shaped electrical connector that pushes into or is bolted/clamped to a matching shape.

**bleed:** to drain a vehicle working hydro/pneumatic system of fluid prior to maintenance or replenishment.

**bleed screw:** a form of threaded valve usually with a conical/tapered seat allowing controlled draining of a hydraulic system's working liquid while preventing back-flow (as of air).

**blem:** acceptable abbreviation in the vehicle tire trade to designate a new tire having a minor manufacturing defect usually a cosmetic blemish that does not influence serviceability or safety and that is sold at a significant discount. The letters B-L-E-M are usually etched into the tire sidewall.

**blind spot:** that portion of a vehicle's environment invisible to the driver in normal driving position, creating an area where one is unable to exercise judgment or discrimination.

**blinker:** any of various vehicle lights that flash on and off as clearance or danger warnings. Flasher.

**blister pack:** a parts or component package with a clear plastic covering usually sealed to a sheet of cardboard.

**block:** the casting that contains the cylinders of an internal combustion engine.

**blow-back:** see back-fire.

**blow-by:** excess leakage of engine air/gases past a piston and/or its sealing rings usually due to wear or breakage.

**blower:** vehicle mechanic's generic name for either a turbocharger (exhaust turbine driven) or supercharger (mechanical gear/belt driven) compressor for increasing volume and pressure of intake air into a vehicle engine.

**blow-out:** the sudden failure of a vehicle tire causing an explosive-like outrush of its inflation air.

**blow-out plug:** a bundle of rubber strands designed to be forced into a small blow-out hole in a vehicle tire as an emergency patch. A special inside boot liner held in place by the inner tube pressure is used for larger but manageable sized blow-outs.

**blow torch:** a small hand-held burner using pressurized fuel for small heating jobs on vehicles such as soldering when there is no electric power available.

**blue:** a spray or brush-on coating for metal designed to accept scribed lines to guide various machine cutting operations.

**bluebook:** an association-compiled publication of actual vehicle sales prices used by dealers to establish trade-in values of used vehicles for sale/trade.

**blue law:** a law prohibiting the sale of certain products on Sundays (clearly unconstitutional) but still imposed (1995) against the sale of new vehicles by licensed dealers in some states.

**blueprint:** an assembly/machining drawing using white lines and notation on a blue paper. Engine mechanic's name for the process of totally disassembling an engine, usually new, and verifying that every individual part/piece is exactly sized to the manufacturers specifications and then reassembling to the exact correct tolerances. Sometimes required for all engines to be used in a regulated racing or competitive event.

**BMEP:** brake mean effective pressure is the engine cylinder pressure, derived through calculations, required to give the engine brake horsepower as measured by a dynamometer. BMEP is the quantitative value of the engines' indicated mean effective pressure reduced by the mechanical efficiency of the engine as tested.

**boat tail:** the rear section of an automobile usually a sports coupe/convertible/ roadster that tapers to the rear for aerodynamic improvement in roughly the configuration of a tapered-end canoe.

**bobtail:** the power section of an articulated tractor-trailer vehicle when it is being driven disconnected from its trailer. Shorty.

**body number:** synonymous with the legal Vehicle Identification Number (VIN) or Serial Number (SN) because this number is permanently a part of every vehicle body.

**body shop:** a vehicle repair/manufacturing facility where bodies are repaired or made. Usually includes finishing and painting. Paint and body shop. Paint shop.

**body work:** the usually permanently affixed structural outer covering panelwork of motor vehicles. The repair/replacement of the vehicle outer body.

**bogey:** a heavy vehicle undercarriage usually consisting of multiple axles that are linked, suspended, and sprung as a unit. On a railroad car it is called a truck of wheels.

**bolt-on:** a mechanic's term usually reserved for aftermarket components intended to hotrod/soup-up (boost acceleration, power, and speed) a stock vehicle without major redesign or modification. Just bolt it on and go.

**bomb:** hotrod jargon for the high-performance vehicle that both goes and sounds like a bomb. The calorimeter (a highly-insulated vacuum walled container that resembles a military bomb) that is used to measure and quantify the energy (BTU heat content) of vehicle fuels with extreme laboratory precision.

**bookmobile:** a specially-equipped vehicle (truck, bus, van) that serves as a traveling library for the convenience of outlying and suburban residents.

**boneshaker:** slang but descriptive name for the early bicycles (high-wheelers) and solid suspension motor vehicles (no springs, shocks, or pneumatic tires) that shock everything except when rolling on a glass-smooth surface.

**bonnet:** British name for the usually hinged covering (hood) that provides access to a vehicle engine compartment.

**boom:** the audible pounding of air flow over an opening in a vehicle passenger compartment (window, vent, or sunroof) that creates rebounding impulses. The structural lifting arm of a vehicle wrecker or cargo-handling device.

**boost:** to increase or amplify a pressure or quantity. To fast-charge (boost) a vehicle battery, increase the amperage flowing to the battery. To supercharge (boost) an engine, increase the pressure/volume of the incoming combustion air/gases by conventional compressor action.

**boost start:** to start a vehicle that has a weak on-board battery it is connected to a strong external source of electrical power (another vehicle's battery, a specially designed starting unit, or commercial power system) using auxiliary clamp-on cables (jumpers).

**booster coil:** an auxiliary ignition coil that supplies extra spark (energy) to the vehicle engine's spark plugs during the cranking operation.

**boot:** the British name for the rear luggage storage compartment of a passenger automobile (trunk). A flexible enclosure sealed around movable junctions to prevent leakage of unwanted fluids or contaminants to the surrounding area. Grease boot, hydraulic cylinder boot, shift-lever boot, axle boot, et al.

**bore:** the internal diameter of a cylinder. To make a round hole with a drill or cutting tool. To enlarge or straighten (as removing a taper) a vehicle cylinder (brake, engine, or pump).

**borescope:** a diagnostic viewing device that allows a vehicle mechanic to visually inspect interior cavities through small openings (engine cylinder through the spark plug hole). A small-diameter usually flexible tube equipped with lights, mirrors, and optics.

**boring bar:**  a rigid cutting tool holder designed for machining large diameter cylinders/holes.  An align-boring bar is for boring main bearings or camshaft bearings installed in an engine block.

**borrow pit:**  an excavated area usually alongside a roadway from which fill material was removed to fill nearby road depressions.

**boss:**  an enlarged section of a shaft to facilitate the mounting of a wheel, gear, or pulley.  A strengthening mass of material usually at any mating juncture or mounting fastening.

**bottled gas:**  pressurized gases, usually vehicle fuels as butane, propane, or compressed natural gas and shop gases such as acetylene, oxygen, helium, or argon used primarily for welding.

**bottom dead center:**  the position of piston travel where the piston is nearest to the crankshaft axis and farthest from the cylinder head.

**bottom end bearing:**  the connecting rod-to-crankshaft bearing. Big end bearing.

**bottom gear:**  the transmission gear giving the lowest ratio of wheel velocity to engine speed (the highest ratio of engine rpm to roadspeed) and the highest torque to the vehicle's driven wheels.  Low gear.  First gear.

**bottoming tap:**  a machine threading tool designed to cut a full thread to the very bottom of a drilled hole.  Finish tap.

**bottom out:**  to extend a vehicle suspension to its extremity from which it begins to rebound.

**bounce test:**  a mechanic's evaluation of a vehicle's suspension/shock absorbers by depressing then suddenly releasing each corner of a vehicle and observing the damping of the rebound oscillations.

**Bowden brake:**  a vehicle mechanical brake actuated by a sheathed (Bowden) cable.

**Bowden cable:**  a mechanical control system utilizing a usually stranded cable in tension within a flexible housing to operate mechanical brake, accelerators, chokes, dampers, et al., that require relatively light push-pull motions.

**bow tie:**  known to every Chevvy chauffeur as the real name of the celebrated Chevrolet marque that resembles a man's formal neck-band.

**box beam:**  a closed section structural member fabricated from thin sheet material into very strong and light members capable of withstanding shear and torsion loads.

**box-van:**  a cargo truck with a rectangular freight compartment mounted behind the cab.  Cube-van.

**bra:**  the flexible usually fabric protective covering stretched over the front nose section of sports cars ostensibly to protect the paint finish from pebble pings or other roadway debris--actually to bloat the car owner's ego to a size XL-56-FF cup. Can one really stuff a VW's bra with falsies until the Beetle becomes a Bugatti Royale?

**brain box:**  mechanic's slang for the sophisticated on-board computer in today's vehicles that contains the programs, the memory, the reactive capability to use exhaust-sensed information to computer control the engine to give the maximum performance/efficiency and the minimum exhaust pollution.

**brake:**  any of various mechanisms to retard and/or to stop the motion of a vehicle or to prevent inadvertent movement when parked.  An engine dynamometer utilizing a friction (prony) brake and torque arm to measure output horsepower.  British name for a utility passenger vehicle usually with external wood construction popular with society hunters for carrying dogs and sporting equipment.  Shooting brake.  Station wagon.  Estate car.

**brake anti-roll-back:**  a gravity-enhanced check valve in a vehicle hydraulic brake system allowing the driver to release pedal pressure when stopped on an uphill slope without the vehicle rolling backward while waiting to go again.  Starting forward immediately releases the brake pressure.  Studebaker and Hudson advertised this brake feature as the "Hill-Holder".

**brake caliper:**  in a disc brake system the mechanism that holds the brake friction pads in position and uses a pressure clamping action to apply braking forces to the disc system.

**brake cylinder:**  the hydraulic cylinder (master and slave) in which the piston generates and applies the pressure that actuates the force against the friction surfaces that stops the vehicle.

**brake fade:**  the loss of braking effort resulting from over-heating of the brake's friction surfaces.

**brake fluid:**  the liquid used to transfer braking force to the friction elements that stop and or slow vehicle motion utilizing the noncompressibility of liquids theory.  Early ground vehicles usually used vegetable oils, aircraft and racing cars soon adopted petroleum oils, and most modern brake fluids are specially compounded synthetics.

**brake hone:** a polishing abrasive grinder used to remove pits and imperfections from the interior surface of a hydraulic brake cylinder.

**brake lever:** the hand-operated vehicle brake control that complements the foot-operated brake control pedal. Emergency brake, hand brake, parking brake.

**brake light:** see stop light.

**brake mean effective pressure:** see BMEP

**brake pad:** the pressure plate faced with a block of friction material that applies the stopping force when pressed against the brake disc.

**brake pedal:** the foot-powered control that actuates vehicle braking action.

**brake return spring:** the tension spring that returns the vehicle brake pedal past its free play insuring against unwanted brake drag. The brake shoe retractor.

**brake shoe:** the arcuate internally expanding semicircular metal base to which the friction lining is attached to mate with the brake drum friction face.

**brake thermal efficiency:** the ratio of the actual energy (horsepower) output of an engine to the actual energy (fuel) input supplied to the engine.

**braking ratio:** the percentage of the total braking effort of the front wheel pair to the total braking effort of the rear wheel pair. Percentage of total vehicle braking distribution.

**brand name:** a product name having a reputation and a loyal following of users/purchasers. Trade name.

**brass:** an alloy consisting primarily of copper and zinc. Widely used in vehicle bushings. Formerly used for aesthetic trim embellishment.

**braze:** to solder with any nonferrous metal or alloy that melts at a lower temperature than that of the metals being joined.

**breakdown:** to stop functioning because of breakage or wear. To become inoperative or ineffective. Likely the source of automobile cliches: "If it ain't broke don't fix it . . . drive it 'till it breaks . . . make a one-horse-shay outa that car".

**breaker:** generic name for the mechanism known variously as breaker assembly, points, breaker contacts, breaker plate, et al., that for so many years has been the source of every spark plug firing. The breaker (points) closes the electrical circuit that builds up the energy reserve in the coil that the same mechanism then releases as the burst of fire that ignites the vehicle engine's fuel by breaking the circuit. High-tech evolution will soon erase the word breaker from our automobile vocabulary as breakerless ignitions are phased into the system. No-moving-parts ignitions are just over the horizon.

**break-in:** an initial period of conservative operation of a new vehicle to allow parts to wear to a better fit. Once essential, modern precision machining has removed the need for extensive break-in periods.

**breather:** a vented opening to a closed container as a tank to allow vapor/gas to escape and dissipate to the outside air.

**Brewster:** early-American builder of prestige automobiles and custom coachwork until 1934.

**brick yard:** the race driver's name for the Indianapolis Speedway 500 Race Track because for many years the track's oval driving surface was paved with bricks.

**Brighton Run:** the annual historic automobile race for early-day automobiles from London to Brighton (England). Many other races mimic the Brighton Run in honor of our first automobiles as a largely society social event to show off ego vehicles-- not to go-fast race.

**Brinnell hardness:** the hardness of a metal or alloy as measured by pressing a hardened steel ball under a standard load into specimen surface. The area of the resulting indentation is converted to a relative number (Brinnell Number) identifying the degree of hardness. Developed by Johann A. Brinnell (Swedish engineer) about 1925.

**British thermal unit:** the quantity of heat required to raise the temperature of one pound of water one degree Fahrenheit at a specified temperature (as 39° F). A universal energy (heat) measurement unit used to rate and evaluate the energy content of vehicle fuels. BTU. Calorie.

**broach:** any of variously-shaped cutting tools used under heavy pressure to cut internal and external shapes (usually matching) as internal and external splines on shafts/collars.

**broadside:** to hit or be hit directly from the side as by another vehicle. Head-on.

**bromate primer:** a protective coating for metals utilizing various bromic acid combinations. Zinc bromate is particularly effective in preventing salt corrosion of metals.

**bronze:** an alloy of copper and tin ideally suited as bushings or any sliding-friction contact particularly with steel/iron pieces. Also widely used for functional/ornamental castings and as a protective coating for other metals. Bronzed.

**brougham:** an automobile design/body-configuration evolved from the horse-drawn carriage with the driver outside in front. Some coupes especially when adorned with landau irons are called broughams but more formal sedans with no (or a retractable) roof over the driver's seat are considered the true brougham.

**brushed finish:** various exterior metal surfaces particularly the relatively non-tarnishings (aluminum, brass, bronze, stainless steel, et al.) that are left uncovered or clear-coated after the exposed surface has been marked with fine parallel scratches as with an abrasive of 80-160 grit.

**bubble balance:** a simple but effective simple machine for static balancing a vehicle wheel by adding peripheral weights until the bubble at the wheel hub is centered.

**bubble top:** any of specially built vehicles having a clear plastic spherical-shaped roof to provide visibility or special protection for the usual celebrity occupant (Pope, President, entertainment stars).

**buckboard:** an open horse-drawn four-wheel vehicle that was mimicked by the early automobiles that evolved from the buggies. Many early gas-buggies were in fact identical to their previous horse-drawn twins.

**bucket-of-bolts:** mechanic's slang for a motor vehicle that has been terribly abused and/or neglected to the extent that it is literally falling apart.

**bucket seat:** a usually low, deep, and contoured individual vehicle seat with some side restraint to provide occupant constraint in fast cornering.

**bucking bar:** a riveting tool of heavy metal used as the anvil against which the rivet end is upset by the hammering action of the rivet gun.

**bucking dolly:** a heavy mass of metal usually fitted for hand holding and shaped to serve as a contour against which a vehicle body panel is hammered to remove dents/bumps.

**buff:** car lingo for the dedicated automobile enthusiast about whom some would say "cars are his life or he lives for cars". An automobile aficionada(o).

**buffing compound:** an abrasive paste or powder applied to the pad on a spinning or oscillating machine to polish (buff) a vehicle finish. Buffing rouge is a very fine abrasive.

**buffing pad:** a pad of fabric or synthetic material designed for application and "rubbing out" of an abrasive/chemical compound for polishing/smoothing of a painted or metallic surface.

**buffing wheel:** a powered rotating wheel with a surface designed to finish/polish parts that are held and pressed against the rotating surface. Either the wheel surface or an applied abrasive compound provide the cutting material.

**buggy spring:** slang for a leafed spring usually mounted transversely to the vehicle/axle as did the horse-drawn buggy of yore.

**built-up crankshaft:** a crankshaft assembled from many separate parts usually splined and bolted together to the same configuration as the traditional one-piece forged/machined units. The Bugatti 8-cylinder crankshaft is likely the epitome of this design.

**bulb horn:** an early vehicle air horn whose air blast was produced by a rubber bulb squeezed by the driver's hand.

**bulldog:** the hood/radiator ornament on a Mack truck as the company's marque. Often attached to much smaller trucks as an ostentatious ego expression.

**bumper:** a horizontal structural member mounted transversely at the front and rear of a vehicle to prevent or reduce damage from low speed impacts.

**bumper bolt:** a round-head bolt like a carriage bolt with a locking square section beneath the head to stop its rotation during tightening. Both functional and ornamental.

**bumper jack:** a usually post-type hydraulic or mechanical ratchet jack that attaches under the vehicle bumper and first raises the body/fender and then a wheel for emergency tire replacement.

**bungee:** an elastic stranded cord with hooks at the ends of various lengths for tying light cargo or fabric coverings in place on vehicles. In endless loops like belts bungee cord was once used for support springs for ground vehicles and early airplanes.

**Burma Shave:** remembered as one of the first outdoor sign advertisers along our first highways using a succession of one-word signs ending with the trade name on the last sign.

**burnish:** to polish by rubbing the finished workpiece with any of various burnishing tools that used friction to impart the desired gloss finish.

**burled walnut:** a prized walnut-grained wood finish used for instrument panels (dashboards) and interior trim on prestige automobiles.

**burn rubber:** an excessively fast start or any rapid acceleration of a motor vehicle that results in spinning, slipping, smoking tires.

**bushing:** a cylindrical sleeve forming a bearing surface for a shaft or pin.

**butane:** either of two isomeric flammable gaseous paraffin hydrocarbons ($C_4H_{10}$) obtained from natural gas or petroleum and used extensively as a pressurized vehicle fuel.

**butterfly valve:** a disc/plate valve pivoted about its diameter/centerline and acting as a throttle in a pipe or chamber/duct. The intake air throttle valve in virtually every carburetor in every automobile throughout history.

**Butyl:** trademark name used for any of various synthetic rubbers made by polymerizing isobutylene.

**bypass:** a channel/conduit carrying a fluid around a part and back into the main stream.

**bypass filter:** a liquid filter, such as an oil filter that filters only a portion of the full flow, assuming that all system liquid will ultimately pass through the filter. A full-flow filter that has a bypass around the filter to insure liquid (as oil to an engine) flow albeit unfiltered if the filter should become totally clogged or with severely restricted flow.

**bypass valve:** a valve that may be manual, automatic, or flow-actuated by direct liquid flow through a bypass.


LAGNIAPPE

**blue smoke:** visible blue color in an engine exhaust that always indicates burning oil, usually from ring blow-by or worn valve stems.

**brake lathe:** a machine tool that spins brake discs or drums and sizes/smoothes the friction faces with cutting tools/grinders.

**breaker bar:** a longer than normal socket handle that provides extra torque for "breaking loose" tight fastenings.

**burette:** a precision laboratory measuring device as a long slender glass container for liquids with scribed markings indicating cubic centimeters, and used to determine the volume of an engine cylinder head by adding increments of liquid until full and using this value added to the cylinder displacement to determine compression ratio.

**burn-out:** spinning the wheels to roughen and warm the tires before starting a race, sometimes using bleach or water to clean the tires.

**business coupe:** before World War II, an inexpensive coupe without rear seating, favored by outside salesmen and house-call Doctors.

## THE BETTER MOUSETRAP

As immutable as Natural Laws, the "Mousetrap Theory" has lost credibility in today's technically illiterate society. Modern man, driven by greed and embracing hedonism, has lost the country logic and perceptiveness of our "gas buggy" forebears.

Best we reinstate the "Better Mousetrap Theory" to its rightful place as our Guardian Angel of all that is good about the automobile and as the infallible test of all technology--ancient, contemporary, and future.

The proponents and purveyors of "alternative fuel" and "snake oil" scams (water fuel, air fuel, and the appurtenances that purport to burn or to produce them) cannot survive the mousetrap test. Neither can any political administration's "most favored fuel". All disingenuously disinform society. They lie!

Back about 1783 another dictionary, Noah Webster's, defined "alternative" as "what we use when we can't get what is most desirable or best". Clearly, the use of any alternative fuel is sheer insanity because choosing something that is demonstrably inferior (ersatz) is injurious to the health and happiness of the automobile and its environs. All alternative fuels--past, contemporary, and visionary--flunk the mousetrap test. Except **HYDROGEN**! It's **BEST**!

Webster's contribution to the "alternative" fuel dilemma is "broke" but ready to be "fixed". It's easy! Just name hydrogen as the best fuel. Because it is! Utopian! Plentiful: Count every atom in our universe--93% of 'em will be hydrogen. Weigh the universe--78% of it will be hydrogen. That's a lot of stuff. Hydrogen! Recyclable: Instantly, in a no-residue (no ashes) process. Hydrogen "burns" (rapidly combines, chemically, with oxygen) releasing its heat (energy) and becoming the purest of water. Water (with energy input) separates into hydrogen and oxygen (both benign, each ready to do an immediate chemical flip-flop and be water again). Zero-polluting: you saw it do it in the previous sentence--and why. Energy dense: a pound of hydrogen has three times the energy of a pound of gasoline or diesel and only slightly less than three times as much as butane, natural gas, or propane. Four and one-half times the energy of ethanol and six times the energy of methanol. Safe: despite its greater energy density hydrogen is the safest vehicle fuel (energy carrier) to produce, to store, to transport, and to use.

Deep six all "alternatives" (including petroleum). Revert OPEC to a Bedouin lifestyle. Forget the Hindenburg! Crown hydrogen as our nation's "most favored fuel".

Indulge in deja vu. In 1981 Ronald Reagan, prompted by Archer, Daniels, Midland, Astronaut Gordon Cooper, and his personal pilot (when Governor of California), read from his Teleprompter that ethanol is our "most favored fuel". 'Twas for 8 years. But didn't shrink OPEC, bleach LA's smog, enrich the farmer, or restore our energy independence. More of Nancy's crystal-ball decisions?

George Bush, parroting the "Oil Patch" party line (1989) choose that other alcohol--methanol that's feedstocked from fossil fuel as his "most favored fuel". Clearly, a predictable decision. OPEC burgeoned. We shriveled to inanition. Both also predictable!

Bill Clinton (1993) blown along, predictably, by the "gas passers" (Gore, McClarty, and O'Leary), named natural gas our "most favored fuel", insuring OPEC's "most favored nation" role. **WHOOPEE!**

All three omniscient heads of state proclaimed "their" fuel the answer to our energy dilemma, promised the country's conversion to their stuff because it was cheaper, cleaner, and better--eliminating our foreign trade imbalance. Each perpetuated our nonexistent national energy policy, myopically viewing energy only over the five-foot distance "from the filler-pipe to the tail-pipe". OPEC profited. We paid. Had Ronnie, George, or Billiary a "mouse-trap"?

It's embarrassing to admit that feckless leaders of our great nation and their fellow-traveling camp-followers can hoodwink our entire society with such outlandish lies. One of reasonable mind must question why not one "whistle-blower" in our Department of Energy--or the scientific community--exposed or opposed this mammoth fraud by our inept leaders--for sixteen years?

The bottom line: no fuel--that must be aggrandized and subsidized, that is irrationally price-compared with some fuels assessed add-on taxes of over 40 cents per unit (gallon) and others taxed at zero-pennies, that has only a fractional quantity of energy (vehicle distance-making ability) of other fuels--can ever be a better mousetrap. That Natural Law is chiseled in stone!

The reality: Isn't/wasn't it obvious that each/either of the politically "chosen fuels" could not be the best for our country? That none was? Clearly our country has no energy policy, but a leadership steeped in stupidity and a lemming-like newsmedia leading us inescapably, into a technically illiterate future society.

Best we amend Uncle Sugar's Constitution, re-establishing the "Better Mousetrap Theory" as America's Icon, placing the "trap" prominently on the Presidential Seal, replacing bumbling bureaucrats with technocrats to guide our new technocracy, and installing the daily "Mousetrap Pledge" at the beginning of every day at every level of education.

Let the "Mousetrap" lead us!

**C-Cars:** The letter "C" clearly stands for cars, all of them, and is proud to start such great names as Cadillac, Chevrolet, and Chrysler, as its All-American Team and to name Citroen as the shining star (certainly deserving a Heisman Trophy) and the team captain of the world team of the 425 other players that have "C" names. America's "Standard of the World", Cadillac, was created in 1903 by Henry M. Leland, then associated with Henry Ford, so it was no mere coincidence that for a few years Cadillacs and Fords were indistinguishable--some might say, identical twins. Cadillac was introduced to Britain in 1908 when F. S. Bennett conducted a "standardization test" at Brooklands. He completely dismantled three new Cadillacs and had the pile of parts indiscriminately scrambled, then reassembled three cars and raced them on the famed Brooklands race course. The Royal Automobile Club awarded Cadillac its vaunted Dewar Trophy for this achievement--a conclusive verification of complete parts interchangeability. Cadillac's original Ford three-pedal planetary transmission gave way to a conventional 3-speed gear box and clutch, with a two-speed rear axle, in 1914. Just a few more mileposts along the road to Cadillac's supremacy: the synchromesh gearbox made its world debut in the 1929 model; 1930 brought the 7.4-litre V-16 engine with overhead valves complemented by an equally impressive 6-litre V-12 in 1931; tail fins first appeared on the 1948 fastback coupe; Cadillacs with their new 5.4-litre oversquare engine were raced at Le Mans in 1950 by Briggs Cunningham against the world's finest race cars; Cadillac, with Lincoln, pioneered four headlights that later became universal in the U.S.; and so many more. Chevrolet, nurtured with Cadillac, under the General Motors umbrella wore a lot of Cadillac "hand-me-downs" that helped establish the BowTie marque as General Motors' least expensive car and as the world's best seller. Walter P's Chrysler was a late-starter behind Ford and General Motors (1923) and is still running third in the American car Great Race.

**car:** Warning! This word is out of its alphabetical order--deliberately. Because it's the most important word in the American lexicon--the first word spoken by nearly every American man-child. If you don't already know, it's the automobile, gas buggy, gas-guzzler, Tin Lizzie, flivver, bucket-of-bolts, limo, hot-rod, junker, clunker, rod, dragster, strip-down, rust bucket, hog, dog, money-pit, draggin' wagon, hack, cab, towaway, taxi, cammer, dreamboat, love bug, chariot, cafe racer, rattle-trap, high boy, deuce, four-banger, caddy, woodie, lowrider, beetle, classic, fast-back, turtle back, dual-cowl, and wheels. Although often said with a lisp, they all mean CAR.

**cab:** this word comes first--after car. Meaning the compartment containing the controls and appurtenances necessary for management and operation of a motor vehicle and occupied by the driver of the vehicle--particularly as of a truck or commercial vehicle. Taxicab. Cab. Hansom cab. Locomotive cab.

**cab-alongside-engine:** the location of a single-occupant cab alongside the vehicle's engine on some off-highway and specialty vehicles to provide the driver a more forward location for precision maneuvering or positioning of vehicle and its on-board devices as a crane, aerial ladder, or boom-arm work-bucket.

**cab-behind-engine:** typical of most cars and trucks the engine is located in an easily recognizable hooded enclosure, comppletely forward of the windshield of the driver's cab.

**cabbie:** a taxicab chauffeur or driver. Cabby.

**cable car:** (1) A car made to be towed along a railway by an endless (looped) cable-powered by a stationary engine/motor activating a cable reel/winch usually on a very steep slope as the world famous San Francisco cable cars. (2) Cars suspended from cables and cable-powered as scenic passenger carriers over mountain gorges or otherwise impassable terrain, and large enclosed ski lift gondolas.

**cableway:** the suspended cable that serves as the track along which cable cars are pulled. Tramway. Ropeway.

**cab-over-engine:** a vehicle with all or most of the engine located beneath the driver's cab, which is hinged at its front so the entire cab may be tilted up at the rear to provide access to the engine and transmission for maintenance, repair, and servicing. COE. Lift-cab. Tilt-cab.

**cable brake:** a vehicle brake operated by an open cable in tension or by a Bowden sheathed cable actuated by a foot pedal, lever or pull-handle. Now obsolete except for emergency/parking brakes.

**cabriolet:** a passenger car with a fabric/synthetic usually padded top, roll-up side windows, and sometimes landau irons used as hinges when folding/retracting the top, but sometimes non-functional (decorative only). Convertible. Drop head.

**cab stand:** a waiting area where taxicabs regularly pick up passengers, often at an airport, hotel, rail or bus station, or sports arena.

**caddy:** (1) A pouch, belt, or small container, sometimes wheeled, used by vehicle mechanics to carry miscellaneous small tools and parts when working on jobs away from their tool box or work bench. (2) Abbreviation for Cadillac.

**Cadillac:** the great American prestige automobile. Caddy. See C-cars.

**cadmium:** a bluish white malleable ductile toxic bivalent metallic element widely used in vehicles as a protective coating and in bearing material alloys.

**cad-plated:** vehicle parts, tools, and trim pieces that have a usually electroplated thin coating of cadmium as a surface protectant.

**CAFE:** Corporate Average Fuel Economy is a federally mandated vehicle fuel consumption standard imposed upon all manufacturers selling vehicles in the United States in an attempt to improve fuel economy, reduce our dependence upon imported fuel, and reduce vehicle exhaust pollution of the atmosphere. Failure to meet the fuel economy by a manufacturer results in a significant monetary fine per vehicle sold.

**cafe racer:** usually applied to motorcycles that have added gadgetry to make them look like racing vehicles but which, in fact, do not necessarily improve performance.

**cage:** the enclosure containing the planetary or epicyclic gears as in a vehicle transmission.

**caleche:** a two-wheeled horse drawn vehicle with a driver's seat on the splashboard that was associated by its peculiar design only with Quebec, Canada.

**calibrate:** to verify the accuracy (against accepted standards) of readings from any mechanic's measuring tool or vehicle's instrument, to insure its useability and to make its readings comparable to all other similar tools and instruments. If readings are accurate the tool or instrument is certified, if not, the necessary adjustments are made. If unable to adjust, a calibration sheet of corrections is prepared to accompany the tool or instrument.

**caliper:** in a disc brake system, the component, usually a casting, that contains the hydraulic cylinders/pistons and friction pads that bear upon the disc to create the braking force for stopping the vehicle. Also as a mechanic's measuring tool, caliper is a telescoping/sliding two-part scale with one fixed jaw and one sliding jaw, both configured to show inside or outside linear distances/measurements with great precision on a dial indicator, digital read-out, or vernier (usually to the ten-thousandth of an inch or metric equivalent).

**call-back:** a recall by a manufacturer of a recently sold automobile for correction of a defect. Recall.

**calorie:** the amount of heat (energy) required to raise the temperature of one gram of water one degree centigrade--a small calorie or gram-calorie. A kilogram-calorie (1,000 gram-calories) is equal to 3.968 BTU, a conversion factor used to convert "American" to Metric measurements of energy/heat.

**cam:** a profiled shape (somewhat resembling a pear) that when rotated around its shaft-center produces linear or angular motion or lift to a follower in rubbing contact with the profiled shape (cam lobe) that is used to actuate a vehicle engine's poppet valves (intake and exhaust). Eccentric. Lobe.

**cam-actuated brake:** a shoe or pad, usually internally-expanded by the rotation of an elongated cam lobe around a fixed center that exerts force to move the friction surface against a drum.

**cam and roller gear:** a helically-cut waisted cam that converts shaft rotation into lever linear motion through tapered disc(s) that engage (mesh) with the helical cut.

**camber:** the inclination (slant) of the vertical plane of a vehicle wheel to the true vertical plane of the vehicle. Camber is called positive when the wheel leans out (from the vehicle center) at the top and negative if it slopes inward. Measured in degrees or inches.

**camber angle:** the angle in degrees between the plane of a vehicle wheel and the vertical axis of the vehicle when viewed from the front or rear.

**camber tire wear:** a wear pattern on the tread of a vehicle tire in which one side is evenly worn as the result of the "lean" of the wheel.

**cam brake:** a vehicle brake usually a drum-type in which the shoes are spread (pressured) against the drum by rotation of a cam.

**cam contour:** see cam profile.

**camel-back:** an uncured compound composed of reclaimed or synthetic rubber used for recapping or retreading motor vehicle tires, using heat to effect the bonding.

**cam follower:** a lever or rubbing block that follows (rides on) the lobe's contour surface thus converting rotational force into linear force. Tappet. Valve lifter.

**cam-ground piston:** a piston ground slightly out-of-round (oval shaped) to counteract thermal expansion of the piston material thus providing a more concentric fit in the cylinder bore.

**cam-lock bearing:** a ball or roller bearing whose inner race is locked to its shaft by an inner cam (eccentric) locking ring that is tightened over the race extension.

**cammer:** race car slang for an engine that has cams with high lift and long duration of valve-opening (usually called race cams) that give the engine a noticeable increase in power, particularly at the design speed for peak cam effect ("when the cam comes in").

**camper:** a vehicle with an enclosed truck/van body with sleeping and other living facilities.

**camper jack:** (1) A jacking device used to level a camper (trailer) when parked on uneven (sloping terrain). (2) A set of four (one-for-each-corner) tall telescoping jacks used to lift and store (until next use) a camper shell from a pick-up or other truck.

**camper shell:** a lightweight roof and side enclosure that fits a pick-up or other light truck cargo body for occasional use for camping and for protecting cargo.

**camping trailer:** a usually low-profile trailer (some may be expanded upward and outward when parked) that can be erected and/or supplemented by folding tents and that stores camping equipment and supplies, towed behind a light vehicle (passenger car) to campsites.

**camshaft:** a shaft on which cam lobes are machined or positively locked in place with one lobe for each valve to be operated. A camshaft on a four-cycle engine is operated at one-half crankshaft (engine) rpm.

**camshaft grinder:** a lathe-like machine tool that rotates a camshaft as an attached grinding wheel follows a profile of the finished lobe and grinds the spinning lobe to the shape prescribed by the profile. A technician who grinds camshafts.

**camshaft pump:** a vehicle's gasoline pump (as a diaphragm) operated usually by a hinged follower, or an engine oil pump (as a piston) operated usually by a plunger or a push-rod from a special eccentric cam on the valve camshaft.

**canard:** a horizontal control or stabilizing airfoil section attached to the front of a racing vehicle. Wing.

**cancer:** mechanic's slang for rust or corrosion of a motor vehicle or its parts particularly when unsightly or adversely affecting operation or performance.

**candescence:** the visible glowing of a material that is heated to extremes. Red hot. White hot. Incandescence.

**candlepower:** luminous intensity expressed in candles (foot-candles). One candle equivalent produces one lumen of luminous flux. Long without a scientifically acceptable definition, in 1940 one candle was refined to represent the luminous intensity of 1/60th of a square centimeter of a black body radiator operating at the temperature of solidification of pure platinum.

**candy-apple red:** a high-gloss vehicle exterior paint finish that resembles the appearance of a candied apple.

**canned horsepower:** a derisive description used by competent vehicle mechanics to describe any of the additives that claim to increase vehicle performance (fraudulently) or reduce exhaust emissions. Tune-up-in-a-can.

**cannibalize:** to take salvageable parts/components from a disabled/wrecked vehicle for use in building or repairing a like vehicle. Wrecking yard. Salvage yard. Recycled parts.

**canopy:** the streamlined transparent driver's windshield of a race car. A temporary open-sided roof commonly used for shade or protection in the pit areas of vehicle race tracks.

**cantilever:** a projecting beam or structural support member that is firmly anchored at only one end.

**cantilever spring:** a vehicle suspension spring, usually a quarter-elliptical leaf that is rigidly attached to the chassis/frame at one end and carrying the undercarriage (axle, wheels) at its other flexing end.

**cap:** any of several covering devices used to close/protect openings in vehicles/components as: radiator cap, oil-filler cap, gas-tank cap, tire valve-stem cap, et al.

**capacitance:** the property of some electrical nonconductors that permits the storage of energy as a result of electric displacement when opposite surfaces of the nonconductor are maintained at a difference of electrical potential (voltage). Electrical charge.

**capacitor:** a device capable of giving/receiving capacitance that usually consists of foils or plates separated by a dielectric (as air or mica) with the plates on opposite sides of the dielectric layers--being oppositely charged by a voltage and the electrical energy of the charged system stored in the polarized dielectric separators. Condenser.

**capacitor discharge ignition:** a vehicle ignition system that stores its primary energy (to create the ignition spark) in a capacitor.

**capacity:** in a vehicle engine, the displacement (measured swept volume) of its pistons acting through a complete operating thermodynamic cycle (2-revolutions of the crankshaft for a 4-cycle engine). One piston through one intake stroke gives one cylinder's displacement which multiplied by the number of cylinders equals engine displacement.

**capsizing perturbation:** a directional disturbance of a moving vehicle, that if uncontrolled becomes an increasing oscillation that can overturn the vehicle.

**captain's chair:** an individual vehicle seat that usually reclines, rotates, is adjustable in height, with sumptuous upholstery, is readily removable, and that is frequently used as a replacement for stock bus or van bench seats to provide more passenger comfort on long trips.

**captured nut:** a machine nut for a bolt that is imbedded in a hex- or square-shaped depression (or otherwise locked and secured against turning) in a vehicle component to eliminate the need for a wrench on the nut when tightening a bolt or stud into its threads. Usually used in locations unaccessible to a wrench.

**car:** see the first c-word, after C-cars.

**caracature:** a style of car-tooning by graphic artists who depict a car sometimes as resembling a person, animal, or thing other than a car, while retaining identifiable car characteristics. Caricature.

**caravan:** a group of vehicles traveling together over a common route to the same destination that follow each other in an orderly file or established line position.

**car bed:** (1) A portable crib for an infant or small child with provisions for securing against crash forces in a vehicle. (2) Vehicle seating that can be adjusted vertical to horizontal to provide bed-like comfort for some passengers.

**carbide:** (1) A binary compound of carbon with a more electropositive element. (2) A very hard material made up of carbon and one or more heavy metals. (3) Calcium carbide ($CaC_2$) and sodium carbide ($Na_2C_2$) mixed with water form acetylene, a welding gas and the gas used for pre-electric automobile lights. Silicon and tungsten carbide are used in many machining operations and vehicle operations because of their extreme hardness.

**carbide lights:** early automobile acetylene-gas headlights were fueled by a carbide/acetylene generator usually running board mounted on the vehicle.

**carbon:** with atomic number 6, symbol, C, and atomic weight 12.010, carbon is known in three forms: carbon black, diamond, and graphite, and found as pure carbon in nature as diamond and graphite, and combined with innumerable other elements, most notably as hydrocarbons and carbohydrates. Space Ship Earth's primary fuels for machine and for man. Who can say whether carbon's benigness offsets its malignancy? Without carbon there could be no man or vehicle, which working together may pollute both into oblivion.

**carbonaceous:** meaning anything/everything that is rich in carbon as a constituent.

**carbon black:** used as a paint pigment, as an ingredient in most vehicle tires, and in a variety of compounds essential to motor vehicle materials and use. Soot.

**carbon cycle:** the life cycle of carbon in living things (and aped by energy-using machines) in which carbon dioxide ($CO_2$) is fixed by photosynthesis to form organic nutrients (fuels) and is ultimately restored to the inorganic state by respiration and protoplasmic decay (metabolism/burning/oxidation) as the original carbon dioxide. Entropy.

**carbon dating:** the determination of the age of old material/ objects by means of its content of carbon 14. Carbon-date.

**carbon dioxide:** a heavy colorless gas ($CO_2$) that does not support combustion, can be considered the ultimate entropy (ashes) of the burning of carbon but is recycleable by the photosynthesis process designed by nature using living plants as part of the carbon cycle.

**carbon 14:** a heavy radioactive isotope of carbon with a mass number of 14 (compared to carbon's 12) used especially in tracer studies and in historical age-dating of archaeological and geological materials.

**carbonize:** to convert into carbon or a carbonic residue as an internal combustion engine does when burning hydrocarbon fuels forming the well-known carbon deposits that are the bane of the motor vehicle mechanic.

**carbon monoxide:** a colorless odorless very toxic gas (CO) that further oxidizes (burns) to carbon dioxide ($CO_2$) with a blue flame and that is formed by incomplete combustion of carbon. One of our most common motor vehicle exhaust pollutants but which is being conquered by modern fuel and vehicle technology. Exhaust pollution.

**carbon pile:** a device consisting of a container of granular or powdery carbon with a means of changing its density as by pressure/squeezing that is used as a variable load/resistor particularly in voltage regulation.

**carbon steel:** a steel in many degrees of hardness and amenability to control of related characteristics by heat-treating. Steel with 0.04% to 0.25% carbon is called low-carbon and used for drawing and stamping sheets, for nails, rivets, structural shapes, and machine parts to be surface carburized and heat-treated (in the order listed as to strength/hardness). Steel with 0.25% to 0.75% carbon is called medium-/intermediate-carbon and used for high-strength structural shapes, forgings, heat-treatment, railroad car axles and wheels, steel springs, and shock-resisting tools (again in listed order/strength). Steel with 0.75% to 2.25% carbon is high-carbon and used for cold-drawn music wire, drill rod, cutting tools, dies, drills, ball bearings, drawing dies, files, etc., listed in a progression of toughness to hardness. Heat-treated.

**Carborundum:** the trademarked name for a significant number of carbon-based abrasives and grinding devices (wheels, papers, powders, and rouges).

**carboy:** a large bottle of about 5 to 15 gallons liquid capacity that is made of glass or of various synthetic plastics and widely used at motor vehicle races for storing, mixing, and servicing racing fuels.

**carburetion:** the act or operation of atomizing and/or vaporizing liquid fuels and mixing them in ignitable/combustible proportions with an oxidizer (usually air) in a vehicle carburetor. Carburetor.

**carburetor:** a device designed to effect carburetion, the vaporization of a liquid fuel and mixing the fuel and charge air as a near perfect chemical ratio (stoichiometric) to provide burning efficiency to an internal combustion engine. Carburetion.

**carburetor chamber:** the fuel reservoir, maintained at an exact level (constant) by a float-valve to insure desired fuel/air ratios to an engine. Float bowl.

**carburetor choke:** a fuel enrichment device as an air-damper (throttle valve) that restricts the charge-air-flow thus increasing the ratio of fuel-to-air (used when first starting an internal combustion engine and particularly when very cold).

**carburetor ice:** the freezing of the moisture in the air as the velocity of the charge air flowing through a carburetor venturi reduces the ambient temperature below 32° Fahrenheit. An inherent problem of carbureted engines on cool, high-humidity days.

**carburetor stove:** a heat-transfer device utilizing engine coolant heat through a coil or engine exhaust heat through a heat-exchanger/radiator in the carburetor/intake manifold assembly to warm the incoming charge air sufficiently to prevent the formation of carburetor ice. Carburetor heater.

**car carrier:** (1) A truck or tractor-trailer usually with open sides and a frame with wheel-ramps/treads designed to transport multiple-vehicle loads. (2) A usually lightweight 2-wheel trailer/dolly and hitch for lifting and supporting only one end of another vehicle for towing behind a passenger car or light truck. The driving wheels of the towed vehicle are normally borne on the trailer to protect the gearing, allowing the non-powered wheels to roll freely. Car hauler. Car dolly.

**carcass:** see casing.

**car corral:** car slang for a used car lot, shopping center parking area, sports arena parking, et al.

**car cover:** a fabric or synthetic flexible covering tossed over and tied in place to protect a parked or stored vehicle from dust and environmental deterioration.

**car cradle:** a structural support device/machine in which an entire automobile can be securely fastened, raised, and rotated into almost any position to facilitate access by a mechanic as for maintenance, repairs, or painting.

**cardan joint:** a vehicle universal joint that uses a cruciform member coupling two yokes.

**car hop:** slang name for the server at various drive-in facilities as of drinks or fast food.

**Carlisle:** a nation-wide vehicle and parts swap-meet held at Carlisle, Pennsylvania, each year that has become a Mecca for automobile collectors, restorers, and aficionado lookers and sellers.

**car lot:** car jargon for a used car sales dealer's place of business usually with a significant number of for-sale vehicles displayed and sold at an open-air parking area.

**car-of-state:** a prestige limousine chosen by the heads-of-state as the favored vehicle for use by the president, king, emperor, or ruler and their entourage and family. Cadillac, Citroen, Daimler, Lincoln, and Mercedes are among the marques that have been favored by many world political leaders.

**car-pool:** a usually informal arrangement by several individuals who live and work in convenient locations so that they can share rides (and rotate whose vehicle will be driven on equitable schedules) for mutual benefits of all.

**car pound:** a storage area maintained by a government entity as a county or municipality to store vehicles that have been in accidents or statute violations pending a legal disposition allowing the vehicle's return to its owner or its sale at public auction.

**carriage bolt:** a threaded machine bolt with a rounded head that is prevented from turning in wood or similar material by a square section of bolt beneath the head and which is retained by a usually square nut. Used on early buggies/wagons and motor vehicles making extensive use of wooden structures before the advent of modern hexhead machine bolts of stronger materials.

**carriage trade:**  car slang for the affluent buyer/owner of prestige motor vehicles, who also takes meticulous care of all maintenance and appearance requirements of his vehicles.

**car sick:**  a malady that causes dizziness and stomach upset for some susceptible individuals with Meniere's Syndrome or an ear-canal canalith problem when the individual is subjected to repetitive motion as in a vehicle that creates certain G-forces (gravity) that disturb the balance senses as on a road with many sharp curves.

**car-top carrier:**  a closed box or open-frame rack enclosure usually temporarily affixed to a vehicle roof particularly of a station wagon and used for carrying extra luggage or packages. Lighter carriers are frequently used to haul sporting equipment as lightweight boats, bicycles, or skis.

**car wash:**  a usually open bay area with water-under-pressure spray equipment and floor drains for waste water disposal where vehicles can be conveniently and efficiently cleaned.  A part of most vehicle shops and widely available as do-it-yourself facilities for private owners of vehicles.

**case harden:**  to make the surface layer of a metal harder than the interior metal usually by heat treating and/or by chemical exposure as dipping, quenching, or spraying.

**casing:**  the main structure of a motor vehicle pneumatic tire for road wheels to which tread and sidewall rubber are bonded. Carcass.

**castellated nut:**  a machine nut that has opposing slots cut across one face (resembling the battlements of a castle parapet) so that it may be safetied from loosening by pushing a cotter key or safety wire through a nut castellation and a hole through a stud or bolt-end.

**caster:**  the trail of a steerable vehicle wheel, usually defined and measured as the longitudinal distance at ground contact-level between the projected vertical axis through the wheel spin-axis and the projected point of intersection of the vehicle steering axis with the ground.  Caster off-set. Caster trail.

**caster action:**  the tendency of a vehicle steerable wheel to self-center (roll in the exact direction of the vehicle's direction of motion) when attributable to caster.

**caster offset:**  the longitudinal distance between the projected intersection of the steering axis and the road surface and the center of tire contact and that is considered positive when the steering axis intersection point is ahead of the tire contact center. See caster.

**casting:** a metal shape for a vehicle part that is formed by pouring or injecting molten metal into a suitable mold and allowing it to harden by cooling.

**cast iron:** a commercial alloy of iron, carbon, and silicon that is hard, brittle, nonmalleable and incapable of being hammer-welded but amenable to fusible welding, brazing, and shaping with metal-cutting machine tools.

**catalyst:** a substance whose presence can enhance the rate or amount of a chemical reaction but does not participate by combining with the chemicals and thus is not consumed by the reaction.

**catalytic converter:** a muffler-like vehicle exhaust system component that uses a catalyst to cause the completed combustion of undesirable toxic gases formed during engine operation thus converting them (burning) into less dangerous exhaust gases as carbon dioxide ($CO_2$). Emissions control.

**Caterpillar:** a major American manufacturer of industrial vehicles (particularly earth-excavating and highway construction) and engines for fixed and mobile uses.

**Caterpillar track:** a proprietary, continuous linked-metal chain of a track-laying vehicle named after the manufacturer. The term is often loosely used to describe any similar track or track-laying tractor. Crawler.

**cattle gate:** an arrangement of spaced parallel pipe imbedded transversely at highway surface-level with a depression between each adjacent pair of pipe to let vehicles proceed unimpeded but that prevents cattle from crossing. Obviously a barrier gate would be impractical. Cattle guard.

**caution light:** a yellow warning light (as the center light of a traffic signal) that warns of a problem that is expected to occur shortly but does not indicate an immediate need to take action or a likelihood of a dangerous occurrence.

**cavitation:** the formation of partial vacuums (usually as air bubbles) in a liquid by a swiftly moving solid such as a propeller or rotating vane pump that adversely affects pumping efficiency that can lead to vehicle damage as a cavitating engine water pump can cause overheating and engine stoppage or total failure.

**CB radio:** a citizens band two-way radio authorized for mobile use in a motor vehicle and widely used by frequent vehicle users (particularly professional truck drivers) for emergency as well as friendly communications. Appears likely to be re-placed by cellular telephones and satellite radio-links.

**C-clamp:** a holding device with many uses during vehicle main-tenance and operations that consists of a C-shaped frame of considerable strength that has one fixed holding pad and a mov-able/tightenable matching pad that is usually screw-propelled or lever-clamped to hold parts in place during assembly, drilling, machining, or tightening/welding.

**cell:** (1) A single container or unit or as a part of a multi-cell battery for storing and releasing electrical energy by electrochemical reactions. (2) The combustion chamber of a Wankel rotary engine. (3) A leak-proof crash-resistant fuel tank liner that is required for all vehicles competing in sanctioned auto races.

**center bore:** to use a boring tool to enlarge the center of a workpiece chucked in a lathe as may be needed to insert a prop-erly dimensioned piece.

**center console:** a storage area or mount for vehicle controls and accessories placed between the front individual bucket seats of many cars and vans and that often is the mounting platform for the earlier floor or stick-shift transmission gear change lever. Console shift.

**center drill:** a starting drill bit usually with a small-diameter lead for accurate centering or locating on a mark with a larger tapered section that makes accurate starting of a larger sized drill easier. Also used to establish a tapered center hole in a shaft for holding it on a lathe dead-center or live-center.

**center finder:** any of several spiral indicators or locators for determining the exact centering of workpieces and cutting tools for lathe or milling machine work.

**center of gravity:** the center of mass (as of a vehicle) through which the effective force vector is assumed to be applied. Useful in vehicle design and in determining handling and stability parameters of existing vehicles. Balance point.

**center of tire contact:** the intersection of a wheel plane and the vertical projection of its spin axis onto the road surface.

**center point steering:** steering geometry with the steering axis projection meeting the plane of the steered wheel at road level thus eliminating any lateral pull by the rolling wheel against steering effort by the driver.

**center punch:** a hand punch consisting of a short steel bar with a hardened conical point at one end and used for marking the centers of holes to be drilled.

**centi-:** prefix word meaning one one-hundredth part of its suffix.

**centigrade:** often called "metric temperature". Each degree represents one one-hundredth of the temperature scale between the standardized freezing temperature of water (0° C.) and the boiling temperature of water (100° C.).

**centimeter:** one one-hundredth of a meter (0.3937 inch).

**centimeter-gram-second:** the metric system of units based on the centimeter as the unit of length (distance), the gram as the unit of mass (weight), and the solar second as the unit of time. CGS.

**central chassis lubrication:** a vehicle's central grease/oil reservoir whose content is pressurized and piped to all chassis moving points requiring periodic lubrication, sometimes automatically accomplished by an integrated vehicle-mileage triggering device which in non-automatic systems presented a dash-mounted reminder to the driver. Once standard on many expensive vehicles--now extinct. "Rolling grease job."

**centralizing steering:** to describe the steering of a vehicle whose steering geometry causes the steerable wheels to "want" to go straight ahead and which return to that position when steering force is removed. Straight-ahead tendency. Inherent steering stability.

**centrifugal force:** the force that tends to impel anything with mass (weight) outward from a center of rotation.

**centrifugal advance:** a vehicle ignition distributor that employs centrifugal force from rotating flyweights to mechanically advance the ignition point opening (and the angular position of the high-tension rotor) to cause the spark to occur earlier as engine rpm increases.

**centrifugal caster:** the tendency of a rotating wheel to self-center (as if its caster effect were increased).

**centrifugal clutch:** a drum, disc, or expanding-Vee pulley actuated by the centrifugal force from rotating weights acting upon/through linkage to engage/disengage the friction elements of the clutch as the rpm of the driver element (engine/motor) increases or decreases about a pre-set value. The expanding-Vee pulley continues to use centrifugal force to change the diameter of the driver/driven pulleys as changes in engine/load rpm dictate.

**centrifugal filter:** a hollow spinning-element as an oil-containing cavity attached to/or-part-of an engine flywheel or crankshaft and in the oil-flow path from the engine pump through the bearings, that uses centrifugal force to fling particulate or heavy contaminants outward into a peripheral containment area of the rotating oil container. The collected particulate/contaminants are removed at oil-change intervals by removing a cover-plate and scraping or dissolving with solvent the accumulated residue.

**centrifugal turbocharger:** the most common type uses the centrifugal forces acting upon the radially-flowing mass of the gases both to drive the turbine and to charge (compress) the outgoing flow of the fuel/air to the engine intake-manifold.

**centripetal force:** a force created by rotation/spinning that represents the "equal-and-opposite" of the centrifugal force vector, e.g., the tension force exerted upon a spinning weight by its tether that pulls in the direction of the center of rotation to prevent the weight from flying outward from centrifugal force.

**ceramic:** of or relating to a material formed by firing (very high-temperature baking) of non-metallic minerals as clay. Widely used in vehicles as baked-on or sprayed protective coatings, as insulation (both against heat and electricity), and as specialized abrasives.

**cetane:** a colorless oily hydrocarbon ($C_{16}H_{14}$) found in petroleum.

**cetane enhancer:** a diesel fuel additive used to raise or improve its cetane rating.

**Cetane Index:** a rating scale for diesel fuels derived from theoretical mathematical calculations that only approximates the actual engine-run Cetane Number but is not accurate enough for scientific matching of a diesel fuel to a specific vehicle application. Cetane Number.

**Cetane Number:** a scientifically acceptable rating of diesel fuel done by actually burning the fuel under laboratory test protocols in a certified test engine in comparison with a known cetane standard (usually a mixture in which the percentage of cetane ($C_{16}H_{14}$) to the percentage of alpha-methyl napthalene that must be mixed to exactly match the combustion parameters of the test sample of fuel defines the Cetane Number). This number is a measure of ignition delay time (after injection spray of the fuel into the engine combustion chamber), with higher Cetane Numbers representing shorter ignition delay time. Cetane Index.

**CFR engine:** a controllable variable-compression ratio engine developed by the Cooperative Research Committee (CFR) which is used to determine a scientifically acceptable octane rating (Octane Number) of fuels for spark-ignition vehicle engines.

**chafe:** injury or damage caused by friction or rubbing when there is no or insufficient lubrication as of a vehicle bearing or bushing.  Gall.

**chain:** with many vehicle applied uses: (1) the interlinked ovoid or other-shaped metal rings used in tension for lifting, pulling, securing, or towing in myriad ways.  (2) A series of paired flat links interconnected at their joints by hinge pins which can carry separator-spacers as rollers of hardened steel that engage sprocket-wheel teeth for transmission of power without slippage thus providing exact synchronous or ratio-rotational timing of connected units.  (3) A roller chain with added machined teeth for meshing with gears (toothed wheels) in lieu of sprocket-wheels for transmitting very high loads (power) and timing functions.  (4) A roller chain with extra (two or more) sets of parallel links and rollers for carrying higher loads than single-row chains (as duplex chain, triplex chain, or higher).

**chain and sprocket drive:** the transmission of power by a roller chain that engages two or more toothed wheels (sprockets) and  most used on bicycles and motorcycles for primary propulsion and in other vehicle engines to drive camshafts from the crankshaft. Chain drive.

**chain case:** a usually solid metal plate covering a chain drive for safety reasons and to contain the chain lubricant.  Open mesh or ventilated coverings are used for safety only, protecting the chain drive from debris and individuals from injury. See chain guard.

**chain drive:** See chain and sprocket drive.

**chain driven:** applied to vehicles and other mechanisms whose operation is powered by chains and sprockets.

**chain guard:** a partially-open chain-drive covering that is not oil tight.  See chain case.

**chain jack:** an over-the-center hinged lever with chain hooks that is used to shorten thus tightening and locking, under tension, a securing chain.

**chain tensioner:** a spring-loaded or hydraulically-pressured idler sprocket or rubbing block (slipper shoe) pressed against the return side of an endless (looped) chain to prevent thrashing by maintaining a uniform tension throughout the chain length, essential with pulsating loads such as camshafts or piston pumps.

**chain track:** a continuous chain of hinged flat links supporting the bogies (wheels) of a track-laying vehicle.  See Caterpillar track.

**chain wheel:** any cam-like, oblate, ovoid, round, or other-shaped pulley or sprocket around which a chain runs, particularly when toothed around its periphery.

**change gears:** to shift a transmission's gear ratio (automatically or manually) by selecting and meshing another ratio (usually of a higher or lower ratio). Gear-shift. Down-shift. Up-shift.

**change-speed-gearbox:** a transmission with multiple-and-varying-ratio sets of gears capable of changing the speed (and torque) ratio between its input and output (drive and driven) shafts that may be selected and shifted at will (automatically or manually) by the operator.

**Chapman strut:** a telescopic suspension similar to the MacPherson strut and mostly used for vehicle rear suspensions only. See MacPherson strut. Both are trade names.

**charabanc:** an obsolete term for "bus" or "motorcoach" from the French char-a-banc.

**charcoal:** a dark or black porous carbon product usually resulting from burning (charring) animal or vegetable matter (as wood) in a kiln with severely restricted air availability and having many uses as a fuel, a filter medium, and a chemical feedstock.

**charcoal canister:** a container of charcoal granules used to capture fuel fumes evaporating from a vehicle fuel system to prevent their escape into the ambient atmosphere as undesirable pollution, and to condense and return the fuel as a liquid to the fuel tank.

**charcoal filter:** a medium in many forms that traps particulates and chemically deactivates many toxic gases and living organisms (as bacteria) in filterable fluids.

**charge:** with many vehicle-related meanings: (1) The usable electrical energy, chemically stored in a battery or capacitor (condenser). (2) To impress or to increase the electrical energy stored in a battery or capacitor--with a battery charger of any type or a vehicle alternator or generator. (3) An expression representing the state or degree of charge in a battery. (4) The quantity or mass of air (charge air) and/or the amount of the fuel and air mixture entering an engine during each intake cycle (summation of cylinder intake strokes).

**charge air:** the amount of air entering an operating internal combustion engine's induction system.

**charge cooling:** the removal of heat from an engine's incoming induction charge (charge air) using a heat exchanger/radiator (air-to-air or air-to-liquid) to increase the density/mass of the charge thus increasing the volumetric efficiency and power output of the engine. Essential for deriving maximum benefit from supercharging. Intercooler. Intercooling.

**charge current:** the electrical current (ions) stated as amperes flowing to a vehicle battery when the system is charging.

**charger:** (1) an electrical/electronic device for flowing electrical energy to a battery at the proper voltage and current to satisfy the battery's needs (state of charge). (2) A fluid compressor designed to supply liquids or gases under pressure for storage or use as needed. Supercharger. Turbocharger.

**charging stroke:** the first "stroke" of an internal combustion engine (two-stroke/cycle or four-stroke/cycle) that initiates the thermodynamic fuel-to-heat-to-power cycle of the engine. Intake stroke. Intake.

**charter bus:** a passenger bus available to and used only by nonscheduled groups traveling to a common destination or touring a common route and returning together to the original starting point.

**chase:** to machine threads on a bolt or stud usually using a hand-held stock (handle) and die (chaser), called chasing threads.

**chassis:** originally meant as the vehicle frame, power train, and running gear that could be driven by sitting on a temporary bench--as a seat. Few light vehicles today have a discernable chassis because of the almost universal shift to uni-body construction. The Model T Ford, often sold as a chassis, was complete from fire wall forward (radiator and its shell, engine hood, front fenders, and headlights) and with gasoline in the fuel tank which served as a seat (until 1926-27) for driving it home on four new tires (no spare), all for under $200.00--and any blacksmith could build a serviceable all-wood body onto that chassis in a few days. Alas, the "good old days" and the vehicle chassis are gone forever! Simplifying dictionary definitions. Simplistically!

**chatter:** to operate with a repetitive irregularity that causes intermittent noise or vibration, as brakes or a friction clutch whose surfaces are too rough to engage smoothly, sometimes aggravated by inept vehicle drivers.

**checkered flag:** a hand-held signaling flag of alternating black-and-white squares that is used to signify a winner when the first car in a competitive automobile race crosses the racecourse/race track finish line.

**check strap:** usually a loop of very strong webbing around a vehicle moving part as a lever, axle, or suspension member that is dimensioned to limit movement to a certain distance. Limit strap. Rebound strap.

**check valve:** a one-way-flow fluid valve that is tension- or pressure-loaded against a seat, stopping (checking) fluid movement beyond that point until a stronger force (higher pressure fluid) from the other side or a manual override opens the valve.

**cherry:** vehicle mechanic's slang to describe a car (usually a used car) that "catches the eye" because of its striking appearance and condition. Perfection.

**cherry picker:** originally used to designate a mobile crane equipped for lifting a worker in a bucket-like enclosure at the end of a boom but now applied generically to many similar-appearing small hydraulically-powered lifting arms used to remove or to replace vehicle engines or similar heavy loads.

**cherry rivet:** the ubiquitous pop rivet started life as a "cherry" rivet because of its developer/manufacturer, the Cherry Company. Pop rivet.

**chicane:** a close-spaced series of tight turns in opposite directions in an otherwise straight stretch of a road-racing course usually a standard feature in international vehicle road racing courses as well as in the short distance amateur sports car autocross events.

**child seat:** a safety seat for infants and small children when riding in a motor vehicle usually designed to be held in place by the adult passenger safety belt harness restraint system with special fastening devices. Car seat.

**chiller:** a heat exchanger usually a coiled fuel pipe in an insulated housing surrounded by ice water or dry ice to cool fuel entering the engine to increase its unit mass, increasing the horsepower as for a race car. Fuel coolie.

**chipper:** a truck-mounted wood grinder/shredder (chip-maker) that is used to reduce large tree sections to chips for easier disposal or industrial usage.

**chlorofluorocarbon:** as Freon (tradenamed), the almost universally-used refrigerant in vehicle air conditioners since "air" was first used but now being phased out because of its damage to the Earth's protective ozone layer.

**chock:** a device, usually shaped as a concave-upper-sided wedge placed under the downhill edge of a vehicle wheel's curvature when parked to provide an added anti-roll device should on-board holding systems (brakes and in-gear compression) fail.

**choke:** a butterfly-type or hinged-damper valve that restricts the flow of charge-air entering a vehicle engine's intake/induction system thus increasing the fuel-to-air mixture ratio for starting and running when cold.

**choke stove:** an engine exhaust manifold heated area with a bimetallic spring that opens the choke valve of an automatic choke as the engine warms and allows the choke valve to close for cold starts.

**choked:** an engine operating with its choke valve partially or fully closed.

**chopped top:** mechanic's slang for the lowering in height of a vehicle's hard top by chopping sections out of all surrounding body panels and glass. A hot-rodders modification to customize a stock-bodied vehicle.

**chopper:** (1) A motorcycle that has been customized, usually by lowering. (2) An electrical switch that interrupts an electrical circuit at short regular intervals. (3) Slang for helicopter.

**Christmas tree:** drag racer's name for the standardized starting light composed of a vertical tier of spaced lights that start from the top with several yellow lights coming on and culminating with the green light at the bottom telling the waiting driver to "go".

**chrome:** a material such as metal or plastic that is electroplated with a thin decorative and protective coating of chromium and extensively used as vehicle bumpers and trim pieces.

**chrome moly:** a steel alloy with chromium and molybdenum used especially for race car and airplane tubing and structural shapes in their frame structures.

**chrome steel:** steel/chromium alloys that are hard, strong, and rust resistant in varying degrees depending upon the composition. Stainless steel.

**chromium:** a blue-white metallic element used especially in alloys and electroplating.

**chuck:** an attachment or device for holding a workpiece or tool in a drill press, milling machine, or lathe.

**chute:** abbreviation for the drag chute used for slowing high-speed race cars or landing airplanes or for a parachute used by airmen for escape or routine jumping from airplanes.

**CI engine:** a compression ignition vehicle internal combustion engine. Diesel engine.

**cigarette:**  a cylindrical insulating tube used when passing high-voltage (ignition) wires through a metal panel of a vehicle.  Most common on older vehicles before the perfection of better dielectric coatings for such wires.

**circuit:**  the complete path of an electric current from the positive (+) battery terminal through the necessary switches and controls to the working load (as lights, ignition, horn, radio, et al.), and then back to the battery negative (-) terminal, usually through the vehicle structure as a common ground.

**circuit breaker:**  an electrical device/switch that disconnects/interrupts an electrical circuit when the current exceeds a predetermined amperage flow.  The breaker can be manually reset after the cause of the overload has been resolved.

**circulating pump:**  an electrical or mechanical pump on a motor vehicle that circulates a working or cooling fluid, e.g., the water pump that circulates engine coolant through the vehicle radiator (cooling); the air-conditioner compressor (working), and the power-steering pump (working).

**citizens band:**  a range of radio frequencies officially allocated by the federal government for private radio communications.  CB radio.

**city cycle:**  a standard motor vehicle test cycle (to establish miles-per-gallon ratings under city driving conditions) that scientifically reproduces the driving habits of the typical city driver.  See CAFE.

**cladded:**  a metal bonded with a covering/coating/film of another metal having more effective resistance (usually harder) to corrosion or wear.

**clamp:**  a device designed to bind, constrict, or press two or more parts together during assembly, machining, or welding operations as in a vehicle maintenance/repair facility.

**clam shell scoop:**  an external air inlet/exit opening (through the body panels) that is designed to feed ambient air into a vehicle interior for cooling/ventilation or to become engine combustion-air, and when reverse-oriented to extract interior air to enhance cooling/ventilation, so-named because of its familiar shape.

**classic car:**  a term without an acceptable definition but widely-used, often to mislead the consumer by implying that a vehicle is different, special, and superior to other identical production models.  The original and likely first meaning/use of "classic" applied to automobiles was the Classic Car Club of America's designation that excluded all production-line automobiles from deserving the designation and identified the models and model years of those truly deserving the "classic" title.

**claw hammer:** a hand tool with one end of the hammer-head forked for extracting or "pulling-out" nails.

**clay model:** used by automobile manufacturer's design divisions during the design/development phase of every new vehicle model, a sculpted, usually clay and full-size or large-scale version of the car to check car styling, location of exterior appurtenances, and the fit, finish, and appearance of trim and moldings.

**clearance light:** a warning light that marks the upper corners (right, left, front, and rear) and at intervals along the longitudinal roof-line of long vehicles thus providing visual verification of overall height, length, and width of the vehicle.

**clearance height:** (1) the unobstructed distance between the roadway and the lowest underside member of a vehicle. (2) The highest point of an empty vehicle above the roadway. (3) The posted height on a bridge/overpass indicating the maximum height of a vehicle that can safely pass underneath the structure.

**clearance volume:** the volume of a combustion chamber when its piston is at top dead center of its operating stroke.

**clear coat:** usually the final coat of paint of the same formula as the "color coats" but without the pigment additives thus giving a protective covering that adds an appearance of depth to the finish.

**clerestory head:** an engine cylinder-head with extended combustion areas over the intake valve on one side of the crankshaft axis and the exhaust valve on the other side.

**clicker brake adjuster:** a drum brake adjusting device using a round threaded nut that is turned to spread the shoes and is locked by a spring-loaded pawl or bar engaging external teeth on the nut.

**climatic wind tunnel:** a test facility that can vary temperature and humidity of the high velocity air flow used in aerodynamic testing of full or scaled-sized vehicles.

**closed cycle turbine:** a gas turbine that recirculates its working gases.

**closed-loop dwell control:** stabilizing and control of the build-up of magnetic flux in a vehicle ignition coil by using electronic data feedback to correct system current/ voltage fluctuations.

**closed-loop engine control:** vehicle automatic engine management using data fed back by sensors to adjust/correct engine operation within specified limits.

**closed-loop fuel control:** the adjustment of fuel/air (equivalence/stoichiometric) ratio and reduction in undesirable exhaust gas pollutants by electronically sensed feedback from exhaust gas analyzers (oxygen sensor, et al.) that correct the fuel/air mixture and or ignition spark timing.

**closed shop:** as a vehicle maintenance/repair shop in which the employer/owner, by mutual agreement, hires only union members in good standing.

**cloverleaf head:** a vehicle engine cylinder-head for a four-valves-per-cylinder engine that resembles the four-leaf clover.

**club coupe:** an automobile resembling a coupe in having only two doors but with a full-width rear seat accessible by tilting the front-seat backs forward.

**cluster gear:** mechanic's name for the set of gears fixed (or an integral part thereof) to a manual transmission's countershaft.

**clutch:** a mechanism as in a vehicle for connecting and disconnecting the transmission of power from the driver (engine) to the driven (transmission) providing smooth engagement and disengagement when starting and stopping vehicle motion and rapid disengagement when changing gear ratios (shifting gears).

**clutch brake:** usually found only on high capacity (horsepower) clutches a device that slows the rotation of a driven clutch plate to make gear engagement easier.

**clutch cover:** the bowl-shaped metal cover that contains the rotating components of a vehicle friction clutch and is normally peripherally bolted to the engine-flywheel, thus rotating at engine speed.

**clutch disc:** the driven plate, a rotating clutch component to which friction material is attached for making the driving contact with the engine flywheel and transmitting that torque as the clutch driven-plate. Clutch plate.

**clutch drag:** a rubbing effect that continues to carry some torque even when the clutch pedal is fully depressed, possibly caused by insufficient free play or bad cylinders if the clutch is hydraulically-actuated.

**clutch fluid:** usually the same liquid as the brake fluid of a vehicle with a hydraulically-actuated clutch. Hudson used a fluid to cushion clutch operation. Wet clutch.

**clutch housing:**  the clutch connecting (from the engine to the transmission) and protective covering that is usually a casting, also known as the bell-housing because of its shape. Hog's head on the Model T Ford.

**clutch pedal:**  the foot pedal that actuates the engagement/ release of a clutch through a hydraulic or mechanical linkage.

**clutch pedal free play:**  the distance that a clutch pedal moves in overcoming slack in its linkage before actuation of the clutch disengagement process begins.

**clutch pressure plate:**  the heavy metal disc whose strong springs press the clutch-disc friction surface against the engine-flywheel, transferring engine torque through the clutch to the transmission input shaft.

**clutch throwout bearing:**  a free-running bearing around the transmission input shaft having a thrust face that presses against the clutch release levers (usually through a matching circular-plate), compressing the clutch springs to release the clutch-disc friction contact, thus disconnecting the transmission from the engine.

**clutch throwout fork:**  a lever that has a forked-end operating inside the clutch housing to move the throwout bearing utilizing force transferred from the foot-pedal linkage to its single-end extending outside the clutch housing.  Clutch release fork.

**clutch servo boost:**  a compressed-air-operated diaphragm that multiplies the force from the foot pedal to overcome the heavier clutch springs in large vehicles (trucks).

**clutch shaft:**  sometimes applied to the transmission input shaft because engine torque is transferred to it from the clutch through the clutch-disk splined hub.

**clutch shudder:**  a jerky, rough vibration imparted to a vehicle drive line during starting (clutch engagement) usually caused by grease/oil on the clutch-disk friction surface or a heat-warped disc itself.

**clutch slip:**  a condition caused by worn clutch friction surfaces, weakened clutch springs, or radical maladjustment of free-play resulting in inability of the clutch to transmit the engine torque to the transmission, initially under heavy-pulling, but rapidly deteriorating into total inability even to move an empty vehicle.

**clutch springs:**  radially-spaced coil springs or a diaphragm spring whose force presses the clutch disc between the flywheel and the clutch pressure plate with sufficient force to develop enough friction to transmit the full engine torque to the vehicle transmission for propelling the vehicle and its load.

**clutch start:** to push a vehicle with a manual transmission "in gear" with clutch engaged--or disengaged to be engaged with the vehicle rolling--causing the engine to be rotated with ignition "on" until it starts. Push start. Jump start.

**coach:** a term sometimes applied to a multi-passenger vehicle as a passenger bus, generally with a modifier. Motor coach. Passenger coach.

**coachwork:** a term typically reserved for the vehicle outerbody that is more ornate or custom designed/constructed than a production or stock body.

**coal gas:** a gaseous fuel, mostly carbon monoxide (CO), formed as combustion gas originally derived from incomplete burning of coal with restricted combustion air. The original name has been retained to apply to similar fuel gas produced from such burning of many other carbonaceous materials such as garbage or as by-product gas from many industrial processes. City gas. Flue gas. Manufacturer's gas.

**coal oil:** the original name for the fuel, now called kerosene (one of and similar to various diesel and jet/turbine fuels), that is a distillate of petroleum (crude oil).

**coarse grit:** abrasive particles of relatively large size used for rough grinding and sanding during many vehicle maintenance and repair operations.

**coarse threads:** a classification of machine threads involving fewer threads per linear inch than do the fine(r) threads with the exact number of threads-per-inch dependent upon the diameter of the threaded part.

**coast:** a condition of rolling by a vehicle without the application of engine/propulsive power such as: downhill; with transmission gears disengaged (in neutral position); when "free-wheeling" an overdrive gear; or with clutch disengaged as when decelerating.

**coast-down:** a vehicle test protocol employing only a stopwatch, the vehicle itself, and a flat stretch of roadway, to determine various horsepowers such as that required to accelerate or to maintain any particular speed under known conditions of such variables as vehicle weight, altitude, temperature, wind, and ambient air density. Imponderables needed for engineering computations will depend, for accuracy, upon the knowledge/experience/sophistication of the tester(s), e.g., acceleration can be determined from elapsed time and starting and final speeds (as from 0 mph to 60 mph in 9.8 sec.) or using the deceleration (coast-down time) from 70 mph to 60 mph to calculate the steady-state horsepower needed to go about 66 mph constant speed. Using smaller speed increments such as from 65 down to 60 to calculate the horsepower required to go about 63 will give more accuracy as will averaging multiple timed runs. A "horsepower curve" (calculated horsepower at the "mid-points" vs roadspeed) will give a plot about as accurate as an actual instrumented dyno-horsepower run in a full-scale wind tunnel.

**coat:** a layer (usually thin) of one material as a paint or metal applied over another material for decorative or protective purposes.

**coaxial cable:** an electrical transmission line consisting of an outer cylindrical conductor separated from an inner solid wire conductor by a dielectric insulator and intended for low-loss transmission of high-frequency electricity such as television signals or any radio-frequency (RF). Coax.

**cobalt:** a tough lustrous silver-white magnetic metallic element and used to alloy other metals as in cobalt steel.

**cobbled up:** mechanic's slang for a vehicle repair as done by an inexperienced and clumsy worker and that is below the accepted standard of excellence of the profession.

**cock:** a usually small fluid valve often requiring only 90° of rotation from full-on to full-off. Drain cock. Petcock.

**cockpit:** the usually one-person driver's seat and its enclosure in a race car or airplane.

**cocktail-shaker piston:** a piston that has an oil reservoir above the pin boss that collects engine oil and sprays (tosses) it up against the piston-head to provide extra cooling. The upward shaking/spraying of the oil apes a cocktail shaker.

**coefficient:** a number that represents a constant factor that is a measure of some property or characteristic of a material, device, or process, e.g., the coefficient of expansion of a metal with temperature changes.

**cog:** a tooth on the rim of a gear or wheel or on the working surface of an endless belt or a flat bar/strip.

**cogged belt:** a toothed rubber or synthetic material timing belt.

**cog railway:** a steep mountain railroad that has a rail with cogs engaged by a cogwheel on the locomotive to ensure traction.

**cogwheel:** a wheel with peripheral cogs or teeth. Gear. Sprocket.

**coil:** a descriptive term indicating a wound (usually circular) length of electrical wire but most commonly used generically to mean the ignition coil (transformer) used to create the fuel-igniting energy for a spark ignition (SI) internal combustion engine. A series of loops or a single loop of a spiral-wound spring, or hose, pipe, or tube.

**coil spring:** a helical/spiral-wound spring, used to react to compression loads as in clutch assemblies and suspensions or to react to tension loads as carburetor throttle, brake pedal/shoe, or clutch pedal return springs.

**coil spring clutch:** a clutch with its driven friction plate positioned and pressured by a number of compression coil springs spaced around its outer perimeter.

**coil spring suspension:** (1) With independent wheel suspension a coil spring reacting in compression between an A-frame/wishbone and the vehicle chassis. (2) With beam axle suspension a coil spring reacting in compression between each side of the axle and the chassis with fore-and-aft and side-to-side positioning/stabilization by A-frame/wishbone or leading/trailing arm and transverse arm.

**coke:** mechanic's term for the undesirable combustion chamber deposits of incompletely burned fuel and oil or of noncombustible contaminants.

**cold chisel:** a chisel made of tool steel of a shape, strength, and temper suitable for chipping or cutting cold metal using hand hammering.

**cold cranking rating:** the maximum amperes that a vehicle battery can supply to the engine starter under specified temperatures and elapsed time, e.g., 400 amperes for 5 minutes at 0° Fahrenheit.

**cold patch:** an emergency roadside repair of a leaking vehicle tire/tube by cementing a usually flat section of rubber over the leak-site/hole.

**cold plug:** a vehicle spark plug having a relatively high heat range index number indicating that it has a significant resistance to causing fuel detonation and is therefore suitable for use in high-performance, high compression-ratio engines.

**cold rolled:** flat metal shapes or sheet (usually of steel) formed by forcing between pressure rollers (without heating) until the desired shape or dimension is attained.

**cold rubber:** a wear-resistant synthetic rubber compounded at a low temperature (usually about 40° Fahrenheit) and used primarily for vehicle tire treads.

**cold soak:** exposure of a vehicle to a cold environment long enough for all vehicle parts to have dropped in temperature to that of the ambient surroundings.

**cold start:** the starting of a vehicle engine that has been exposed to cold temperatures long enough for any residual heat from its last use to be lost.

**cold start ballast:** a heat-sensitive ballast resistor designed to allow a higher current to flow in a vehicle's ignition primary circuit when it is cold (just starting) to provide a hotter spark during engine starter cranking drain and then to reduce the primary current as the ballast resistor and the engine warm up and the system voltage from the alternator/generator charging is high enough to supply the necessary primary current to the ignition process. Ballast resistor.

**cold start enrichment:** the use of either a partial blockage of incoming charge air to an engine or the addition of extra fuel supplied by an injection pump and injector nozzle discharges both of which increase the ratio of fuel to air during engine starting when cold to insure that each cylinder's incoming charge fires consistently.

**cold sticking:** the binding of a piston ring in its groove when cold (or when overheated) because of the different coefficients of temperature-change expansion of the different materials of the two entities.

**collapsed piston:** a severe reduction in physical dimensions, most usually a smaller skirt diameter, of an engine piston caused by the loss of tensile strength (temper) when overheated beyond its yield-point (of temperature) causing a failure of the piston to help the rings seal against compression (blow-by) and usually indicated by power loss and significant knocking/slapping noises.

**collar:** a usually strong metal ring or flange used on a shaft to prevent axial movement of a wheel, gear, pulley, sprocket or bearing and usually secured by threads, drive pins, key/keyways, set screws, or lock-rings and often with a thrust-face to counteract axial forces or shaft movement.

**collectible:** a term applied to a vehicle possessing characteristics that make it more desirable and therefore more valuable, e.g., age, rarity, previous celebrity ownership, performance record, et al.

**collector:** most usually applied to engine exhaust system large pipes/sections into which smaller pipes (as from individual cylinders) flow their exhaust gases but applicable to any system handling fluid flow.

**collet:** a ferrule, flange, or collar for holding the workpiece or the cutting tool during machining operations. Chuck.

**colloid:** a substance of such small particulate-size (smaller than 250 millimicrons) as to be too small to be visible with an ordinary light microscope.

**colloidal suspension:** the mixing (suspension) of particles so small that when dispersed in a gaseous, liquid, or solid medium will not "settle out" but exhibit continuous random movement-- the so-called Brownian Movement--throughout the medium and are not filterable by vehicle-quality filters.

**color chart:** a usually wall-mounted chart in a dealer showroom or a vehicle body-and-paint shop showing examples of available paint colors and the names assigned to those colors.

**color chips:** small painted rectangles showing the exact colors available for vehicles so that customers may select or so that the painter can compare a chip to a vehicle color for exact color matching when painting only a portion of the vehicle.

**color code:** the practice of using distinctive colors (or com- binations) to identify electrical wires to facilitate circuit tracing and troubleshooting; or to identify fluid piping for tracing and for safety considerations (red denotes combustible fuel, yellow denotes lubricants as oil, green means oxygen, and brown means an inert nonflammable gas); or to identify vehicle liquids to prevent improper servicing of closely-grouped filler-pipe openings.

**color match:** to compound a paint by adding coloring pigments so that the final painted finish looks exactly like adjacent paint work on a vehicle or a color visualized by a customer. Color matching, originally done by the practiced eye of an ex- pert, can now be done by computerized color scanners.

**color temperature:** the temperature at which the light from a complete radiator (black body) matches in chromaticity the light from the source being evaluated. Used in the heat- treating (tempering) of metals, e.g., when steel is heated, a faint red glow becomes perceptible at about 500° C., becoming bright red at around 800° to 900° C., and reaching "white" heat at about 1500° C.

**color tune:** a procedure for tuning (adjusting) the fuel/air ratio and ignition timing by observing the color of the combus- tion flame in an operating engine through the quartz viewing window of a special spark plug designed for this purpose with accompanying instructions as to what needs to be adjusted based upon flame color.

**Combined Fuel Economy:** a combined weighted average of urban cycle fuel consumption (mpg) and highway cycle fuel consumption (mpg) with the proportion of each type driving extracted from the latest national statistics to get the CFE which is published for every new model automobile to give purchasers comparisons with other cars.

**combustion:** a chemical process involving rapid oxidation (burning) of a fuel (energy carrier) by air (as the oxidant) evolving the energy as usable (to do work) heat and light.

**combustion chamber:** the enclosed part of an engine in which fuel-burning takes place, in a reciprocating engine, the volume between the piston head (as floor), the cylinder head (as ceiling), both fixed areas, and the variable area of the exposed cylinder walls. In some engines as a compression ignition (diesel injection) engine (with a "hot spot" injection swirl chamber) or a "lean-burn" engine with a third-valve rich mixture chamber with spark plug, these flame-initiation-chamber's volume is added to the main combustion-chamber volume for compression-ratio calculations.

**combustion chamber surface-to-volume ratio:** in an IC engine the amount of surface wall area varies with piston-stroke position (as does volume) and influences the quench (fire extinguishing action/cooling) effect of cool exposed wall areas upon the formation of unburned hydrocarbon (fuel residue).

**combustor:** the fuel-burning chamber of a gas turbine engine between the turbine and compressor where energy is released from the fuel to further expand the gases that turn the turbine whose output shaft powers the vehicle wheels.

**come along:** a mechanic's name for a small hand-lever ratcheted cable winch used for pulling vehicles up ramps onto car-hauling trailers and for light hoisting from overhead beams or lashing heavy cargo against shifting in transit.

**come back:** mechanic's name for a repair job that was unsatisfactory to the customer who comes back to the shop with his vehicle to have the work done again.

**Comet head:** a tradenamed cylinder head for diesel engines developed by Ricardo using a small chamber with a heated plug and the injector nozzle for the initial firing of the fuel.

**comfort station:** a roadside facility providing traveler conveniences such as drinks, food, information, rest rooms, picnic area, and telephones. Rest stop.

**command car:** an open lightly-armored military vehicle radio-equipped and designed for reconnaissance and capable of negotiating rough terrain.

**commercial vehicle:** a vehicle, other than passenger carriers, that is for hire or operated for profit to transport goods and

cargo and that is licensed and taxed for commercial use.
Truck. Delivery van. Furniture van.

**common carrier:** a corporation or individual licensed to use vehicles to transport cargo, messages, or people for hire.

**common ground:** an electrical return circuit such as a vehicle frame that returns a number of electrical paths such as from fans, ignition, lights, radio, and starter to the power source (battery) without separate wiring conductors.

**commutate:** to reverse every other half-cycle of an alternating current (AC) thus forming a unidirectional current (DC).

**commutator:** the series of insulated bars (segments) mounted around the shaft of a vehicle generator that act as a rotating electrical switch through fixed brush contactors that selectively "pick off" half waves (cycles) of the full waves (AC) induced in the rotating coils (connected to appropriate commutator bars) thus forming the unidirectional direct current supplied to the vehicle's electrical system and storage battery.

**compact car:** a statutory size-classification of automobiles, making it easier for purchasers to compare the fuel economy (mpg) ratings of comparably-sized cars. Subcompact; compact; mid-size; large; and very large.

**company car:** an automobile supplied to an employee by his employer for use in furthering the company's interests.

**compensating axle suspension:** a tandem axle with the axles supporting the vehicles through a hinged beam that insures an equalizing transfer of load between the axles or by utilizing hydraulic or pneumatic support cylinders that are interconnected to effect load equalization.

**compensating jet:** a jet or tube in a carburetor that adds air to the fuel during high-power operation to maintain a better fuel/air ratio preventing overrich operation. Emulsifier tube.

**composite:** any of various man-made synthetic materials (many are lighter-weight and stronger than naturally occurring elemental materials) used in motor vehicles to increase efficiency, performance, safety, and useful life.

**Compressed Natural Gas:** natural gas in on-board pressurized tanks is seeing increased use for fleet vehicles. The addition of hydrogen makes CNG a much better fuel. Liquid Natural Gas (LNG) use and Liquid Petroleum Gas (LPG) are gaining in favor because their tanks are smaller, expanding the range of CNG-equipped vehicles.

**compression:** a force and its resultant that shortens the distance between the points of force/load application with the amount of shortening a function of the compressibility of the material undergoing compressive forces. The increase in internal pressure of an engine cylinder as the piston travels toward the cylinder head during the compression stroke (the second stroke of the four-stroke engine).

**compression ignition engine:** a reciprocating engine using the heat of compression to ignite the fuel/air mixture (normally pressure-sprayed/injected into the combustion chamber in precise quantities with exact timing of the fuel pulses) and usually called a "diesel" because in 1892 Dr. Rudolf Diesel patented such an engine that operated on the Carnot Cycle. CI engine.

**compression ratio:** the volume of an engine cylinder + combustion chamber at bottom-dead-center (BDC) of the piston stroke compared to the volume at the top-dead-center (TDC) with the TDC volume assigned an arithmetic value of one (1) in the ratio, e.g., 1 volume at TDC and 6.8 volumes at BDC will be stated as a ratio of 6.8 to 1 or 6.8:1. Though called "compression" ratio the actual pressures in the cylinder will not conform exactly because of the Gas Laws governing pressure-temperature-volume relationships and leakage losses.

**compression ring:** the top ring or rings on a reciprocating engine's piston whose primary function is sealing (minimizing leakage), assisted by oil-control and oil-scraper rings variously located below the compression ring(s).

**compression stroke:** the piston stroke in a reciprocating engine during which the charge air or the fuel/air mixture is compressed prior to ignition. In a four-stroke engine it is the second of the four: intake, compression, power, and exhaust (repetitively sequenced, as long as rotating).

**compression temperature:** the increase in temperature with the increase in pressure of a gas as governed by the Gas Laws.

**compression test:** a diagnostic procedure involving measuring the maximum pressure attained while rotating a piston engine at cranking speed (usually by the engine starter) whose value depends upon the knowledge, skill, and technique of the mechanic-diagnostician. Largely superseded by the "leakage test" using external pressurization of an engine's closed cylinder (valves closed) and differential pressure gauges.

**compulsory insurance:** the statutory requirement in most states that every vehicle driver and or vehicle must have certain insurance coverage (varies from state-to-state) usually at least protection against personal injury to others and property damage to other than the insured (liability insurance).

**concentric:** things having a common axis or common center. Concentricity is found in vehicle practice as coaxial electrical conductors and planetary gear systems.

**concept car:** a car conceived and presented for public comment by a manufacturer's design research team, usually involving the latest "state-of-the-art" in materials and engineering breakthroughs. Usually one-of-a-kind and nonfunctional.

**concours d'elegance:** literally a competition of excellence, typically as a vehicle display or exhibition of vehicles and accessories for the judging of their excellence of appearance.

**condensation:** a chemical/physical reaction involving union between molecules (from temperature or pressure changes) usually increasing the substance density as steam (water vapor) from the gaseous state to the liquid state as water (condensate).

**condenser:** (1) An apparatus/device used to condense a gas or vapor into a liquid. (2) An electrical capacitor that stores and apparently condenses an electrical charge. Points-and-condenser ignition.

**condition number:** an arbitrary rating scale (1 through 5) used by many major automobile auctions to indicate vehicle condition (1 being highest).

**conductance:** the ease or readiness with which a conductor transmits (carries) an electric current. The reciprocal of electrical resistance.

**conductor:** a substance, material, or body capable of transmitting (carrying) electricity, heat, or sound.

**conduit:** (1) A natural or artificial channel through which something (as a fluid) is conveyed. (2) A pipe, tube, or tile for protecting electric wires or cables.

**cone clutch:** a system using the engagement of conical surfaces of driver and driven elements to transmit vehicle power to the drive train or to disconnect the engine-to-drive train. Conical matching rings do the same thing in the synchronizing of gears in synchromesh transmissions.

**configure:** to change or shape a material or device to fit a particular requirement or space.

**conical:** a geometrical shape with many vehicle applications as cone-section roller bearings to carry axial and radial loading. Tapered roller bearings.

**conk out:** mechanic's slang for a sudden break-down or stoppage of a vehicle, usually without apparent cause.

**connect:** to attach or join two or more things. To complete an electrical circuit.

**connecting rod:** a rod that transmits power from one rotating part of a machine from/to another reciprocating part, most common is the piston rod connecting the power from the piston to the crankshaft.

**connecting rod bearing:** the crankshaft-end (big-end) bearing of a vehicle engine piston rod that attaches and secures the rod to the crank-throw journal of the crankshaft.

**connector:** any of various devices used for joining vehicle parts, e.g., cable connector, electrical connectors, hose connectors, pipe/tube connectors.

**conservation of charge:** a scientific (physics) principle: the total electric charge of an isolated system remains constant irrespective of whatever internal changes may take place.

**conservation of energy:** a scientific (physics) principle: the total energy of an isolated system remains constant irrespective of whatever internal changes may take place with energy disappearing in one form reappearing in another form (but equal in amount).

**conservation of mass:** a principle in classical physics: the total mass of any material system is neither increased nor diminished by reactions between the parts--called also the "conservation of matter" (nothing can be created or destroyed).

**consignment sale:** a sale as of vehicles and parts in which the title to the for-sale items remains with the current owner until sold by the agent/representative authorized to consummate the transaction for the owner. Consignment auction.

**console:** a small cabinet/enclosure between the bucket (individual) seats of a vehicle, usually for storage or convenient mounting of controls and instruments or accessories.

**constantan:** an alloy of copper and nickel used for electrical resistors and in thermocouples whose resistance remains constant under changes in temperature.

**constant mesh gearbox:** a transmission in which all forward-gear pairs remain in mesh with the selected driving pair being engaged by a clutch or a synchromesh mechanism.

**constant velocity joint:** a universal joint whose output shaft rotates at a constant angular velocity with no cyclic variations (judder), given a constant input-shaft speed.

**constant vacuum carburetor:** a carburetor with a variable section venturi (to accommodate varying charge-air flow rates) that maintains a constant intake manifold vacuum (pressure).

**constant voltage control:** a voltage regulator that maintains a preset voltage in a vehicle electrical system to control and stabilize battery charging and electrical component operation irrespective of fluctuations in load and alternator/generator speed (within limits).

**constantly variable transmission:** See continuously variable transmission.

**constriction:** an obstruction of fluid flow as by a contaminant build-up, a crushed conduit, or a deliberate reduction of conduit cross-section by valving or squeezing.

**contact breaker:** the distributor cam-operated electrical contacts (spring-loaded closed) that close (make) and open (break) the vehicle's primary ignition circuit that induces the high-voltage spark at the spark plug.

**contact breaker points:** the special alloy (to resist hammering wear and electrical erosion) electrical switching contacts (one fixed and one pivoted and cam-operated) that open and close a vehicle's primary ignition circuit. Set of points.

**contact cement:** a chemical adhesive applied to two matching surfaces that bonds instantly when they are brought together.

**contact coupling:** a quick-disconnect fluid pressure-line-coupling device usually with a tapered male and female cam-locked joining designed for connect/disconnect with virtually no leakage of the fluid, e.g., shop compressed-air lines to air-tools; pressurized gaseous fuel servicing lines to vehicle tanks; hydraulic, pneumatic, or vacuum brake connections as between tractor and trailer vehicles.

**contact patch:** the contact area between a vehicle tire and the roadway and generally somewhat oval in shape. Tire print. Footprint.

**containerization:** the grouping of odd shapes and packaged cargo for packing into one large shipping container that can be transshipped via large flat-bed truck-trailer vehicles, railroad flat cars, or as trans-ocean cargo-ship deck-loads.

**continental kit:** an aftermarket accessory spare tire-mounting kit with metal protective cover that emulates the distinctive spare tire of Lincoln Continental coupes.

**continental spare tire:** the famous spare tire mounting faired into the trunk lid and with a full-metal covering as pioneered by the Lincoln Continental coupe.

**continuous spray injection:** fuel injection for relatively small spark ignition vehicle engines using a continuous fuel spray discharged at a central location in the induction system usually near the air throttle. Throttle body injection.

**continuously variable transmission:** a vehicle transmission which provides an infinitely variable ratio of driver (engine) to driven (wheels) speed ratios throughout the working speed range of the vehicle.

**control arm:** any lateral swinging arm of a suspension member such as the upper end/or lower arms of a double A-frame that control the camber of the wheel.

**control box:** the housing containing the current and voltage regulators of a vehicle electrical charging system. Any box containing automatic or hand-operated levers/switches for controlling vehicle operations. When such "box" is not repairable but is a throwaway/replacement it is called a "black box".

**control lever:** the console, floor, or steering column mounted lever for selecting gear ratios in a manual or automatic transmission. Stick shift. Stick.

**control ring:** an oil-return or oil-scraper piston ring in an engine.

**controlled separation:** the use of deliberate changes in a vehicle outer-body shape to cause boundary layer flow of air over a moving vehicle to separate (move away from the surface) thus disturbing laminar flow.

**converter:** a mechanic's abbreviation of either catalytic converter or torque converter.

**convertible:** an automobile with a foldable top that can be stowed on-board while retaining roll-up windows (in contrast to a roadster without windows).

**coolant:** the working liquid used to transport heat from any machine that requires cooling, usually to a radiator (heat exchanger) for dissipation to ambient air before returning to the machine (as a continuous closed loop operation).

**coolie:** mechanic's slang for an on-board fuel cooler used to increase the density/mass of a volume of fuel thus increasing its energy content usually used only in specialized race cars, e.g., straighaway world landspeed record contenders.

**cooling system:** the components required and used for cooling an engine or other devices usually comprising a heat-exchanging jacket, appropriate working-fluid (usually liquid as a coolant), circulating pump, pipe and hoses, temperature regulating thermostat, and a radiator/heat exchanger.

**copper:**  a common reddish metallic element that is ductile and malleable and one of the best conductors of electricity and heat.

**copper asbestos gasket:**  a sealing plate of two thin copper sheets encasing a layer of asbestos and used where both leak prevention and interruption of heat flow between gasketed parts is essential, e.g., cylinder-block-to-cylinder-head and from either to exhaust or intake manifolds.

**copper-clad:**  a gasket of various materials as steel with a thin coating of copper because of its softness (malleability) making a better seal than the harder materials that it coats. Copper klad.

**cornering force:**  a dilemma definition: so-called cornering force derives from well-known natural laws modified by too many imponderables defying simple explanation.  Vehicle "roll-overs" during cornering are not "accidents" because they are <u>caused</u> by the driver: excessive speed or out-of-control.  The inescapable centrifugal/centripital forces resulting from rotation around a center, the height and lateral (as well as transverse) location of vehicle center-of-gravity, the weight distribution by wheel, steering geometry shifts when cornering, aerodynamic-flow directional shifts, tire/road friction, tire design, and wheel/tire slip-angle, all affect G-force effect upon a direction-changing vehicle.

**Cosmoline:**  trademarked name for petrolatum formulated specifically for coating machine parts to prevent corrosion/weathering particularly when stored or not in use.

**cotter pin:**  a usually half-round metal strip bent to form a split pin with a looped enlarged head whose split ends can be flared after it is pushed through matching holes in a threaded bolt and nut to safety against loosening.  Also used through holes in small control rods to retain small parts such as levers, springs, et al.  Cotter key.

**counterbalance:**  any use of weight to offset imbalance in a rotating system.  Heavier mass imbalance and higher rotation speeds make the problem critical and immediate.  Failure to counterbalance engine crankshafts will cause catastrophic failure.  See counterweight.

**counterbore:**  the hole or the act of creating the hole that is slightly larger than, for instance, a bolt-hole that is machined to a depth allowing the bolt head to be recessed below the surface of the bolted item.

**countershaft:**  a shaft carrying pinion gears that parallels the mainshaft in a manual transmission and serves as the power path between the selected gear ratios.

**countersink:** to make a funnel-shaped taper (enlargement) at the outer end of a drilled hole to receive a matching-taper of the head of a bolt/screw or other fastener thus recessing the head to or below the material surface

**counterweight:** the weight added to an out-of-balance mechanical system to overcome the imbalance for smoother operation and to reduce vibration. See counterbalance.

**coupe:** an automobile body style usually closed (sometimes convertible) with two doors sometimes for two occupants, sometimes with folding front seat backs providing access to a back seat accommodating 2-3 additional occupants.

**coupling:** (1) Any of various devices for joining mechanical components such as rotating shafts, air hoses, pipe, et al. (2) Any of various means of fastening a vehicle trailer to a tow unit.

**cover:** a short name for various vehicle items as: car cover, engine cover, fender cover, tire cover, radiator cover, et al.

**coveralls:** a one-piece full-length full-zippered outer garment with copious pockets that is favored by many vehicle shops/ mechanics as a shop uniform and that makes a useful addition to every vehicle emergency kit (to wear as protection over travel clothes should minor vehicle repairs be needed en route).

**covered bridge:** an early-day vehicle bridge with closed side-walls and top throughout its length with many retained in service today because of their historical significance as a part of the quaint beauty of our first rural highways.

**cover glass:** the transparent protection over vehicle instrumentation, sealing against dust and grime and preventing contact with delicate dial pointers (heads). The protection against road debris over vehicle light bulbs or an aerodynamically-shaped streamlined covering over vehicle headlights.

**cow-catcher:** a sturdy low-mounted inclined structural frame on the front of railroad locomotives or urban trolley cars for throwing obstacles off the track and preventing smaller vehicles and animals from being run over and crushed beneath the heavy vehicles.

**cow college:** a vehicle engineer/mechanic/technician's derisive term for an agricultural school.

**cowhide:** a leather made in many vehicle upholstery grades from the hide of a cow. Leather seats.

**cowl:** the top portion of the front part of an automobile body extending from the two front doors to the engine fire wall and carrying the windshield and instrument panel (dash). Also the second unit of a dual-cowl phaeton extending rearward from the back of the front seat over the laps of rear-seat occupants and usually carrying a second foldable windshield.

**cowl vent:**  a usually hinged openable section of an automobile body panel along the top or sides of the cowl to provide ventilation to the front seat floor area.

**crabbing:**  a vehicle whose longitudinal centerline axis is at a distinct angle to its direction of motion, usually the result of distortion of the normally rectangular chassis/frame into a parallelogram from collision damage (uncorrected, and sometimes called a "Z-eed" frame).  Dog-legging.

**crack down:**  slang to describe a police concentrated effort as against traffic law violators.

**cracked block:**  an engine cylinder block casting that has a crack through a cylinder or coolant-containing wall usually caused by freezing expansion forces or by drastic overheating expansion.

**crackle finish:**  a painted surface as an instrument panel or interior door/window frame or sill marked by a network of cracks on an otherwise smooth surface, not as a defect but from a special crackle paint compounded to surface-contract (shrink) upon drying to form the decorative crack network of lines.  See crinkle finish.

**crack-up:**  slang meaning to smash up or wreck a vehicle.

**cradle:**  a structural framework designed for lifting, suspending, and rotating an entire vehicle to facilitate repair work or painting on underneath areas.

**cramp:**  to turn the steering wheels of a vehicle hard left-or-right and to hold at that angle.

**crane:**  a machine (fixed or mobile) for raising, shifting, and lowering usually heavy weights by means of a projecting swinging arm (boom) or with the hoisting apparatus supported on an overhead track (traveling crane).

**crank:**  (1) The bent part of an axle or shaft or an arm keyed at right angles to the end of a shaft by which circular motion is imparted to or received from the shaft or by which reciprocating motion is changed into circular motion or vice versa. (2) To turn by hand a crank or starting handle fitted to an engine to initiate its operation.  (3) To start a vehicle engine into its running mode by means other than a hand crank, e.g., by an electric, air, or small-engine powered starting motor (starter); by towing by another vehicle; or by pushing or downhill rolling, in gear.  (4) To manually raise (crank up) or

lower a window (crank down) using a crank.  Crank is often used
with "up" even as to "crank up" a vehicle engine.

**crankcase:**  the lower enclosed section (often structural) of
an engine that houses, protects, and supports the crankshaft,
main bearings, and often the camshaft, while acting as an oil
supply reservoir.

**crankcase dilution:**  the leakage of fuel usually past the piston rings/cylinder wall, condensate from combustion gas blow-
by, or other vehicle fluids escaping into the crankcase oil
supply.

**crankcase emissions:**  the build-up and escape of combustion
gases and leakage of other engine fluids from the crankcase
vent.

**crankcase emission control system:**  equipment evolving from
positive ventilation to contemporary devices that reduce or
eliminate the combustion process contaminants from the crankcase without venting to the outside atmosphere.

**cranking enrichment:**  the adding of extra fuel by whatever
means (restricting/choking the charge-air, or injecting fuel)
to increase the fuel-to-air ratio while starting an engine.

**cranking motor:**  an engine, air-motor, or electric motor connected to the engine to impart rotation only during starting,
until it begins to run under its own power.

**cranking speed:**  the rotational speed needed to be attained by
an engine before it will continue running on its own power.

**crankpin:**  the stub-shaft journal (bearing surface) acting as
the crank of the engine crankshaft on which the piston rod big-
end bearing is attached and runs.

**crankpin end:**  the big end of a piston connecting rod that attaches to the crankshaft throw journal and transmits/translates
the piston's reciprocating force into crankshaft rotational
force.

**crankshaft:**  the rotational-power delivery/acceptance shaft of
a reciprocating engine/compressor (pump) where linear (reciprocating) force from a piston is translated into a rotational
force imparted to the shaft through a crank/offset arm/throw
or vice versa.  The crankshaft has a crank/throw for each operating piston connected to the piston through a piston rod and
associated bearings/bushings/pins and is itself supported by
main bearings secured by/in the cylinder block structure.

**chrankshaft-end bearing:**  the operating bearing between the
piston rod and the crankthrow journal.  Rod bearing.

**crankshaft grinder:** a lathe-like vehicle shop machine tool capable of spinning an off-center workpiece and applying a large-diameter powered grinding wheel for sizing crankshaft main bearing and rod bearing journals. The technician who operates a crankshaft grinding machine.

**crankshaft journal bearing:** a large bearing at the shaft axis operating between and supporting the crankshaft to the engine block. Main bearing.

**crank throw:** the radius distance from the crank (throw) center to the rotational center of the crankshaft. One-half the distance of the piston stroke. Crankshaft throw.

**crank web:** the usually structural flat section arm that supports the crank-pin journal and as a diametric support for couterweights as balance. Crankshaft web.

**crash:** to wreck a vehicle in a violent and usually disastrous manner or the result of such action.

**crash barrel:** a flexible (as plastic) barrel containing energy-absorbing material to mark and separate temporary vehicle lanes particularly in highway construction/repair areas as well as to prevent vehicle collisions with immovable structures as bridge/overpass abutments or supports.

**crash box:** a vehicle transmission using square-cut spur gears on coaxial driving and driven shafts that are shifted by sliding axially along a shaft into mesh with countershaft gears to effect ratio changes (without the benefit of synchronizers) resulting in frequent clashing/crashing sounds during shifting (ratio changes).

**crash fence:** a protective fence of strong energy-absorbing mesh used along the outside border of a precipitous road to prevent out-of-control vehicles from going over a cliff or used on the outside corners of vehicle race tracks for spectator safety.

**crash helmet:** a strong protective head covering/enclosure required to be worn by each driver/occupant of a race car in a sanctioned event and by law for motorcyclists in many states as additional protection against head injuries if in a wreck.

**crash pad:** an impact-absorbing cushion strategically placed inside a vehicle (as a padded dash, headrest, or steering wheel) to minimize injuries to occupants in the event of a wreck.

**crash rail:** a barrier usually of energy-absorbing construction/materials separating traffic lanes and road shoulders and protecting against out-of-control vehicle crossovers.

**crash restraints:** on-board safety devices such as seat and shoulder belts, headrests, and air bags to minimize occupant injuries from vehicle crashes.

**crawler:** (1) A Caterpillar tractor. (2) Any track-laying vehicle. (3) A very slow-moving vehicle. (4) A vehicle with very low gearing suitable for climbing steep hills and hauling heavy loads--at slow speeds. See crawler tractor.

**crawler tractor:** a usually off-highway vehicle with traction and suspension by continuous chain tracks in lieu of wheels. See crawler.

**creature comfort:** the modern automobile now offers all the comforts of home with amenities such as air conditioning, automatic climate control, no-draft ventilation, heated seating, 4-way adjustable seat positions. That's real "down home" creature comfort stemming from human engineering and ergonomics.

**crew cab:** a pickup or other truck with a second seat (sometimes with doors) behind the driver's seat to carry additional workers to job sites.

**crimp:** to press, pinch, or squeeze together as a wire terminal fitting is affixed around the end of a wire.

**crimping pliers:** a tool for hand-applying the pressure to press terminals onto electrical wires to produce the necessary bonding for permanency and good conductivity.

**crinkle finish:** another name for crackle finish. See crackle finish.

**critical speed:** a rotational speed (as of a flywheel) or linear speed (as of a piston) at or above which natural forces may cause catastrophic failure as an exploding/disintegrating flywheel from centrifugal force or a stretched/broken piston rod from acceleration/deceleration forces.

**Crosley:** an American small automobile (1939-1952) developed by radio pioneer Powel Crosley that competed successfully in the American marketplace where few other such small cars were ever accepted.

**cross flow:** a flow pattern most prominent in a hemi-cylinder-head but present with valving on opposite sides of the cylinder bore in any engine.

**crosshead:** a metal connector block sliding between two parallel guide rails while pinned to the angular-oscillating push/pull of an engine's piston rod, converting it to a linear push/pull movement. Every reciprocating piston epitomises the crosshead.

**crossover:**  a vehicle roadway that crosses over another lower-level road.  Overpass.  Fly-over.

**crossroad:**  a road that crosses a main road at the same level.

**cross-pins:**  four bearing journals spaced 90° apart in a cruciform that carry the needle bearings of a universal joint or the pinion gears of a differential.

**cross scavenging:**  the use of a wedge-shaped deflector on the dome of a two-stroke engine's piston to establish a gas flow pattern from the intake port on one side of the cylinder toward the exhaust port across from it.

**cross section:**  a cutting of a device at right angles to its main axis or a drawing thereof.

**cross talk:**  an unwanted electrical voltage from one circuit impressed or induced upon another circuit by electrical leakage or inductive coupling as an engine's high-voltage spark jumping to a nearby wire.

**crossthread:**  to start a nut onto a bolt with the threads misaligned so that one thread cuts across another and usually damages the whole piece/part.

**crosswalk:**  a specially paved or marked path for pedestrians to use in crossing a vehicle road or street.

**cross wind:**  a wind blowing from a side direction not parallel to a vehicle's path.

**crowbar:**  an iron or steel bar that is usually wedge-shaped at the working end for use as a pry or lever and often with a crook on the other end.

**crowfoot wrench:**  a box-end or open-end stub with an off-set receptacle for a ratchet drive extension to be fitted into for working in close spaces.

**crown:**  (1) An engine piston head with a slight convex curvature (dome).  (2) The slight convex transverse curvature of a highway surface.

**crown saw:**  a saw having teeth around the edge of a hollow cylinder used for sawing holes with relatively large diameters. Hole saw.

**crown wheel:**  the larger bevel gear of a differential gear and pinion gear set.

**crucible steel:**  a durable hard cast steel made in pots that are hoisted from the furnace before the metal is poured into molds.

**crude:** abbreviated term for crude oil (natural petroleum—hydrocarbons), known to West Texas wildcatters as "black gold", that can be fractionally refined and reformulated into various vehicle fuels and lubricants as well as myriad feedstocks for our petrochemical industries.

**cruise control:** a vehicle speed control system that can be pre-set to adjust engine power and automatic transmission gear ratios automatically to maintain a specified speed and that can be overruled by the driver at any time.

**cruising gear:** a term usually applied to an overdrive gear but generically to any gearing combination that gives the fewest engine revolutions-per-mile.

**crush zone:** parts of a vehicle designed to absorb energy of collision forces by controlled structural collapse to reduce the transmission of these forces to vehicle occupants, e.g., collapsible steering wheel and steering column, 5-mile-an-hour front bumper, and front body/chassis units built to collapse from head-on impacts.

**cryogenic:** of or relating to the production of very low temperatures, the use of material at very low temperatures, and the storage of substances at very low temperatures. Each of these scientific specialties is likely to burgeon as motorized America inevitably embraces hydrogen as Space Ship Earth's "fuel of the future"--there is no other!

**cubage:** the cubic content, displacement, or volume used with actual physical dimensions as an expression of the size of the cargo area of a commercial vehicle and correspondingly the size of cargo items to be loaded on such vehicles.

**cubic centimeter:** the metric measure of engine displacement/volume in which one cubic centimeter (c.c.) equals 0.06102 cubic inch (cu.in.) and one thousand cubic centimeters (one liter, 1 L.) equal 61.02 cubic inches and usually expressed/written, e.g., 5.0 L. or 302 cu.in. (a popular contemporary Ford V-8 engine, using the manufacturer's "round-off" of digits).

**Cuda:** car buff lingo for the popular Plymouth performance/sports car model first introduced in 1966.

**cul-de-sac:** a street that is closed at one end and usually marked with a sign at its entrance warning "No Exit".

**curator:** one in charge of a collection of valuable automobiles as those in a designated museum.

**curb:** a raised edging (as of concrete) built along a street or roadway to form part of its drainage (gutter) and to delineate the outer limits of its width.

**curb feeler:** a wire spring attached to the lower right side of a vehicle that "feels" a curb when parking and emits a sound audible to the driver warning of the curb proximity. Curb marker. Curb warning.

**curb service:** service extended (as by a restaurant) to persons sitting in parked automobiles usually in a "drive in" facility.

**curbside pick-up:** a small cargo/delivery truck with sides to the cargo floor that hinge downward to form loading ramps or access from the side (as a sidewalk/streetside) as the tailgate does for rear-loading.

**curb weight:** the weight of any vehicle with standard equipment and serviced with coolant, fuel, and oil but without driver or occupants on board, also called "empty weight" or "tare weight".

**current:** the "flow" of an electric charge/amperage/electrons over/through a conductor (as a wire) or the rate of such "flow" whether alternating (AC), direct (DC), or pulsating ("chopped" DC).

**current regulator:** usually one-half of a vehicle's current/voltage automatic control device that prevents the current from alternator/generator exceeding a pre-set value thus preventing overheating of wiring and overcharging the battery.

**cushioned clutch:** a vehicle clutch with cushion springs in the disc to minimize the shock of clutch engagement. Almost universal.

**cushion spring:** flat annular strong springs incorporated in the clutch friction disc hub to cushion the shock of engagement.

**Cushman:** a trademarked usually three-wheeled scooter used for personnel transport and light delivery in and around manufacturing, maintenance, and military facilities.

**custom car:** a production-line automobile modified to fit the personal tastes of the owner, most usually by special quality exterior paint and often with elaborate and unusual designs and mixtures of colors. Customized.

**custom rod:** a production-line automobile, light truck, or van that has been radically altered in appearance and shape, often by lowering (chopping) the overall height and the ground clearance as well as changing the fender, hood, roof, and trunk contours before applying a "wild" paint scheme. Hot-rodded. Street rod.

**cut glass vase:** a usually door-post or window-frame mounted ornate flower vase found in the ostentatious limousines of yesteryear.

**cut-in speed:** the rotational speed at which an alternator/ generator voltage exceeds the vehicle system/battery voltage by a specified margin and the current/voltage regulator begins to feed its power into the vehicle circuits.

**cut-out:** (1) Any device, usually automatic, that stops the operation of a mechanical device or opens an electrical circuit, e.g., the magnetic switch (now electronic solid-state devices) that prevents feed-back through an alternator/generator when their voltage drops below battery/system potential or when the vehicle electrical/ignition is "off". (2) A valve in an engine exhaust system that vents to atmosphere ahead of converters/ mufflers, ostensibly to eliminate their restriction and reduce exhaust backpressure.

**CV-joint:** abbreviation for constant velocity universal joint.

**CVT:** abbreviation for continuously variable (ratio) transmission.

**cycle car:** a very light passenger vehicle usually with bicycle wheels and often as a three-wheeler, normally found only in financially-deprived populations.

**cylinder:** the tubular chamber in which the reciprocating piston of a compression engine or pressure pump works.

**cylinder block:** the usually heavy casting that contains the cylinders with water jackets for cooling; mountings (main bearings) for the crankshaft; valve guides, ports, and seats; and camshaft bushings and drive mechanisms. Block.

**cylinder head:** the assembly, sometimes with valves and camshaft(s), that is fitted to the cylinder block to close the cylinder end(s) and provide a coolant path from/to the block or cooling system plumbing. Head.

**cylinder-head gasket:** a sealing material fitted between an engine cylinder block and cylinder head to prevent leakage of coolant and of combustion gases.

**cylinder hone:** a rotating set of abrasive stones or pads used to smooth and polish the inner wall of a cylinder to reduce friction and provide a more leak-proof fit between the cylinder, piston, and rings.

**cylinder sleeve:** a thin-walled cylinder liner that can be pressed into an engine block that has been overbored to a prescribed diameter to repair cylinder-wall damages and restore the cylinder size to new specifications. Cylinder liner.

**C:** (1) The chemical symbol for carbon, atomic weight of 12 and one (with hydrogen) of the two most available and used elemental sources of heat energy (fuel). (2) When followed by a period, **C.** denotes Celsius, the SI scale of temperature.

**calorimeter:** an insulated laboratory test chamber where a material can be burned and the amount of heat given off accurately determined. Adiabatic calorimeter and bomb calorimeter are the most common types.

**cam duration:** the time in degrees of crankshaft rotation that the engine exhaust or intake valve is held open by the cam lobe.

**canister:** a usually carbon-filled can that collects fuel vapors for return to the vehicle tank, thus preventing venting pollution.

**cape chisel:** a metal cutting chisel configured to work in narrow channels and grooves as a keyway or slot.

**Carryall:** trade name of the large station wagon on a truck chassis that was the predecessor of the General Motors Suburban.

**catch can:** an onboard container in a car used to catch (collect) spilled or overflow fluids and retain them for proper disposal.

**cathode:** the negatively charged electrode from which current (electrons) flows through conductors, or a vacuum to a positive (+) point.

**ceton filter:** a wicking sock-filter that "wicks" diesel fuel through its filter media while effectively barring the passage of water.

**chassis dyno:** a vehicle horsepower measurement device where the wheels drive rollers connected to a load absorber (water, air, prony brake using friction) to evaluate and record actual road horsepower.

**chassis punch:** a metal die designed to cut round or square holes in sheet metal.

**chrome-moly steel:** a steel alloy of chromium and molybdenum that is favored by many race car builders for use in fabricating frames using welded tubing to be covered by aluminum sheet or formed plastic outer panels.

**clean room:** a contaminant/dust-free work area usually reserved for precision fitting and assembly especially of precision devices.

**Clenet:** a French-designed California-built neoclassic of the 1970s/1980s era that appeared to borrow style from several great classics but failed to stir the mixture into a homogeneous composite.

**cloud point:** the temperature at which the wax in diesel fuel and waxy oils begins to separate (solidify) and become visible.

**closed course:** a vehicle racecourse or track that completes a circular path with the finish line being the starting line.

**coefficient of drag:** for aerodynamic drag $C_d$ represents, as a fraction, the effective flat-plate resistance of the vehicle to the measured area of the hole that it pushes through the air (frontal area or dimensional flat-plate area).

**coil-over shock:** a telescoping shock absorber mounted inside a compression coil spring to increase the load-carrying capacity.

**coke bottle shape:** a vehicle body shape that is somewhat smaller near the middle (front-to-rear), a shape that reduces skin-drag (Reynolds Number) of high-speed aircraft but has neglible and questionable effect at typical automotive speeds.

**color sand:** using a very fine-grit wet sanding of newly-painted surfaces to blend variations in the final color shading to a uniform color throughout.

**cream puff:** a vehicle in outstanding condition of appearance and mechanical performance.

**crocus cloth:** a very fine-grit cloth-backed abrasive used to final polish lathe-work while spinning and to polish bearing journals.

**cross hatch:** a deliberate cross pattern from abrasive honing of cylinder walls to leave sufficient roughness to promote better oil-film adhesion and to inhibit the drain-back of oil to the crankcase when the vehicle sits idle.

**CRT:** cathode ray tube, a visual display vacuum tube with a flat screen accepting electron streams from "guns" that are computer directed to "paint" visual pictures or graphics.

**cycle fender:** a motorcycle-like covering attached to, and moving with (up-and-down and steering), the wheel.

### EXCUSES, EXCUSES
(From Traffic Court Records)

I collided with a stationary truck coming the other way.

An invisible car came out of nowhere, stuck my sports car and immediately vanished.

I was thrown from my car as it ran off the highway shoulder and was later found in a nearby ditch by some stray cows.

The oncoming car was weaving all over the road. I had to swerve a number of times before I hit him headon.

In my attempt to kill a fly, I drove into a telephone pole.

# PRONUNCIATIONS
(Is your mouth shaped right to say 'em?)

| | | | |
|---|---|---|---|
| Ballot | bal-oh | marque | mark |
| Beaulieu | bew-lee | Maybach | my-bock |
| Bollee, Leon | bowl-lee, lee-own | Michelin | mish-lan |
| Bouton | boo-tone | Modena | mow-den-ah |
| brogham | broh-ham | Molsheim | mole-sime |
| Cibie | cee-bee-ay | Mugello | moo-jello |
| Citroen | cee-tro-en | Napier | nape-year |
| Connaught | con-nawt | Panhard | pon-ahr |
| coupe | coo-pay | Petre | pet-tree |
| Cugnot | kewn-yo | Peugeot | pe-joe |
| Darracq | dar-rack | Porshe | por-sha |
| Decauville | de-co-vil | Renault | re-no |
| De Dion | de-dee-own | Salmson | sam-son |
| Delage | de-laj | sans soupape | sahn-soo-pap |
| Delahaye | del-a-aye | Saoutchik | sow-chick |
| Fournier | foor-gnay | Steyr | shtire |
| Gregoire | gray-gwar | Talbot-Lago | tal-bo lah-go |
| Grosvenor | grove-ner | Vanden Plas | van-den plahs |
| Horch | whore-sh | Veritas | ver-a-tahss |
| Ickys | icks | Vignale | vee-gnal-ay |
| Jaguar | jag-you-are | Voisin | vwa-zan |
| Junek | you-neck | voiture | vwa-teur |
| Lancia | lan-she-ah | voiturette | vwa-teur-et |
| landaulette | lawn-doe-lay | Wankel | vahn-kell |
| Le Mans | le-mawn | Veymann | way-man |
| Levassor | le-vass-or | Zandvoort | zand-vort |

**D-Cars:** Of 293 of 'em only one is a "Duesy". There may never be another. And there's not a single "dog" among them but a lot of little "dogs" with very little bark to be heard and absolutely no bite to be felt by society. Historically, the "D"-marque left few impressions; however, the "winged-8" or "Flying-D" initial that adorned the massive radiators of Augie and Fred Duesenberg's motoring masterpieces left an imprint that will never disappear. The brothers graduated from bicycles to race cars in 1904, building a Mason racer and then Duesenberg race cars and engines for nearly two decades before forming the Duesenberg Motor Company, Indianapolis, IN, and building their first Model A in 1920. A 3-litre Duesenberg racing car with a single overhead camshaft and three vertical valves per cylinder won the 1921 French Grand Prix. Duesenbergs chased Millers around the brickyard for several years until a centrifugal blower was installed on the straight-8 and won the 1924 Indy-500. While Sir Malcolm Campbell was setting world landspeed records with his "Bluebird" streamliner at Daytona Beach, FL, and Bonneville Salt Flats, UT, he was also a star salesman of Duesenbergs back home in England. And the Mayor of Salt Lake City, UT, was setting dozens of world records in his own backyard, also the Bonneville Salt Flats, as the "Mormon Meteor" driving his "Mormon Meteors I, II, and III" --all mammoth racing machines, and all proudly wearing the Duesenberg Marque. Ab Jenkins, the mayor, roared around a 50-mile-diameter blacklined circle painted on the white salt (sometimes still visible from the air) for 24-hour periods and dashed across the straightaway "flying mile" --many times each and always at new world record speeds, like a true meteor.

**D.A.F.:** In 1958 the Netherlands-built D.A.F. became that country's first serious entry into automobile manufacturing since the demise of the Spyker in 1925. D.A.F. had built commercial trailers and a military 4 x 4 since 1928. The D.A.F. introduced the ingenious and jerk-free Variomatic transmission, a fully automatic using a centrifugal clutch and V-belt drive giving an infinitely-variable drive ratio into a limited-slip differential.

**damper:** a device, usually as an elastic, hydraulic, or spring system capable of absorbing and dissipating the energy from rebound or rotational vibration energy, making a vehicle quieter and smoother while preventing material failure.

**damper springs:** coil springs situated within a vehicle clutch plate hub to absorb the shock loads of engagement.

**damping:** the dissipating of energy from a vibrating system, usually by mechanical friction, counter springing, or the flow of fluid through a restriction.

**damping tensioner:** a device operating against the slack side of a chain drive carrying pulsating loads to maintain tension and damp oscillation or whip of the chain as when the lobe of a camshaft passes the peak resistance point of a valve spring.

**dash:** a short fast vehicle race that usually precedes the main events as a Trophy Dash or qualifying heat race. Contemporary name for dashboard.

**dashboard:** a transverse panel (below the windshield) across an automobile/truck, et al., usually containing instruments and hand-operated controls/switches.

**dashpot:** a cushioning device for damping the stopping of a moving mechanical part to reduce shock.

**Day-Glo:** trademarked fluorescent coating used for instrument marking and various safety and informational signals and signs.

**dead axle:** a non-driven axle as the rear axle of a front-wheel-drive vehicle with the rear wheels turning freely on the integral spindles on each end of the axle. de Dion axle. Beam axle.

**dead center:** the position of the top-most point of a piston in a reciprocating engine when at either extreme of its stroke-- top dead center at the top of the stroke and bottom dead center at the bottom of the stroke. Also a stationary tapered shaft in the tail-stock of a lathe that supports the rotating work-piece during machining.

**dead heat:** a vehicle race in which two or more of the fastest racers finish exactly together with no discernible winner. Photo finish tie.

**dealership:** a factory authorized new vehicle sales agency. New car dealer. Factory dealer.

**decanter cars:** whiskey containers moulded as miniature models of very special automobiles as "Indy 500" winners and intended, with contents, as gifts to automobile aficionados.

**decarbonize:** removal of carbon deposits from vehicle engine combustion chambers, or exhaust components, by scraping, spray blasting, or wire brushing when disassembled or by use of carbon removing additives during engine operation.

**deceleration valve:** a valve that allows extra air to enter a vehicle induction system during deceleration to prevent back-firing.

**decibel:** a unit for expressing the relative intensity (loud-ness) of sounds on a scale from zero (for the average least perceptible sound by the human ear) to about 130 (for the beginning of pain level to the human ear). Vehicle interior sound levels and exhaust sound levels are given in decibels for comparative evaluations and for establishing statutory limits.

**deck:** the floor of a cargo or passenger-carrying vehicle, e.g. a double-decker (for two floor levels) or flat bed for one.

**deck lid:** trunk opening door (lid).

**decompression valve:** a vehicle driver-controlled valve (normally closed) that can be opened when starting a diesel (usually small displacement) to release compression air thus allowing the starter to spin the engine faster and store more cranking energy in the flywheel to facilitate starting. The decompression valve is closed as soon as sufficient starting speed is attained.

**decriminalize:** to remove or reduce the criminal classification or status of a law as is the contemporary trend with traffic violations. Reasonable minds should reject and oppose this liberalization, recognizing that speeding does kill (more than any other crime), that speeding is deliberate, that automobile "accidents" aren't <u>accidents</u>, but are caused--usually by speeding.

**dedicated fuel vehicle:** a vehicle designed and manufactured to use only one specific fuel. Dual fuel.

**deductible:** a clause in a vehicle insurance policy that re-lieves the insurer of responsibility for an initial specified amount of the cost of judgments or damages incurred under the policy provisions, which the policy holder (vehicle owner) must pay.

**deep cycle:** the practice of completely discharging a battery before fully recharging. With electric vehicle batteries, bat-tery design may dictate adherence to this practice to prevent "battery memory" from shortening vehicle distance traveled per battery charge.

**deep socket:** a socket wrench whose cylindrical length is suf-ficient (usually 2-3 inches) to allow it to slip over a bolt that extends that distance beyond the nut to be removed.

**deep well:** a formed or machined cylindrical hole in a machine that provides access for installation, removal, or servicing of a component such as a spark plug, sensor, drain plug, or retaining bolt that must be recessed below the outer limits of a machine's outer surface. Shallow well or recessed hole is one countersunk enough to permit such as a bolt head or nut to be just below or even with a machine's outer surface.

**deflection:** the flattening effect of load or low inflation pressure on a vehicle tire that produces the visible sidewall bulge above the tire footprint.

**deflector head:** the wedge-shaped piston dome (head) in a two-stroke engine that deflects the intake and exhaust gas flow from/to their respective cross-flow valve ports.

**defroster:** a vehicle system using heated air directed against windshield/window glass or electric heating elements imbedded in the glass to melt outside surface ice/snow or to evaporate inside fog/frost.

**degreaser:** a chemical solvent used to spray or immerse vehicle parts to remove grease and grime before inspection, shop work, and/or assembly.

**delivery van:** a cargo delivery vehicle usually without windows but with low threshold doors for easy curbside access and primarily intended for short hauls. Delivery trucks.

**demagnetize:** the removal of magnetic properties from a magnetized vehicle part to prevent unwanted electromechanical effects, usually by the use of a controllable alternating field. Degauss.

**demountable box:** a cargo carrying box with structural integrity. allowing it to be dropped off at a shippers to be picked up after being loaded, for shipment by truck, rail, or ocean deckload. Container box. Roll-off.

**Denver Boot:** a law enforcement tool patented in Denver, CO, and used worldwide by police to disable vehicles whose owners have outstanding traffic violations that are unsatisfied (unpaid fines, et al.). The device is a massive casting clamp that locks a vehicle wheel against movement until removed by a law enforcement officer.

**depot:** a facility for storing vehicles/cargo. A building for on/off-loading of cargo/passenger vehicles.

**depot hack:** a usually wooden-bodied multi-passenger motor vehicle used during the passenger-train heyday to deliver/pick up train travelers.

**depth-gauge:** a mechanic's measuring tool with a retracting extension for reaching into holes and providing micrometric accuracy to depth measurements. Often part of an external measuring caliper.

**desiccant:** a chemical drying agent used in strategically placed porous bags or breathable plastic containers in and around stored machinery and parts to remove ambient moisture to prevent corrosion damage.

**desmodromic valve:** an intake or exhaust valve that is positively/mechanically opened and closed by a cam or linkage and sometimes assisted to a better seal upon closing, by a spring. Used in some high-speed racing engines.

**detent:** a device as a dog, pawl, or spring-operated ball for positioning and holding one mechanical part in relation to another but allowing some extra force to release the detent locking force. Typical are the detent balls that retain manually shifted vehicle transmission gears in proper mesh until forcibly overcome for ratio changes.

**detergent:** a chemical, different from soap but able to emulsify oils, act as wetting agents, and hold insoluble particulates in suspension. Used as additives in vehicle fuels and oils to clean and protect internal parts by preventing deposition of, and by suspending potentially damaging residual products of combustion and environmental contaminants which may then be removed by proper filtering or fluid changing.

**detonation:** too-rapid combustion in an engine caused by a fuel with inadequate octane rating (number), excessive compression, excessive load, too-high manifold pressure, or ignition spark time too far advanced, thus resulting in lost power and potential material damage/failure from detonation-created stresses.

**deuce:** mechanic's jargon for a 1932 Ford, especially the roadster or coupe that became the Icon of the American hot-rodder-- and still is.

**diagnostic shop:** a vehicle facility or sub-section, usually equipped with state-of-the-art automated and computerized machines for the testing of complete vehicles or any component system, to verify operation to design parameters or to detect any malfunction or maladjustment. When staffed by competent technicians, vehicle diagnosis is indispensable to preventive maintenance and economical and effective repairs or replacement. Positive pin-pointing of a problem is essential prior to starting any work.

**diagonal brake system:** the use of two brake master cylinders with one operating the brakes on the left front and right rear wheels and the other master cylinder operating the right front and left rear wheels, thus providing safety redundancy should there be a failure in either of the split brake systems.

**Diamond T:** a large and powerful automobile built in Chicago, IL (1905-1911), with the name continuing as the Diamond T commercial trucks.

**diamond wheel:** an abrasive (grinding) wheel faced with diamond particles allowing it to cut very hard materials and to impart a very smooth highly-polished finish.

**diaphragm:** a flexible disc or membrane that deflects under fluid pressure, imparting a linear movement to a rod or lever attached to the diaphragm, or the imparting of deflection to a diaphragm (creating pumping action to a fluid) by the same type of rod or lever mechanical input.

**diaphragm carburetor:** a carburetor utilizing one or more diaphragms to regulate fuel mixing, rather than depending upon the level of fuel in a float bowl, thus allowing operating in any position and with vibration and inertia forces without affecting metering accuracy. Pressure carburetor.

**diaphragm chamber:** a pressure-tight chamber housing a diaphragm with linkage to serve as a pressure or vacuum-powered servo to operate brakes (as with power-brakes) carburetor chokes, or air-duct damper valves.

**diaphragm clutch:** a vehicle clutch that uses a diaphragm spring in lieu of coil compression springs to supply power to hold the pressure plate in contact with the friction plate to prevent slippage.

**die:** a sharp tool resembling a slotted nut and used for cutting external threads on screws, bolts, studs, and pipe. A device used to obtain plastic flow of metal as in wire drawing.

**die casting:** a manufacturing process involving forcing molten metal or liquid plastic into a suitable die form or mold and maintaining the pressure until the casting medium cools or chemically hardens. This insures smooth finishes and intricate detail in the finished casting.

**die grinder:** a usually high-speed electric or pneumatic drive motor with a selection of shaped grinding wheels to allow shaping a die or machine tool to an exact shape and finish.

**die sinker:** a specialized tool-maker who designs and makes cutting and shaping dies.

**Diesel cycle:** the thermodynamic-cycle (Carnot Cycle) engine invented and patented in Germany by Dr. Rudolph Diesel, 1892, that theoretically compresses intake air adiabatically until the temperature is well above the ignition point of the diesel fuel. Fuel is injected at the peak pressure and continues partially through the power stroke with the heat from the burning fuel expanding the combustion gases and maintaining a high working-pressure throughout most of the power (down) stroke. The subsequent exhaust and intake strokes complete the cycle. True adiabatic compression and expansion cannot be attained because of the necessity for cooling the engine for proper lubrication to prevent material failure.

**diesel-electric:** a motive power system used for locomotives, large industrial power sources, and some off-road utility vehicles as in mining and hauling coal and earth loads, in which a diesel engine running at optimum speed drives an electric generator that delivers power to wheel-traction motors more efficiently and controllably than through a geared transmission drive.

**diesel engine:** a two or four-stroke compression-ignition engine operating on the Diesel thermodynamic cycle. Considered capable of extracting more useful work out of each fuel heat unit (BTU) than any other type of engine in the world.

**Diesel Index:** a measure of diesel fuel quality, now being replaced by the more meaningful Cetane Number (Index). Octane Number is for spark-ignited fuels.

**dieseling:** the continued operating (running) of an internal combustion engine (whether it is compression ignition or spark ignition) after the ignition is turned off. In spark-ignition engines it usually indicates low octane fuel, overheating, or excessive combustion deposit build-up in the combustion chamber --in diesels, failure of fuel to shut off.

**diesel rattle:** the gravelly sound (tapping) present during idle and high loads on most diesel engines that is aggravated by low quality fuels (low Cetane Number). Engine knock.

**differential:** the "rear end" of a vehicle that changes direction (from the driveshaft) of the engine's motive power by 90° and divides the power equally to the left and right drive wheels. The internal gearing is designed to differentiate between the differing wheel speeds when cornering, because the outer wheel must revolve faster to travel the extra distance of its larger radius of turn.

**differential angle:** the very small angle between the mating angle of a poppet-valve head (as of an exhaust or intake valve of an I.C. engine) and angle of the seat in the cylinder block/head that insures more positive sealing against fluid flow.

**differential carrier:** the forged (sometimes cast) assembly that carries the final drive pinions in a vehicle differential (rear end).

**differential housing:** the central covering (of a vehicle rear axle) to which the outer tubular axles are riveted or welded, sometimes called the "banjo" because of its bulbous shape that houses the rotating differential gearing assembly.

**differential whine:** the high-pitched noise produced by a vehicle rear end when there is excessive wear on either the power or coasting side of gear teeth, causing whine during either acceleration or deceleration but usually not under both conditions unless the vehicle has many miles of operation or has lacked proper lubrication.

**digger:** mechanic's slang for a high-powered or low-geared vehicle that spins the rear wheels excessively when starting thus grinding (digging) softer road surfaces and throwing showers of particulates behind the wheels.

**dikes:** a vehicle mechanic's lingo for one of his favorite hand tools, diagonal side-cutting pliers.

**dilution air:** excess ambient air introduced into a vehicle exhaust system to dilute the unwanted contaminants in the exhaust gases and as appropriate to assist exhaust catalytic converters in oxidizing certain carbon contaminants.

**dilution factor:** a comparison of actual vehicle exhaust contaminants to the theoretical values resulting from chemical computations for combustion of stoichiometric mixtures (chemically balanced) of air and fuel (equivalence ratio = 1.0).

**dimmer switch:** a hand or foot-operated (by a vehicle driver) electrical switch that turns off the high-beam and turns on the low-beam of the headlights for added safety when meeting another vehicle at night or driving in fog.

**diode:** an electron tube or its analogous solid-state semiconductor, each having a plus (anode) and a minus (cathode) terminal and the ability to rectify alternating current to direct current.

**dioxide:** an oxide containing two oxygen atoms in each molecule of the compound, e.g., carbon dioxide ($CO_2$) is the desired remainder when burning carbon--ultimate entropy.

**dipper:** a scoop or cup-shape on a rotating device that dips through a pool of liquid lubricant to force the lubricant into bearing surfaces that are not pressure-fed.

**dipstick:** the marked rod or flat metal strip that visually shows the upper level of lubricant in a vehicle reservoir, as an engine crankcase or gear-train housing when the rod/stick is removed for viewing.

**direct current:** an electric current flowing in one direction only through a conductor at a substantially level value (amperage) unless modified intentionally.

**direct drive:** a power transmission mode as in a vehicle where the engine speed and the driveshaft speed are identical, as a mode that is typical of a vehicle running in high gear with a 1:1 gear ratio. Sometimes the only operating mode as in many small boats and airplanes.

**direct injection:** a vehicle engine fuel system, sans carburetor, that injects pulsed and-timed correct amounts of fuel directly into the engine's combustion chamber.

**direction indicator:** the flashing warning light at each exterior corner that indicates the driver's intention to make a turn in that direction. Turn indicator.

**directional control:** the accuracy and quality of response by a vehicle to a driver's steering effort.

**directional stability:** the ability and willingness of a vehicle to maintain an established direction (whether straight ahead or in various rates of turning) when external and extraneous forces act upon the vehicle, e.g., braking, cross winds, road surface imperfections, or steering geometry. Inherent stability.

**director plate:** a shaped orifice in a fuel injector discharge nozzle that forms the fuel's spray pattern.

**dirt bike:** a usually small motorcycle designed, geared, and suspended primarily for use on unpaved surfaces. Off-road.

**disc brake:** a vehicle wheel brake composed of an appropriate metallic plate rotating between caliper elements containing cylinders, friction pads, and pistons using hydraulic pressure to clamp the pads from opposing sides of the disc creating the friction stopping force.

**discharge tube:** the passage through which an air-fuel mixture within a carburetor is emulsified and discharged into the venturi throat. Emulsifier tube.

**disc valve:** a rotating plate usually with an arcuate port that indexes with a matching aperture(s) in a stationary sealing plate to time the flow of fluid to designated receptors.

**disc wheel:** a wheel presenting a solid surface from inner hub to outer rim.

**dispersant:** a chemical additive used in vehicle fluids (as engine oil) to disperse and hold in suspension unwanted contaminants until removed by filtration or draining.

**displacement:** the theoretical volume (usually stated in cubic inches or cubic centimeters) of incompressible working fluid that is drawn into (or displaced by) an engine during one complete cycle (exactly two crankshaft revolutions for a four-stroker or one revolution for a two-stroker). Swept volume.

**dissociation:** the chemical process of breaking or separating complex compounds into simpler entities that occurs naturally in the combustion chamber of an engine when a hydrocarbon fuel is broken into the hydrogen and carbon so that each can combine with oxygen, releasing the heat energy that propels the vehicle. On-board dissociation of a fuel (outside the combustion chamber) is a loser, but frequently promoted by charlatans and special interests who take advantage of the public's scientific illiteracy. Possibly the most fraudulent is the claim that water in a vehicle tank can be "dissociated" ($H_2O > H_2 + O_2$) and the hydrogen used as the "wonder fuel"--which it really is! But impossible to do economically, efficiently, or practically.

**distillate:** a viable liquid (as a fuel) that is separated by fractional boiling and condensing the vapors or by catalytic "cracking" of a complex compound (as crude oil) into simpler and more usable or situation-friendly fluids (as gasoline, et al.).

**distortion angle:** the angle between the plane of a vehicle wheel and the direction of vehicle motion. The difference between the intended (steered) path and the actual path of a steerable vehicle. Slip angle.

**distributor:** a rotary high-voltage switch driven at one-half crankshaft speed by a four-stroke engine--at crankshaft speed by a two-stroke engine--that delivers (distributes) the high voltage energy from the ignition coil to each spark plug in firing order and at the exact right moment to create the spark.

**distributor cam:** a multi-lobed (one lobe per cylinder) cam within the distributor that operates a breaker contact switch to initiate the spark to each cylinder in firing order.

**distributor cap:** a tightly-fitted cover to a vehicle distributor that contains the terminal contacts for each spark plug wire arranged in a circle with the coil input contact in the center from which the rotor contactor delivers the coil high tension energy in firing order.

**distributor pump:** a high-pressure rotary fuel pump that also meters measured volumes in firing order to each individual cylinder injector nozzle of a multi-cylinder diesel engine. A wobble-plate-piston pump is also a distributor and high-pressure pump that does the same functional job.

**distributorless ignition:** Of two types, the electronic-switching of the high voltage energy in timing sequence is accomplished with no moving parts. The second type, popularized by the Model T Ford had a coil for each spark plug. Each coil acted as a transformer-like Tesla Coil and was energized in timing order by a low-voltage rotary electrical switch. Of course, each type "distributed" the spark to the right spark plug at the right time.

**ditchdigger:** a special purpose vehicle usually with tracked wheels and an excavating device such as an endless-belt assembly of scoops or an articulated-arm bucket/scoop/ shovel used for digging often narrow and deep trenches in the terrain surface. Trencher. Clamshell.

**dive:** the strong and sometimes violent downward plunge of a vehicle front-end when brakes are applied forcefully. The motion results inevitably from the gravity-force of deceleration as influenced by vehicle weight-distribution (center-of-gravity), brake force distribution (percentage front-and-rear), and suspension strength and geometric design.

**Doble:** Abner Doble's great American steam-powered automobile (1914-1931) was likely the most conventional and most sophisticated steam car in world history though only a limited number were ever manufactured. The Model E. Tourer (there's a 1925 model in the Henry Ford Greenfield Village Museum) had a 4-cylinder horizontal (flat) engine, acceleration, hill-climbing, and top speed that was outstanding even when compared with all other steamers, could have steam power to drive in less than 90 seconds after turning the switch, and had a driving range of 1500 miles per tank of water (24 gallons). All of this plus elegance and luxury nonpareil for $8,000, and with a 3-year factory warranty.

**dock:** a vehicle unloading/loading facility usually a platform or porch-like raised-level floor that is easily accessible to commercial vehicles.

**dock height:** usually applied to the cargo floor height of a commercial vehicle that matches the level of a warehouse servicing dock.

**doctor's coupe:** an automobile two-door coupe without a rear passenger seat and that was favored by doctors in the "house-call era" of medical practice.

**Dodge Brothers:** in the beginning, John and Horace, the Dodge Brothers, financed Henry Ford's manufacturing efforts while building and selling Henry their engines for his cars. The Brothers produced the first car wearing their name with the Star of David marque in 1914 and their tough automobile became the star of General "Black Jack" Pershing's 1916 Mexican Expedition, remaining popular as ambulances, staff cars, and trucks in the American military services. In July, 1928 Walter P. Chrysler bought the Brothers for $175,000,000. A good buy!

**dog bones:** automobile jargon for the horizontal shaft/handle with decorative/functional ball-ends that became the industry-wide standard grip for unscrewing and removing vehicle external radiator caps.

**dog cart:** a small lightweight 2-wheeled vehicle with back-to-back transverse seating and usually dog- or pony-drawn.

**dog clutch:** a toothed-fitting (dog) for shaft ends that mesh with a mirror-image fitting to impart no-slip turning effort while allowing total disengagement when physically separated.

**dog leg:** a sudden sharp bend in a vehicle roadway or race-course. A long-handled tool that has a sharp bend (about 90°).

**DOHC:** vehicle mechanic's abbreviation for double-overhead-cam. Twin cam.

**dolly:** a low platform with casters, rollers, or wheels for moving heavy objects. A two-wheeled towable platform for lifting either the front or the rear wheels of one vehicle, for towing behind another vehicle. A heavy cupped-end bar for holding against a rivet-end when the rivet-head is hammered by a rivet-gun.

**domed piston:** an engine piston with a semicircular crowned head for added strength and for fitting into a hemispherical cylinder head to increase compression ratio. Dome head.

**donkey engine:** a small usually portable auxiliary engine for industrial/construction purposes. A small locomotive usually for yard-switching of rail cars.

**donor:** a metal used to donate or give up one of its components (as an atom) as in a vehicle coolant to prevent the erosion of similar metal from a major casting exposed to the coolant.

**doorpost:** the vertical structural support and closure member from floor-to-roof at the front or rear of a vertical door-opening. Some turret-top automobiles have no center doorpost. Hardtop.

**dope:** a chemical additive to vehicle fluids that purports to enhance or add desirable properties such as higher octane, anti-freezing, better lubricity, lower unwanted emissions. Some do. Most don't. Sometimes illegal. Mechanic's jargon used in lieu of complex chemical nomenclature.

**do-si-do:** an early day automobile with back-to-back transverse seating for occupants. Dos-a-dos.

**double-acting:** an engine or pump whose piston does work in both directions of its reciprocating stroke. Common practice in steam engines and fluid compressor pumps.

**double-barrel carburetor:** a vehicle carburetor usually with one float bowl and two air ducts (barrels) with venturis each supplying fuel/air combustible mixture to three cylinders of a 6-cylinder engine or four cylinders of an 8-cylinder engine. Two-barrel. Four-barrel.

**double-cardan joint:** a constant velocity universal joint using two properly-oriented cardan joints in series but that does not attain true constant velocity response.

**double clutch:** the use of two de-clutch/clutch sequences to equalize gear speed allowing no-clash/grinding of gears when changing gear ratios in an unsynchronized-gear sliding-mesh transmission (crash-box). Also prevents potential transmission gear damage when down-shifting a syncromesh transmission at high vehicle speeds.

**double-decker:** a bus having an upper passenger floor (deck) above the lower passenger floor (deck), roughly doubling the passenger-carrying capacity of the vehicle.

**double-nut:** the practice of using a second nut torqued against the primary nut securing a bolt- or stud-assembled piece against vibrating or rotational loosening forces. Pal nut.

**double-park:** to park a vehicle alongside (on the moving-traffic side) of a row of automobiles, already parked parallel to the roadway.

**double-pivot steering:** the conventional system of all modern vehicles utilizing a king-pin for each steered wheel. Some early vehicles used single-pivot steering like buggies/wagons.

**double-reduction axle:** a usually heavy vehicle having two stages of speed-reduction (torque amplification) between the drive-shaft (propeller shaft) speed and the drive axle speed to assist in hill-climbing and/or heavy-hauling.

**double-row bearing:** a low-friction bearing having two rows of balls or rollers (needles) for greater load-carrying capacity.

**double-trailer:** a high-capacity vehicle cargo-hauler attained by adding a second towed trailer (fully suspended on wheels at all four corners) behind a conventional tractor-trailer ("18-wheeler"). Usually restricted to freeway service and sometimes augmented by a third trailer unit behind the "double". Triple-trailer. Trailertrain.

**double wide:** an overwidth trailer house usually transported to its "trailer park" on special over-the-road truck-tractor transporters.

**double-wishbone suspension:** a stacked A-frame (one above the other) usually used for vehicle independent front suspensions with the stub axle supported at its steering center by upper and lower ball-joints at the apex of each A-frame. A-frames may be equal length (parallel) or unequal-length (nonparallel) thus determining the handling response from the suspension geometry. Double-wishbone support is also used for the rear axle(s) of some race cars.

**downdraft carburetor:** a vertically-oriented vehicle carburetor through which the intake air travels downward into the engine's intake manifold. Sidedraft. Updraft.

**downpipe:** the first pipe usually downward from the vehicle engine exhaust manifold to the under-side muffler or catalytic exhaust converter. Sidepipe.

**downshift:** when a vehicle driver selects and deliberately shifts into a lower transmission gear ratio (either automatic or manual gearing) to obtain more pulling power or to use the engine compression for slowing (braking) the vehicle's progress.

**downsize:** the contemporary trend in passenger cars (reducing exterior dimensions and weight) in an effort to save fuel. Future concomitant benefits are certain to accrue as vehicle population burgeons and parking space shrinks.

**downstream injection:** a vehicle fuel system that sprays the fuel (injects) at some point in the intake system after the air throttle usually as near as possible to the engine intake valve port or opening (port injection). Throttle-body injection. Direct (combustion chamber) injection.

**downwash:** descriptive term for the airflow pattern over a curved-top (streamlined) vehicle body where nonturbulent air flow is desirable to attain decreased air drag.

**drag:** the total of the air and road resistance (friction) to vehicle movement that represents, with inertial losses (acceleration), the useful work done by the fuel burned in the engine. Air drag increases exponentially with increased speed while road drag is a straight-line (linear first-power) increase.

**drag chute** a parachute carried by race cars (Bonneville land-speed racers and dragsters) and deployed for rapid deceleration at the completion of a high speed run until the vehicle brakes become effective.

**drag line:** a vehicle-mounted excavating machine that uses a cable-pulled scoop/shovel/bucket that digs into the surface and is drawn toward (dragged) the machine with its load and dumped.

**drag link:** the vehicle steering system member connecting the Pitman Arm from the steering gear box to the steering arm of the steerable stub-axle (directly or through intermediate linkage).

**drag race:** a competitive vehicle event usually involving two special-built race cars (dragsters) or one single vehicle competing against the clock (time) to determine the fastest (speed) and quickest (lowest elapsed time) over an electronically-timed distance (usually one-quarter-mile).

**dragster:** a special-built race car or modified stock vehicle with increased horsepower and drive-train gearing and tires selected for maximum acceleration/speed and lowest elapsed time over a short race course (usually one-quarter-mile). Rail. Show-room-stock. Funny-car.

**drag strip:** a short (usually one-quarter-mile) vehicle race-course with nearby seating for spectators, electronic speed/ timing devices, starting lights (Christmas Tree), and pit areas for maintenance, preparation, repair, and service of competing race cars.

**drag strut:** a structural member either in compression or ten-sion that resists and transfers forces resulting from vehicle drag (either aerodynamic or road drag).

**drainback:** a hose/pipe/tube in a vehicle recirculating fluid system, e.g., the oil gallery in a V-block engine, the oil re-turn from a turbocharger, that returns fluids to the reservoir or supply tank.

**drain plug:** a removable usually threaded sealing device that allows fluids to be drained from any vehicle system such as crankcase, differential, transmission, radiator, fuel tank, et al.

**drain valve:** usually a 90° from off-to-on valve for draining any vehicle fluid-containing system so equipped.

**drawbar:** a transverse structural member on the rear of a tow vehicle to which towed vehicles or machines are attached. A rigid bar or structural shape (A-frame) that is hinged to a tow vehicle (tractor) for towing and steering a full trailer.

**drawbar combo:** a tractor vehicle and a drawbar-towed full trailer.

**drawbar pull:** the pulling force (usually expressed in pounds) exerted by the drawbar when towing any load at a particular speed by a tow vehicle.

**drawbar trailer:** a full trailer (totally self-supported--not a semi-trailer) with a drawbar assembly for towing and steering when attached to a tractor power unit.

**drawbridge:** a vehicle bridge across a navigable waterway that can be raised, lowered, or drawn aside (turned or swung) to permit selective passage of vehicles or boats/ ships.

**dray:** loosely used to describe various cargo-carrying vehi-cles, e.g., a horse-drawn 2-wheel farm cart; a flat-bed (low-boy) heavy-duty semi-trailer.

**drip molding:** the narrow gutter above the side window area of a passenger vehicle, usually extending from the windshield to

the rearmost roof dimension, that serves to protect the side
windows from roof run-off.

**driveability:**  the degree of ease/difficulty in operating and
controlling a vehicle. Driver friendliness.

**driven plate:**  the clutch friction plate that is splined to the
transmission input shaft and friction-locked to the engine flywheel friction-face when the clutch is engaged.

**drive pin:**  a hardened steel pin that is driven through
tightly-fitting matching holes of two parts to lock them together in a fixed relationship.  Roll pin.

**drive plate:**  the vehicle engine's flywheel friction-face.

**drive plug:**  a sealing plug that is driven into an appropriately shaped/sized opening to seal against leakage.

**driver's field of view:**  the horizontal range of visibility
through the vehicle windshield, side and rear windows, and
inside/outside mirrors.

**driver's license:**  a questionable certificate of an individual's authorization to drive a motor vehicle legally.  Literally inherent to the issuance of such a privilege is the pre-
sumption that the licensee has been tested to verify competency.  Not so, because none of Uncle Sugar's states uses a
practical or written test that verifies competency.  License
is thus degraded to "identification card".

**drive shaft:**  in a rear-wheel-drive vehicle, the shaft(s) from
the transmission output shaft to the differential that transmits engine power to the wheels.

**driveshaft tunnel:**  the raised tunnel-shaped (hump) floor
center-section from front-to-rear that houses a rear-wheel-
drive vehicle's driveshaft.

**drive train:**  the conduit/path of the vehicle power from the
engine to the drive wheels.  With rear-wheel-drive, the clutch/
transmission, drive shaft, differential, rear axles.  With
front-wheel-drive, the transaxle and constant velocity joints.

**driving axle:**  a vehicle axle, front or rear, that imparts a
turning force to a wheel.  Live axle.

**driving beam:**  the so-called high beam of a vehicle's headlights because of its intent--to provide nighttime visibility
farther down the road than does the bow-beam (passing beam,
city beam, dipped beam).

**driving mirror:** an inside or outside vehicle mirror designed to give a clear view of the traffic and the roadway behind the vehicle.

**drop axle:** a dead (non rotating) axle with its central span lower than the axis of the wheels thus lowering the vehicle's center of gravity or providing additional underbody space as for suspension, steering, or propulsion equipment. Dropped axle. Lowered axle.

**drop cloth:** a flexible covering to protect shop equipment, other vehicles, or floor areas when spray painting, grinding, welding, et al., in a vehicle shop.

**drop forge:** to forge metal into shape with or without heat by exerting the force of a drop hammer or punch press upon appropriate dies.

**drop hammer:** a power-operated hammer that is raised and released to free-fall against material on an anvil surface or between dies.

**drophead:** British term for a convertible vehicle roof.

**droplight:** a portable shop work-light usually encased in a protective cage and suspended, or on an extension cord (often with a retractable cord reel).

**drop seat:** a hinged (fold out of the way) seat for occasional overload passengers as in a taxi cab or limousine normally providing greater interior room when not needed. Jump seat.

**drowned out:** to describe an engine stoppage caused by excess fuel making a mixture too rich to ignite. Water as rain, splash, or leaks on electrical equipment/wiring that causes short-circuits.

**drum brake:** a vehicle brake with an interior or exterior friction surface and secured to a road wheel or drive shaft that is acted upon by an internal-expanding brake shoe (the most common) or an external-compressing brake band (primarily on drive shafts as emergency/parking brakes).

**drunkometer:** a chemical analysis device for measuring the alcohol content in the blood (as of a suspected drunk vehicle driver) by analyzing the breath. Breathalyzer.

**dry cell:** an electrical battery that uses non-liquid chemicals to produce electrical energy, usually as an emergency backup for another electrical system. Yesteryear's source of ignition energy for vehicles. Hotshot battery.

**dry-charged battery:** a lead-acid battery whose plates have been charged for extended dry storage with battery acid solution to be added when placed in service. The added solution activates the full capacity and strength of the battery's chemical-to-electrical potential for delivering energy as needed.

**dry clutch:** the most common vehicle clutch using dry friction materials in lieu of the oil-bath sometimes used with multi-disc clutches.

**dry hole:** a well that has been drilled to prospect (search) for fossil hydrocarbon fuel deposits but discovers none. Wildcatter.

**dry lakes:** a series of lake beds left when ancient lakes/seas disappeared leaving hard, perfectly level, and smooth surfaces large enough for high speed automobile racing. Too many to name, the best known is Bonneville Salt Flats (UT), followed by El Mirage and Muroc Dry Lakes (CA), and Black Rock Desert (NV) where Englishman Richard Noble set the current World Landspeed Record of 633 miles-per-hour in 1983. The Lake Gairdner, Australia, lake bed appears to be leading as the preferred race track for vehicle speeds near and above Mach I (the speed of sound, 741 mph at standard conditions).

**dry sleeve:** a cylinder liner or insert of hardened material that is pressed or heatshrunk into a softer metal as an aluminum cylinder block in a manner that exposes none of the sleeve to the engine's liquid coolant. Wet sleeve.

**dry sump:** an engine lubricating oil system in which no oil is carried in the engine as in the crankcase but is stored externally in a tank or reservoir with the main oil pump supplying pressured oil to bearings and the sump/scavenger pump returning the bearing spill-over to the supply tank usually through an oil-cooler. This arrangement allows an engine to run inverted or in any other orientation (essential for airplanes) and reduces internal drag in very high speed racing engines by preventing the impingement of oil droplet, foam/froth, or mist by the rotating crankshaft or reciprocating components.

**dry tank:** an empty fuel tank. Dusty tank.

**dual axle:** a vehicle with two close-spaced rear axles (for a truck) to provide better traction and for better load distribution to the road surface.

**dual beam headlight:** a single vehicle headlight-enclosure that contains two individually-lighted filaments to provide either a high-beam or a low-beam for longdistance or short-distance illumination of the roadway. Single beam headlight.

**dual cab:** a truck driver's-compartment (cab) that is enlarged to provide extra seating or sleeping space. Crew cab. Sleeper cab.

**dual carb:** a vehicle engine with two carburetors whose controls are linked together and synchronized for better fuel/air mixture distribution to all cylinders.

**dual-control car:** a passenger car with two complete sets of duplicate operating controls for emergency use or for giving driving instruction, with either the instructor or the student able to drive the vehicle safely from either side.

**dual-drive tandem:** a tandem-axle vehicle in which both axles are driven.

**dual exhaust:** a vehicle engine using two separated exhaust conduits (pipes, mufflers, and catalytic converters) from the engine exhaust manifold to the tail-pipe exhaust exit.

**dual-fuel engine:** a vehicle engine adapted to run on two distinctly different fuels, e.g., gasoline and natural gas--each requiring separate supply tanks, delivery systems, and fuel/ air mixing devices.

**dual side-mounts:** a vehicle having fender wells in both front fenders, each for carrying a spare tire/wheel.

**dual valves:** an engine with two intake or exhaust valves for better breathing and/or scavenging.

**dual valve-springs:** a vehicle engine having two concentric compression coil springs on each valve providing a spring-rate that permits higher speeds without valve bounce.

**dual wheels:** two close-spaced wheels with tires mounted on each side/end of a vehicle axle to carry increased weight.

**duct:** a channel, pipe, or tube capable of carrying a fluid substance.

**ductible:** capable of being drawn, rolled, or hammered into a thinner section as with a soft metal.

**Duesenberg:** the great American car and the brothers, Augie and Fred, who built them.

**dump body:** the tiltable body of a dump trailer or truck.

**dump trailer:** a full-trailer or a semi-trailer with a tilting body or underneath-opening doors for dumping its load (as sand, gravel, et al.).

**dump truck:** a truck with tiltable body for dumping its load.

**dump valve:** an emergency valve that actuates the brakes of a full- or semi-trailer in the event of its separation from its tow vehicle.

**dune buggy:** any off-road or recreational vehicle equipped with large tires and a suspension suitable for driving on sandy or muddy surfaces without "digging in".

**duplex chain:** a roller chain with two parallel sets of rollers used to provide longer life to timing chains carrying pulsating loads as does a camshaft drive-chain.

**duralumin:** a light, strong alloy of aluminum, copper, magnesium, and manganese that resists corrosion.

**durometer:** an instrument for measuring hardness of a material.

**dust cover:** a protective cover with many vehicle uses, e.g., a fabric cover enclosing the entire vehicle, a metal or plastic plate over an opening into a component's interior, or a hubcap.

**dwell:** the period during which electrical power is supplied to a vehicle's ignition coil (points/primary circuit closed) allowing the build-up of the coil's magnetic field toward or to its maximum strength. Measured in degrees of distributor shaft rotation or in milliseconds of elapsed time. Dwell angle. Dwell time. Dwell duration.

**dwell extenders:** dual distributors, dual points, multiple coils (up to one per cylinder), electronic devices. All can help by improving dwell and allowing higher engine speeds.

**Dymaxion:** one of Space Ship Earth's first (and possibly the foremost) truly aerodynamic and super-efficient automobiles, Buckminster Fuller's nonpareil Dymaxion, built in the former Locomobile factory at Bridgeport, CT (1933-1934), bequeathed two examples to society, one in the Harrah Automobile Museum, Reno, NV, and the other (purchased by Leopold Stowkowski for his wife and driven 300,000 miles) in the Museum of Transportation and Industry, Chicago, IL. Though larger than a Cadillac, the front-wheel-drive, rear-engined, rear-steering Dymaxion, with Henry Ford's 1932 flathead V-8 85-horsepower engine was timed, fully-loaded, at 130 miles-per-hour and 50 miles-per-gallon fuel economy. The Dymaxion was touted for its ability to parallel park in a space only $1\frac{1}{2}$ inches longer than its length--without jockeying.

**dynamic balance:** the balancing of rotating vehicle parts using a sophisticated electronic machine. Particularly important for wheels, crankshafts, and fly-wheels.

**dynamic compression:** checking the compression of each individual cylinder of an engine while running by using a dynamometer and sophisticated electronic measuring and computing devices. The procedure involves shorting out the spark plug of the cylinder being tested and the computer using the power-loss shown by the dyno to calculate the compression that it would require to develop that horsepower.

**dynamic supercharging:** using the resonant properties of the intake system (air from inlet to carburetor, the carburetor itself, the intake manifold, and the inlet valve ports) to take advantage of the kinetic energy of the incoming induction air to obtain slight gains in intake manifold pressure thus improving volumetric efficiency of an engine. Tuned intake. Tuned pipes. Acoustic tuning.

**dynamo:** the British name for the automobile D.C. generator now almost totally replaced by the more efficient A.C. alternator on contemporary vehicles.

**dynamometer:** a vehicle diagnostic/testing device that is invaluable to every vehicle maintenance shop. An engine dynamometer is used for engines removed from the vehicle and a chassis dynamometer tests the complete vehicle under exact simulated driving conditions. The shop technician can measure horsepower, fuel consumption, and exhaust emissions with scientific precision for any load at any desired speed. Being able to "drive" the vehicle while working alongside makes it possible to duplicate the same highway conditions at which reported malfunctions were experienced by the driver. With the dynamometer-matched test instruments and integrated computers, malfunctions are readily pin-pointed and all repairs and adjustments can be evaluated and performance verified under anticipated driving conditions.

**dyno:** a mechanic's abbreviation of dynamometer.

**dyno-tune:** to operate an automobile on a chassis dynamometer at the loads and speeds where it is desired to be driven and use the dynamometer's measuring instruments to "peak out" (maximize) the operating parameters of every appropriate tuneable system and component. Race tuning. Peak tuning.


### LAGNIAPPE

**DA:** body shop lingo for a powered dual-action hand sander also called a "jitterbug".

**dB:** standard abbreviation for decibel.

**DC:** direct current (electricity) AC.

**deck plate:** aluminum or steel plate usually about one-quarter inch in thickness with a surface marked by slightly raised ridges of metal to prevent sliding of cargo when used as vehicle floor.

**degree:** an increment-measure of angularity and temperature indicated as deg. or the superscript "°" after the value as 45°. The temperature-increment is subject to further definition/delimitation--the angularity-increment is fixed as 1/360 of a circle.

**dial:** a visual presentation/readout of data usually on a circular face with "hands" pointing to the continuously variable physical quantities--remember when we all "told time" from the positions of the "little hand and the big hand"?

**dial indicator:** the indication of minuscule dimensional changes and values on a simplified circular scale pointed to by a rotating "hand" (pointer).

**DIN:** the German Institute for Standardization is analogous and similar to our Society of Automotive Engineers, setting industry-wide measurement standards.

**direct ignition:** distributorless timed electrical impulses (sparks) to the spark plugs from an electronic module just like the Model T Ford did it mechanically--and so well!

**DNF:** code symbol used throughout motor sports and automobile racing in reporting the race-end finishing position of competitors, meaning literally "Did Not Finish".

**dual ignition:** an engine with two spark plugs per cylinder each fired by a totally separate independent electrical circuit.

**ducktail:** an upswept panel usually above the trunk lid rear section ostensibly to produce down-force but of doubtful value. Porsche's whale tail.

**duct tape:** a usually silvered fabric-backed joint sealing tape that adheres well and widely used around race cars for temporary fixes. Racer's tape.

**Dykem blue:** trade named blue coating for metals designed to be scribed to show places for cutting and machining.

**Dzus fastener:** trademarked quick release locking fastener for sheet metal panels or access openings of race cars (borrowed from aircraft use after years of successful service).

### NO KIDDIN'

The world's youngest automobile dealer? Floyd Clymer, whose father financed new-car dealerships for Cadillac, Maxwell, and Reo marques in Floyd's name at Berthoud, Colorado, was eleven years old when he sold the first of 20 new cars during his first year as a dealer. Floyd later became a motorcycle dealer and racer, invented his Throughthe-Windshield-Spotlight, wrote his first Clymer Book, and became the world's largest publisher of automobile literature. President Theodore Roosevelt traveled to Colorado to meet Floyd Clymer and acclaimed him as the "World's Youngest Automobile Dealer" during an official proclamation in 1907.

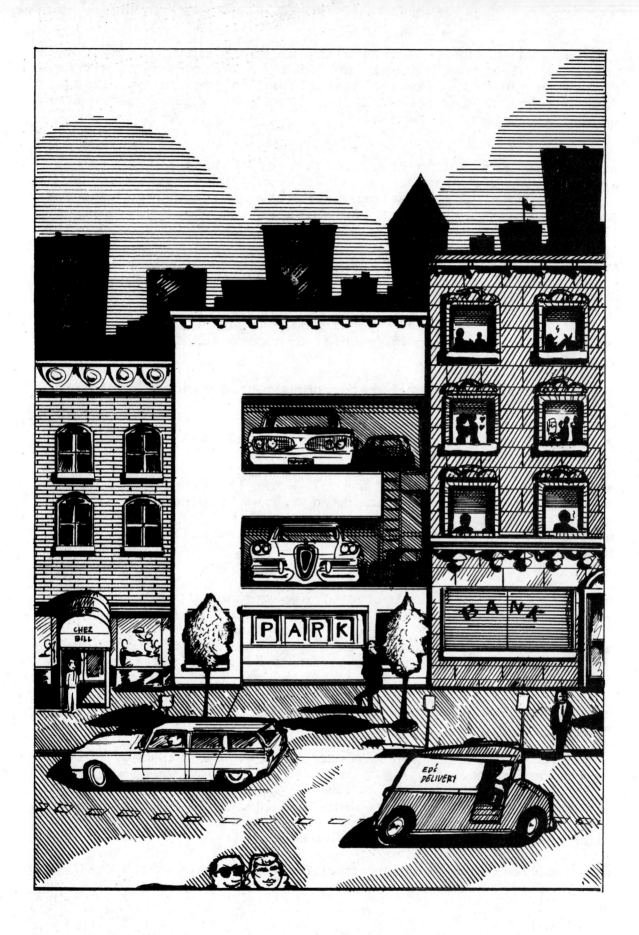

**E-Cars:** among the 198 cars with the first initial "E", there were 19 electrics but only one Edsel. There are likely more Edsels in the U.S. Census registration and the Mormon Genealogy Vault (about a quarter-million) than any other E-car. Henry Hudson's Essex maybe ran second.

**eccentric:** not having the same center. Deviating from a circular path. Off-center. A rod with one end attached at the eccentric point and whose other end is constrained to move in a straight line will convert the circular eccentric motion to a reciprocating motion at the constrained end.

**ecofreak:** an overzealous environmentalist--used disparagingly.

**Edsel:** a Ford-built marque produced from 1957 through 1959 and discontinued 1960.

**econocar:** designed to operate at low cost for fuel and maintenance.

**economizer valve:** a carburetor component designed to reduce fuel usage where operating modes permit.

**eddy current:** an electric current induced in a conductor by an alternating magnetic field.

**edge:** the cutting side of a tool. The line where an object or area begins or ends. Pavement edge, blacktop edge.

**efficiency:** the quality or degree of being efficient. The ratio of the useful energy delivered by a dynamic system to the energy supplied to it.

**egg car:** vaguely descriptive of short rounded vehicle shapes also called "bubble" cars. BMW, "600", Isetta.

**egged-out:** a circular hole in a part that has been worn unevenly to an oval or elliptical shape. To deliberately shape such a hole.

**ego-mobile:** another synonym more truly descriptive than automobile.

**ego trip:** "cruising" on Main Street. Show-off Sunday drive to the drive-in.

**eight:** an eight-cylinder engine or automobile. It's an eight.

**eighty-eight:** a memorable Oldsmobile.

**elapsed time:** the actual time taken to travel over a specified course (as in racing).

**elasticized:** made with elastic thread or inserts. Stretchy seat covers.

**elastomer:** any of the various elastic substances resembling rubber.

**elbow grease:** human energy vigorously exerted as in hand-polishing a car.

**electret:** a dielectric body in which a permanent state of electric polarization has been set up.

**electric car:** an automobile propelled by an electric motor supplied energy from storage batteries or a fuel-cell.

**electrical:** relating to or operated by electricity.

**electric eye:** photoelectric cell. A miniature cathode ray tube used to determine a condition (as of radio tuning).

**electro analysis:** chemical analysis or system analysis by electrolytic methods.

**electro chemistry:** a science that deals with the relation of electricity to chemical changes and with the interconversion of chemical and electrical energy.

**electrode:** a conductor used to establish electrical contact with a nonmetallic part of a circuit.

**electrodeposit:** to deposit (as a metal or other material) by electrolysis. The deposited material. Electroplating.

**electrodynamometer:** an instrument that measures current by indicating the strength of the forces between a current flowing in fixed coils and one flowing in movable coils. Ammeter.

**electroform:** to form shaped articles by electrodeposition on a mold.

**electrohydraulic:** of or relating to a combination of electric and hydraulic mechanisms.

**electrolysis:** the producing of chemical changes by passage of an electric current through an electrolyte.

**electrolyte:** a nonmetallic electric conductor in which current is carried by the movement of ions.

**electromagnet:** a core of magnetic material surrounded by a coil of wire through which an electric current is passed to magnetize the core.

**electromechanical:** of, relating to, or being a mechanical process or device actuated or controlled electronically.

**electrometallurgy:** a branch of metallurgy dealing with the application of electric current either for electrolytic deposition or as a source of heat.

**electromotive force:** something that moves or tends to move electrcity. The amount of energy derived from an electrical source per unit quantity of electricity passing through the source.

**electron:** an elementary particle consisting of a charge of negative electricity equal to about $1.602 \times 10^{-19}$ coulomb and weighing about 1/1836 that of a proton.

**electroplate:** to plate with an adherent continuous coating by electrodeposition.

**electrostatic:** of or relating to static electricity or electrostatics.

**electrostatic painting:** painting with a spray that utilizes electrically charged particles to insure complete even coating.

**eliminator:** applied to a heat race, preliminary race, or timed competitive run by a vehicle to eliminate slower vehicles to insure more competitive action in the final race event composed of the remaining fastest vehicles.

**elliptic:** applied to certain leaf springs because of their shape or a segment of an ellipse. Buggy spring.

**elongate:** to stretch out or to lengthen as of a part. Extrude.

**embankment:** a raised structure of soil or rock used to carry a roadway.

**emblem:** a device, symbol or figure adopted and used as an identifying mark. The marque of a brand of automobile sometimes as a medallion on the front, rear, or sides and sometimes as a radiator cap ornament. Usually replicated on horn buttons, control knobs, and hubcaps.

**embrittle:** to make or become brittle. Surface embrittlement of a metal can occur when exposed to other material (usually gaseous) and heat.

**emery:** a hard abrasive powder consisting essentially of corundum used for grinding and polishing. Used as a powder, a slurry, a paste or bonded to paper or cloth or cast into stonelike wheels and blocks.

**E.M.F.:** a car built by Everitt-Metzger-Flanders, Detroit, MI, (1908-1912) and marketed by Studebaker whose marque disappeared when Studebaker began to manufacture in addition to being just a selling organization.

**emissions:** combustion products (usually environmentally harmful) discharged into the air by vehicle engines.

**emissions controls:** vehicular on-board equipment designed to reduce combustion emissions and to neutralize harmful substances.

**emissions tampering:** altering, deactivating, or removing emissions controls legally required on a vehicle. May result in varying penalties.

**emulsion:** a system consisting of a liquid dispersed with or without an emulsifier in an immiscible liquid, usually in droplets larger than colloidal size. Oil and water mixed by violent agitation or with a surface-active agent or soap.

**encapsulate:** to coat or completely wrap as with plastic often heat-shrunk to totally seal and isolate from the surroundings.

**enchain:** to bind or hold cargo to a vehicle using chain fastenings usually with a tightening device as a chain jack.

**encumber:** to burden with a legal claim (mortgage) the title to a vehicle sold on credit or repairs done on credit to insure the debt until legally discharged.

**end float:** the amount of end-to-end movement occurring in a system usually limited to a small displacement increment. End clearance, end play.

**endless:** as a belt or chain joined at the ends making a continuous loop.

**enduro:** a long race for automobiles or motorcycles stressing endurance and durability rather than speed.

**engage:** to cause mechanical parts to mesh as with transmission gears. a starter pinion gear with a flywheel ring gear, a clutch pressure plate with a disk and flywheel surface, or brake pads and shoes with discs and drums.

**engine:** a machine for converting any of various forms of energy into mechanical force and motion.

**engine dynamometer:** a test instrument for measuring the horsepower of various engines in an environment outside the vehicle and for adjusting engine performance, fuel consumption, and exhaust emissions in isolation from vehicle involvement. See chassis dynamometer.

**engine stand:** a support frame for holding an engine in convenient positions and heights during assembly, storage, and disassembly.

**engine turning:** a technique for metal surface finishing using a circular stone or pad with appropriate abrasives spinning in contact with the metal to impart concentric circular patterns that can be overlapped to create an endless number of designs. Spot polishing.

**enrich:** to increase the amount of fuel in relation to the amount of combustion air being supplied to a vehicle engine. A rich mixture sometimes called "fat" has an excess of fuel contrasted to a lean mixture which has an excess of air when compared to the chemically perfect (stoichiometric) fuel/air or air/fuel ratio for combustion.

**enshroud:** as to enclose or surround an engine, manifold, radiator, or fan to direct air for cooling/heating.

**entrain:** to draw in and transport as solid particulates or a gas by the flow of a fluid.

**epicyclic:** a train as of gears to have one or more gears travel around the circumference of another fixed or revolving part. A planetary gear system

**epoxy resin:** a flexible usually thermosetting resin made by polymerization of an epoxide and used chiefly in coatings and adhesives.

**equipoise:** a counterbalance to attain a state of dynamic or static equilibrium (balance).

**equivalence ratio:** a numerical value to represent the fuel/air or air/fuel ratio with the stoichiometric (chemically perfect) ratio for vehicle fuel combustion comparisons.

**ergonomics:** human engineering. The design of a vehicle to fit the people who will use it and to make the controls friendly to man.

**ersatz:** being usually an artificial and inferior substitute for what is best or most desirable. An apt description of most so-called "alternative" vehicle fuels.

**ess:** resembling the letter "S" in shape as a S-shaped curve in a road. The deliberate esses in a sports car race track.

**estate car:** the British counterpart of the American station wagon. A sporting version for the gentleman hunter was called a "shooting brake".

**estimate:** a statement of the cost of work to be done. A legal requirement in many states is that a written estimate of cost be given to a vehicle owner prior to a garage/shop beginning repair work.

**ethanol:** ethyl alcohol usually made from fermenting sugar-containing agricultural crops, then distilling the resultant beer into 200-proof (100%) alcohol. With about two-thirds the energy content of gasoline, ethanol is widely used straight or as an additive to gasoline as a vehicle fuel. Very high in octane rating but notoriously hard-starting with cold ambient temperatures.

**ether:** a light volatile flammable liquid ($C_4H_{10}O$) used chiefly as a solvent and anesthetic. Used as a starter fluid spray to assist in starting balky vehicle engines during very cold weather. Various ether derivatives and ethanol are added to vehicle gasoline to reduce exhaust pollution.

**Ethyl:** trademarked additive tetraethyl lead, $P_b(C_2H_5)_4$, used as an antiknock agent added to vehicle gasoline to increase its octane number (rating). Being discontinued because of airborne lead contaminants in vehicle exhausts.

**ethylene glycol:** a thick syrupy liquid alcohol $C_2H_6O_2$ widely used as a vehicle cooling system antifreeze and in making polyester fibers.

**exact science:** a science (as physics, chemistry, or astronomy) whose laws are capable of accurate quantitative expression and exact repeatability.

**exhaust:** the escape of combustion gas or vapor from a vehicle engine. The gas or vapor thus escaping. The pipe and muffler system through which the gases escape. The fourth stroke of the four cycle internal combustion engine.

**expanded metal:** sheet metal with ribbon cuts expanded into a lattice and used for protective enclosures or wrapped around heated components as heat dissipating surface or for safety.

**explosive rivet:** a rivet with an explosive charge that expands the end used in "blind" areas inaccessible to backing or "bucking" tools.

**explosive squib:** an explosive actuator or trigger that initiates a much larger action. Like the percussion cap in a rifle or gun shell. The air bag operation is initiated by a shock (impact) detector sending a electrical signal that ignites the squib whose explosion fires the gas-former that fills the larger air-bag.

**export:** a vehicle manufactured in one country or jurisdiction and sold in another.

**expressway:** a high-speed, multilane, divided highway for through traffic with access fully or partially controlled and with grade separations at intersections.

**extension cord:** an electric cord fitted with a plug at one end and a receptacle at the other end to connect tools or lights to a power source at a distance from the work site.

**external combustion engine:** a heat engine that derives its heat from fuel consumed outside the engine cylinder as a steam engine or Stirling-cycle engine.

**extractor:** a tool to remove broken, damaged, or jammed parts from a machine such as an internal expanding device for removing broken studs or bolts. Easy-out. Stud remover.

**extrusion:** a form or shape created by forcing raw material through a die. The forming of wire and many structural members represent the process.


### LAGNIAPPE

**ECM:** the electronic control module, providing ignition optimization.

**econobox:** slang term for the small boxy economy vehicle. Econocar.

**EFI:** electronic fuel injection, either throttle-body or port.

**EGR:** exhaust gas recirculation, the system and the valve.

**EMF:** electromotive force. Voltage, analogous to the pressure in the commonly used electricity/water analogy.

**endothermic:** a chemical reaction that requires the input of heat to insure the combination or separation of the chemicals involved in the reaction. Exothermic.

**EPA:** Environmental Protection Agency the U.S. agency charged with setting and monitoring vehicle emissions limits and providing verification of Corporate Average Fuel Efficiency (CAFE) in addition to regulating toxic wastes.

**ET:** the elapsed time from start through finish of a vehicle race.

**exhaust headers:** usually smooth steel tubing sized to take advantage of the inertia of exiting exhaust pulses to enhance scavenging gases.

**exothermic:** a chemical reaction that gives off heat. Endothermic.

**eyeball:** to estimate dimension/distance visually without measuring.

**eyes:** photoelectric cells that sense data (as movement or light).

## EVER WONDER WHERE YOUR VEHICLE FUEL GOES?
### (What it _really_ does in your car?)

For the first three-quarters of this century automobiles kept secret what they did with the white gas, Ethyl, premium, regular, or unleaded that we poured down their filler-pipes. Now we know. But too few care.

Came the CAFE Law and the window sticker mileage ratings revelation. To obtain the Corporate Average Fuel Economy for the manufacturers' aggregate and for the individual make-and-model mpg figures, the EPA initiated the most sophisticated, scientific, state-of-the-art, and computerized testing programs to provide accurate results to the thousandth of a mile-per-gallon. All designed to encourage and let the American public select and buy the most economical and efficient vehicle.

But then the EPA blew it by the cockamamie classifications of car sizes in which the "SUBCOMPACTS" Aston Martin (8 mpg), Jaguar (10 mpg), and Rolls-Royce (10 mpg) cast a bigger shadow, cost more, and were tons heavier that the "LARGE CARS" Oldsmobile Delta 88 (21 mpg) and Chevrolet Malibu Station Wagon (22 mpg). While wasting mega-tax-dollars exhorting the public to "buy smaller cars"!

The EPA Test Cycle Data (next page) are invaluable if either the government or the public would consider them. Instead our Department of Energy gave 55,000 tax dollars to Nutronics Corporation of Longmont, CO, to promote the sale of the "Alter Break", claimed by them and Colorado U.S. Senator Bill Armstrong to "improve fuel mileage 32%, reduce pollution 64%, and save 14½ Billion Dollars in each month of OPEC oil imports. All because the "Alter Break" deactivated the alternator/generator from charging during vehicle acceleration. Inarguably outright lies because the extensive tests by the EPA show that the alternator, running full-time, only uses 0.5% of the vehicle fuel.

A Federal Court, acting upon the author's complaint charging fraud, accepted a _nolo_ _contendere_ plea from Nutronics and a "Consent Agreement" to cease and desist the fraudulent claims, but required no restitution of our tax dollars.

There are hundreds of similar scams being sold to technically illiterate vehicle owners every day when reference to the EPA Data would belie the outrageous claims by the charlatans. Refer to them!

Possibly the most egregious example has been the regular appearance of Claude Wild III, the Federal Trade Commission District Director for the Rocky Mountain Region on Denver radio station KOA's "Consumer Protection" talk show that was sponsored by CLM, an oil additive that claimed as much as "94% improvement in fuel mileage" by reducing engine friction. WHOOPEE! When the EPA Data show total engine friction losses to be only 7½%. The author's many complaints against the fraudulent claims and the government fox mandated to watch our henhouse were ignored! Not even answered!

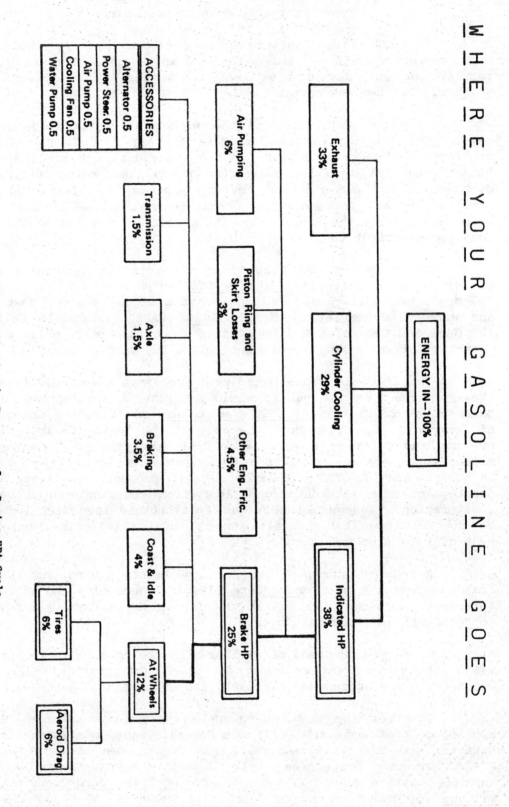

Energy Distribution in Passenger Car During EPA Cycle

**F-Cars:** although 200-strong, F-marqued cars have spawned not a single "Duesy", but every Ford fan can genuflect to Henry Ford with confidence and reverence as the true Icon of the Twentieth Century for his "Tin Lizzy", "999", Greenfield Village, and the two-passenger Thunderbird. Beginning with his first car in 1896, Henry literally "put the world on wheels" and started Space Ship Earth rolling into "The Era of the Automobile". No historian will question Henry's dominance for the First Century of Automobiles and every economist "odds-maker" will tout "Ford Futures" for the next century, confidently predicting their rolling along in the ruts already imprinted by the Taurus and the Contour models. A close second finisher in the formula-race to lead the F-clan would have to go to the Double-FF conglomerate team of Fiat- Ferrari. They are likely to be strong contenders for the checkered flag on the last lap of the Second Century of Automobile competition. With an F-marqued "Formula T"?

**fabricate:** typically descriptive of the assembly/construction of an automobile implying the completion of the roll-out model by assembly-line bolt-on or minor welding of many diverse but standardized components to form the finished automobile.

**fabulous:** the most overworked word in the vocabulary of automobile advertising copywriters.

**faceplate:** a disc fixed with its face surface at right angles to the spindle of a lathe for the attachment of the workpiece to be machined. The friction face of a vehicle clutch.

**factory:** a building or collection of buildings equipped for manufacturing as of vehicles.

**fade:** the fading or reduction of braking from overheating of friction surfaces or from other transient effects of vehicle wear and tear in normal use.

**F-head engine:** a vehicle with the intake valve in the cylinder head (overhead) and the exhaust valve in the engine block (side).

**fairing:** a vehicle outer body panel member or structure so designed as to produce a smooth outer contour to reduce air drag by streamling air flow over and around the moving vehicle.

**false positive:** as with human ailments, the erroneous diagnosis of a vehicle's mechanical defect/malfunction because of imperfect test procedures/diagnostic equipment or incompetent/ unqualified diagnostic technicians. Either leads to unnecessary expense/surgery.

**false start:** a premature start (race horse, from a standstill) or an out-of-position location (flying start) of one or more contestants in an automobile race.

**fan:** one of various devices for moving air in vehicles for engine/radiator cooling, defrosting, heating, and ventilating the passenger interior using multi-blade (propeller) cylindrical/tangential, or centrifugal/radial technology.

**fan belt:** an endless belt of flat, multi-V, or V cross-section that transmits power from the engine to the cooling fan.

**fan clutch:** a viscous or electromechanical clutch that transmits power to the engine/radiator fan only when needed thus saving the unnecessary parasitic loss of energy and improving vehicle fuel consumption.

**fascia:** the panel or molding just below a vehicle windshield where the accessories, air vents, instruments, and control switches are located. Dash. Instrument panel.

**fastback:** automobile with a downward sloping rear-roof section, back window, and trunk to improve vehicle aerodynamics.

**fast idle:** the deliberately high idle speed programmed into a cold engine's control system to prevent stoppage until properly warmed up.

**fast lane:** the leftmost lane of a multi-lane roadway where passing and higher vehicle speeds are allowable and attainable.

**fast track:** a sanctioned vehicle race track designed with turn radii and banked surfaces permitting higher than normal vehicle speeds.

**fat-man wheel:** a vehicle steering wheel that tilts or is hinged upward to allow easier access/egress to and from the driver's seat.

**Federal bumper:** a vehicle bumper that meets U.S. Federal Safety Regulations currently requiring the absorption of the energy of a 5 mile-per-hour impact without damage to the vehicle.

**Federal emissions:** the body of laws/regulations specifying the allowable limits of harmful emissions from a vehicle and allowing more stringent standards if individual states wish to impose such within their jurisdictions.

**feedback:** the return to the input of a part of the output of a machine system or process (as for producing change in an electronic circuit that improves performance or in an automatic control device that provides self-corrective action). The oxygen sensor in a vehicle tail-pipe that feeds back exhaust gas information to the engine control computer is a classical example.

**feed pump:**  a fuel pump that supplies usually low-pressure fuel to an engine's high-pressure injector pump.

**feeler guage:**  a selection of accurately-ground metal strips of various thickness that are inserted into the space between two adjacent surfaces to determine the dimensional distance between them as in valve clearance or spark plug gap.

**fender:**  a fixed panel or formed sheet metal shape that covers or partially shrouds a vehicle road wheel.

**fender bender:**  mechanic slang for a minor automobile accident.

**fender cover:**  a padded nonslip protective sheet placed over a fender to protect nearby painted surfaces while a mechanic does maintenance, repair, or service work near the fender.

**fender flare:**  a graceful outward winglike curve to a vehicle fender surface.

**fender mount:**  a bracket or lug for attaching a vehicle fender to the chassis or frame.

**fender skirt:**  a usually flat removable panel that covers all or part of the fender cut-out thus covering more of the normally-exposed wheel side for better streamlining.

**fender well:**  a semi-circular depression in a portion of a fender top for carrying a side-mounted spare tire/wheel.

**fender welt:**  a folded fabric strip with a raised rib-edge sandwiched between the fender-to-body joining surfaces to hide alignment imperfections, to quiet, and to seal the joint.

**fiber glass:**  glass in fibrous (strand) form that can be used as a filter or insulating medium or woven into glass cloth that can be formed into structural shapes and hardened by coating with an epoxy-like material.

**fiber optics:**  thin transparent fibers of glass that when enclosed in a material of lower index of refraction transmit light throughout their length by undistorted internal reflections.  When bundled such fibers can transmit visual images of instruments or warning lights over long distances from remote locations or allow a vehicle mechanic to visually inspect the entire inside of a tank or engine cylinder through small openings.

**field magnet:**  a magnet that produces and maintains a magnetic field in an electric alternator, generator, or motor.

**field of visibility:** the arc around a driver describing the area that he can see effectively. The angle through which a vehicle signal or warning light is visible to an observer.

**field winding:** the conductive wire winding that surrounds a field magnet in an electric alternator, generator, or motor. Field coil.

**fifth wheel:** the weight-supporting circular plate mounted near the rear of a tractor that supports and secures the tongue-weight of a towed semitrailer. An accurately calibrated distance/speed measuring wheel that may be clamped to a test vehicle to verify the accuracy of its speedometer.

**filler cap:** a manually installed/removed sealing cover to the filler pipe (tank opening) of a fuel tank, radiator, or other fluid reservoir.

**filler pipe:** a vehicle fuel tank servicing opening usually accessible to a supply hose at a convenient location on the outside of the vehicle or beneath a protective hinged cover similarly located.

**film strength:** a measure of the ability of a lubricant (oil) to cling to a friction surface between periods of operation and to resist being squeezed out of the lubricated area.

**filter:** a canister containing a porous sheet or mass through which a fluid (such as air, gasoline, oil, or water) is passed to remove suspended particulates. An electrical/electronic circuit that cancels or minimizes unwanted frequencies (noise) in/to an operating device. A transparent material (as colored optical glass) that absorbs (blocks) light of certain frequencies.

**filter element:** a replaceable component of appropriate filter media (ceramic, fine wire mesh, metallic granules, or porous pleated paper, et al.) shaped to fit a permanent filter canister, allowing the disposal of a lower-priced item in lieu of discarding the entire filter canister.

**fin:** a thin metal plate attached to or an integral part of hot devices to cool the device by increasing the square area of hot surface exposed to cooling air (as an air-cooled engine cylinder/head or a cooling radiator). The vertical airfoil appurtenance to the rear fenders or trunk top of an automobile that ostensibly improves directional stability.

**final drive:** the final geared assembly in a vehicle's transmission system (drive line), usually the differential.

**final drive ratio:** the ratio between the rotational speeds of the propeller shaft (drive shaft) and the driven wheel axle shaft (rear axle).

**fine tune:** to adjust an engine's controllable variables especially ignition energy strength and timing and fuel/air mixture to insure absolute peak performance. Race tune.

**finning:** the arrangement of cooling fins on the hot surface of an engine or radiator.

**finish line:** a line marking the completion of an automobile race (also usually the starting line).

**fire engine:** a vehicle specially designed and equipped for fighting fires. Fire truck.

**"Fire Ring":** trade name of a spark plug that fraudulently claims to dramatically increase power, speed, and fuel economy for vehicle engines. But does not!

**fire wall:** the panel separating a vehicle engine from the passenger compartment that is designed to protect occupants from engine fires.

**firing order:** the numbered sequence in which the cylinders of a multi-cylinder engine fire. Spark timing.

**firing stroke:** the working (down) stroke of an internal combustion engine during which the ignited fuel burns, expanding the gases that transfer energy into pushing the piston.

**fish-eye:** bubbles in a newly-painted exterior surface of a vehicle usually attributable to contaminants in the paint, in the high-pressure air, or on the vehicle surface and that are usually preventable by careful preparation/application and the proper additive to the paint.

**fitted luggage:** travel cases (luggage) sized and shaped to fit into a vehicle trunk and to minimize shifting or sliding of the individual pieces.

**five mile-an-hour bumper:** see Federal bumper.

**fixed-cam brake:** a drum brake with the shoe-expander cam fixed to the backing plate insuring equal movement (but not equal pressure) of the primary and secondary shoes.

**fixed head engine:** a vehicle engine with an integral cylinder block and cylinder head thus reducing cylinder head leakage but complicating maintenance and repair operations. The Crosley and Meyer-Drake (Offenhauser) engines are notable examples.

**flame arrestor:** a barrier to burning gases usually consisting of metallic screen or a labyrinth of metal shavings as at the breather opening to a crankcase or valve cover. Flame trap.

**flame front:**  the leading edge of a propagating (expanding) area of combustion as the mixture of fuel and air burns in a vehicle cylinder.

**Flame Spray:**  a trademarked process used to spray molten metal (as paint) to apply a protective coating to metal surfaces or to build up worn surfaces to a larger dimension.  Powder coat.

**flare nut:**  a fastening nut shaped to compress and seal a flared tube-end over an appropriate cone-shaped fitting.

**flare-nut wrench:**  a box-end wrench with a segment cut out to allow slipping it around a tube to access a flare nut for assembly or removal.

**flasher switch:**  an electromechanical or electronic switch that causes turn signals or emergency lights to flash at regular intervals as a warning to other vehicles.

**flat battery:**  a fully or partially discharged storage battery that lacks the power to start a vehicle's engine or provide lighting energy.  Dead battery.

**flatbed:**  a truck or trailer with a flat cargo floor without side panels.

**flat engine:**  a vehicle engine with two banks of horizontally-opposed cylinders as in a flat-twin, flat-four, flat-six, flat-eight, or flat-twelve number of cylinders.

**flat head:**  an engine cylinder head without a profiled depression above the cylinder bore (contour, hemisphere, or wedge) with the combustion area volume determined solely by the height to which the piston rises in the cylinder.

**flat rate:**  the standardized time in hours/minutes required for an average vehicle mechanic to accomplish a definable maintenance or repair operation.  The basis for estimating the cost and the amount charged to the vehicle owner (as multiplied by the established/published hourly rate for a particular vehicle repair facility).

**flat spot:**  a momentary reduction in engine power especially during acceleration manifested by a noticeable hesitation in engine speed.  Most often caused by reduced spark or fuel mixture to the engine.

**flat torquerer:**  an engine that produces good torque values throughout its speed range and particularly at slower engine speed.  A good lugger, the opposite of peaky (power).

**flawless:**  a part or component that has been measured and tested within state-of-the-art parameters and found to be free from any detectable defect.

**flea market:** a commercial sale usually involving a wide selection of products offered to the general public for sale or barter in a relatively unstructured (informal) sales environment.

**flexible hose:** a fluid-handling conduit that will move in unrestricted directions without leaking its contents when connecting fluid fittings on rigid devices which move in relation to each other. Some examples: brake line from wheel to chassis, fuel line from vehicle frame to engine, radiator hose from engine to radiator, et al.

**flexible joint:** a disc or hose made of tough flexible material fastened between two flanges/spiders or clamped to two butting shafts and capable of transmitting torque between two rotating shafts through a limited angular misalignment of the shafts.

**flivver:** a small, cheap, and usually nondescript automobile.

**float:** a buoyant or evacuated sealed canister that will remain on a liquid surface and through a hinged lever operate a valve to maintain the liquid level or transmit a signal from within a tank to a remote instrument to indicate the liquid level.

**float bowl:** a fuel reservoir as an integral part of a vehicle carburetor casting whose fuel level is maintained at an exact height by a float-operated valve that replenishes the fuel as it is metered into the engine intake system.

**float level:** the level of fuel in a carburetor maintained just below the exit opening of the carburetor jet to prevent siphoning but near enough to allow the venturi air pressure depression during intake strokes to discharge a metered quantity of fuel into the venturi for vaporization.

**floating caliper:** a disc brake caliper so-mounted that it can move to equalize and center the opposing pads against the brake disc when brake pressure is applied.

**floating cam brake:** a drum brake in which the expander cam mechanism is not fixed to the backing plate allowing both shoes to shift enough to apply even braking pressure.

**floating power:** in the 1930s many automobiles, for the first time, shock-mounted engines from the chassis to reduce the excessive vibration from hard-mounted engines in previous years. Some companies advertised their cars as having floating power smoothness.

**flood car:** a used car that has been underwater then recovered and the marks from the flood repaired or camouflaged. Such history must be revealed at dealer wholesale auctions but is sometimes concealed from unsuspecting retail purchasers.

141

**flooding:**  too much fuel supplied to an engine causing a fuel/ air ratio too rich to be ignited by the spark energy at the spark plugs.

**floor mat:**  the factory original covering (rug) for a vehicle floor or a wide assortment of aftermarket coverings used to replace or to supplement the original.

**floor shift:**  a transmission (gear) shift selector lever that is mounted on the vehicle floor or transmission tunnel (hump).

**flow bench:**  a system of jigs, ducts, sensors, and indicator (meter) recorders that measure the breathing (flow) efficiency of vehicle induction system, including the air inlet (scoop), filter, carburetor, intake (induction) manifold, cylinder head and valves, valve porting, exhaust manifold (pipes), exhaust tubing, and mufflers all the way to the tail-pipe exit.

**flower car:**  a funeral service vehicle configured to transport cut flowers and wreaths to/from mortuary, church, cemetery, et al.

**flow meter:**  a measuring device for sensing, displaying, and recording fluid flow velocity (speed), volume, and mass (weight).

**flower vase:**  the holder, usually cut glass, that once adorned the doorposts of limousines of the elite, ostentatiously flaunting the self-image and wealth of the vehicle owner.

**fluid clutch:**  the use of hydrodynamics principles to transmit power from a driver to a driven unit without a positive mechanical lock-up thus always at the expense of some efficiency loss due to heat (energy) loss and slippage.  Fluid coupling.  Fluid flywheel.

**fly-cut piston:**  a piston that has machined relief areas in the piston head to prevent contact with overhead valve heads particularly at high rpm when there is a significant valve overlap.

**flying mile:**  official designation of the world record distance with calibrated approved timing devices through which aspirants must establish a two-way averaged speed under controlled conditions (level starting [acceleration] distance, level timed-mile), and regulation specified wind velocities and starting procedures for each vehicle classification.  American mile.  Metric "mile" (kilometer).

**flying start:**  the start of a vehicle race characterized by all competitors crossing the starting line at high speed (initiating the timing system at the instant that the leading element of the vehicle crosses the line).  In a multi-vehicle race each is assigned a starting position in the field of qualifiers and must be in that location when the pack crosses the starting line, usually led by a "pace car" to stabilize positions/speed to prevent "racing" before the official start. Race horse start. Standing start.

**flywheel:** a heavyweight wheel or disc usually bolted to an engine crankshaft that stores inertial energy from the combustion (power stroke) of the engine to continue the rotation through the exhaust, intake, and compression strokes until the next power stroke thus smoothing the intermittent power pulses from the engine to its working load. The flywheel ring-gear is the input power connection from the starter and smooths its pulsed load with the flywheel serving as the friction member that transfers power through a mechanically-clutched transmission. The inherent power-pulse dilemma is most pronounced with a single-cylinder engine, reducing in impact as numbers of cylinders increase.

**flywheel magneto:** common to small two-stroke engines with the rotating spark-generating and timing components located within the flywheel structure.

**fog light:** a supplementary vehicle light using a color frequency (in the yellow portion of the visible light spectrum) that maximizes the penetration and minimizes the reflectivity of fog or mist.

**follower:** that part of a mechanism that is directly driven by rubbing contact with a cam lobe and imparts motion to other parts of the mechanism. Tappet. Cam follower.

**foot brake:** a vehicle brake operated by foot-power applied through a pedal.

**foot-pound:** a unit of work equal to the work done by a force of one pound acting through a distance of one foot in the direction of the force.

**foot-pound-second:** the system of units based upon the foot as length, the pound as the unit of mass (weight), and the second as the unit of time. Defining horsepower as 1 horsepower equals 33,000 foot-pounds-per-minute or 550 foot-pounds-per-second.

**footprint:** the shape and area of the contact between a vehicle tire and the roadway surface.

**forced lubrication:** lubricant delivery to friction points using pressure from gravity, a spring, piston, or a pump.

**Ford:** the Icon of automobiliana, both the car and the man behind it.

**Fordson:** one of our earliest American farm tractors.

**forged:** metal that has been shaped and hardened by heating and hammering either by hand or by mechanical or hydraulic presses and drop hammers.

**forged crankshaft:** an engine crankshaft that has been hammered or pressed into shape and then machined to exact dimensional tolerances.

**forged piston:** an engine piston that has been hammered or pressed into shape and machined to exact dimensional tolerances.

**forklift:** a cargo/equipment warehouse transporter with two parallel flat lifting arms at the front that can be hydraulic lifted and tilted for moving and stacking heavy items with ease and accuracy because of its rear steering.

**formula car:** a race car classification conforming to pre-scribed specifications as to the size, weight, and engine-size (displacement) and usually having a long streamlined body, open wheels, a single-seat open cockpit and with the engine in the rear.

**forward control:** a commercial vehicle (truck) with the cab and driver situated ahead of the engine and front axle to improve parking and maneuvering in congested warehouse areas. Cab-over-engine. COE.

**fossil fuel:** hydrocarbons as coal, peat, natural gas (meth-ane), petroleum (crude oil), and tar (heavy crude) recoverable from the earth and used au naturel (unrefined) or refined for specific uses from fossil feedstock formed many centuries ago by the natural heating and compressing of decaying animal and plant organic matter.

**fouled plug:** an engine spark plug that has become electrically "shorted" (unable to produce a spark) by conductive contamina-tion as moisture, carbon from combustion, or deposited (on the gap electrodes) fuel additives.

**four-banger:** a four-cylinder engine designation, usually applied to a four-cylinder in-line cylinder arrangement.

**four bolt main:** an engine main bearing (crankshaft) having four retaining bolts rather than the usual two and providing a stiffer and stronger "lower end" for high-horsepower high-speed (racing) engines.

**four-on-the-floor:** a vehicle with four-speed transmission manual shift with a floormounted gear-shift lever.

**four-stroke cycle:** the thermodynamic cycle of an internal combustion piston engine composed of four 180° strokes of the piston: intake (induction), compression, power (combustion), and exhaust requiring two complete revolutions (720°) of the crankshaft.

**four-wheel-drive:** a vehicle power-transmission arrangement that delivers engine power to all four wheels.

**frameless construction:** a vehicle with an integral body, chassis, and frame without the conventional heavy beam structural supporting members. Unibody. Unitary construction, Monocoque. Birdcage. Space frame. Tube-and-skin.

**frame-off:** descriptive phrase for a vehicle restoration involving taking the body off the frame, total disassembly, then followed by refurbishing (to new condition), replacing of all defective parts with new and refinishing to the original factory tolerances and appearance. A complete or total restoration.

**front-line car:** auto dealer slang for a used car (purchased or trade-in) that looks sharp enough to be displayed in the front row of the stock of used cars to attract the attention of passers-by as an enticement to stop, look, and hopefully buy.

**Franklin:** American built (1901-1934) as the world's most sucessful air-cooled engined automobile/truck (subsequently challenged by the Volkswagen) with many notable firsts and innovations. Its great engine has continued to be manufactured for airplanes and helicopters with a helicopter engine used in the Tucker automobile (1946-48).

**free-floating bushing:** an intermediate plain sleeve bearing that rotates freely outside (around) a shaft and inside a another sleeve bearing thus allowing higher rpm than is possible with a shaft journal rotating directly within one sleeve bearing. Commonly used on turbochargers.

**free-inertia:** the primary cause of unbalance in an engine containing reciprocating and rotating masses.

**free-power turbine:** a gas turbine engine whose turbine that provides output shaft power is not mechanically connected to the primary compressor turbine or its shaft.

**free travel:** in a brake or clutch mechanism, the amount (distance) of lever or pedal movement before the working mechanism is activated. Free play. Slack.

**freeway:** an expressway for vehicles, usually a multi-laned divided high-speed roadway with fully-controlled access but without any crossing traffic or mainstream stop signals or signs.

**free-wheel:** the overrunning clutch (or other disconnect) that disengages the vehicle engine from the drive-train to the wheels whenever the drive force is reversed as going downhill or deceleration coasting. Dog clutch. One-way clutch.

**free-wheeling fan:** a vehicle radiator cooling fan that is disconnected from its drive when not needed to enhance cooling of the engine. The use of a temperature-sensed electro-friction or viscosity clutch are most common. A continually driven fan is often a parasitic power user that reduces a vehicle's road-fuel-mileage.

**freeze-plug:** a safety seal in an engine block or cylinder head coolant casting outer wall that retains liquid coolant but pops out to relieve the tremendous expansion force developed from low-temperature solidification (freezing), thus preventing catastrophic cracking damage to expensive engine components.

**Freon:** trademarked flourohydrocarbon (gas or liquid) propellant/refrigerant widely used since World War II but now in disfavor because of its extensive proven damage to our protective upper atmospheric ozone barrier against adverse solar radiation.

**Fresnel lens:** an optical lens, named for its inventor/originator Augustin J. Fresnel (1848), that has a surface consisting of a series of concentric lens sections allowing a dimensionally thin lens with a very short focal length ratio to lens diameter making it ideally suited for light enhancement and beam focusing as for headlights and/or spotlights.

**friable:** material prone to crumbling, making it easy to shatter and pulverize.

**friction:** the rubbing of one material against another dissimilar or similar substance that causes resistance to relative motion between the two bodies when in physical contact, creating heat and therefore wasting system energy unnecessarily. Ameliorated by proper lubricants.

**friction clutch:** a vehicle clutch in which the energy-transmission-connection is effected through sliding friction between two pressure plates against a friction-material-coated disc with the ultimate goal of a solid "lock-up" of the moving parts to  each other.

**friction drag:** the primary expenditure by a vehicle of available fuel energy that is nonrecoverable goes to overcoming friction drag with the largest bite taken by air drag caused by air being displaced and rubbed by the moving vehicle. Some other identifiable drag losses are to rolling/scraping/sliding bearing contact, scraping/sliding piston-ring/cylinder-wall contact, valve hammering/sliding contact with valve seats/ guides, chain/gear tooth pressure/sliding contact, flexible belt hysteresis/friction with pulley contact, and tire hysteresis or friction contact with the road surface. All of these energy losses return to nature's entropic ash heap as heated surrounding air and roadway surface. Totally and irrevocably wasted.

**friction horsepower:** that part of a vehicle's horsepower that goes to overcoming the aggregate, but partially reducible, friction encountered when in operation.

**friction lining:** the usually molded or woven material with high coefficients of friction and resistance to friction wear and that is used as the contact surface of clutches and brakes.

**friction plate:** the brake pad or shoe or the clutch member/disc to which the friction material is bonded or riveted utilizing the structural rigidity/strength of the plate to extend useful life of the assembly.

**frontage road:** a local street usually parallel to and often the predecessor of a current freeway that accommodates slow-moving local vehicular traffic and provides access to businesses/local property near the expressway. Service road. Alternate city route.

**frontal area:** the effective flat-plate area (in square feet, the size of the hole that a moving vehicle punches through the air) that is the dominant cause of aerodynamic drag that is only slightly reduced percentagewise by aerodynamic shaping.

**front-end loader:** a dirt excavator/loader bucket/scoop attached to the front of a tractor-type industrial vehicle designed for excavating and loading bulk material onto disposal/removal trucks.

**front marker lights:** warning lights marking the corner widths and roof heights of vehicles (automobiles, trailers, and trucks) as specified by applicable laws usually white or amber in color and visible from straight-ahead to 90° outboard (left and right).

**front-runner:** a race car that is currently leading the pack of contestants in an on-going race or a race car that is known for its past record as a winner and is therefore predicted to be the front-runner in a future race with known competitors.

**front-wheel-drive:** a vehicle power transmission system that delivers engine output only to the front wheels.

**fuel:** combustible (burnable) material usually in a liquid or gaseous state that can be converted into heat (energy) by burning within an internal combustion engine, allowing the expansion energy from the heat to propel the vehicle.

**fuel cell:** a cell that continuously changes the chemical energy of a fuel (usually the hydrogen of the fuel) and an oxidant (air or oxygen) into electrical energy. Fuel cells are unquestionably destined to replace batteries in electric cars as their technology and efficiency improve because of their much lighter weight.

**fuel consumption:** the rate of usage of fuel by a vehicle, usually expressed in units as miles-per-gallon, kilometers-per-liter or pounds-per-brake-horsepower-per-hour (most precise and meaningful from a pure engineering perspective).

**fuel gauge:** a quantity-indicating instrument that shows the amount of fuel in a vehicle tank.

**fuel injection:** injection of fuel under pressure into the in-take manifold, directly into the engine's combustion chamber, or indirectly into each intake valve port.

**fuel injector:** a nozzle and valve assembly that injects fuel in metered quantities into the combustion air of an engine.

**fuel pressure regulator:** a pressure sensitive diaphragm valve that maintains a pre-set value above atmospheric pressure in a fuel supply system to an engine.

**fuel pump:** an electrical or mechanical diaphragm, piston, or rotary pump designed to move fuel from a vehicle supply tank to the engine's carburetor or fuel injection system.

**fuel starved:** the restriction or stoppage of an engine's fuel supply for whatever reason that its power output is reduced or stopped.

**fuel system:** the total components comprising the complete de-livery system for insuring an engine's satisfactory performance such as adequate fuel storage tank, all fuel and vapor return hoses, lines, and valves; pumps; pressure regulators; filters; carburetor or injector mechanisms; vents; and evaporative emissions controls and devices.

**fuel tank:** a fuel supply reservoir of adequate volume that is so mounted as to provide adequate protection from the rigors of vehicle operation and exposure.

**fuel throttled:** a fuel flow metering system to an engine that complements the air-flow metering control to maintain the optimum fuel/air equivalence ratio of 1.0.

**fulcrum:** a center, pivot, shaft, or support about which a lever turns and from which its torque amplification or mechanical advantage is calculated.

**fuller's earth:** an earthy substance that consists chiefly of clay mineral but lacks plasticity and that is used as an absorbent, a filter medium, and as a carrier for catalysts.

**full-floating axle:** a rear-drive vehicle whose drive-axles transmit torque but carry no weight or handling forces which are totally supported by the outer axle housing through bearings directly carrying the load/forces to each driven wheel.

**full-flow filter:** a filter through which the total volume of liquid flows, with a by-pass circuit that allows continued flow when the filter media becomes clogged or overloaded.

**full house:** mechanic's slang for any engine that has extensive hot rod modification to increase its power and performance, but lacks the internal machining and technical improvements such as flow-bench peaking. Not quite a race car--but a hot street rod.

**full-load enrichment valve:** a carburetor valve, usually at or near the bottom of the float bowl that supplies extra fuel through the carburetor barrel during full-throttle operation.

**full-time four-wheel-drive:** a four-wheel drive vehicle that has no provision in the drive system for disengaging any axle from driving. All four drive all the time.

**funeral car:** any vehicle designed or modified to support funeral activities/services as a flower car, hearse, or sedate limousine.

**fuse:** an electrical safety device (replaceable in whole or in part) consisting of or including a strip of wire or fusible metal whose resistance heating causes melting and breaks (interrupts) the circuit when its amperage rating is exceeded by the electrical current in the circuit.

**fuse box:** a collection of fuse holders/fuses in an easily-accessible location for ease in checking, replacing, and servicing.

**fuse rating:** the number of amperes and the time required before "blowing" (melting and interrupting the circuit) that a fuse can withstand and protect its electrical circuit, e.g., "25 Amps., instantaneous", or "25 Amps. slow-blow".

**fusible:** capable of being fused (reduced to a liquid) by heat.

**fuzz:** slang for "police officer".

**fuzz buster:** slang for a radar speed detector warning device to alert a vehicle driver that vehicle speeds are being monitored by police using radar in the vicinity.

**fuzzy dice:** usually oversized replica gambling dice that are often dangled from rear-view mirrors by teen-age mentality drivers, possibly as a show of rebellion against common sense --and some laws. Such driver distractions are illegal in some jurisdictions.

**F.:** Fahrenheit, the thermometric scale of the 180 degrees from the freezing point of water (as 32° F.) to the boiling point of water (as 212° F.). Centigrade. Gabriel D. Fahrenheit (1783).

**face angle:** the angle of the seating surface of a poppet valve head.

**factory team:** a racing team financed by and representing (advertising) a vehicle manufacturer.

**factory tool:** a tool configured and sized to facilitate one maintenance/repair operation on one specific model vehicle.

**fillet:** the radiused configuration of the Vee of a machined angle to relieve metal stresses common to such a juncture. Also the "filling" of such a joint with a welded bead.

**fire bottle:** mechanic jargon for any on-board or portable fire extinguisher.

**fishtail:** repetitive side-to-side weaving of an out-of-control vehicle.

**flared fender:** wing-like raised edges around a vehicle wheel-well.

**fliptop:** the 1957-59 Ford retractable hardtop that hinge-folded beneath the rear deck.

**formula libre:** a vehicle race allowing any kind of vehicle to participate. No restrictions as to body or engine configuration, size, style, or type.

**Funny Car:** a drag racing class of cars using a true dragster chassis underneath with a very light passenger car replica body on top that is usually hinged at the rear with the entire body opening at the front like a front-engine hood.

## FAST WOMEN--DISTAFF DRIVERS
### (Could I be Wrong?)

Alberta Elizabeth Jeffryes (Mrs. David R. Griffith), Trinidad Colorado, was the first woman to drive the World Landspeed Record course at Bonneville Salt Flats, UT, in September 1931. A licensed airplane pilot, Alberta bought an Amos Northrup-designed 1932 REO Royale coupe that Amos guaranteed to "do 120 mph". She did 116.493 mph at the "Flats" (recognizing that at the 4,250-foot elevation this probably equalled the Northrup promise), and later exceeded 120 mph on a newly-opened low-altitude section of the Pennsylvania Turnpike. Zack Brinkerhoff, Denver car collector, now has the fully-restored REO Royale which has won many "Best-of-Show" national honors with 100-point scores.

Marcia Holly (Don Vesco's wife) drove into the Bonneville 200 mph Club in 1978 (the first woman to go over 200 mph) with 229.36 mph that she later increased to 272.013 mph. Followers: Tanis Hammond 251.750 mph (1987); Juli Burkdoll 204.586 mph (1990); Sylvia Hathaway 202.301 mph (1987); and Pat Zimmerman 200.355 (1992).

Lee Breedlove was the first to "spool up" a jet (308.221 mph) in Craig's Spirit of America at Bonneville. Kitty O'Neal, who timed a rocket dragster at over 300 mph and a low 5's ET, may have gone 512 mph in the SMI Motivator at Alvord Dry Lake, OR (this jet car, with phony claims of "Mach I" as the Budweiser "Beer Can", has been accused of many spurious speed claims). Paula Murphy, who drove Tony Fox's Pollution Packer Rocket to about a 300 mph and 5½ sec ET quarter, also drove Walt Arfons' Avenger jet over 200 mph when Betty Skelton drove brother Art Arfons' Cyclops jet about 300 mph at Bonneville in 1962.

Shirley Muldowney leads the distaff dragster drivers Trophy Dash with three National Championships plus a passel of lowest ET's and fastest quarters. Shelley Anderson is the current "Drag Queen" with an ET of 4.718 seconds (the second quickest ever) at the NHRA 1994 Winston Finals at Pomona, CA complementing a 302.11 mph quarter.

Janet Guthrie drove into the "First at Indy 500" slot, (1977), qualifying at 188.4mph, dropping out in the twenty-seventh lap with a cracked valve seat. Returning in 1988, Janet finished in ninth place becoming the first woman to finish the entire race. The second woman, Lynn St. James, drove 176 laps in 1993 and finished in 1994 in a Lola with a top lap speed of 211 mph. Kudos, Ladies!

## WHEN YOUR CAR WON'T START

It's either 100° in the shade and your car's in the sun or it's 30° below and you're in a snowbank. Laws chiseled in stone.

First think good thoughts, be calm for at least 3 seconds, then blow your top. Call the worthless hunk of junk every vile and filthy name you know--at the top of your voice . It won't start the car but it may stave off a coronary. Guaranteed!

If the car's hot push it under the nearest shade tree, raise the hood and go fishing. Tomorrow, the shade tree'll start it first time. No further warranty--expressed or implied.

If it's cold sit on your hands. That way your fingers won't freeze to the keys and you can't beat your brains out. Get your bagpipe out of the trunk and play until the neighbors push-start you around the block. Warranteed!

The bottom line: always park under a shade tree with your hood up and keep your bagpipe inflated on your roof-rack. Better yet, get regular tune-ups and buy low Reed-Vapor-Pressure fuel in the summer and high R-V-P fuel in the winter. No guarantee!

**G-Cars:** gee-whiz, not a single great G-car among the 209 "G" marques. The Graham, because of the 1940 Hollywood model stamped from the Cord 810/812 body dies, can be found in a few specialty collector's portfolios. The Russian GAZ started in 1932 with considerable help from U.S. Ford engineers so the GAZ-A was a near-carbon copy of Henry's Model A. The GAZ Gorky Works were once the largest automobile plant in Europe.

**gadget:** a usually small mechanical or electronic device with a practical use but often thought of as an unneeded novelty. Often applied to the fraudulent gimmicks sold with claims of fuel savings, performance improvement, or pollution reduction that fail to meet their promises.

**gage:** a variation of gauge.

**gal:** a unit of acceleration equivalent to one centimeter per second per second--used especially for values of gravity. See G-force.

**gall:** to fret, scratch, or wear away by friction.

**gallery:** usually a gutter-like duct or conduit within an internal combustion engine crankcase to distribute lubricating oil to needed areas.

**gallium arsenide:** a synthetic compound of the metallic element gallium used especially as a semi-conducting material.

**gallon:** in liquid measure a unit of liquid capacity equal to 231 cubic inches or four quarts. The American measure of liquid vehicle fuels.

**gallop:** the fast natural 3-beat gait of the horse whose sound is that of an engine running unevenly, erratically, or misfiring.

**galvanic couple:** a pair of dissimilar substances (metals) capable of acting together as an electric source when brought in contact with an electrolyte.

**galvanize:** to coat iron or steel with zinc usually by immersion in molten zinc to achieve a protective layer to resist rusting (corrosion). A common treatment for vehicle sheetmetal panels prior to painting.

**galvanometer:** an instrument for detecting or measuring a small electric current by movements of a magnetic needle or of a coil in a magnetic field.

**gamma ray:** a photon or radiation quantum emitted spontaneously by a radioactive substance.

**"gang":**  to assemble or operate simultaneously as a group.  A gang of electrical switches connected by a bar to insure that they act as one.

**gap:**  the space between adjacent components.  Sometimes essential and to be maintained within close dimensional tolerances: spark plug electrode gap; ignition point gap.  Sometimes undesirable and to be avoided: a gap in a door or window closure; a gap between body sheet metal panels or fender to body or hood to body.

**gap gauge:**  a device for measuring the width of a gap opening.  Usually a tapered thickness flat plate to insert into the gap, a selection of flat plates of differing thickness, or a selection of round rods (wires) of differing diameters.

**garage:**  a protective shelter or repair shop for vehicles.

**garage man:**  one who works in a garage.

**garage sale:**  usually a sale of used household or personal articles held in or adjacent to the seller's garage.  Sometimes by an actual vehicle garage to reduce inventory.

**garnet paper:**  an abrasive paper using crushed garnet as the abrasive.

**gas:**  a fluid (as air) that has neither independent shape nor volume but tends to expand indefinitely.  A combustible gaseous mixture or single gas used as a vehicle fuel:  natural gas; methane; hydrogen.  Short for gasoline.  To fill the fuel tank of a vehicle often suffixed with "up" --as "gas up".

**gas charged:**  a component pressurized with gas (usually inert) to supplement and sometimes to protect or preserve other components: an air/oil or gas/oil shock absorber; a diaphram divided accumulator/tank that separates the gas charge from the working gas/fluid.

**gas chromatograph:**  an instrument used to separate a sample into components in chromatography.  For analyzing gases and identifying constitutents.

**gascolator:**  usually a glass cup/jar (sometimes inverted) in a fuel supply line that provides a visual inspection of fuel flow and fuel filter condition.  Common on older vehicles and airplanes.  Rare today.

**gaseous:**  having the form of or being a gas.  Remaining free from suspended liquid droplets.  A vapor not in contact with its own liquid.

**gas-guzzler:**  usually a large or a high-performance vehicle that gets relatively poor fuel mileage.

**gasify:** to convert into a gas from a liquid or from a solid.

**gaslight:** light made by burning a gas. Early vehicles used on-board generated acetylene gas before electric lights became available.

**gasphol:** a blend of gasoline and alcohol usually consisting of 90% gasoline and 10% ethanol (ethyl alcohol) used to reduce vehicle exhaust pollutants through more efficient fuel combustion.

**gas oil:** a hydrocarbon oil used as a fuel oil with a boiling range and viscosity between kerosene and lubricating oil.

**gasoline:** a volatile flammable liquid hydrocarbon distillate used as the most common fuel for vehicle engines and usually blended at the refinery from several products of natural gas and petroleum crude oil.

**gasoline alley:** often applied to the fuel servicing area of the pits at an automobile race track.

**gasometer:** a test laboratory apparatus for holding and measuring gases.

**gas operated:** usually a piston/cylinder arrangement using gas pressure to actuate or to damp a component movement such as a vehicle trunk lid or a door closer.

**gas turbine:** an internal-combustion engine in which the expanding gases from the combustion chamber drive the blades of a turbine. The turbo of a turbocharger.

**gas works:** a plant for manufacturing fuel gas from coal or industrial/municipal wastes/garbage.

**gate:** a door, valve, or other device for controlling the passage, especially of fluid. A signal that makes an electronic circuit operative for a short period. A controlled access or directive pathway for the movement of certain machine controls used as gates in early manual transmissions to insure clash-less meshing of the various gear ratios.

**gauge:** in vehicle parlance any of many dash-mounted instruments that sense, measure, and display various vehicle functions and conditions: oil pressure and temperature, fuel quantity, engine coolant temperatures, speed and distance, electical functioning and condition.

**gauntlet:** early-day driving gloves with large extended cuffs to protect the motorists sleeves from the vehicle grime.

**gauss:** the cgs unit of magnetic induction (magnetic field strength).

**gear:** a toothed wheel that when engaged (meshed) with another with matched teeth can transmit power/speed at prescribed ratios. One of two or more adjustments of a transmission that determine mechanical advantage, relative speed, and direction of travel.

**gear box:** transmission, gearing.

**gear ratio:** the numerical relationship of the numbers of teeth on each of two engaged (meshed, mating) gears. A gear with twice the number of teeth will turn at one-half the speed of the gear with one-half as many teeth. A ratio of 2-to-1 or 1-to-2 dictated by the direction of power flow.

**gear train:** gearing, a train of two or more gears in mesh with each other.

**gear shift:** a mechanism usually a lever by which the trans-mission gears in a power-transmission system are engaged and disengaged.

**gear wheel:** a toothed wheel that gears or meshes with another piece of a mechanism. Cogwheel.

**Geiger counter:** an instrument for detecting the presence and intensity of radiations as cosmic rays or particles from a radioactive substance by measuring the ionizing effect on an enclosed gas producing a pulse that is amplified and fed to a display device giving a visible or audible indication.

**gel:** a colloid in a more solid form than a sol. To change into or to take the form of a gel. Important in gasketing and sealing materials.

**gellant:** a substance used to produce gelling in a gel.

**gender:** everyone knows that an automobile is always a "she". No one ever called a car a "him". Who can explain the prolif-eration of the genus without procreation?

**generator:** a machine by which mechanical energy is changed into electrical energy. The direct current generator for vehi-cles has been replaced by the alternating current "alternator" in contemporary vehicles.

**genuflect:** the mark of courtesy and respect due your auto-mobile each day in recognition of its dominance of our very being.

**genuine:** overworked and trite meaning simply that a "genuine" article is actually produced by or proceeds from the alleged manufacturer. Genuine Ford parts.

**geometric progression:** a change in value or dimension that is predictable with mathematical certainty, usually exponentially.

**German silver:** a silver-white alloy of copper, zinc, and nickel. Nickel silver.

**gestalt:** the automobile represent the ultimate gestalt with properties not predictable by summation of its parts.

**get-a-bigger-hammer:** an expression of desperation by a mechanic used when all conventional procedures for repairing a vehicle defect have failed. Whap it!

**get-up-and-go:** used to describe the acceleration and top speed of a vehicle.

**geyser:** a descriptive term used in the days before the pressurized and sealed vehicle radiator systems to describe an overheating vehicle.

**G-force:** for purposes of standardization, the acceleration due to gravity adopted by international agreement is: g equals 980.665 centimeters per second per second.

**gimbal:** a device that permits a body to incline freely in any direction or suspends it so it remains level when its support is tipped. To provide with or to support on gimbals.

**gimcrack:** a glitzy object or device usually supported by false or misleading claims but having little or no value or being of no practical use. Typical: gas saving devices, pollution reducing devices. Gimmick is similar.

**gimlet:** a small tool with a screw-point, grooved shank, and cross handle for boring holes.

**give:** capacity or tendency to yield to force or strain, implying flexibility.

**give-off:** emit as an odor, smoke, or toxic fumes.

**glancing:** having a slanting direction as a vehicle collision other than head-on or from a distinct side direction.

**gland:** a device for preventing leakage of fluid past a joint in machinery. The movable part of a stuffing box by which the packing is compressed against the joint.

**glassine:** a thin transparent paper-like material highly resistant to the passage of air and grease. Widely used as windows in the curtains of early vehicles.

**glass pack:** a muffler designed to allow a straight-through passage for the exhaust gases surrounded by an area packed with glass fibers. The true race car makes its loud exhaust from its horsepower. The amateur Sunday driver hopes that the glass packed muffler will simulate the sound of the real thing.

**glass wool:** glass fiber in a mass resembling wool and used as insulation and air filters.

**glaze:** a smooth glossy or lustrous finish sometimes applied as a final coating to vehicle painted surfaces sometimes created by polishing with very fine grit or various waxes.

**glove box:** a sealed box having holes to which are attached protective gloves for use in handling objects sometimes dangerous within the sealed compartment.

**glove compartment:** a small storage cabinet in the dashboard of an automobile.

**glove leather:** a very fine soft flexible leather used to upholster only the finest of prestige automobiles. Sometimes ostentatious by intent.

**glow lamp:** a gas-discharge electric lamp in which most of the light emanates from the glow of a gas near the cathode. Used in some early cars for low-level lighting such as instruments.

**glow plug:** a heating element in a diesel-engine cylinder to preheat the air and provide a hot spot to facilitate starting. Also used with other than diesel fuel in the compression ignition engine. Model aircraft two-cycle engines.

**glycol:** a related alcohol containing two hydroxyl groups. See ethylene glycol.

**go:** functioning properly· being in good and ready condition. The pit crew assured the race driver that all systems (on the car) are "go".

**go-ahead:** a sign, signal, or authority to proceed; green light.

**go-cart:** though once a walker, stroller, or hand-cart now any of several designs of small high-performance race cars.

**gofer:** an employee whose primary duties include running errands.

**goggles:** protective glasses set in a flexible padded frame that fits snugly against the face. Necessary for motorcycle riders and open-car race drivers before the advent of the racing helmet and face shield.

**going-over:** a thorough examination/inspection of a vehicle usually visual to verify its readiness for service.

**Goldbug:** a famous "airport roadster" built by the Kissel Car Company. Amelia Earhart left her Goldbug at the airport when she took off on her last flight. Car is currently (1995) in the Forney Museum of Transportation in Denver, Colorado.

**gold leaf:** a thin sheet of gold foil ordinarily varying from four to five millionths of an inch in thickness and used for decorative gilding in fine automobiles.

**gold plated:** a synthetic plastic or base metal coated with a fine layer usually electroplated for the decorative value of gold. Used functionally to increase the electrical conductance and prevent wear of ignition points, spark plug electrodes, and electrical connections.

**golf cart:** a motorized cart for carrying the more affluent golfer and his equipment around the golf course.

**go-no-go:** a measuring device that is designed to go into or not to go into the hole size that is to be measured.

**goof-off:** to describe the mechanic who evades work or responsibility even to the extent of sleeping under a vehicle on his mechanic's creeper.

**go-pedal:** slang for the vehicles's accelerator pedal or trottle.

**gosport:** a flexible one-way speaking tube for communication between the limousine passenger and the chauffeur up-front beyond the glass divider between the front and rear seats.

**gouge:** a chisel with a concave-convex cross section. To scoop out with as or if with a gouge.

**governor:** an attachment to a machine (as a gasoline engine) for automatic control or limitation of speed.

**grab:** a sudden snatch or engagement as of a clutch or brake, tending to grab.

**grade:** ground level, a datum or reference level, a sloping road, the degree of inclination of a road or slope, to level off to a smooth or sloping surface.

**grade crossing:** a crossing of highways, railroad tracks, or pedestrian walks or combination of these with all on the same level.

**grade separation:** a highway or railroad crossing using an underpass or overpass.

**gradient:** the rate of regular or graded ascent or descent. Change in the value of a quantity (as temperature, pressure, or concentration) with change in a given variable and especially per unit distance in a specified direction.

**gradiometer:** an instrument for measuring the gradient of a physical quantity.

**grain alcohol:** ethanol, a vehicle fuel and fuel additive.

**grainy:** resembling or having some characteristics of grain, not smooth or fine.

**gram:** a metric unit of mass and weight equal to 1/1000 kilogram and nearly equal to one cubic centimeter of water at its maximum density.

**grand:** having more importance than others, having higher rank than others bearing the same general designation, marked by a regal form and dignity. Never grandiose.

**grand prix:** one of a series of international formula car races. Grand Prix.

**grandstand:** a usually roofed seating area for spectators at a vehicle race course.

**grand tour:** an extended tour of the Continent (European) that was formerly part of the education of young British gentlemen.

**grand touring car:** usually a 2-passenger coupe designed for long-distance high-speed touring.

**granny low:** an extra low-low gear intended for extremely hard pulling at very slow speeds.

**granny knot:** an insecure knot resulting from an improperly tied square knot. To be avoided when tying down cover tarps or truck cargo.

**graphite:** a soft black lustrous carbon that conducts electricity used in crucibles, electrolytic anodes and as a lubricant.

**graphitize:** to coat or impregnate with graphite. Some sintered bronze sleeve bearings are so impregnated. Oil additives use graphite to coat bearing surfaces. A favored dry lubricant in powdered form for locks, speedometer cables, and other flexible drives.

**grappling iron:** a tool with hooks or claws used to search for and retrieve vehicles underwater or otherwise inaccessible places.

**grating:** a partition, covering, or frame of parallel bars or cross bars. Used in front of radiators, lights, or windows for protection against flying objects. To cover floor or wall openings to restrain passage of solid objects while allowing fluids to pass.

**grave:** to carve or shape with a chisel flat surfaces or use in hand metal-turning.

**gravel:** loose rounded fragments of rock commonly used alone or with a binder to surface vehicle roadways. A major filling and strengthening component of concrete.

**graveyard:** a storage space for worn-out things as parts or complete vehicles. The work shift beginning at or around the midnight hour.

**gravimeter:** a device similar to a hydrometer for determining specific gravity as of battery acid or liquid fuels.

**gravity:** the quality of having weight. The height of the center of gravity (weight) is cruical to vehicle stability as is the force measured in relationship to gravity (G-force) resulting from acceleration, decelleration, or rate of turning.

**graze:** to touch lightly in passing as the fenders barely grazed in the near-accident.

**grease:** a thick lubricant as a heavy oil, semi-solid, or solid substance.

**grease cup:** a threaded cap for forcing grease through an opening into a bearing area. Becoming obsolete.

**grease fitting:** an attachment for accepting the discharge of a grease gun to force lubricant into a bearing area. Alemite, Zerk.

**grease gun:** a container of grease designed to pump or force grease (using hand or mechanical power) into a lubricated area through appropriate connective devices.

**grease job:** usually the complete lubrication of a vehicle including checking and/or changing fluids as coolant, engine oil, brakes, transmission and differential, steering, battery, and windshield washer.

**grease leak:** any unacceptable loss of lubricant usually indicated by amounts on the floor or ground, deposits on the vehicle underside, or smears around or near moving parts.

**grease monkey:** prejoratively applied to a vehicle mechanic usually implying a low level of competence and slovenly appearance.

**grease pit:** an underground excavation allowing vehicles above it to be serviced by mechanics standing upright. Used for greasing.

**grease seal:** a sealing material to retain grease within a moving joint. Retainer.

**green horn:** an inexperienced vehicle attendant, driver, or mechanic. A newcomer to the profession.

**green house:** car jargon for a vehicle with excessive glass or window/roof openings. A race car canopy or tour-bus roof.

**Green Monster:** the name given by race great Art Arfons to each of his many record-holding dragsters and landspeed racers.

**green silicon carbide:** an abrasive to cut some of the hardest materials used in machines.

**gremlin:** a small gnome blamed by vehicle mechanics for otherwise unexplainable manfunctions of equipment.

**Gremlin:** a competitively-priced automobile by American Motors.

**Greyhound:** the trade-named national bus company. Many people-carrying buses are generically known as "Greyhounds".

**grid:** the starting positions of cars in a competitive race.

**grid-lock:** a traffic jam in which a grid of interconnecting streets or highways is so completely congested that no vehicular movement is possible.

**grill:** a protective sometimes decorative covering of parallel bars usually vertical in front of a vehicle radiator or other inlet for the flow of air.

**grind:** to wear down, polish, or sharpen by friction. An act of grinding. To turn by hand as with a crank. To turn as with a motor--to let the starter grind.

**grinder:** a machine or device that grinds. A workman who operates a grinder.

**grinding compound:** an abrasive powder in paste or a liquid used to grind (lap finish) mating surfaces for a better seal against leakage. Vehicle valve faces and valve seats are routinely finished by lapping with grinding compound.

**grinding wheel:** a flat circular usually cast wheel using various abrasive materials adapted to grind the particular type of material to be processed.

**grind out:** to produce in a repetitive mechanical way. The production line grinds out engines.

**grindstone:** a flat circular stone of natural sandstone that rotates on an axle-shaft and is used for shaping, grinding, or smoothing.

**grit:** the structure of a stone or synthetic that adapts it to grinding. Grit is usually related to hardness and fineness when a rating value is stated.

**grommet:** a reinforcing eyelet of firm resistant material used to strengthen or protect an opening or to insulate or protect something passed through it. As a grommet in a flexible cover for tie-down or through a metal firewall or panel where hoses or wires pass through.

**groove:** a long narrow channel or depression sometimes circumferential as on a piston for rings or a shaft for oil-flow or snap-rings (locking devices).

**gross:** an overall total exclusive of deductions as the gross weight of a vehicle.

**ground:** the total metallic mass of a vehicle used as one "side" of its electrical system usually the negative polarity side. To attach to a ground.

**ground crew:** the mechanics and technicians who maintain and service an airplane or a vehicle. Pit crew for race cars. Maintenance crew for large vehicles.

**ground effect:** the support provided by the cushion of air underneath a vehicle that can be artificially created with aerodynamic devices to totally support the machine's weight. A vehicle utilizing aerodynamic devices to control its ground effect.

**ground glass:** glass with a light-diffusing surface produced by etching or abrading. Used in vehicles for privacy and for soft reduced-glare interior or warning lights.

**ground loop:** a sharp uncontrollable spinning turn usually on a race course or slick roadway. Spin-out.

**ground-off:** a mechanical part that has literally been totally disintegrated by wear or misuse.

**ground out:** the use of a jumper cable or any conductive device to short circuit an electrical system or an entire vehicle for test procedures or as an emergency deactivation.

**ground up:** from top to bottom; entirely new or afresh; thoroughly applied to vehicle inspection, repair, or restoration meaning perfection in every respect.  Also frame-off and frame-up.

**growl:**  a vehicle sound of wear, maladjustment, or lack of lubrication resembling the growl of a living animal.  An engine growl or roar from the exhaust usually denotes power.

**growler:**  an electromagnetic testing device with two adjustable pole pieces used for finding short-circuited coils (particularly in starter and generator armatures) by the tone of its "growl" and also used for magnetizing and demagnetizing.

**grueling:**  a competitive endurance vehicle race that taxes both man and machine to the point of total exhaustion or failure.

**grungy:**  descriptive of a vehicle or a worker that is shabby or dirty in character or condition.

**G-suit:**  a protective suit designed to counteract the physiological effects of acceleration, deceleration, or centrifugal G-forces on a race driver or vehicle test driver.

**GT:**  Grand Turismo.  Grand Touring Car.

**guarantee:**  whether expressed or implied an assurance of the quality of or of the length of use to be expected from a product or a repair offered for sale often with a promise of reimbursement, additional repair, or replacement.  Warranty.

**guard:**  a device, enclosure, or mechanism for protecting a machine from damage or an operator from injury.

**guard rail:**  a railing or barrier for guarding against damage, injury, or trespass in a vehicle work/storage area.

**gudgeon pin:**  a pin to allow a reciprocating partially rotating motion as with a piston pin or shaft.

**guesswork:**  work performed or results obtained based upon a guess (usually educated) when adequate test results or historical data are unavailable.  Usually considered an expedient to the proper procedure.

**guide:**  a device for steadying or directing the motion of something as a valve guide in a vehicle engine.

**guidebook:**  a book of information for travelers usually containing maps, traffic information, service facility locations, and food and lodging information.

**guidepost:**  early highways in the U.S. were marked by mileposts for distances and guideposts that were informational.  The Michelin Tire Company funded and implemented much of this early marking program.

164

**Gullwing:** trade-name of the mid-1950s 3005L Mercedes GT Coupe marked by its top-hinged upward swinging (opening) passenger doors.

**gullwing:** an upward swinging (opening) passenger door as pioneered by the Mercedes Gullwing.

**gusset:** a plate or bracket for strengthening a corner in a vehicle frame. Usually triangular and welded but sometimes bolted into place.

**guy:** a rope, chain, rod, or wire attached to something as a brace or guide. Usually at an angle.

**gymkhana:** a timed contest for vehicles featuring a series of events and maneuvers designed to test driving skill.

**gypsy cab:** a taxicab licensed only to answer calls and allowed to cruise in search of passengers.

**gyro:** abbreviation for gyroscope.

**gyroscope:** a wheel or disk mounted to spin at high speed about an axis and also free to rotate about one or both of two axes perpendicular to each other and to the axis of spin so that a rotation of one of the two mutually perpendicular axes results from application of torque to the other when the wheel is spinning and so that the entire apparatus offers considerable opposition, depending on the angular momentum to any torque that would change the direction of the axis of spin.

## LAGNIAPPE

**g.:** the proper abbreviation (though often misused as a capital "G") gravity force (G-force) with 1 equalling an acceleration of 32.2 feet-per-second-per-second.

**galvanic action:** the production of electricity by chemical reaction or fluid friction involving dissimilar materials.

**gas class:** a competitive auto racing class restricted to using gasoline only (usually of a specified formulation) by all entrants.

**Gilmer belt:** tradenamed timing belt using a cogged engagement interface with matching gears or pulleys for no-slip power transmission.

**glaze breaker:** an abrasive or cutting tool for removing an overly slick or polished surface (from rubbing contact) as a cylinder wall to create a better lubricated seal with the piston/rings.

**Go Kart:** once a specific marque, now generically applied to various small open-wheel vehicles usually with engines under 15 cubic inches displacement.

**green flag:** universally used to signal the start of competitive vehicle speed events--the exception, the international Formula One Grand Prix uses the host country national flag for starting.

**GTO:** technical ("politically correct") usage indicates a homologated Grand Touring car but loosely used as an advertising aggrandizement.

**guide hone:** an abrasive tool used to smooth and impart a desired finish to valve guide interior bores.


### CAR WARS--A LOOK BACK--AND AHEAD
(Which automobile will prevail/survive:  Electric, Gasoline, Steam?)
(Remains Unanswered for Over Two Centuries.)

Which came first?  Most likely, Frenchman Nicholas Cugnot's 1769 _fardier_ (cart) and his 1770 Carriage, steam-powered _automobiles_ led/lead the parade of cars.  Either an English clergyman, William Cecil, or a Swiss engineer, Issac de Rivaz, almost certainly built the first car with an internal combustion engine--both long before Austrian Siegfried Marcus' car in 1865 or Germany's Karl Benz's tricycle in 1885 and Gottlieb Daimler's four-wheeled one in 1886. American Thomas Davenport _may_ have built the first battery-powered electric automobile in 1834.

Cecil entered Magdalene College, Cambridge, about 1810. While a student, he built and demonstrated to the Cambridge Philosophical Society a hydrogen-fueled internal combustion atmospheric engine (the world's first ICE) and _may_ have used it to propel a vehicle.  After his ordainment in 1820, Cecil devoted his life to the Church of England.  Another Britisher, Samuel Brown, as reported in the May 1826 MECHANIC'S MAGAZINE, drove a one-ton four-wheeled carriage up an eleven percent grade, powered by his internal combustion engine burning coal-gas.  Brown demonstrated a 36-foot boat powered by his engine at seven to eight miles per hour _upstream_ to the British Admiralty and also sold many successful water pump engines that operated at less than half the cost of steam engine pumps.  Would you believe 3,000 gallons per minute?

Opt for the inarguability of the documentation that Issac de Rivaz drove his _grand char mechanique_ (unquestionably an automobile, by definition) at Vevey, Switzerland, 18 October 1813.  Recorded data reveal that Issac's over one-ton automobile attained a speed of 3 mph and climbed a 12 percent grade, burning marsh gas/coal-gas (essentially methane) and getting 2 miles per tank-full. His electric-spark ignited gas-fueled internal combustion engine (Patented in France, 30 January 1807) powered numerous successful self-propelled _chars_ (chariots) _automobiles_ from 1805-1813.

Rivaz advocated the establishment of coal-gas filling stations along potential travel routes.  What foresight--in 1813! With about one-half pound of coal required to produce enough coal-gas to propel his car one mile the _grand char_ fuel consumption was two miles per pound of coal.

National Pride and Santayana's warning be-damned, let the world disown and forget Benz as the "Father of the Automobile"!

Jousting for the favor of a fickle public has been a see-saw battle. The steam car dropped out of favor early-on and "Boss" Kettering in 1911 took the heart of the electric car--its motor, downsized it, and taught it to start the Cadillac engine and every other "hand-cranker"--forevermore! The winner of the automobile Great Race seemed settled in favor of the gasoline car.

Now, after years of uneasy truce and smoldering cold war, recent skirmishes brought on by concern about atmospheric pollution and depletion of the gasoline automobile's traditional finite fuel supply, the electric car may be positioned to make another try for the lead in the three-way race. Don't discount the "steamer", if our "New Age" investigates the wide variety of fuels that can heat a boiler, the ability of tailor-made working fluids, and the vast potential of high-speed turbines in a closed-loop energy system.

There are a number of imponderables hidden in the car-choice dilemma. Let's take a look back and see if Santayana's cliche about "history repeating itself and dragging man along for the ride" is, in fact, a truism. Unquestionably, every reasonable mind can ration-alize the common sense of his wisdom by re-reading vehicle history.

Early-on, the electric car was the front-runner because society's elite, the ladies, the genteel dandies, the rich, liked to simply turn a switch and GO--dependably, efficiently, and quietly with no muss of their finery or sweat of the brow. Let the proletariat stoke the fire of the steamer and spin the crank of the gasmobile. The electrics even went FAST, with the first world speed record of 39.24 mph set in 1898 by Comte Laubat in his Jeantaud electric racer. The next year, two other Frenchmen, Jeantaud and Jenatzy, raised the world record 5 times to 65.79 mph. Another French driver, Louis Rigolly, driving a Gobron Brillie 103.56 mph in July 1904 put gasoline cars in the lead again--briefly.

Came Fred Marriott to Daytona Beach, Florida, in 1906 and drove a Stanley steamer Beetle over 127 mph to put steam out front in the Great Race. Fred returned to the beach sands in 1907, dying in the crash of his Stanley Steamer when it became airborne at over 150 mph. The 127 mph remained the steam car speed record until 1985 when the Barber-Nichols Steamin' Demon ran 145.607 mph, setting the current (1995) record for steam cars. The boiler produced 900° Fahrenheit and 900 pounds per square inch superheated steam, while burning 1½ gallons of kerosene per minute. That's 1.6 miles per gallon of fuel--and a Helluva lot of water because it exhausted to the atmosphere (non-condensing). The turbine turned 65,030 rpm at 150 mph, delivering 120 horsepower to the drive-wheels. The turbine was originally built by Barber-Nichols, a Denver, CO, engi-neering company, and had been used for a year-long government test by Bill Lear (of Learjet) in steam buses on the San Francisco hills.

When Sir Henry Segrave's British Sunbeam roared across Daytona Beach at 203.790 mph, March 29, 1927, macho man's machismo put gasoline into the lead position again--remaining there today (1995).

Between Segrave's famous milestone--the first automobile to exceed 200 mph, a goal once believed unattainable--and the onset of World War II, a number of British speed-merchants raised the world landspeed mark several times--every one of them fueled with gasoline and wheel-driven. Although aircraft engines were used exclusively, none used the reaction <u>thrust</u> that made the airplanes go so fast.

Malcolm Campbell's Sunbeam turned 206.960 mph (1928), losing to Segrave's Golden Arrow at over 231 mph (1929). Campbell's new Bluebird raised the ante to 253.968 mph (1930) at the "Beach", moved to Bonneville (1935) and topped the "Big 3" at 304.311 mph (Campbell had his last fling) with Brit John Cobb ending up with 369.70 mph.

After the Big War, American Craig Breedlove's Spirit of America jet "broke 4" at 407.45 in 1963 and Bob Summers' Goldenrod with four Chrysler piston engines did 409.277 mph. Know the rest?

In 1961, Dr. Nathan Ostich, a California physician, became the first to pilot a jet automobile across the Bonneville Utah Salt Flats at 360.000 mph. Dr. Henry Linden, a physicist who headed the American Gas Association, was project officer for the Jet racer that Gary Gabelich drove over 622 mph burning natural gas augmented by hydrogen peroxide to obtain rocket-like thrust--similar to afterburning in a jet.

A number of jets with sufficient power to exceed Mach I (the speed of sound wave travel through the air at sea level) may succeed in breaking the "sound barrier" in 1995 if a suitable surface is available. Several possibilities exist: Bonneville Salt Flats in Utah; Black Rock lakebed in Nevada; Lake Alvord Dry Lake in Oregon; several dry lake beds in the Australian outback.

Can your Cibie driving lights pierce the fog of future uncertainty? Or your crystal-ball come into sharp focus onto vehicle-future? Is there <u>deja vu</u> ahead?


## EXCUSES, EXCUSES
(From Traffic Court Records)

What I thought was a large truck way up ahead was, in fact, a small Volkswagen just a few feet from me.

I was planning ahead while backing up until a lamp post smashed my rear fender.

This accident would not have happened if I had overslept, as I usually do.

**H-Cars:** Maybe a few of the Thunder Road "rum-runners" who outdistanced the Feds with a few jugs of "white lightning" in the trunk of a Hudson Super-Six in the 1920s thought that driving a "Super-Six" was like "living in Hog Heaven", but virtually none of the other 231 H-marques left great impressions upon automotive history. Certainly the British Hillman and Humber will have a place in the hearts and minds of Limey car lovers. The Hispano-Suiza built concurrently in Barcelona, Spain and Paris, France is a favored showpiece in many world-class automobile museums because of the luxurious Alfonso XIII limousine, named to honor Spain's King and remembered by the world aviation community for the "Hisso" airplane engine, a workhorse teammate of the American Curtis "OX-5" engine. The German Horch (1900-1939) was a prestige large automobile that may have lost the race to greatness to the Daimler and Mercedes marques. Back to the Hudson Super Six, one of its never-to-be-bested accomplishments was the first round-trip transcontinental automobile trip (New York to San Francisco and return) in 1916, and driver Ira Vail's ninth place finish in the Indianapolis 500-Mile Race in 1919.

**hack:** common abbreviation for hackney (a vehicle for rent).

**hackney:** a colloquial expression for an automobile that is for hire or rent. Taxicab.

**hacksaw:** a fine-toothed saw with a replaceable blade under tension in a frame that is used for cutting hard materials as metals.

**hairpin clip:** a U-shaped retainer pin that passes through a drilled hole in a shaft or rod (or that fits into a machined grove around such a shaft or rod) to hold small linkages in proper relationship to allow desired movement. C-clip.

**hairpin spring:** a spring with two extensions out from a half-loop or coil that can provide either a compression or tension force to close an engine valve in lieu of a coil spring.

**hairspring:** a slender spiral-wound spring recoil device used to return, to stabilize, or to calibrate the hands (pointer) of various vehicle instruments.

**half-axle:** the shaft that transmits power from a differential or transaxle to one wheel of a vehicle. Half shaft.

**half-midget:** a class of open-wheel race cars that are smaller (about half-size) and race on a shorter (usually one-eighth-mile) oval race track when compared to the more popular full-midget.

**half-moon-key:** a key for locking two pieces together to prevent rotational slippage (relative movement) usually with the circular segment fitted into a crescent depression (keyway) in a shaft and the diametric flat segment fitted into a matching keyway in a pulley, hub, or wheel.

**half-track:** a vehicle with steered front wheels and a continuous track rear support package providing better traction and preventing sinking into the mire when driving off-road. Common to military combat vehicles and oil exploration and well-drilling vehicles.

**halogen:** any of the five elements: astatine, bromine, chlorine, fluorine and iodine that form part of Group VII-A of the periodic table and used extensively in motor vehicles with halogen (quartz iodide) headlights being best known to the non-scientific vehicle owner.

**ham-handed:** descriptive of a vehicle mechanic lacking dexterity and skill in doing detailed work on delicate or intricate vehicle parts. Epitomized by his philosophy in solving difficult repair operations: "get a bigger hammer!" Ham fisted. Heavy-handed. Klutzy. All thumbs.

**hammered-finish:** an exterior or decorative metal surface that has a distinctive pattern of hammer blows impressed into its finish.

**hammer mill:** a large rotating cylinder in which materials (usually junk or worn out machines) are ground or crushed into small pieces by swinging hammer-like heavy weights or steel balls. Ball mill.

**hand brake** a vehicle brake applied by a hand-operated cable or lever. Emergency brake. Foot brake. Parking brake.

**handcar:** a small four-flanged-wheel railroad rail-bed service vehicle powered by a hand-pumped ratchet device or a small engine/motor.

**handfeed:** a metal-cutting machine whose cutting tool's depth or rate of cut is controlled by a hand-operated feed screw, e.g., drill press, lathe, or milling machine.

**hand fit:** to make minor changes in the dimensions of an assembly part by filing, grinding, or polishing to an exact match with its adjoining part.

**handhold:** a sturdy handle or strap attached to a vehicle's structure for occupants to hang onto when traversing rough terrain or to assist in entering or leaving the vehicle.

**hand hole:** an opening through the outer surface of a vehicle providing access for a mechanic to reach inside to adjust, maintain, repair, or service components.

**handicap:** the advantage given to slower vehicles in either starting time or distance to insure a more competitive and closer race to please the spectators. Staggered start.

**hand lap:** to polish to close dimensional tolerances or to a high shiny finish using a lapping compound (as jeweler's rouge) as the abrasive applied with a pad or lap.

**hand rubbed:** to describe the process of attaining a high-gloss smooth finish on a painted surface by applying multiple light coats and wet-or-dry sanding with increasingly fine grit after each coat has dried, ending with a very fine rouge.

**hand scraped:** replaced by today's sophisticated surface-grinding machines, the technique of using a triangular-shaped scraper to obtain near-optically-flat surfaces for precision machine tools, e.g., lathe, milling machine, grinder, or shaper ways or work table surfaces. Scraped ways.

**hand start:** to start a vehicle engine by using a crank turned by arm/hand strength of the mechanic. To start a stationary internal combustion engine by hand-turning the open flywheel. To push a vehicle with driver using forward momentum and en-gaged clutch/gears to turn the engine. Hand crank. Push start. Jump start. Bump start.

**hard case:** a ferrous metal whose surface has been hardened against wear by heating and quench-cooling in an appropriate chemical bath as of cyanide. Case hardened. Shot peened. Peened.

**hard chrome:** an electroplated surface on a part subject to rubbing wear, as a shaft journal or its bearing, using a chrome alloy resistant to such wear, that is machined to the desired clearance, fit, and tolerance.

**harden:** to change a material's hardness by metallurgical tech-niques such as annealing, heating-and-cooling, chemical dip-ping, forging, hammering, or peening. Temper. Hard finish.

**hard-hat:** a protective head covering worn by construction workers and by vehicle mechanics in high-bay shops where falling material can happen.

**hard rubber:** a dense non-flexible rubber usually with a hard shiny surface like plastic made by vulcanizing natural rubber with high percentages of sulfur. Gutta-percha.

**hard seat:** a valve seat (ring) with high resistance to heat and erosion wear (as for an engine exhaust valve) that is machine-inserted into the softer, less-resistant metal of block or cylinder-head castings to extend an engine's operating life-time.

**hard-seat-grinder:** a valve/valve-seat machining tool equipped with stones/grinding wheels specified for cutting the particular alloy in the seat insert.

**hardtop:** a sports car with a fixed or removable rigid top, designed to resemble a foldable or removable soft top (convertible or roadster), or any automobile having a fixed rigid roof.

**hardtop hoist:** a usually webbing strap sling in a private garage to lift the removable hardtop from a sports car and hold it suspended overhead until needed again.

**hardware cloth:** a rugged galvanized square screening with meshes of usually two, four, or eight squares to the square inch.

**harmonic balancer:** an oscillating or rotating device (counterbalance) that generates vibrational forces in opposition to the harmonic (integral multiple) frequencies of an engine's fundamental vibrations. Sometimes accomplished by separate rotating masses or by attaching appropriate spring or hydraulic dampers directly to major rotating masses such as a crankshaft or flywheel. Harmonic damper. Shake quencher.

**harmonic intake:** an engine whose entire induction system (air horn, carburetor, intake manifold, and intake port) length, cross-section area, radius of bends (curves), interior obstructions and interior surface finish are modified to take advantage of the inertial forces and pulse-timing of the incoming airflow at some particular engine rpm (usually within a narrow range of rpm). Tuned pipes. Acoustic tuning.

**harness:** a collection of electrical wiring usually bundled or enclosed in a conduit for removal or servicing as a unit rather than dealing with each individual wire. An occupant safety restraint system such as the combined seat (lap) belt and diagonal or crossed shoulder belt. Wire bundle. Safety harness. Wiring harness.

**hatchback:** a two-door or four-door automobile usually with a downward-sloping rear roof section that is hinged to be lifted from the rear, exposing the trunk and sometimes the rear interior for access.

**Hat-in-the-Ring:** famous logo insignia used by World War I ace, Captain Eddie Rickenbacker on his combat airplane and later as the manufacturer's marque on his Rickenbacker automobile (1922-1927), the first low-priced American car with four-wheel brakes, that had a 4.4 litre engine that propelled his large sedan smoothly (the engine used two flywheels) at 90 mph.

**hay bales:** the tightly bound bundles of animal feed used as course markers and crowd barriers at sports car road races in urban locations because of their resiliency and shock absorbency if hit by a race car traveling at high speed.

**hay burner:** a vehicle mechanic's derisive slang expression to describe that one-horse power automobile, the four-footed horse.

**hazard warning lights:** flashing signal lights at the extreme corners of a vehicle that is stopped on an active roadway or parked alongside such. Flashing signs.

**H.D.:** mechanic's abbreviation for heavy duty as applied to a vehicle, a tool, a vehicle jack, a vehicle tire, et al.

**head:** mechanic's jargon for an engine's cylinder head.

**headache bar:** mechanic's slang for a vehicle roll-bar or roll-cage as required in most sanctioned vehicle racing events.

**header:** the large conduit (exhaust pipe) into which the individual cylinder exhaust pipes of a multi-cylinder engine merge. Header pipe.

**header tank:** a larger volume liquid tank at the highest point in a system of pipes or devices that insures that the remainder of the system is always filled with liquid as with the top tank of a vehicle's coolant radiator.

**heading angle:** the angle by which the longitudinal axis of a moving vehicle (apparent direction of motion) deviates from its true direction of travel. Yaw. Yaw angle.

**headlight:** the forward-aimed front lights (two) on a vehicle that illuminate the roadway ahead during nighttime driving.

**headlight dimmer:** the driver-operated foot- or hand-switch that changes the high beam (bright) of a vehicle headlights to the low beam (dim) when approaching another oncoming vehicle at night or to reduce glare when driving in fog or smog at night.

**headliner:** the fabric covering the inside (underside) of the roof (top) of automobiles--or any motor vehicle. Ceiling liner. Roof liner.

**head/port matching:** making the exact size and outline shape of the intake manifold opening fit the cylinder head intake port opening perfectly, and likewise for the cylinder head exhaust port to the exhaust manifold opening to insure the smooth flow of the intake and exhaust gases, uninterrupted by turbulence caused by sharp edges or mismatched mating surfaces at the cylinder head port/manifold juncture. This matching is done with a die-grinder using appropriate grinding wheels and polishing compounds. Porting. Flow peaking.

**head restraint:** a padded headrest cushion on the back of each passenger seat adjustable in height to suit the occupant and designed to absorb G-forces (gravity) from front or rear collisions, thus mitigating against whiplash injuries to passengers.

**heads-up display:** a system being adapted from fighter aircraft to automobiles that projects all instrument readings as if onto the windshield, allowing the vehicle driver to monitor all instruments without shifting his eyes from the road ahead. Intended to reduce accidents caused by driver inattention to the road ahead.

**head start:** the practice in automobile races of allowing slower vehicles to leave the starting line earlier or to start a specified distance ahead of the faster cars to insure closer finishes and more competition during racing.

**hearse:** a sedate specialty vehicle used to transport the deceased as needed. Funeral car.

**heat block:** an annular slot or a poor heat-conductor-insert below the head (crown) of an engine's piston to reduce the conductive heat flow from the piston top to the piston skirt and pin-boss area.

**heat control valve:** a thermostatically controlled valve that by-passes exhaust heat to the carburetor base/intake manifold area for better fuel vaporization during cold starts and to prevent carburetor icing on cold days with high humidity.

**heat crack:** a metal fatigue or stress crack that occurs in an engine casting or other part that is exposed to repeated heating and cooling as with an exhaust manifold that is not properly torqued to its mating block or head.

**heated intake:** an engine's intake manifold that is heated selectively by by-passed exhaust or coolant to assist in vaporizing the fuel/air mixture and/or to prevent carburetor icing during conditions of cold and high humidity.

**heat engine:** any engine that converts the energy stored in a fuel by burning the fuel and converting the heat into rotation or thrust that translates into useful work in propelling a vehicle. Some examples of internal combustion: piston engines, turbines, jets, or rockets; external combustion: steam piston engines, steam turbines, or electric motors powered by steam-generated electricity.

**heat fade:** loss of a vehicle's braking power when brakes become overheated from prolonged use (as on a long downhill run) causing glazing of friction surfaces and sometimes vapor lock in the hydraulic system from heated brake fluid.

**heat gun:** a device with an electric heating element and a fan to force air across the heat source and direct the stream of hot air through a nozzle to dry and to heat localized areas during vehicle maintenance, repair, or service. The most common type is a hand-held pistol-shaped device similar to a small hair dryer.

**heat lamp:** a single prefocused reflector electric bulb designed to emit heat (light in the infrared spectrum) to be used for drying or heating localized areas during vehicle maintenance, repair, or service. Often used in banks of multiple lamps or with separate reflectors as when drying ("baking") large painted areas. Baking oven. Drying oven.

**heat range:** a rating of spark plugs' operating temperatures on a scale that allows the selection of a proper spark plug for a particular engine. A colder plug dissipates combustion heating through a shorter path to the engine's coolant while the hotter plug has a longer dissipation path to transfer its heat to the coolant.

**heat range index:** a numbering system for indicating the effective heat range (from hot to cold) of vehicle spark plugs. The index number is derived from the time required in seconds for the plug to begin to cause fuel detonation when operated under the standard test protocol in a "knock-test" laboratory engine.

**heat shield:** a usually thin shiny heat-reflective surface (as chromium plated or stainless steel) or a low heat-conductive material (as asbestos) used to keep the heat from "hot spots" (as exhaust manifolds or pipes/mufflers) from overheating nearby heat-sensitive areas/equipment.

**heat shrink:** the assembly/mating/joining process involving the heating (thus expanding the size of an interior hole) of one part and placing it around/over another part that is cool then cooling the heated part until it shrinks tightly onto the cooler part making a very strong joint comparable to welding. A reversible process if the assembled parts have the proper coefficients of heat-expansion.

**heat sink:** a mass of material with good heat absorbing capacity or with fins with good heat dissipation ability used to prevent overheating of very localized heat-producing devices as a solid-state diode rectifier in a vehicle alternator circuit.

**heat stress:** heat-caused forces within a material (particularly metals) that can cause weaknesses, cracks, or total failure. Modern metallurgy has solved many of our earlier problems in this area by compounding better alloys.

**heat transfer:** a broad technology concerning the theoretical and practical movement and control of heat energy involving using, storing, concentrating, dissipating, blocking, et al.

**heat treat:** the science and technique of altering the characteristics (ductility, hardness, strength, et al.) of a metal by controlled heating, cooling, and quenching.

**heavy duty:** a vehicle of any type designed and built to withstand service and use far beyond the normal intended use parameters of the standard vehicle. Light duty.

**heel pad:** an extra strength/wear section or separate part of a vehicle floor near the accelerator, brake, or clutch pedals to resist/withstand the heavy repetitive contact from the driver's foot/heel.

**Heli-Arc:** tradenamed welding system using an electric arc from an electrode (usually tungsten) as the heat source while surrounding the weld area with a protective flow of the inert gas, helium, to prevent atmospheric contamination (especially oxidation) of the weld.

**helical:** of, relating to, or having the form of a helix. Spiral spring.

**Heli-Coil:** tradenamed device for repairing, replacing, or strengthening damaged threads in a hole in a variety of materials, involving drilling to an exact diameter and using a special tool to insert and lock the hardened coil spring that essentially becomes like-new threads.

**helium:** a lighter-than-air inert nonflammable gaseous element (#2 in the periodic table) whose properties make it useful in many vehicle-related operations.

**helmet:** a protective covering for a vehicle driver/occupant's head when engaged in dangerous/hazardous activities. Required for all participants in sanctioned vehicle competition events (racing). Crash helmet. Head bucket. Head sled.

**helper spring:** an added spring, coil or leaf, to an existing vehicle suspension system that becomes effective when the normal spring deflection exceeds the amount allowed for standard loads.

**hemi:** mechanic's abbreviation of hemispherical.

**hemihead:** an engine cylinder head with its combustion area having a hemispherical shape. Dome head. Flat head. Wedge head.

**heptane:** any of several isomeric hydrocarbons ($C_7H_{16}$) of the methane series, especially the liquid normal isomer naturally occurring in petroleum and used as a solvent and as a comparative standard for establishing fuel octane ratings/numbers.

**hermetic seal:** an airtight seal that is impervious to external influence.

**herringbone gear:** a machine gear wheel whose teeth are of a repeated parallel-vee configuration and known for heavy-load carrying ability.

**Hershey:** the annual nationwide swap-meet (flea market) for automobiles and parts, accessories, and supplies at Hershey, PA, that has become the automobile aficionados' Mecca.

**hertz:** the unit of frequency equal to one cycle per second.

**hexane:** any of several isomeric volatile liquid paraffin hydrocarbons ($C_6H_{14}$) found in petroleum.

**hex-head:** the gripping area of a bolt, nut, or screw having the six flats of a hexagon around its periphery.

**hex wrench:** a mechanic's wrench that has a box (loop) end or socket with six flat gripping areas joining to form its interior shape.

**hi-fi:** abbreviation for the high fidelity sound reproducing systems (as radio and recording players) available for motor vehicles to entertain and inform the occupants while traveling.

**high bay:** a vehicle shop or storage facility with higher than normal ceiling heights.

**high beam:** the long-range focus of a vehicle headlight.

**high blower:** with a two-stage (two-speed) supercharger, the use of the second stage that produces a higher manifold pressure. The use of any engine supercharger that produces higher than usual or typical manifold pressures.

**high boy:** a recognized racing class of/for vintage vehicles of the 1920s-1930s, usually roadsters that have larger-than-stock engines and that run without fenders, tops, windshields, or any added streamlining. High boy heritage likely started with "street rods" in their era that graduated to the California Dry Lakes (El Mirage and Muroc) speed trials, hot rod drags, the half-mile "stockers", and are now recognized among the Bonneville Salt Flats, UT, elite world landspeed racing classes.

**high center:** a roadway surface anomaly (as a hump or depression) or an obstruction that a vehicle cannot drive over without interference with its underside to the extent that one or more wheels teeters in the air, losing road contact.

**high cube:**  vehicle lingo for an enclosed truck body that has a higher than average interior ceiling and cargo cubage space.

**high frequency:**  a radio frequency between very high frequency and medium frequency.  (HF: 3 to 30 megahertz).

**high gear:**  the highest gear ratio in a multi-speed transmission that results in the highest vehicle forward speed at a given engine rpm.  Tall gear.  Cruising gear.  In high.

**high lift cam:**  an engine camshaft with a lobe profile that creates more lift (for a wider opening valve) and usually greater duration (longer time of valve opening) than production cams to provide better engine breathing, thus increasing power and performance as for sports and racing vehicles.  Racing cam.  Long duration cam.

**high octane:**  a vehicle fuel having a high octane number and hence good anti-knock properties.

**high-powered:**  a vehicle having significantly greater than normal acceleration, pulling power, and speed.

**high rise:**  a deprecatory description of a pickup or otherwise stock vehicle that has been altered with various lift devices to raise the body/chassis significantly above its normal stock suspension height.

**high speed:**  a vehicle operated or adapted for operation at faster than usual speeds.

**high technology:**  current technology involving the production or use of the most advanced or sophisticated devices available for motor vehicles.  High tech.  State of the art.

**high tension:**  having a high electrical voltage or relating to apparatus to be used at high voltage.  High tension (spark plug) wires.  High tension (spark) coil.

**highway cycle:**  any standardized motor vehicle test cycle that replicates or simulates typical driving on the open road as routinely done by the average driver of like vehicles.  Highly sophisticated computer programs are used by government agencies and vehicle testers to assure comparability of test results to highway driving.

**hill climb:**  a road race for motor vehicles in which competitors are individually timed up a hill.  Pikes Peak (CO) Hill Climb is the world's premier such event.

**hinge joint:**  a joint at the juncture of two levers that permits motion in only one plane.  Ball joint.  Universal joint.

**hit-and-run:** being or involving a motor vehicle driver who does not stop after being involved in an accident.

**hitch:** the connection between a towed vehicle and its source of motive power (tractor). Trailer hitch.

**hitchhike:** to travel by securing free rides from passing motor vehicles. Bum a ride. Thumb a ride.

**hob:** a rotating cutting tool that is used in a milling machine or as an accessory lathe attachment to cut gear teeth as in gear wheels or gear worms. Gear hob.

**hogged out:** a hole as a bolt/stud hole or a bearing/bushing that is badly worn or misused so that its original round shape and dimensions are severely distorted and enlarged, requiring major remachining or total replacement of the affected part. Chewed out. Egged out.

**hogshead:** the casting that encases the Model T Ford's fly-wheel/magneto and the planetary gearing and controls for the transmission. So named because of its resemblance to a hog's head.

**hoist:** a common vehicle-shop device designed to lift entire vehicles or major components as complete engines/transmissions for repair or replacement and to allow mechanics to work conveniently and efficiently on a vehicle's under-body components. Post hoist/lift (hydraulic). Cable/chain hoist. Crane. A-Frame. Overhead traveling crane.

**hold-down:** any securing device for holding vehicle components or cargo in place with the most familiar type likely to be the battery hold-down. Tie-down. Chain jack. Cargo strap. Bungee.

**Hollywood:** Graham's final fling or swan song was the 1940 Hollywood whose stylish body was stamped from the Cord 810/812 dies as was the Hupmobile Skylark, its near-identical twin. A number were built but the company became a casualty of World War II, with Graham's president, Joseph Frazer, joining with Henry Kaiser in 1946 to build their namesakes.

**hollywood pipes:** any of various vehicle exhaust systems of the 1940s that were sold as aftermarket bolt-ons that emulated the loud exhaust sounds of the California hotrods which became the centerpiece of so many post-World War II movies. Smittys. Glass packs. Dual pipes.

**home-built:** an automobile built-from-scratch (almost) or from various kits that is touted as the hands-on product of the backyard builder, but isn't. The concept smacks of our childhood Erector Set or Tinker Toy because nothing is built--simply bolted together from purchased parts.

**home stretch:** that part of a vehicle closed racecourse (race track) between the last turn and the finish line.

**hone:** a tool for enlarging holes to precise tolerances and for finish polishing by means of rotating abrasives. A fine-grit stone for hand-sharpening cutting tools.

**hood:** the movable metal body section (usually hinged) that covers the engine of traditional front-engined motor vehicles. Bonnet (British).

**hood lacing:** a fabric woven strip that was laced to the metal flange on a vehicle fire wall and to the flange on the radiator shroud where the engine hood rested when closed thus forming a padded seal. Largely replaced in contemporary vehicles by self-adhering foam or other synthetic weather stripping to seal the juncture of the hood and containing body panels.

**hood latch:** a usually two-step positive holding device that is spring-loaded to prevent motion between the hood and its mating enclosure, and that is released by a hand-lever or cable-pull from the driver's position as the first step and finally by manually releasing the second safety latch at the latch site at the hood opening.

**hood pin:** usually two pins securely attached to the vehicle body structure that protrude through reinforced grommets in the hood sheet metal so that a locking spring clip can be pressed through a hole in the main pin. Though functional as a supplementary safety latch to the main hood latch in racing vehicles, it is usually an ostentatious ego piece of the amateur sports racer.

**hand release:** the inside driver-operated hand-lever or cable-pull that is usually complemented by the latch-site manual release.

**hood stay:** the usually-hinged stowaway rod that supports the weight of the hood allowing hands to be free while checking, repairing, or servicing engine compartment components.

**hood strap:** a usually sturdy leather or woven belt/strap (secured by a buckle/latch) that encircles the hood near its longitudinal center from anchors at each chassis siderail as a safety retainer for hoods on early-era race cars and on contemporary off-road vehicles and to authenticate vintage race cars.

**hood vent:** an entry or exit opening for cooling or ram air through an engine-hood surface. Air scoop. NACA scoop. NASA Vent. Side-vent.

**hop up:** the mechanic's slang for increasing a vehicle's power/performance usually by adding aftermarket devices or special engine tuning. Race tune.

**horizontal engine:** a vehicle engine with cylinders lying in the horizontal plane (flat) for installation under large vehicles as under passenger buses or in automobiles to allow lower body profiles. Flat engine. Slant engine. Inverted engine.

**horizontally-opposed engine:** one with cylinders arranged horizontally (flat) on both (opposite) sides of the crankshaft. Flat engine. Boxer (because of the appearance of the opposing pistons/rods punching at each other). Porche/Volkswagen cars popularized this engine configuration for automobiles. Most light aircraft use such.

**horn:** an audible warning device for vehicles, formerly air, exhaust, or steam-powered sound waves but currently almost exclusively electrical/electronic sound generators/ amplifiers with a wider range of frequencies/tones. Siren. Whistle. Klaxon. Bulb horn.

**horsepower:** the historical Anglo-American measure of power/ work by comparison with a horse's ability/strength using an arbitrary, but inaccurate, unit of one horse's work equaling 33,000 foot-pounds-per-minute. The metric approximate unit is one kilowatt (1,000 watts of electrical energy). One horsepower = 0.7457 kilowatt.

**horshoe vortex:** a vortex directly behind a moving vehicle formed by the combined transverse and outer surface trailing vortices and lying between the main-flow vortices formed at the rear sides/top of the moving vehicle. This phenomenon is more pronounced behind a vehicle with a boxy (squared-off) rear. "U" or "V" vortex.

**hot bulb ignition:** for compression-ignition (diesel) engines, a supplementary ignition source employing a heated (sometimes incandescent) element, usually electrically, for starting and sometimes for sustaining efficient fuel combustion. Glow plug. Hot spot. Semi-diesel.

**hot patch:** a form of repair to a pneumatic vehicle tire or tube leak using a section of rubber/synthetic that is compatible with the tire/tube and applying heat and pressure to essentially "weld" the patch over the damaged spot thus sealing/stopping the leak.

**hot plug:** a low-numbered spark plug (hot) whose center and ground electrodes remain hot (by design) to prevent plug fouling in low-compression engines.

**hot rolled:** a class of steel used throughout industry that is produced at the steel rolling mill by heating red hot and passing through rollers at increased pressure for each pass until the steel has been squeezed to an exact thickness dimension. Cold rolled.

**hot rod:** a production car, usually several years old, that has been modified to increase acceleration, performance, and speed usually by adding "bolt on" after market gadgetry. The exterior configuration and paint scheme are usually changed to make it look like a currently popular professional race car.

**hot shoe:** a race driver who has the knack or the luck of always going faster than his competitors, even when he drives their vehicles. Hot foot. Heavy foot.

**hot shot:** a multi-cell dry-cell battery that was often clipped into the ignition circuit only during cranking to overcome the vehicle system voltage loss because of the heavy current draw by the engine starter.

**hot soak:** with the contemporary sound-insulated and non-ventilated (except when driving) engine compartment, the tendency for heat to build up under the hood after parking a vehicle that has been operating at normal temperature. As the under-hood heat increases, areas that normally are cooler with operating ventilation overheat enough to cause starting difficulties, e.g., residual fuel boils causing vapor lock until overcome by start-up fuel pressure and temperature-sensors can confuse the engine-control computer with overheat signals. Under-hood fumes from excess heat create a dilemma for the emissions regulators.

**hot spot:** a localized heated area, deliberate and desirable when needed to enhance fuel vaporization and carburetor de-icing, but unforeseen and undesirable when a carbon build-up or red-hot metal (as a sharp-edged valve head or seat) in the combustion chamber causes fuel detonation (fuel-knock) that loses power and overheats the entire engine.

**hot wire:** mechanic's lingo for using an electrical jumper-wire to by-pass (bridge) an open-circuit (accidental, as a broken wire or poor terminal connection) or a normal "open" as a switch that can't be closed (turned on) for whatever reason (as lost or missing keys). A "hot wire" is the favored tool of the car thief who uses it to bypass a locked ignition and "jump-start" the engine's starter motor.

**hot wrench:** mechanic's slang for using a welding torch to join or tighten parts or assemblies that cannot be mechanically secured or the use of a cutting torch to separate (cut apart) parts that cannot be separated mechanically using loosening tools (wrenches).

**hourglass worm:** a waisted (smaller middle-diameter between its ends) worm gear for better meshing with a pinion, sector gear, or roller to accomplish an angular direction-change of a force.

**Hovercraft:** trademarked vehicle that can traverse almost any terrain or water, supported by a cushion of air.

**HT paint:** a vehicle paint for accessories/components that operate at relatively high temperatures as radiators, engine cylinder blocks, and cylinder heads. VHT paint (for very high temperature such as exhaust manifolds, mufflers, and exhaust pipes).

**hub:** the center assembly of a gear or wheel that contains the bearings/bushings for a free-running unit or the locking mechanism (threads, keyway, or splines) for power transmission.

**hub cap:** a covering both decorative and functional for protecting the bearings of a hub only or totally covering a road wheel's rim diameter for streamlining and for displaying the vehicle manufacturer's marque or model designation.

**hub plate:** the usually riveted and splined center-section of a vehicle's driven clutch plate/disc.

**hub reduction:** the use of epicyclic (planetary) gears within a wheel hub (usually a heavy-vehicle road-wheel) to provide speed or torque multiplication.

**huckster wagon:** a horse-drawn or motorized vehicle designed for the sale of various products to door-to-door purchasers. Apple cart. Bakery wagon. Pie wagon. Milk wagon. Vegetable wagon. Depot hack.

**huffer:** mechanic's slang for a supercharger (mechanical or turbo) that is located below (downstream) of the carburetor/fuel-mixer thus pulling (sucking) the combustion air as contrasted to pushing the charge-air (a puffer) into and through the carburetor.

**human engineering:** the science of making vehicles more user-friendly, e.g., attention to occupant comfort as seating design, climate control (heating and cooling), ventilation, visibility, sound control (reduction), ease of entry/egress, safety (air bags, body restraints, head rests, padded structure, et al.), interior decor, vibration damping, audio/communications (radio, cassette/disc/tape recorder), and driveability ergonomics.

**Hummer:** this recognized marqued vehicle is best described as an oversized Jeep, originally intended as a military personnel carrier, the Hummer is now sold as an off-road (street legal) general purpose 4-passenger vehicle retailing in excess of $50,000.

**hump:** the raised longitudinal center section of a vehicle floor that provides underbody space for the drive-shaft, transmission, et al., allowing a lower center of gravity and lower overall vehicle height.

**hunting:** the usually repetitive (and annoying) fluctuation in frequency or speed of an engine or other vehicle component that is not accurately/properly adjusted or is insufficiently internally governed/regulated. The offending unit seems to be seeking but not finding a stable operating mode.

**hush kit:** mechanic's lingo for a post-production or aftermarket modification utilizing a number of noise-suppressing materials and components supplied and added as a group to make a motor vehicle quieter, inside and/or outside.

**hustle shop:** a vehicle mechanical shop or parts store that specializes in modifying vehicles or providing parts to the do-it-yourselfer owner that are designed to make a stock vehicle accelerate or go faster. Hot rod shop.

**hustle stuff:** race car driver/mechanic slang to denote any chemical additive, part, or procedure used to make a car accelerate or go faster. Speed stuff. Bolt-on speed. Bought speed.

**hybrid engine:** an internal combustion engine that can operate as a compression-ignition engine (Diesel cycle) or as a spark-ignition engine (Carnot cycle). An engine combination such as an internal combustion engine powering an electrical generator that supplies electric power to motor(s) that propel the vehicle wheels or an industrial load. Future engines are likely to use a number of hybrid modalities in the search for better fuel efficiency and/or lower vehicle emissions.

**hybrid vehicle:** any motorized vehicle propelled by a hybrid engine or combination thereof.

**Hydragas suspension:** a tradenamed vehicle suspension system using pressurized gas as the weight supporting spring and shock absorber supplemented by a diaphragm-separated hydraulic pressure system usually employing pistons to control and adjust vehicle height and vertical wheel bounce/travel.

**hydraulic brakes:** vehicle brakes actuated by usually foot-powered hydraulic pressure.

**hydraulic clutch:** a vehicle mechanical clutch engaged/disengaged by a foot-powered hydraulic master cylinder that actuates the clutch mechanism through a hydraulic pressure-actuated slave cylinder.

**hydraulic damper:** a vehicle shock absorber that utilizes controllable/fixed viscous fluid-flow orifices to mitigate the transfer of wheel-road rebound/shock to the suspended chassis.

**hydraulic gauge:** an instrument that displays/indicates/records hydraulic pressure or volume usually transmitted hydraulically through a connecting passage/hose/pipe/tube from pressure/volume sender-source to instrument.

**hydraulic lifter:** a small hydraulic cylinder/piston actuator designed to operate exhaust and intake valves of an engine either directly or through a mechanical linkage with zero-lash (clearance). Hydraulic tappet.

**hydraulic lock:** the total stoppage of an engine's rotation by a volume of liquid (as oil, water, or fuel) that is as effective as a mechanical blockage because of the inherent incompressibility of all liquids. Hydraulic lock can cause catastrophic material failure when a piston is forced upward into a cylinder full of liquid.

**hydraulic pump:** a device for moving or pressurizing liquids. The pump may be mechanically or electrically powered, utilizing positive displacement gears or pistons or a wide variety of turbines or vanes.

**hydraulic retarder:** a usually transmission-mounted turbine-like device that dissipates power by using fluid friction to retard the speed of a vehicle thus saving the mechanical brake system's wear and extending brake life.

**hydraulic transmission:** a vehicle transmission that employs a hydraulic torque converter to complement the gears in providing torque-multiplication ratios and to eliminate the necessity for a mechanical clutch.

**hydrazine:** a colorless fuming corrosive strongly reducing liquid base ($N_2H_4$) used especially in fuels for rocket and jet engines and usually limited to use in dragster and landspeed racing cars.

**hydride:** a compound of hydrogen usually with a more electro-positive element or group. The storage of hydrogen in hydride is the safest (though heavy) way to store any practical motor vehicle fuel.

**hydrocarbon:** a chemical compound consisting of the two elements, carbon and hydrogen, in a wide variation of atomic ratios, loosely used to apply to all fossil fuels. Virtually all energy derived from combustion as heat (synonymous with energy) comes from "burning" (oxidation) of either carbon or hydrogen. All combustion (fuel) pollution comes from burning carbon with zero pollution from burning hydrogen, whose only exhaust product is the purest of water ($H_2O$).

**hydrocarbon emissions:** the undesirable exhaust products resulting from incomplete chemical combustion of a hydrocarbon-containing fuel consisting of unburned or partially burned fuel having the same molecular composition of the original fuel or a wide variety of chemical compounds consisting of varying ratios of carbon and hydrogen and combinations with other exhaust chemical elements. The ultimate product of carbon entropy (burning) is carbon dioxide ($CO_2$), of incomplete burning of carbon is carbon monoxide (CO), and of hydrogen is pure harmless water ($H_2O$). Nitrogen oxides, most commonly nitrous oxide ($N_2O$) is not fuel-related but a result of heat and pressure at anytime air is present because ambient air is about 78% nitrogen and 21% oxygen just waiting to hold hands when heated and/or squeezed.

**hydrocracking:** the refining of crude oil (petroleum) into motor vehicle gasoline by chemically cracking the hydrocarbons in a hydrogen-rich atmosphere.

**hydroforming:** the process for producing high-octane gasoline from petroleum napthas by catalytic dehydrogeneration and aromatization in the presence of hydrogen. The process of forming sheet metal into shapes as body parts for vehicles using dies and hydraulic pressure. Hydro stamping. Die formed.

**hydrogen:** the lightest and smallest element in our Periodic Table of chemical elements, the most plentiful element by weight and by actual atom count in our universe, the highest energy-dense chemical fuel, totally non-polluting when burned, and instantly recyclable The fuel of Space Ship Earth's future.

**hydrogen peroxide:** the unstable hydrogen/oxygen compound ($H_2O_2$) used as an oxidizing and bleaching agent, a medical antiseptic, and as a propellant in rocket motors.

**hydrometer:** a graduated floating instrument for accurate determination of specific gravities widely used in motor vehicle shops to measure the state of charge of an electric storage battery, the freezing point of coolant (anti-freeze) mixtures, and the correct portions of racing fuel mixtures such as methanol and nitromethane.

**hydronic:** of, relating to, or being a system of heating or cooling that involves transfer of heat by a circulating fluid (as water, oil, or Freon) in a closed system of devices and pipes.

**hydroplane:** the tendency of a vehicle tire to lose physical contact with the road surface when the depth of water and vehicle speed combine to create sufficient support/ lift force to "float" or aquaplane the tire footprint resulting in the total loss of braking or steering ability of the vehicle.

187

**hydropneumatic:**   the technology that combines and utilizes gas pressure and hydraulic pressure in various ways for vehicle suspensions and the mitigation of road/wheel bounce/shock.

**hydrostatic transmission:**   a vehicle drive system usually having a hydraulic motor powering each wheel with the pressurized flow of the working liquid from an engine-driven pump aboard the vehicle and with the return liquid piped back to the pump reservoir.

**hypersonic:**   of or relating to speed that is five or more times that of sound in air (about 741 miles-per-hour at standard conditions).   Mach V+.

**hypoid:**   a vehicle driving axle that incorporates a hypoid differential crown wheel (gear) on the transverse axle and a hypoid pinion (gear) on the longitudinal drive shafts to change the power flow direction 90°.

**hypoid gear:**   bevel gears with the axes of the driving and driven shafts at right angles, but not in the same plane, providing some sliding action between meshing teeth.

**Hyster:**   a tradenamed specialty vehicle with attachments for lifting various materials from ground-level to truck-height and unloading in/on the truck cargo body.

## LAGNIAPPE

**hairpin turn:**   on road or racetrack, a turn usually with a short radius and that is more than 90 degrees, often approaching 180°.

**hardener:**   the catalytic component of a two-part epoxy that assures the chemical setting (hardening) of the mixture.

**hard face:**   to apply or the applied very hard metal or alloy to wear or impact surfaces to reduce rubbing or pounding wear of soft base metal.

**hat trick:**   as for a hockey goalie, three consecutive successive victories in the same automotive competitive event (race).

**heating value:**   of a fuel, the _useful_ energy released during combustion.   In hydrogen-containing fuels the heat absorbed by the water of combustion is subtracted from the "higher chemical heating value" to provide a better assessment of potential work from the fuel.

**Hypalon:**   a special high-voltage insulating covering for ignition wires with excellent dielectric characteristics.

**hygrometer:**   any of several instruments for measuring humidity of ambient air.   Sling psychrometer.

# FEET OF CLAY

Many popular perceived Icons tend to reveal feet of clay when viewed critically at close range. No automobile or other engineering marvel of my acquaintance has ever revealed such a flaw. Not even the consistently meanspirited Ford "Tin Lizzie" that kicked me so many times when being hand-cranked--because I forgot to retard the spark control lever.

Not so with the human component of automobiles/engineering. "Hall of Fame" (lagniappe after the "M" definitions and "Dirty Linen" (after the "Vees" vented the author's "ire pressure" almost back to normal but left the curmudgeon's conscience unrequited. Reducing my "ire pressure" further may be jousting with another windmill. So Be It!

In 1937 the author, as a Junior undergraduate candidate for a degree in Mechanical Engineering, was selected for membership in Tau Beta Pi. In the early 1960s "Red" Matthews, who fathered Tau Beta Pi and was still in Virginia (before he moved to Tennessee, now the Tau Beta Pi headquarters, granted me permission to use our "Bent" fraternal insignia on my landspeed race car. Our mutual goal was to promote and publicize excellence in engineering. The "Bent" served us well, complemented by the car, a 1959 Abarth Zagato (the front-cover car of this Automobile Dictionary), that set several World Landspeed Records, was the first 100% hydrogen-fueled race car to traverse the Bonneville "Flying Mile", the first to do it with an internally-insulated (with plasma sprayed porcelain) engine, and the first to use a porcelain crankshaft.

In 1991, the new-age gurus of Tau Beta Pi refused my request for permission to use the "Bent" on a trophy to be awarded to the winner of the world's first hydrogen-fueled vehicle race. This curmudgeonly author placed an exact replica of the Zagato on the stainless steel trophy--proudly wearing its "Bent", as in the front-page cover picture on this Automobile Dictionary.

After years of internal strife and a few interstate scraps with the Utah Salt Flats Racing Association, The Southern California Timing Association and its subservient subordinate--Bonneville Nationals, Inc.--finally shook hands with USFRA in 1994, deciding to live by the same rules and honor each other's fastest timed speeds at the Salt Flats. The two rivals had been using the same clocks to time cars over the same two-way "flying mile" with neither recognizing the other's speeds.

The rebellion flared again and the "old guard" were voted out of SCTA/BNI management in December 1994. The "old guard" secretly tossed out the vote but the rebels forced a new election, more overwhelming than the first. Sounds good--too good. 'Twas.

The new boys "DISALLOWED ANY AND ALL HYDROGEN POWERED CARS AT THEIR EVENTS". The world's safest fuel, without a single untoward incident in 25 years of racing--OK to run hydrazine and nitromethane!

189

**I-Cars:** Although 70 automobiles wore I-marque names one is hard-pressed to name other than Italy's massive Isotta-Fraschini as noteworthy of mention. The sheer size of the car makes it a popular attraction in a number of car collections.

**I beam:** a metal structural shape with an I-shaped cross-section.

**ID:** abbreviation for identification and for inside diameter.

**ID card:** short for identification card but in actuality a better definition of a driver's license than is "license to drive". Not one of our 50 states' "driver's licenses" is ever validated by written and performance tests that truly determine the potential driver's competency. Insuring that one's license to drive is truly indicative of competency could reduce highway accidents and increase vehicle life to a significant degree. Don't we want to save our national resources and many lives at no cost to society?

**ID grinder:** an abrasive device used to accurately shape and size the inside diameter of vehicle parts such as engine cylinders, brake drums, or hydraulic (brake) cylinders.

**ID hone:** a fine-grit abrasive device used to polish the inside diameters of vehicle parts to reduce friction and provide a better seal between mating parts.

**ID reamer:** a tool with hardened steel cutting edges designed to insure a true inside diameter within a very small size-tolerance. Can be with fixed or adjustable cutting diameters or be tapered to any desired angle.

**idiot light:** a colored light on a vehicle instrument panel to provide visual indication of the operating condition of mechanical or electronic systems in lieu of digital or analog instrument readings. Green--normal or within limits. Yellow--warning of marginal performance or impending failure. Red--danger or immediate action required. Ideally, lights and finite instrument readings are complementary but too few vehicle operators possess the technical know-how to understand and interpret the significance of instrumented values--hence the idiot light.

**idle:** the state of an engine running so slow or so disconnected from the wheels (clutch disengaged or transmission in neutral) that power is not being used for useful work.

**idle screw:** an air or fuel metering adjusting screw that regulates engine speed or the mixture fuel/air ratio to insure smooth continuous engine operation within the manufacturers' specifications.

**idle speed:** the correct speed (rpm) of an engine to provide operation as dictated by the conditions or engine specifications.

**ignition:** the process or means of igniting a fuel mixture. The vehicle system that supplies the electric spark to the sparkplugs to ignite the fuel/oxidizer mixture that releases the heat energy within the internal combustion engine. The process has evolved from constant flame sources through the Rube Goldberg make-and-break mechanical monstrosities and points-condenser-coil combinations to today's solid-state computerized electronic marvels, some of which even have no moving parts.

**immersible fuel pump:** an in-tank pump designed for use when completely or partially submerged in the fuel thus preventing suction sub-pressures that can cause fuel vapor-lock.

**impact:** to impinge or make forcible contact as if in the collision of two vehicles or with a fixed object.

**impact socket:** usually with a six-point hex much stronger than hand-tightened sockets to withstand and transmit the torque that mechanical tightening machines develop.

**impact wrench:** an air or electric impulse hammering action converted to rotational torque for tightening or loosening bolt, nuts, or screws.

**impedance:** the apparent opposition in an electrical circuit to the flow of alternating current that is analogous to the actual resistance to the flow of direct current.

**impervious:** the characteristic of a material that prevents the entry of another substance. New automotive synthetic hoses are impervious to alcohols and solvents that damaged earlier natural rubber products. New paint finishes are impervious to the damaging effect of the ultraviolet rays of sunlight that once faded and bleached automobile paint finishes.

**import iron:** a disparaging colloquialism applied to foreign cars.

**impound:** the legal seizure and retention of a vehicle resulting from its violating applicable laws or being involved in certain accidents.

**incher:** that which has a dimension of a specified number of inches. Big-incher implies a large cubic-inch displacement engine usually meaning more than 350 cubic inches.

**incline:** any grade or slope making an angle with the horizontal.

**inclinometer:** an instrument for measuring the inclination to the horizontal or an axis of a vehicle. Also used for the leveling of a trailer or motorhome when parked. Used in maintenance shops for leveling machines.

**independent suspension:** a springing or suspension allowing each wheel to move independently of the other three in response to road surface imperfections.

**index:** a pointer or mark on an instrument or scale that serves to indicate a value, a quantity, or a limit.

**indicator:** an instrument that indicates a measurement, pressure, volume, or a material such as litmus (paper) that can indicate an acid or basic condition by color change.

**indium:** a malleable fusible silvery metallic element used in plating for bearings such as main bearings and rod bearings in vehicle engines.

**inductance:** the property of an electric circuit causing an electromotive force (voltage) to be induced by the variation of a current in itself or in an adjacent circuit. Sometimes called "crosstalk" between closely-spaced high voltage wires such as those to spark plugs.

**induction coil:** the typical ignition coil consisting of a primary coil through which flows the low voltage direct current that has been "chopped" (interrupted) by the ignition points causing the secondary coil windings to transform the low voltage into induced high voltage to "fire" the spark plugs.

**inert gas:** a noble gas inherently deficient in active qualities preventing its reaction or combination with other materials. Two such gases, argon and helium, are widely used in welding to shield the welding process from contamination from its surroundings.

**inertia:** the property of matter by which it remains at rest or in uniform motion in the same straight line unless acted upon by some external force.

**infield:** the area within the oval, round, or other-shaped automobile race course (track) usually reserved for garages, pit areas, and emergency safety vehicles and those involved in specific race support activities. Sometimes spectators who pay extra for the privilege are allowed access to the infield when there are suitable facilities.

**infrared:** light frequencies lying outside the visible spectrum at its red end with wavelengths longer than those of visible light.

**ingenious:** is there a better synonym for automobile? Marked by originality, resourcefulness, and cleverness in conception or execution--is it a man or a machine?

**inject or injection:** to forcibly insert fuel into the combustion chamber, the intake manifold ports, or the throttle-body of an internal combustion engine. The modern onboard computer talking to electronically timed injector nozzles can guarantee an exact fuel/air ratio as dictated by preprogramming the computer to respond appropriately to every possible driving condition.

**in-line engine:** an internal combustion engine with its cylinders arranged in one or more straight lines.

**inner tube:** a flexible air container fitting inside a tube-type tire providing a leak resistant seal to retain the air under pressure to support the weight of the vehicle and to help absorb road shock providing a smoother ride.

**input shaft:** the shaft transmitting power at engine/motor speed into a transmission that usually modifies the rpm as needed by the vehicle wheels for efficient performance.

**insert:** the bearing metal sleeve that is placed within a clamping holder to rub against the rotating journal to accept the wear of use and to be replaceable, thus preventing the replacement of a more expensive part.

**instrument:** an electrical or mechanical device used to provide observation, measurement, or control of vehicle functioning that is not normally available directly to the operator.

**instrument panel:** normally the dash (from dashboard) containing the vehicle instrumentation, sometimes supplemented by instrument clusters mounted nearby.

**insulate:** to separate conducting, radiating, or receiving bodies by means of nonconducting material so as to prevent transfer of electricity, heat, sound, or vibration.

**insulation:** nonconducting material used to separate conducting, radiating, or receiving devices.

**insurance total:** a vehicle damaged so extensively that the insuring agency agrees to pay the owner a specified amount, takes title to the vehicle, and sells it for reusable parts or to be rebuilt.

**intake manifold:** the ductwork that takes the incoming charge of air from the carburetor and directs it to the individual cylinders of an internal combustion engine. Sometimes cast/ machined into the cylinder head/engine block but usually a removable bolt-on assembly.

**intake stroke:** the downstroke of an internal combustion engine that takes in the charge of air and fuel to begin the engine cycle that converts fuel energy into motive power.

**intake valve:** the opening/closing device separating the combustion chamber of an engine from the outside air. Valves may be poppet, quill, reed, rotary, or sleeve designed to allow the incoming charge to enter before sealing the route so that the compression stroke can follow.

**intercooler:** a device for cooling a fluid (as air) between successive interconnected heat-generating processes. Commonly used to cool the incoming charge air heated by the compression of a turbo/supercharger before it enters the engine for the further compression stroke. A cooler incoming charge air improves efficiency and reduces unwanted fuel detonation.

**internal combustion engine:** a heat engine in which the combustion of fuel that generates the heat energy takes place inside the engine instead of in an external furnace.

**interrupter:** a device for periodically and automatically interrupting an electrical current. The distributor points of a vehicle ignition system or the flasher switch for turn signal or emergency flashing lights are two examples.

**interurban:** as a bus operating between cities or towns.

**inverter:** a mechanical or electrical device that converts direct current into alternating current.

**inverted engine:** an engine designed to run "upside down" with the crankshaft on the top end rather than the bottom end. Used in aircraft to provide better visibility by raising the center-line of the propeller. The Menasco and the Ranger are among the better known examples.

**inverted start:** the start of a vehicle race where the slower cars start in the first rows of vehicles and the faster cars--based upon qualifying event speeds--start in the rear rows. Intended to insure closer race finishes and more competition by the faster cars doing more passing.

**ion exchange:** the underlying principle of the fuel cell/ hydrolyzer concept. A reversible interchange of one kind of ion with another of like electrical charge. The fuel cell takes in hydrogen or other fuels and an oxidizer (oxygen or air) and gives off electricity or in reverse it uses an electrical input and produces hydrogen and oxygen from water.

**isooctane:** a flammable liquid octane used as a reference standard in determining the octane number (rating) of vehicle fuels. Octane number of a fuel indicates its ability to resist detonation (fuel "knocking").

**icing:** the formation of ice in the carburetor throttle and venturi area resulting from decreased temperature from fuel vaporization and humid ambient air that restricts charge-air flow causing engine power loss and stalling.

**idiot box:** a derisive but implausible descriptive slang expression for the automatic transmission. It's smarter than you--or I!

**ideal fuel/air ratio:** the chemically correct proportions of fuel (as one pound of gasoline) and air (14.7 pounds) necessary for complete combustion. Easily attainable but rarely attained.

**Iron Duke:** the marque of honor bestowed by many mechanics upon the American Pontiac four-cylinder, 151 cubic inch cast iron engine that has served so many cars so well for so many years. This engine has proven to be virtually indestructable.

**Iron Horse:** since coined in 1840, the railroad aficionado's pictured definition of a locomotive, especially a steam one. Some automobile aficionados have called the Bugatti Royale and the Maybach Zeppelin "Iron Horses" because of their sheer size and weight.

## THE IDEAL AUTOMOBILE

In Nirvana, the car that's outlived its mortgage and front-end depreciation, with a history of TLC and preventive maintenance and service by a technically literate driver/owner in communication with his machine--you! Only in Nirvana.

In Everytown of the Real World of Automobiles we've always known so many things that were wrong--but correctible. And we failed to address them. Since the completion of the very first four-stroke cycle or two-stroke cycle, fuel efficiency has been atrocious (about one-third of the fuel energy doing useful work) with one-third lost as heat out the exhaust and one-third wasted just cooling the engine. As small gains have been made, modern man has demanded more creature comfort, creating parasites that consumed more energy than the small efficiency improvements gained. Possibly the largest energy spendthrifts: air conditioning, climate control, softer ride, plush interiors, and power steering.

Utopia. Kill these parasites and their fellow-travelers: all power assists, cooling fan, mechanical distributor and valves, and water pump. Reduce drag, size, and weight to the irreducible. Internally insulate engines. Lengthen power stroke--shorten intake, compression, and exhaust. Dual, smaller tandem ICE <u>and</u> electrical, hydrogen-fueled power. Regenerate braking energy into flywheel <u>and</u> hydrogen storage. Gyro-stabilize. Optimize highway and vehicle speed compatibility. Perfect road/street directional/informational signs and automated vehicle locus establishment. Any "lost" driver represents 100% wasted energy (fuel)--0% vehicle efficiency.

**J-Cars:** 88 of 'em, but only three are noteworthy or remembered by our society: Jaguar, Jeep, and Jordan.

**jack:** any of various portable mechanisms for exerting pressure or lifting a heavy body a short distance. Something that supports or holds in position. A female fitting in an electrical circuit used with a plug fitting to make a connection with another circuit.

**jacket:** a covering or casing. A thermally insulating cover that encloses an intermediate space through which a temperature-controlling fluid circulates. Water jacket around a cylinder block or cooled exhaust manifold. To cover.

**jackleg:** a mechanic characterized by unscrupulousness, dishonesty, or lack of professional standards.

**jackrabbit:** the unnecessarily sudden and fast starting of a vehicle, usually in a reckless manner.

**jackscrew:** a screw-operated jack for exerting pressure or lifting.

**Jag:** colloquial shortening or abbreviation of the car named Jaguar.

**Jaguar:** a post-World War II British automobile noted for its style, performance, and excellent handling. With stately comfortable sedans and sporty roadsters and Grand Touring Coupes the Jag became the favorite of many affluent car enthusiasts.

**jalopy:** a dilapidated old automobile or airplane frequently like a member of the family to those needing cheap transportation.

**jam:** a crowded mass of vehicles that impedes or blocks traffic. To push forcibly. To make unworkable by jamming. To apply vehicle brakes suddenly and forcibly.

**japan:** any of several varnishes yielding a hard brilliant finish. Japan black in a baked-on hard coating of asphalt and a dryer as a metal covering. Often used to provide a dust and oil resistant finish for under-the-hood parts.

**jargon:** as with other technical/scientific disciplines automobile mechanics/aficionados have developed their own technical terminology or characteristic idiom to set themselves apart. The "inside" slang and ethnic slurs lead to frequent misunderstandings between car maintainers and uninitiated car owners.

**jato:** jet-assisted take-off rocket bolted to competition drag racers to impart rapid acceleration thrust force.

**jaw:** either of two or more opposable parts that open and close for holding and crushing between them. Vise or adjustable opening wrench or clamp are typical examples.

**jaywalk:** to cross a street carelessly or in an illegal manner so as to be endangered by vehicle traffic. Usually crossing at other than at a right angle or at other than at street corners or designated crosswalks.

**jeep:** originally a small general-purpose motor vehicle with 80-inch wheelbase, 1/4 ton capacity, and four-wheel drive used by the military services in World War II. Since applied to many similar vehicles for universal use.

**Jeep:** trademark name now used to identify civilian automobiles having characteristics of the military jeep under the Chrysler banner. Even their 4-wheel drive 4-door family sedan bears the family resemblance of the original military jeep.

**jeepney:** a Philippine jitney (5¢ fare) bus converted from a military jeep.

**jerk:** a single quick motion of short duration. Jerky, moving along with or marked by fits and starts as a vehicle that sporadically but repeatedly stops and goes because of a mechanical malfunction or an inept driver.

**jerrican or jerry can:** World War II German-designed narrow flat-sided 5-gallon liquid container configured to be strapped to the sides of military vehicles to carry extra fuel or water.

**Jesus clip:** in various sizes a usually hairpin-like retainer used in assembly of rod and linkage systems for easy removal or adjustment. The smaller sizes have a propensity for jumping into dark inaccessible openings eliciting the mechanic's expletive: "Oh, Jesus", "bejesus", or just plain "Jesus!"

**jet:** a usually forceful stream of a gas or liquid discharged from a narrow opening or a nozzle. An orifice that accurately meters or regulates liquid or gas flow. Carburetor jets metering gasoline flow are the most common. Jet thrust.

**jig:** a holding device used to maintain mechanically the correct positional relationship between a piece of work and the tool or between pieces of work during assembly.

**Jimmy:** colloquial slang for a General Motors vehicle particularly a GMC pick-up truck or 4-wheel drive utility vehicle. Gimmy.

**jitney:** slang for a 5-cent piece (nickel). A small bus that carries passengers over a regular route but according to a flexible schedule. With the original fare of a nickel it logically became the jitney.

199

**jitterbug:**  a handheld sander/polisher, air or electric-powered, that imparts jerky irregular random movements to the abrasive  pad so that no marks or pattern are formed on the area being polished.

**jobber:**  a vehicle parts and supplies wholesaler, usually small, who sells only to retailers or other wholesalers and to institutions at less than list prices.

**job lot:**  a miscellaneous collection of goods for sale as a lot usually to retailers.  A sales ploy frequently used to sell slow-moving stock and by auctioneers to speed up stock disposal.

**Jo-blocks:**  abbreviation for Johansen blocks.

**Johansen blocks:**  very precisely-sized hardened steel blocks of varying thicknesses used to calibrate measuring tools.  Jo-blocks are an intermediate step between the world metric stand-ards maintained in Paris and the American standards of linear measurement at our National Bureau of Standards.

**jog:**  a brief abrupt change in the direction of a road.

**Jordan:**  one of the greatest of all "assembled" automobiles with contemporary European styling and always powered by 6 or 8-cylinder Continental engines.  The Jordan Speedway Eight, and Great Line Eight sedans were topped off by the sporty Tomboy and Playboy rumbleseat convertible cabriolet roadsters all of which are highly-prized as collector cars.

**Jordan, Edward S. ("Ned"):**  "Ned" who conceived the unfor-gettable "Somewhere West of Laramie" magazine advertisement for his great cars will always be remembered for his cars but even better as the genius who introduced Madison Avenue pizzaz into the sale and promotion of automobiles.  His advertising copy creations are taught today as the epitome of promotion art in our leading business schools.

**journal:**  the portion of a rotating shaft, axle, roll, or spindle that turns in a bearing.  Crankshaft journals are most commonly encountered in vehicles.

**joystick:**  a lever capable of motion in two or more directions. Common to airplanes and computers.  Used in vehicles for remote control of small devices such as outside mirrors.

**J-pin:**  a push-pin retainer in the shape of a J with the curl of the J being used to hold it in place and as a handle for removal.

**jug:**  slang for the cylinder of a reciprocating engine.

**jump seat:** a folding seat between the front and rear seats of an automobile.

**jump start:** pushing a vehicle to use its momentum to turn the engine and then jumping into the vehicle and taking over its controls as it starts.

**junk yard:** a yard used to store usually resalable worn-out or wrecked automobiles and their parts.

**junk yard dog:** the inevitable guard dog at every junk yard big, ugly, and mean to guard the widespread cars and parts against pilferage and theft.


## LAGNIAPPE

**jack hammer:** an electrical or pneumatic percussive tool for applying repetitive pounding force. Rivet gun.

**jackshaft:** (1) An auxiliary/intermediate line shaft in a power delivery system. (2) A shaft that allows one large motor that runs continuously to power a number of machine tools by belts from clutch-engaged pulleys (3) A shaft in a vehicle engine, usually driven by the timing belt or chain, that may drive various accessory units.

**jack stand:** a portable sturdy support placed under a vehicle axle to provide safety should the jacking device fail when a mechanic is working underneath.

**jet car:** a reaction (thrust) driven vehicle using the rapid expansion of nozzle-directed combustion gases to provide propulsion force in lieu of wheel tractive force.


## JET SETTER'S THRUST

Dr. Nathan Ostich (MD) pushed his Flying Caduceus jet racer (the first of the racing class of reaction powered cars) to 360.000 mph at the Bonneville Salt Flats, Utah, in 1961. The doctor's speed has since been outstripped by many others: Craig Breedlove's Spirit of America at 526.28 mph in 1964 and by his Spirit of America Sonic One at 600.601 mph in 1965; Tom Green driving Walt Arfons' Avenger at 413.20 mph in 1964; brother Art Arfons Green Monster at 576.550 mph in 1965; Gary Gabelich's Blue Flame jet car, of the American Gas Association at 622.407 mph in 1970; and the current World Land-speed Record holder, Richard Noble of England, who drove his streamliner jet to 633.468 mph at Black Rock, NV, in 1983. Richard Noble is completing a new twin jet (each rated at 50,000 horsepower) car that features rear wheel steering similar to "Bucky" Fuller's 1933 Dymaxion. His speed goal is over 850 mph with plans to run again at Black Rock, NV, late in 1995.

202

**K-Cars:** historically, the letter "K" has not been generous to Automobiliana, leaving only a few memorable car words like Kammback, Kansas jack, Karmann-Ghia, Klaxon, and knee-action and even fewer (118) automobile names. Can you name other than Kaiser and Kissel? The Forney Transportation Museum has a Kissel collection featuring the great Kissel Airport Roadster, "Gold Bug", left on the flight line when Amelia Earhart took-off on her ill-fated Pacific flight intended to circumnavigate the world.

**Kadenacy effect:** researcher Michael Kadenacy's discovery and perfection of the phenomenon that the partial vacuum created by the sudden release of exhaust gases through the exhaust ports in two-stroke engines could improve exhaust scavenging.

**Kaiser:** for eight post-World War II years the Kaiser (the third automobile to wear the name) was the most successful independent car manufactured in the U.S. (1946-1953). Over 800,000 Kaisers were produced in the ex-B-24 Willow Run factory that Henry J. Kaiser, whose shipyards launched so many ships during World War II, and Joe Frazer bought from Henry Ford. Probably over-priced against "Big Three" models, Kaiser production ceased in 1954. The shades of the Kaiser returned to life for four years (1958-1962) in Argentina, but few cars ever rolled off the production line under the name "Carbella" before Renault presided over its demise.

**Kamm-back:** German aerodynamicist W. Kamm developed the technique of truncating the typical tail-cone in a way that reduced vehicle aerodynamic turbulence without the extended protuberance.

**Kansas jack:** a body-shop power tool capable of exerting great push/pull forces to straighten vehicle body panels or chassis frames.

**kapok:** a light resilient upholstery padding, prized for its flotation qualities, extensively used in vehicle cushions before the era of synthetic foams.

**Karmann-Ghia:** the German coachworks Karmann teamed with Ghia in reshaping the VW bug into a stylized convertible and coupe.

**kart:** a miniature automobile popularized as an affordable racing car for the masses. Go-kart.

**keeper:** any of various devices for holding (retaining) parts in place or together.

**kerf:** a notch, slit, or slot made by a saw or cutting torch.

**kerosene:** a flammable hydrocarbon liquid usually obtained by distilling crude oil, used as a fuel, solvent, or thinner.

**Kettering ignition:** the conventional vehicle electrical ignition system named for its originator Charles (Boss) Kettering of General Motors.

**key:** in addition to being the instrument by which the bolt of a lock or switch is turned a key may be a variously-shaped piece of material used to prevent the relative movement of two mating surfaces as the usually square bar used to secure a pulley on a shaft.

**keyhole saw:** a narrow-blade tapered saw used to cut curves of short radius and to start saw cuts outward from a circular drilled hole.

**keyless lock:** a lock as for a vehicle door that uses a mechanical combination, a coded magnetic strip, or an electronically actuated device in lieu of the conventional mechanical key.

**keyway:** the aperture slot in a lock having a flat metal key. The key-matching slot or grove in parts such as a shaft and a pulley that secures the pieces together when the key is in place.

**kick:** graphic description of an engine suddenly trying to run backward when the ignition is timed to fire too early. Kickback.

**kick-down:** the system or procedure used to cause an automatic transmission to shift into a lower gear when needed. Actuated by fully depressing the accelerator pedal.

**kick-over:** to begin to fire, the sporadic firing of an internal combustion engine as it starts to run.

**kick-stand:** a hinged/retractable support stand or arm, foot actuated, used to support two-wheeled vehicles (as motorcycles) when parked.

**kick start:** the act of using the foot-pedal and ratchet starter drive of a motorcycle to manually start its engine.

**kill:** slang for stopping or shutting off an engine.

**kill-switch:** the emergency switch or control used to instantly disconnect and disable operating engines or machinery.

**kilo:** as a prefix meaning 1,000 of its suffix-defined item. In computer language it means 1,024 (as kilobits or kilobytes) because 2 raised to its 10th power or 1,024 is the closest value to 1,000 in computer notation.

**kilogram:** 1,000 grams. The metric pound. 2.2046 U.S. pounds.

**kilometer:** 1,000 meters. The metric mile. 0.621 U.S. miles.

**kilowatt:** 1,000 watts, a measure of power equaling 1.34102 horsepower and becoming widely used in America in lieu of horsepower as we increasingly accept the Metric System of measurements.

**kinetic energy:** the energy associated with motion and all things mechanical. The life-blood of the automobile.

**king bolt:** a vertical bolt by which the forward axle and wheels of a vehicle or trailer or the wheeled trucks of a railroad car are connected with the other parts.

**kingpin:** the vertical or inclined shaft about which a vehicle steered spindle and wheel assembly pivots to determine a vehicle's direction of travel. Generally replaced in today's vehicles by upper and lower ball joints in automobiles and light-service vehicles.

**kink:** a short tight bend, curl, or twist caused by a doubling or winding of a part upon itself. Sometimes done deliberately for a needed purpose but usually indicating an imperfection likely to cause failure or difficulty in operation of the affected part.

**Kissel:** American automobile built in Hartford, Wisconsin, for about 25 years with the best-known model being the Gold Bug Speedster because Amelia Earhart chose one as her "Airport Roadster". Her "Gold Bug" is on display in the Forney Trans-portation Museum in Denver, Colorado.

**kit:** a set or collection of tools for a particular specialist's use. An engine mechanic's kit. A set or collection of all necessary parts for the repair of a particular vehicle component. A carburetor overhaul kit. A hydraulic brake cylinder repair kit. An ignition tune-up kit.

**Klaxon:** trademarked electrically operated vehicle horn or warning device.

**knee-action:** an automobile front-wheel suspension permitting independent vertical movement of each front wheel.

**knobby:** slang for a traction tire (as for mud and snow) using a tread with distinct knob-like protrusions.

**knock:** a heavy pounding noise from an engine usually indicating major engine failure as of a crankshaft main bearing. A light staccato rattle usually indicating fuel knocks from detonation.

**knock-kneed:** slang for severely inward leaning wheels of a vehicle usually from damaged or badly worn front suspension and/or steering components.

**knock-off:** a wheel-retaining hub nut usually affording quick removal/installation by hammering to loosen/tighten as for a race car pit-stop service.

**knock rating:** the number as octane number that indicates the fuel's resistance to detonation. Higher numbers indicate greater resistance to knocking. High/low octane.

**knock sensor:** an instrument that can detect the onset and progression of detonation in an internal combustion engine. The signal is used in modern vehicles to adjust engine ignition timing and fuel mixture to minimize or eliminate the detonation which is always harmful, sometimes destructive.

**knot:** a unit of speed, corresponding to 1 nautical mile per hour or about 1.15 statute miles per hour.

**knurl:** a series of small ridges or beads on a metal surface as of a tool handle to aid in gripping. To machine such a pattern in a metal workpiece.


## LAGNIAPPE

**keeper groove:** the machined groove near the tip of a valve stem into which the tapered valve spring keepers are locked to the stem.

**keyed:** the locking of a gear/pulley/wheel to a shaft with a key.

**kilohertz:** 1,000 cycles (hertz) usually per second of time.

**kit car:** a partially assembled car to be put together by the buyer.


### "HOW TO PICK WOMEN WHO CAN DRIVE CARS"
(Page 58, LITERARY DIGEST, 5 April 1924)
(By a woman motorist expert, Mrs. Edna Purdy Walsh)

Some day a man with a head for statistics is going to show us just how many deaths and disablements women drivers are responsible for, and just how much more, or less, dangerous they are at the wheels of motor-cars than are their brothers of the road. Everybody will concede that some women make poor drivers of automobiles.

Fortunately, every woman can determine, even before she actually undertakes to drive a car, whether she possesses or lacks the qualifications that will make her a successful pilot. This very short course of character reading and then looking into her own mirror will show much that was not clear to her before. The simple truth is that the ability to drive a car skillfully comes mainly from one faculty, namely the Sense of Weight.

How strong this quality is in us may be seen in the size of the eyebrow ridge just above the pupil of the eye. Eyes that have no prominence of eyebrows above the pupil never belong to a girl with a good sense of balance, "an unmistakable sign of a woman's driving ability." So with the ear, "in which the central section is larger." A firm mouth, with closed lips, indicates carefulness, while "full lips and a partly open mouth belong to impulsive women."

Notice the dancer, the flyer, the acrobat, the tight-rope walker, and the racer. In all of them the bony ridge above the eyes is well developed. This is the part of the brain where we take in our first impressions of objects and things seen with the eyes, where we sense color, form, and weight of objects and remember them. When this ridge is flat we do not retain for long in our mind the pictures that we see. The heavy Center of Weight eyebrow causes the brain to remember the balance of everything, its heaviness or lightness. Without it we are unable to balance our own bodies correctly--to make the hands and feet coordinate with the brain.

There are many dancers who make poor car-drivers but there are few drivers who love driving who cannot make good dancers, because the Center of Weight which they use all the time while driving makes them graceful and competent dancers.

The stout woman who takes on her weight mostly at the chest, whose fingers and foot are not too short, usually makes an excellent driver. But the stout woman who takes on her weight at the hips and ankles, and who possesses a smaller chest and smaller shoulders seldom makes a good chauffeur for the safety of herself and the world in general, unless we see on her forehead a good development of the eyebrow region. If the weight is taken on very much below the chest, the fingers and feet and bones of the leg are too small and short to be very efficient at the wheel and the pedals and gear-shifting levers.

Wide and high cheek-bones, in a face tapering toward the chin, means skill in movement of all kinds. The American Indian possesses these wide, high cheek-bones, and we wish he were driving our taxicab today, for he is both cautious and skillful in driving, even tho he may be a poor mechanic. The long and narrow face, narrow between the ears, is seldom skillful at the wheel of an automobile, believes Mrs. Walsh.

Love of praise or the Faculty of Approbation has caused many a woman to speed and to take too quick action in driving so that an accident has occurred, through her desire to show her friend her superior skill. Let's look at her lips to see if she is impulsive and fond of Approbation.

There is no hard and fast rule about light and dark hair as an indication of caution, but, generally speaking, the dark-haired women are slower to act and will pay more attention to detail. Also, as a rule, the deep-seated eye is slower to act than the eye that is very prominent in the face.

Another faculty is important in first-class driving, especially country driving: that is the Sense of Locality. This is seated in the forehead about an inch above the eyebrows and the Faculty of Weight. When the forehead across its central section and about an inch above the center of the eyebrows is hollowed, the driver has a hard time finding her way home, when taken away from the streets on which she habitually drives. She cannot feel her direction.

Would this "politically correct" Op-Ed, written by a woman in that liberal bastion of womanhood, the LITERARY DIGEST, be "politically correct" today? Wanna' bet?


## MYTHOMANIACAL U. S. PATENTS

Everyone knows that "U.S. patented" affixed to an item guarantees that it performs/works as claimed. Like Hell, it does! Will Rogers said it best: "Our problem is not that we don't know so much, but that so much of what we know just ain't true!"

In my basement collection are about a couple hundred fraudulent gimcracks sold as automobile "bolt-ons" that are guaranteed to significantly improve economy, efficiency, exhaust pollution, and performance. Every one is U.S. Patented. Not a damn one works as claimed, clearly violating our "Truth in Advertising" statutes.

About half involve the burning or air or water in your car. Impossible! But millions have been/are being sold today.

Astronaut Gordon Cooper was indicted, pled nolo contendere, and signed a consent decree in Federal Court for selling his patented "G-R Valve", claiming increased mileage and all that "good stuff".

President Gerald Ford was a major stockholder in the gimmick "Webster-Heise Valve" (patented), showcased in the June 1983 READER'S DIGEST as "one of the biggest technological advances in 40 years.... eliminate the need for high-octane gasoline and improve mileage 20%....fewer pollutants....save $300 per car in pollution controls and at least 600,000 barrels of OPEC oil a day, according to Congressional Research Services." And desalinate sea water at half the current cost. Outright lies in 1983 and in 1995 but the "Valve" continues to be widely sold using those same false claims.

The "Lord told" Stanley Meyer, Grove City, OH, how to extract the energy of 2½ million barrels of oil from one gallon of water (patented) in your car and fly an airplane around the world--twice, on one tank of water. Is Stan or his patents lying? Hell yes!

USA TODAY, 6-19-84, reported that George Miller, Johnstown, PA, "burned" 100% air in his Buick and even "made his own Air" when driving! Patented! I know a bridge in England that you can buy!

Where the Hell was/is the FTC? And "Truth in Advertising"?

**L-Cars:** L-marques, 271 of 'em, have an international flavor of greatness with four from Great Britain: Lagonda, Lanchester, Lea-Francis and Lotus, three from "Uncle Sugar": Lincoln, Locomobile, and Lozier, two from Italy: Lamborghini and Lancia, and one from France, the Leon-Bollee. Many of the also-ran "Ls" came close to being mentionable but automobiliana forgot why they should be remembered.

**laboratory:** a place equipped for experimental study in a science or of a technology (such as motor vehicles) or for actual testing and analysis of vehicle equipment. In earlier days cars evolved slowly with major contributions from competitive racing while today most engineering developments are born in the laboratory and proven before the public can buy them. Even with today's computerized sophistication there is rarely anything that is truly new in automobiles--just minor refinements in age-old theories, principles, and practices.

**lace curtains:** a descriptive phrase for paint "runs" on vertical surfaces of a vehicle exterior that form a pattern reminiscent of hanging lace curtains.

**laced spokes:** many early-day wire wheels used a great number of spokes of very small diameter wire requiring a kind of crisscross pattern of interweaving giving the appearance of open-weave lace. Double and triple "lacing" was used for added strength as in racing wheels.

**lacquer:** any of various clear or colored synthetic coatings that typically dry (by evaporation of its volatile solvents) to form a hard, smooth, glossy finish for vehicle exterior surfaces.

**ladder ramp:** an inclined track resembling a ladder with close-spaced rungs for loading on a vehicle or other platform by driving or pulling up the incline. The cross-bars (like rungs) provide lightness and good traction.

**ladder truck:** a special purpose vehicle as the fireman's hook-and-ladder truck designed to carry ladders for various purposes.

**ladle:** a deep-bowled spoon-like container with a long handle used for melting and pouring babbitt (lead) as for bearings.

**lag:** to trail behind or follow as electric current lags the electric voltage when flowing in a circuit whose resistance is predominantly inductive.

**lagniappe:** a small gift or service given to a customer by a merchant to complement a purchase. Something given or obtained gratuitously or by way of good measure. The thirteenth roll of a "baker's dozen".

**lag screw:** a screw with a head (square in early vehicles) allowing the use of a wrench to apply greater tightening torque than is possible with a screwdriver.

**laminar flow:** smooth streamline flow of a fluid (as air) near a solid boundary. Important to the design and construction of all very fast vehicles and inherent to the improvement of the coefficient or aerodynamic drag for all vehicles.

**laminate:** a product made by laminating layers of similar or dissimilar materials cemented or heat bonded under pressure to gain strength, rigidity, or other desired characteristics. Safety glass is usually a laminate of two outer layers of glass with an inner layer of material to resist cracking or shattering.

**lamp:** any of various devices for producing light or heat. Light bulb.

**lampblack:** a finely powdered black soot deposited in incomplete combustion of carbonaceous materials and used chiefly as a pigment in paints and enamels and in industrial/chemical processes.

**landau:** a closed automobile body with a folding top over the rear passenger compartment.

**landau irons:** a gracefully curling S-shaped hinge on each side of a landau top to facilitate the folding of the top.

**landaulet:** a small landau with an open (no top) driver's seat and an enclosed rear section having a folding top.

**landmark:** a distinctive geological formation or shape, an unusual man-made structure, or a specifically designed visible marker that a vehicle driver can use to maintain his place orientation.

**landslide:** the usually rapid downward movement of a mass of natural rock, earth or artificial fill on a slope. A cause for concern where highway routes have been excavated into the sides of hills, ridges, or mountains leaving steeper than natural slopes rising from the highway level.

**land yacht:** a three-wheel wind-driven recreation vehicle consisting usually of a bare-frame structure and a single sail and used on areas of packed sand as beaches and deserts. Used pejoratively but aptly to describe the very large and overly ostentatious automobiles of pretentious public figures seeking undeserved attention.

**lane:** a usually marked strip of a roadway for a single line of vehicles.

**lantern pinion:** a gear pinion having cylindrical bars instead of gear teeth.

**lap:** the complete circuit of a vehicle or other race course. To pass another contestant in a race and to proceed to increase the lead distance until it exceeds the distance of one full circuit of the race course. To shape or fit by working two surfaces together with or without abrasives between them until a very close fit is attained. To join as two sheet metal panels by having a portion of one extend over the edge of the other for fastening by any of several means.

**lap belt:** a vehicle safety seat belt that fastens across the occupant's lap and most effective when complemented with appropriate shoulder belts.

**lap joint:** a joint made by overlapping two ends or edges and fastening them together.

**lap leader:** in a race as with automobiles the contestant who leads the field of entrants at the end of a particular lap. Sometimes prize money is paid to the leader of each lap regardless of his position at the completion of the race.

**lap robe:** a covering as a blanket for the legs, lap, and feet especially of a passenger in early automobiles before the days of on-board heaters.

**lap time:** the elapsed time required for a participant in a closed course race as of automobiles to complete one full circuit of the race track. Timed for each vehicle for each circuit completed.

**large car:** a meaningless classification by the DOE/EPA to indicate the relative size of automobiles. Undue emphasis is given to trunk size resulting in some really big cars being classified as compact or even subcompact when they are in fact bigger than misclassified large cars. A compact Rolls-Royce is much bigger than a large standard Chevrolet in the arbitrary bureaucratic rating system. Many compacts being bigger and heavier than large categorized vehicles completely distorts fuel-mileage comparisons that the rating system purports to make meaningful to the public in choosing an economical vehicle.

**laser:** light amplification by stimulated emission of radiation. Coherent light. The technological basis of many speed and motion-detecting instruments as the laser speedgun used to monitor vehicle speed on our highways. The concentration of energy into a very small beam of laser light makes possible the welding, cutting, drilling, and shapeforming in industrial production never before possible. Military applications of laser include distance measuring, target identification, and weapons direction with extreme accuracy.

**lash:** mechanic's jargon for clearance or size tolerance as in valve lash or gear-train back-lash.

**Lastex:** trade name for an elastic yarn consisting of a core of latex rubber strand wound with threads of cotton, rayon, nylon, or silk used in making flexible stretch coverings as seat covers that will fit a variety of sizes of seats.

**last-in and first-out:** of, relating to, or being a method of accounting that values all stock on hand at the cost of the last lot received.

**latch:** any of various devices in which mating mechanical parts engage to fasten but usually not to lock something. As a vehicle hood latch.

**late model:** a descriptive phrase for vehicle age usually implying new or no more than three years old.

**latent heat:** heat given off or absorbed in a process (as fusion or vaporization) other than by a change in temperature.

**lateral:** to describe a brace, a force, or a movement situated on, directed toward, or coming from a side direction.

**latex:** a plant-produced milky fluid used to make rubber and related materials. A water emulsion of synthetic rubber or plastic obtained by polymerization and used especially in protective coatings (paint) and as adhesives.

**lath:** a thin narrow strip of wood or perforated metal used as a goundwork for plaster, slates, or tile overlays. In early vehicles commonly used to support flexible fabric roof coverings.

**lathe:** a machine in which the workpiece is rotated about a horizontal axis and shaped by a fixed or hand-held cutting tool.

**latitude:** freedom of action or choice as regards a vehicle mechanic's judgment regarding the extent, quality, and cost of required repairs. The geographical and position identification by latitude will become more important as vehicle location becomes possible from on-board computerized outerspace satellite data.

**lattice:** a structural framework of crossed metal or wood strips used because of its light weight and strength.

**launch:** to spring forward or set into motion, sometimes descriptive of the driver who commonly races away from a red light or other stop at excessive speed.

**Lava soap:** trademarked cleansing soap favored by mechanics because its gritty abrasive scrubs the work-related grease from the skin for ease in after-work wash-ups.

**layout:** the act or process of planning or laying out in detail, to mark (work) for drilling, machining, or filing, a step whose precision and accuracy determine the ultimate fit and finish of the end product.

**lay-up:** as in taking a vehicle out of service for extended storage. Also to cover a form with a plastic fabric such as fiberglass cloth prior to applying the resin bonding material for hardening into the permanent shape of the form or mold.

**LCD:** liquid crystal display, a constantly operating display (as of the time, or radio frequency) requiring very little power that contains segments of liquid crystals whose reflectivity/visibility varies according to the voltage applied to them to form the desired numbers, letters or symbols.

**leach:** to dissolve out by the action of a solvent liquid as to flush particulate deposits from a cooling system of a vehicle.

**lead:** the entry edge of a cutting tool as a threading tap designed to initiate the machining in the exact direction desired.

**lead:** a heavy soft malleable ductile plastic but inelastic bluish-white metallic element used in pipes, cable sheaths, batteries, solder, type-metal, and shields against radio-activity. In early vehicles a filler used in smoothing body panel dents prior to painting.

**lead-in:** the length of wire used through a wall barrier such as through a fire wall or an antenna wire through a body panel of a vehicle.

**leading edge:** the foremost edge of any aerodynamic shape, the forward part of something that moves or seems to move.

**lead time:** the time between the beginning of a process, project, or repair and the appearance of final results or completion.

**lead foot or lead shoe:** descriptive slang for the vehicle driver who consistently drives too fast or recklessly, indicating a heavy application of the vehicle accelerator pedal.

**leaf spring:** a vehicle spring made of superposed strips, plates, or leaves. Buggy springs.

**leak:** with so many vehicle fluids (water, antifreeze, fuels, oils, greases, brake, windshield washer, airconditioner, power steering, shock absorbers, batteries, etc.) the seepage and

and escape of these materials becomes the bane of the vehicle mechanic's profession when Murphy's Law "that what <u>can</u> leak <u>will</u> leak" operates.

**leak-down test:** an engine compression/condition test now favored over the old-time compression pressure testing of an engine by cranking with a pressure gauge inserted at the spark plug hole. The leak-down test consists of pressurizing the combustion chamber from an external source and using specially designed pressure gauges to measure the leakage around rings, valves, and other leak-prone areas. An exact diagnosis that identifies a problem and quantifies the extent or magnitude of the problem.

**lean:** a vehicle fuel/air mixture that has a deficient amount of fuel for perfect chemical burning (stoichiometric proportions). Excessively lean mixtures lead to overheating, loss of power, and misfiring although a proper degree of lean-burning can reduce undesirable exhaust pollutants.

**lean-to:** a building or structure having a roof with just one slope. Typical of early-day vehicle garages.

**lease:** a contract by which one conveys a vehicle for a specified term and for a specified rent (as three years at $300 per month).

**lease back:** to invest by purchasing a vehicle and leasing it back for whatever use by the lessee The purchaser usually gains a higher return as the investor and the lessee gains by reducing capital invested and sometimes reduced liability.

**lease/buy:** a method of selling vehicles allowing the purchaser to rent/lease for a specified time period with the option of retaining the vehicle at the completion of the lease by paying an additional specified amount. Lease/buy option.

**leather:** any of many animal skins dressed, tanned, or variously finished and used as a durable, sometimes luxurious, upholstery material for vehicles.

**leatherette:** an inexpensive trademarked substitute for real leather.

**LED:** light emitting diode, a semiconductor diode that emits light when subjected to an applied voltage and that is used as an electronic instrument display as in the digital vehicle instruments of all types.

**left-handed thread:** a screw fastener that has reversed threads requiring counter-clockwise turning for tightening sometimes used to prevent connecting non-compatible systems that could be dangerous when combined. Necessary for retaining wheels, gears, or pulleys whose rotation could tend to loosen the retainer.

**left-handed tools:** tools designed specifically for use by left-handed mechanics to improve efficiency and safety in the workplace.

**legal age:** as the age, prescribed by law that must be attained before a driver's license or right to drive can be given.

**legal steal:** car jargon for the repossession of an encumbered vehicle for nonpayment for the vehicle or for its repairs after an appropriate authority has authorized repossession.

**legend:** an accurate and well-deserved designation for many of our great automobiles of the past. No list can ever be definitive or complete but must include: Duesenberg, Bugatti Royale, Rolls-Royce, Henry Ford's "999", Sir Malcolm Campbell's "Blue Bird", Bucky Fuller's "Dymaxion", Mercedes Gullwing 300SL, Ferrari, Lamborghini, Maserati, Citroen, Porsche, Pierce-Arrow, Henry Ford's Model "T", Art Arfon's "Green Monsters", Stutz DV-32, Stanley Steamer, Rivaz' 1813 grand char mechanique, K-B Lincoln, Maybach Zeppelin,

**leg-room:** space in a vehicle in which to extend the legs when seated. A recognized comparative measurement for evaluating the passenger comfort of a vehicle.

**lemon:** a pejorative car-critic term implying a car that cannot be successfully repaired. Many states have passed so-called "lemon law" requiring a manufacturer to replace or to buy-back any vehicle judged by political standards as deserving their "lemon" label. Every reasonable mind will conclude that such laws are just mean-spirited bashing of our great American institution, Automobiliana.

**Le Monstre:** the name given to a massive race car, for obvious reasons, designed and built to compete in the famous 24-hour Le Mans race by Briggs Cunningham of West Palm Beach, FL. Briggs' best finish was third in the 1954 Le Mans. Though known best for its size the Le Monstre also used water-cooled brakes.

**lengthen:** to extend or to make longer.

**letter of credit:** a letter from a banker to a correspondent as a vehicle manufacturer certifying that the named dealer therein is entitled to draw on him or his credit up to a certain sum.

**level:** a device for establishing a horizontal line or plane by means of a bubble in a liquid that shows horizontal adjustment to the horizontal by moving to the center of a slightly bowed glass tube.

**level crossing:** a grade crossing in which both crossing roadways, railroads, or pedestrian paths (or any combination thereof) cross at the same level.

**level of significance:** the probability of rejecting the null hypothesis in a statistical test when it is true.

**lever:** a bar used for prying or dislodging something. A rigid piece that transmits and modifies force or motion when forces are applied at two points and it turns about a third point. A projecting piece by which a mechanism is operated or adjusted.

**leverage:** the action of a lever or the mechanical advantage gained by it.

**Levi's:** trademarked blue denim work apparel often worn by vehicle mechanics.

**levorotation:** left-handed or counterclockwise rotation.

**liable:** obligated according to law or equity. Subject to appropriation or attachment. Exposed or subject to some usually adverse contingency or action. The stance or standing of a motor vehicle operator that dictates the need for liability insurance protection.

**liaison:** communication for establishing and maintaining mutual understanding (critically needed between vehicle owner/operators and vehicle shop/maintainers).

**license:** a permission granted by competent authority to engage in a business or occupation or in an activity otherwise unlawful. In the world of vehicles operators are universally licensed, all selling dealers are licensed and mostly bonded, but vehicle mechanics are not licensed but should be. A true license implies verification of competency that is based upon knowledge and skill. Vehicle operator licenses do not meet such standards but could and emphatically should.

**licensee:** one that is licensed.

**license plate:** for vehicles a metal plate or tag that attests that a valid legal license has been issued for the vehicle to which it is affixed. Evolutionary needs are arising that dictate the necessity for a national uniform vehicle license. Fragmented accounting and administration of motor vehicles into 50 different approaches no longer serve the needs of the country.

**lickety-split:** the driving of a vehicle at great speed.

**lien:** a charge upon real or personal property for the satisfaction of some debt or duty ordinarily arising by operation of law.

**lift:** an apparatus or machine used for hoisting heavy weights. Typical vehicle shop lifts are usually hydraulic cylinder powered and capable of lifting entire vehicles to the most efficient height for each maintenance or repair operation.

**liftgate:** an upper rear panel (as on a station wagon) that opens upward.

**lift truck:** a cargo truck with an attached load lifter.

**light:** that which makes vision possible. An electromagnetic radiation in the wave length range including infrared, visible, ultraviolet, and X-rays traveling in a vacuum with a speed of about 186,281 miles per second. Traffic light--a red/green control signal.

**light bulb:** incandescent lamp.

**light-emitting diode:** see LED.

**lighten:** to reduce weight as of moving vehicle parts to minimize weight-caused wear or vibration. To use lighter materials throughout a vehicle to reduce gross weight to save fuel consumption.

**lighter:** an electrical resistor-heating device usually vehicle-dash-mounted for lighting cigarettes, cigars, or pipes.

**lighter-than-air:** having less weight than air of equal volume.

**light fast:** resistant to fading or color change when exposed to light, especially sunlight such as vehicle exterior paints and upholstery materials and dyes.

**light guide:** fiber optics usually bundled and used for telecommunications with light waves.

**light meter:** a light-sensitive photocell for measuring illumination and used for the automatic dimming of vehicle headlights when another vehicle with lights is approaching and for turning on safety/clearance lights as daylight fades.

**light pen:** a pen-shaped device for direct interaction with a computer through its cathoderay tube display.

**light pipe:** fiber optics or a solid transparent plastic rod for transmitting light lengthwise.

**ligroin:** any of several petroleum naphtha fractions that boil in the range $20°$ to $135°$ C. and are used especially in solvents.

**like-new:** every used car salesman's fantasy-view and descriptive phrase for every used car on the used car lot.  Like-false.

**limit:** a stop or barrier to restrict the travel, movement, or action at an exact place or time for safety considerations or for proper functioning.

**limit stop:** a positive stop-block to mechanically stop the horizontal movement of a lathe tool holder or to stop the vertical movement of a drill press or milling machine drill chuck or tool holder.

**limit strap:** a leather, cable, or metal loop around an axle and a vehicle frame member to restrict the allowable movement of the axle in the direction away from the fixed frame.

**limit switch:** usually a microswitch that when touched will stop the electrical power to the moving part of a machine thus preventing damage.

**limited access highway:** a high-speed roadway with no grade crossings, stop signs, or traffic signals with entry/egress allowed only at major intersecting roadways by means of traffic circles/ramps that prohibit all cross-traffic.

**limited liability:** liability of investor/owners as frequently specified by statute to be less than the liability of more active participants in a venture.

**limited partner:** a partner in a venture who has no management authority and whose liability is restricted to the amount of his investment.

**limited warranty:** a warranty/guarantee that specifies and offers reduced promises of what will be replaced or repaired on the warranted item.

**limo:** limousine.

**limousine:** a large luxurious often chauffeur-driven sedan that has a glass partition separating the driver's seat from the passenger compartment.  Some are used commercially in specialized scheduled service such as airport passenger pick-up and delivery.

**limousine liberal:** pejorative for a wealthy political liberal.

**linchpin:** a locking/retaining pin as used through a crosswise matching hole in an axle or shaft to secure wheels, gears, or pulleys.  Commonly used to secure removable trailer hitch ball connectors in a matching receiver fitting on the tow vehicle.

**linear:** of, relating to, resembling, or having a graph that is a line and especially a straight line. Involving a single dimension.

**linear measure:** measure of length or a system of measures of length.

**linear motor:** a motor that produces thrust in a straight line by direct induction rather than by the use of gears. New generation tracked vehicles of advanced design use linear motors.

**linear slide rule:** an engineer's calculating device that adds logarithms representative dimensional lengths to solve complex mathematical problems. Contrast with a circular slide rule.

**line-haul:** cargo trucks or passenger buses that operate from fixed-terminal to fixed-terminal with no intermediate stops, pick-ups, or deliveries.

**line-up:** to align pieces for assembly or joining with a proper fit.

**lingo:** the special vocabulary of a particular field of interest. Mechanic's lingo.

**link:** any of various connecting devices as: a chain link, a short connecting rod with a hole or pin at each end, the fusible member of an electrical fuse.

**lip:** the sharp sealing edge of various rotating, wiping, or scraping sealing devices. Lip seals.

**LPG:** liquefied petroleum gas.

**liquefied petroleum gas:** a compressed (until liquid) gas that consists of flammable hydrocarbons (as methane, propane and butane) used as a motor vehicle fuel. LPG.

**liquefy:** to reduce from a gaseous to a liquid state.

**liquid:** neither solid nor gaseous characterized by free movement of the constituent molecules among themselves but without the tendency to separate.

**liquid air:** air compressed and cooled until it reaches the liquid state. Used chiefly as a refrigerant and selectively evaporated to obtain the individual gaseous constituents.

**liquidate:** to settle a debt by payment or other settlement. To convert assets as parts and vehicles into cash.

**liquid crystal:** an organic liquid whose physical properties resemble those of a solid crystal and capable of responding to electrical signals making it useful for instrument displays.

**liquid crystal display:** LCD.

**liquidize:** to cause to be liquid.

**liquid lock:** hydraulic lock. The "locking" of an engine/cylinder/piston because of the incompressibility of a liquid when a confined cylinder becomes filled with a liquid. The reason why the leaking of water, oil, or liquid fuel into an engine cylinder can cause catastrophic failure.

**liquid measure:** a unit or series of units for measuring liquid capacity. Most commonly used in vehicle vocabulary: ounce, quart, gallon.

**list price:** the basic price of an item as published in a catalog, price list, or advertisement but rarely adhered to because of many and varied discounts.

**liter:** a metric unit of capacity equal to the volume of one kilogram of water at $4^\circ$ C. at standard atmospheric pressure. Used throughout much of the world as the standard measure of vehicle fuel and engine displacement. One liter is equivalent to 1.0567 quarts and 61.02 cubic inches.

**litharge:** a fused lead monoxide widely used in early vehicles mixed with glycerin as a sealant and thread-locking medium.

**litmus paper:** a test paper that changes color with Ph of a material touching it indicating the degree of acidity or alkalinity.

**litterbag:** a bag used (as in a vehicle) for temporary storage of refuse awaiting disposal.

**livery:** archaic. Delivery, the act of delivering. Livery barn, a place for storing vehicles.

**living:** implies useful functioning of a vehicle. A race car must remain living until the completion of a race.

**Lloyd's:** an association of underwriters in London specializing in insuring for high risk ventures of almost every conceivable kind such as vehicle races and even crash testing.

**load:** whatever is put in a vehicle for conveyance. Cargo is load that has been assembled or packed as a shipping unit. To place anything aboard a vehicle.

**loading dock:** a floor level at the usual height of truck beds (floors) to facilitate the loading/unloading of the vehicle.

**loading ramp:** an incline fixed or portable from ground-level to vehicle floor height used to move a load aboard the vehicle without vertical lifting. Most used for loads that are mobile or ambulatory: other wheeled-vehicles, livestock.

**load leveler:** an automatic or manual mechanism designed to maintain a vehicle reasonably level with changing loaded weights, usually accomplished with pneumatic/hydraulic cylinders or variable resistance torsion bars/springs.

**lobe:** a curved or rounded projection or division as on an engine camshaft valve-lobe.

**locate:** to set or establish an exact spot or place. The act or process of locating. In vehicle vernacular: to find or determine the center of a workpiece to be machined, to locate a cylinder head for exact fit on a cylinder block, to locate a malfunction or broken part by diagnosis.

**lock:** a fastening as of a vehicle door or trunk operated by a key or combination. To secure in a fixed position or state as to lock the brakes, gears, ignition, or steering.

**locker room:** a vehicle shop room with lockers for mechanics to store work uniforms and other personal effects.

**locking differential:** a mechanism that creates the effect of a solid driving axle thus preventing one wheel from spinning when there's reduced traction. Know as a "locker".

**locknut:** a separate nut screwed down hard on another to prevent it from slacking back, unscrewing, or vibrating loose. Also a nut so constructed that it locks itself when screwed up tight.

**lockout:** the withholding of employment by an employer and sometimes the whole or partial closing of his business establishment to gain concessions from or resist demands of employees.

**locomote:** a colloquial expression for describing the action of a fast-moving vehicle. It really "locomotes".

**lodestone:** a natural magnet (magnetite) possessing polarity. Permanent magnets have wide use in ignition magnetos and magnetic-drag instruments.

**log intake manifold:** an engine manifold resembling a tree-log with 90° branches to the individual cylinders. Appears to create a resistance to smooth gaseous flow but can be very efficient if accurate computations of dimensions consider gas inertia.

**logo or logotype:** an identifying statement, slogan, or design (usually copyrighted or trademarked) known as the marque of a particular make of vehicle.

**London Double-decker:** the two-level buses first used in London as high-density peoplemovers for congested urban areas.

**London taxi:** the small plain-looking but very efficient and utilitarian people-mover.

**longeron:** a fore-and-aft main framing member or beam as part of a vehicle frame consisting of metal tubing. Typical of many race cars.

**long haul:** used to describe bus/truck routes and vehicles operating over great distances as contrasted to urban or city uses.

**long-range:** relating to or fit for long distances.

**long track:** used to describe a racetrack usually longer than one mile and to denote race cars specifically designed for such tracks.

**long wheelbase:** used to describe a vehicle with longer than the average or typical length for its make and model. Usually a special purpose vehicle for hauling long cargo or additional passengers.

**loom:** a sheath or envelope used to encircle and hold a number of separate wires bundled together.

**loop:** a ring or a curved piece used to form a fastening or a handle. A closed electric circuit. To connect electric conductors so as to form a loop.

**loose:** not rigidly fastened or securely attached. Having relative freedom of movement.

**lope:** used to describe the operation of an engine when it experiences a slightly erratic firing of the cylinders.

**lorry:** a long low-bed usually open truck with no sides. Any of various trucks running on rails.

**loud:** descriptive of a vehicle with a defective muffler or operating without a muffler.

**loud pipes:** an exhaust system that amplifies the engine's sound sometimes with expanding megaphone-like shapes.

**louver:** an opening through any outer panel of an automobile provided with one or more fixed or movable slots or fins to allow flow of air but to exclude rain or sun or to provide privacy.

**"Love Bug":** the theatrical name for the Volkswagen automobile featured in the Hollywood motion picture of that name.

**loving cup:** a large ornamental vessel with two or more handles presented as an award for excellence now commonly known as a trophy.

**low ball:** to give a customer a deceptively fictitious low price on a vehicle or vehicle repair with the intent of later raising that price.

**low beam:** the short-range focus of a vehicle headlight.

**low-boy:** a very low heavy duty vehicle trailer designed for loading and hauling heavy equipment or cargo with a minimum of lifting in on-loading and off-loading.

**low drag:** a vehicle of aerodynamic design that minimizes the air drag, lowering the power required for propulsion thus permitting higher economical speeds.

**low end:** to denote the gearing when operating in the power producing ratios of a vehicle transmission.

**lower:** to reduce the overall height of a vehicle lowering the top (chopping) or reducing the road clearance (lower spring fittings, reduced spring tension, dropped-center axles) sometimes for cosmetic reasons or increased stability from the concomitant lowering of the vehicle center of gravity.

**low frequency:** a radio frequency between medium frequency and very low frequency.

**low-low:** to describe the lowest ratio gear in the transmission of a heavy duty truck or tractor: Also called "double low".

**low pressure:** having, exerting, or operating under a relatively low pressure. A low pressure tire that provides a smoother more comfortable vehicle ride.

**low profile:** a vehicle that is physically lower than the average height. A vehicle whose profile is wider than its cross-section height

**low tension:** having a low potential or voltage. The vehicle voltage circuit, usually 12 volts currently, that operates the usual accessories, as contrasted to the high tension or ignition system.

**low test:** applied to vehicle gasoline usually meaning low octane, low volatility, and low price.

**lube:** mechanic's jargon for lubrication and lubricants.

**lubricant:** a substance (as grease or oil) capable of reducing friction, heat, and wear when introduced as a film between rubbing materials.

**lubricate:** to make smooth or slippery. To apply a lubricant to. To act as a lubricant.

**lubritorium:** an ostentatious and rarely used name for a facility for lubricating motor vehicles. Now referred to as "Fast-Lube", "Quick Lube", "Quick Change", "Grease Monkey", "No-Wait-Lube", et al.

**Lucite:** trademarked name for an acrylic resin or plastic consisting essentially of polymerized methyl methacrylate. A substance of exceptional clarity, durability, and usefulness.

**lug:** to operate a vehicle at too low a speed in too high a gear. To move heavily or by jerks. A vehicle wheel attachment fastener. Lug bolt. Lug nut.

**luggage:** suitcases or traveling bags for a traveler's personal belongings and necessities.

**luggage carrier/rack:** an accessory enclosure usually of framework designed to transport additional luggage beyond the capacity of a vehicle's trunk.

**lumen:** a unit of luminous flux equal to the light emitted in a unit solid angle by a uniform point source of one candle intensity.

**luminous paint:** a coating containing a phosphor (as zinc sulfide activated with copper) and so able to glow in the dark.

**LWB:** long wheelbase.

## LAGNIAPPE

**L:** the letter "L" used on an automatic transmission shift quadrant marker for positioning the shift lever in the low-gear position. Usually the bottom or rearmost position of the PRNDL standardized sequence of marking.

**ladder frame:** vehicle chassis frame with parallel side rails and perpendicular cross members.

**lakester:** a recognized Dry Lakes/Bonneville racing class requiring all wheels located outside the widest body section with no wheel aerodynamic coverings allowed. Evolved from the early aircraft belly-tank/drop-tank bodied race cars.

**lambda:** the Greek-letter symbol for air/fuel ratio compared to stoichiometric (chemically perfect with lambda = 1 being perfect, lambda greater than one (lambda = 1+) indicates a lean mixture, and lambda less than one (lambda = -n<1) a rich mixture.

**laminated core:** a magnetic core consisting of stacked thin plates as used in an electrical device utilizing an alternating or pulsating current to minimize losses caused by hysteresis (molecular polarity switching) heating of the core material.

**lateral acceleration:** in a turn, the centrifugal force in g's that pushes a vehicle toward the outside of the turn. Cornering force.

**lead free:** as all highway-legal fuel today (1995) gasoline without tetraethyl or other lead-compound additives.

**leading arm:** an independent suspension with the wheel attached to an arm ahead of the arm's fixed pivot. Several Citroen models used such a front suspension.

**lean burn:** an engine that runs satisfactorily on an exceptionally lean mixture by first igniting a small segment of the air/fuel charge that is over-rich.

**lean surge:** a "hunting" oscillation of an engine rpm when the mixture is excessively lean.

**Le Mans:** the annual 24-hour Grand Prix race in France.

**Le Mans start:** a race begun by requiring all drivers to run a stated distance to their cars, jump in, start up, and Go!

**Lexan:** GE's trademarked plastic that is heat resistant, shatterproof, transparent and widely used for racing canopies.

**L-head:** an engine with exhaust and intake valves on the same side of the cylinder bore in the block casting. The typical flathead.

**liftback:** vehicle body with the rear window an integral part of and opening with an upward-hinged access opening.

**line mechanic:** a large-shop mechanic working "on the line" usually specializing as in engines, electrical, brakes, et al.

**live axle:** a rotating shaft delivering power to the wheels as contrasted to a dead axle, non-rotating with free-turning wheels.

**low rider:** a usually illegal modified suspension, wheels, and body/chassis barely clearing the road surface and often with hydraulic cylinders causing rapid up-and-down motion leading to the disparaging description "Mexican jumping bean".

**LSR:** a racer's abbreviation of Land Speed Record. There are literally hundreds of record classes, usually broadly categorized into types of propulsion (wheel or reaction/jet thrust), type of fuel (gasoline or a mixture of exotic additives such as nitromethane, nitrous oxide, hydrazine, et al.), or body style/type, which include stock coupes, roadsters, sedans, and various trucks. The elite class is the "streamliner", also called the LSR class.

**M-Cars:** M-marques outnumber the number of car-related words that share the letter M on the front end. Mercedes (Germany 1901- ) out of alphabetical order, leads the pack of M-marques in longevity, in numbers manufactured, in innovative/techno-logical impact upon world automobiliana, and in name recogni-tion. The MacDonald (US 1923-1924) is number 1, alphabetically, but Jimmy-the-Greek will give long odds that you never heard of this steam car built in Garfield, Ohio. The little MG (GB 1924- ) has to have the third spot in the front row of any M-car race, certainly as the leader of all unnamed cars (just initials, for Morris Garage). Maserati (Italy 1926- ) quali-fies first in the speed trials with the shades of Alfieri Maserati or Juan Fangio cheering whoever sits behind the wheel. Every big-car-aficionado will vote for a V-16 Marmon (US 1902-1933) to lead the M-field, remembering that Ray Harroun won the first "Indy 500" in 1911 by floor-boarding a Marmon 6. Emil Jellinek started the three-pointed star dynasty and the Mercedes Marque in 1901 when he commissioned Wilhelm Maybach and Daimler to build him a high performance car (today recog-nized as the forefather of the modern cars). Jellinek entered his new car in the 1901 Nice Week Speed Trials and the La Turbie Hill Climb under his pseudonym, Mercedes (his daughter's name). His driver, Wilhelm Werner, won both races, initiating a dynasty of winning ways, highlighted by Ralph DePalma's win-ning the "Indy 500" in 1915 and Count Masetti finishing the 1921 Italian Grand Prix and the 1922 Targa Florio races in front of everybody in essentially the car that had won "Indy" and the first, second, and third places in the 1914 French Grand Prix. And a Mercedes engine did the same hat trick again at the 1994 "Indy 500". Abou Ben Adem said it well of the three-M's, Maserati, Mercedes, and MG, "may their tribe increase".

**macadam:** a bituminous binder used as a surface coat/layer for motor vehicle roadways. Black top. Asphalt.

**macadamize:** to construct or finish a vehicle road by compact-ing into a solid mass a layer of small broken stone/gravel into a convex (crowned) surface and finishing the surface with a binder as asphalt or cement.

**machinable:** the property of a metal or alloy that allows form-ing, machining, and shaping into useful vehicle components/ parts.

**machine shop:** a workshop where metal is machined to size and assembled into mechanical devices. Vehicle machine shops are specialized as to tools and technicians.

**machinist:** a specialized mechanic who is adept with machines/ tools capable of shaping and forming metal.

**MacPherson strut:** a hydropneumatic and sprung suspension member (telescoping) used for independently supporting each wheel/vehicle corner as steerable (front) or fixed (rear) assemblies with the strut upper end fixed to the body shell or chassis frame and the lower end located by beams or linkages, as an A-Frame, to maintain location by counteracting transverse and fore-and-aft movement.

**MAF:** mass air flow, the weight of air entering the vehicle induction system at a given speed.

**MAF sensor:** a measuring device in the air stream in a vehicle intake that telemeters quantitative air flow information to the engine control computer which uses the information to maintain the programmed Fuel/Air equivalence ratio for best engine performance and lowest exhaust emissions.

**mag:** mechanic's abbreviation for magneto.

**Magnaflux:** trademarked name for a testing process using a magnetic field and ferrous particles (iron filings) to reveal hidden cracks/defects in a metal as visible surface patterns. Non-destructive testing.

**magnesium:** a silver-white light malleable, ductile metallic element, abundant in nature, widely used to form lightweight alloys for vehicle structures and components.

**magnetic chuck:** a worktable or holder of pieces to be machined that has a strong electromagnet for grabbing and holding ferrous material/parts for machining.

**magnetic clutch:** a clutch that is engaged/disengaged by an electromagnetic field pulling friction surfaces together or apart.

**magnetic plug:** usually a drain plug as for an engine crankcase, or a differential/ transmission that incorporates a permanent magnet which attracts and holds bits of metal circulating in the lubricant until the next scheduled oil change when the drain plug is removed and the trapped metal is flushed or brushed off.

**magnetize:** to impart magnetic properties to another metallic object by contact with another magnet or by insertion of the metallic object into a magnetic field.

**magneto:** a very high-voltage magnetoelectric alternator that uses permanent magnets with flux-cutting coils to produce (and time) the spark energy for the ignition systems of internal combustion engines. No external electricity needed.

**magnetomotive force:** a force that causes (induces) a flux of magnetic induction.

**magnetron:** a diode vacuum tube whose electron flow is controlled by an externally applied magnetic field to generate power at microwave frequencies.

**main-beam:** the high-beam of a two-filament vehicle headlight that reaches farther ahead, for safety when driving faster at night. Upper beam.

**main bearing:** the alignment, location, stiffening, and support bearings for each crankshaft journal, usually integrally located in an engine block with a bolted halfcap forming half of the bearing and retaining the bearing and crankshaft in place.

**mainframe:** a computer cabinet containing its main components and circuitry usually implying a large fixed unit with the capability to interface with and support satellite computers.

**main jet:** the primary fuel-metering orifice in a carburetor that supports the normal power requirements of a vehicle engine. Idle jet, Power jet, and Accelerator/pump jet.

**main shaft:** mechanic's term for the power-output shaft of a multi-ratio vehicle transmission. Tail-shaft.

**make-and-break:** a realistic depiction of most vehicle ignition systems: an electrical circuit is closed (made) allowing the build-up of magnetic lines of force (flux) in a transformer (coil) and the capacitive build-up in a condenser. The circuit is then opened (broken) causing the decaying magnetic field of the coil's high-voltage windings to induce the voltage-caused spark at the spark plug gap which is augmented by the condenser discharge. Modern electronic devices are replacing the electromechanical ignition systems of yore.

**malfunction:** partial or total failure of a vehicle component or system to function as designed for proper performance.

**malleable:** a material capable of being extruded, formed, or shaped by hand or machine hammering or by pressure as of rollers.

**mandrel:** a usually round or tapered arbor, axle, shaft, or spindle inserted (and locked or secured) into a hole in a piece of material (workpiece) to support it during machining. The shaft and bearings on which a tool (as a circular saw, grinding wheel, or polishing pad) is mounted.

**manhole:** an access hole through which a mechanic may go to work on the enclosed equipment or interior of a large enclosure as an underground storage tank or tanktruck cargo container. Hand hole. Access panel.

**manifold:** a collection or system of ducts, hollow castings, and/or pipes that divides or unites fluid flow from one location for delivery to a number of locations or from a number locations for delivery to one point. Exhaust manifold. Fuel manifold. Intake manifold.

**manifold absolute pressure:** the fluid pressure within a manifold as measured in absolute units, usually taken from a mercury manometer column height reading in inches or millimeters or from an aneroid barometer in pounds-per-square-inch or atmospheres.

**manifold heater:** a heat-exchanger in a vehicle's intake manifold using exhaust temperature or coolant temperature to eliminate carburetor ice and/or to help fuel vaporization under adverse climatic conditions. An exhaust manifold heat-exchanger with ductwork conducting heat to the interior of a vehicle for occupant comfort. Manifold stove.

**manifold pressure:** the difference between the average static pressure within an engine's intake manifold and the ambient surrounding atmospheric pressure. Called negative (depression or vacuum) under virtually all operating conditions with natural asperation and positive (pressure) when using a boosted environment of supercharging. In a computer-controlled engine, sensors/tranducers relay manifold pressures to be used in automatically modifying ignition timing, fuel/air ratios, and exhaust emissions. Manifold vacuum.

**manual brake:** a vehicle hydraulic or mechanical braking system actuated exclusively by the driver's foot or hand strength (unassisted) applied to foot pedals or hand levers.

**manual choke:** a carburetor fuel-mixture enrichment device operated by the driver through flexible push-pull control cables or linkage from the driving position.

**manual shift:** a geared transmission that is shifted by the driver's hand or foot power applied to levers or pedals. Stick shift.

**manual steering:** a vehicle steering system actuated exclusively by the driver's physical strength (unassisted) applied usually through a steering wheel and rarely through a tiller or foot pedals.

**manual transmission:** a multi-gear-ratio vehicle transmission whose gear ratios must be changed (shifted) by a driver-operated (unassisted) mechanism.

**marker light:** a warning light on a vehicle, especially trailers without a powered vehicle's lighting requirements, usually intended to indicate (mark) the external dimensional extremes (height, length, and width) of the vehicle.

**Marmon:**  the great American classic automobile.  See M-Cars.

**marque:**  a manufacturer's name, brand name, or trade name as of an automobile.

**marsh gas:**  methane ($CH_4$) a chemical burnable gas naturally produced by biodecomposition of organic material as in a marsh or swamp.  Swamp gas.

**mass:**  one of the fundamental quantities on which all physical measurements are based. The property of a body that is a measure of its inertia, commonly taken as the amount of material (stuff) that it contains thus causing it to have weight in a gravitational field.  Scientific metrology is totally dependent upon exact definition of mass (weight), distance (length), and time.  Foot-pound-second.

**master cylinder:**  a pedal-controlled hydraulic pressure pump (cylinder) that provides primary power for doing work to one or more slave (satellite) cylinders as used to actuate vehicle brakes or clutches.

**master switch:**  an electrical switch that disconnects a vehicle's entire electrical circuitry and electrically operated components from its electrical supply, usually the vehicle's storage battery, and as near the battery connection (terminal) as practically possible.

**match box:**  a very small but usually accurately detailed model of an automobile, highly prized by children of all ages and by serious grown-up aficionado-collectors.

**matte:**  a usually smooth even surface that is not shiny or reflective but with a dead/dull appearance as frequently used on vehicle interiors and exteriors to minimize unwanted reflections or glare.

**maximum brake horsepower:**  the peak power produced by a vehicle engine while being tested on a prony brake or engine-dynamometer against an air, electrical, or hydraulic load.

**mean effective pressure:**  the average combustion pressure pushing against an internal combustion engine piston throughout its power stroke.

**mean piston speed:**  the average speed usually in feet-per-second of an engine piston throughout one complete stroke (up or down).

**mechanical efficiency:**  in a vehicle engine, the ratio of the output shaft horsepower to the indicated horsepower developed within the engine cylinders.  The difference (loss) is almost totally attributable to pumping losses and friction if the engine is stripped of its parasitic accessories (alternator, fan, water pump, et al.).

**mechanical transmission:** a vehicle with conventional meshing gears that are mechanically shifted and using no electrical or hydraulic components.

**medium speed diesel:** a diesel engine usually of large size operating from 250 to 1000 revolutions in a marine, or stationary industrial, application.

**Merry Oldsmobile:** the song and advertising catch-phrase stemming from the days of the Curved Dash Oldsmobile.

**metal fatigue:** a crack, crystallization, or weakened streak in a metal piece caused by bending, heating, stress, and/or vibration.

**metal shear:** a metal-working tool designed to cut like a scissors and that is used to cut (shear) large metal sheets for forming into panels as for ducts and equipment cabinets.

**metering jet:** a carburetor fuel jet of a size to provide a desired fuel flow through a wide range of engine power requirements.

**metering rod:** a carburetor fuel control rod whose taper or stepped diameters, that when raised or lowered in a fuel metering jet, throttle the flow through the jet to the exact quantity needed to match the air flow through the venturi.

**meter-kilogram-second:** the metric unit statement of the fundamental quantities of physical measurement. The MKS system.

**methane:** our fossilized natural gas ($CH_4$) from underground gas wells, when pure.

**methanol:** a light volatile flammable poisonous liquid alcohol ($CH_3OH$) derived primarily from natural gas as a chemical feedstock, long used as an antifreeze, denaturant for ethyl alcohol (ethanol), and a solvent, now widely used as a vehicle fuel and as an additive to gasoline to reduce unwanted exhaust emissions. Its energy density is about one-third that of gasoline.

**methyl alcohol:** methanol.

**metrology:** the science of weights and measures or of measurement. A system of weights and measures.

**mho:** the backward spelling of ohm, the electrical unit for the measurement of resistance defined in MKS units as the resistance of a circuit in which a potential difference of one volt produces a current flow of one ampere. Numerically, one mho (the practical unit of conductance) is the reciprocal of one ohm.

**micro:** a mathematical prefix meaning one millionth of the suffixed word.

**mid-engine:** a vehicle engine located near the longitudinal center between the axles of a vehicle.

**midget:** a very small version of a thing. A midget race car is about one-half the size of a half-mile or sprint car. The Austin-Healey "Sprite" and the MG "Midget" were highly-desired, widely-sold, and virtually identical midget sports racing roadsters that dominated world-class racing for their sized cars for many years.

**midnight requisition:** mechanic's lingo for the surreptitious theft of gasoline by siphoning from a vehicle tank or the stripping of easily-removed accessories, usually at night. "Bought with an Oklahoma credit card."

**mid-size:** an official vehicle classification by the DOE/DOT/EPA used to compare CAFE fuel consumption ratings that has little resemblance to common sense, e.g., when a Rolls-Royce is classified as a "Compact" and a Chevvy or Ford is classified as "Very Large"--something's rotten in our Puzzle-Palace in the Beltway.

**MIG welder:** Metal Inert Gas welder is an arc welder system that shields the welding flame and molten metal puddle with a gas, usually argon or an argon mixture, and incorporating an automatic wire-feed (fill-rod), freeing one of a welder's hands.

**mike:** the commonly spoken abbreviation for micrometer, the frequently used mechanic's precision measuring-tool. Microphone.

**milli:** a prefix meaning one one-thousandth.

**milepost:** the roadside mileage markers usually placed at one-mile intervals alongside the right side shoulder of major vehicle highways.

**milling machine:** an essential vehicle repair shop machine tool on which material or parts are clamped to a movable surface (carriage or way) to be cut, drilled, or shaped by rotating milling cutters.

**miles-per-gallon:** the accepted standard expression of fuel efficiency for highway vehicles by technical illiterates, the American public. Miles-per-gallon is a phony and unquestionably misleading so-called standard that has no scientific credibility or value. The myriad imponderables involving fuel comparisons falsify every efficiency standard when the fuel is not named, when there is no correction or quantification for comparative energy content, fuel volumes (gallons) are meaningless because size is as flexible as Jello or a rubber band or a leaky balloon. Fuels must be compared by energy content (BTUs) per unit of mass/weight (pound). Linking volumes (gallons) of fuel (a false standard) with miles (a legitimate fundamental standard) guarantees a fallacious and meaningless comparison. A gallon of gasoline contains about three times the energy (BTUs) of a gallon of methanol and therefore will propel a vehicle about three times the number of miles. A gallon of any fuel can have a wide disparity in energy (BTU) content due to the change in weight of a gallon (with changing temperatures) because of its coefficient-of-temperature expansion.

**miles-per-hour:** a scientifically accurate measure if each fundamental quantity (distance/mile and time/hour) is determined accurately.

**mineral oil:** oil, usually for use as a vehicle lubricant, distilled from petroleum (crude oil) or other fossil feedstock as shale, et al.

**mineral spirits:** a petroleum distillate used extensively around vehicle maintenance facilities as a solvent and parts cleaning fluid.

**minibike:** a small one-passenger motorcycle with a low frame and raised handlebars used primarily for short errands as around a large vehicle shop, parking lot, or storage area.

**minibus:** a small bus (usually about three-quarters of full-size) for comparatively short trips and small loads. Minivan.

**Mini Moke:** a small jeep-type front-wheel-drive (and 4 x 4) quasi-military all-purpose light personnel transport and utility vehicle originated by Austin in England in the early 1960s.

**mint:** an adjectival word description of a vehicle implying outstanding appearance and/or condition when compared with all vehicles of its type.

**mirror finish:** a painted or bare metal surface that is so highly-polished that it acts as a mirror to reflect images.

**misfire:** the failure (usually intermittently) of a vehicle engine to fire on one or more cylinders due to lack of sufficient ignition spark and/or ignitable fuel mixture.

**missed shift:** the failure of a vehicle driver to properly select and shift into the next sequential ratio (up or down) when "changing gears" of a manual transmission.

**modulator valve:** an automatic transmission valve that integrates changes in engine manifold vacuum and vehicle driveshaft rotational speed to provide a signal that controls a boost valve in the transmission pressure regulator that modifies output pressure from the hydraulic pump thus controlling transmission output to suit driving conditions.

**module:** a collection of electronic devices (usually solid state) and circuitry (usually printed) in a replaceable "black box" usually attached to the distributor of an engine with electronic ignition to control spark timing and other system operational parameters.

**mohair:** a fabric or yarn made wholly or in part of the long silky hair of the Angora goat, once prized for automobile or other rough-wear upholstery.

**Mohs' Scale:** a scale of hardness of minerals that ranges from #1 (talc) to #15 (diamond), and that is useful in selecting the proper grit to match grinding and polishing requirements for vehicle applications.

**molybdenum disulfide:** the metallic compound $MoS_2$ used as an additive to greases and oils to modify their lubricating properties and as a dry-powder lubricant.

**momentum:** the property of an object as a vehicle that determines the length of time required to accelerate from a standstill to a given velocity or to decelerate from a given velocity to a standstill. Primarily a function of mass plus well-known variables in vehicle design that determine acceleration and braking time and distance.

**monkey wrench:** a wrench with one fixed and one movable jaw at right angles to a straight handle.

**monoblock:** used variously to describe the arrangement of vehicle engine castings, e.g., a cylinder block and cylinder head cast as one inseparable unit, a cylinder block and crankcase cast as one, all cylinders of a multi-cylinder engine cast as one piece, or a Vee-block with such a narrow Vee that only one flat cylinder head is used for both banks of cylinders.

**monocle windshield:** a circular glass vehicle windshield used on early sports cars primarily as an ostentatious showpiece.

**monocoque:** a type of construction of a vehicle body in which the outer skin carries all or a major part of stresses, with the chassis as an integrated part of the body.

**monohead:** a single-casting, flat cylinder head that covers both banks of a narrow-Vee cylinder block.

**monogram:** the owner's sign of identity, usually name initials or coat of arms engraved or in cloisonne on a brass badge affixed to outside doors or badge bars of prestigious automobiles.

**monorail:** a single-rail track, usually overhead, used for high-speed mass transit vehicles.

**moon disc:** a smooth wheel-cover (hubcap) used for improved appearance and aero-dynamics of the wheels on sports and racing cars.

**moon roof:** a usually transparent openable panel, for ventilation and visual pleasure, that is built into the roof of hard-top vehicles.

**Moped:** a trademarked lightweight low-powered motorbike that can also be human-powered (pedaled) by the rider.

**mother-in-law-seat:** a single-passenger seat that required the occupant to face to the rear or the side of an automobile, and located near the rearmost portion of the vehicle and usually uncovered.

**motion sensor:** a mechanical or optical device that can detect motion or objects and utilize this information to alert the driver or to control certain vehicle functions, e.g., the wire feeler attached to a low outboard location around a vehicle periphery that makes an audible scraping noise when it contacts an obstacle (curb warning); the photo cell that detects oncoming other-vehicle lights and automatically dims the headlights; a pressure switch that warns of partially open doors, hood, or trunk lid; the optical scanner that detects the flash from a reflector mark affixed to a rotating flywheel and triggers an ignition timing circuit; and myriad other such applications.

**motocross:** an automobile or motorcycle competitive speed contest (race), usually on a tight closed course often over natural terrain with deliberate challenging obstacles that test driver/vehicle stamina and durability. Autocross. Steeplechase. Obstacle course.

**Motometer:** an engine temperature gauge by Boice in 1913 that used a bulb/capillary thermometer, glass-encased, that attached to the radiator cap and provided a reading visible to the driver through the windshield, and that was standard equipment on the more expensive cars, or available as an extra-cost accessory for cheaper cars, through the early 1930s.

**motor:** another designation, as is "engine", for the motive-power unit of a vehicle. Motor usually denotes electric power and engine is applied to a heat-generating fuel system powered machine.

**motorcade:** a procession of vehicles usually with a common purpose and destination.

**motorcycle:** a two-tandem-wheeled vehicle with one or two rider saddles and sometimes a sidecar with a third supporting wheel.

**motordrome:** a circular (usually portable structure) steeply-banked race track for motorcycles (and rarely for small race cars) that primarily provides thrills (and noise) for carnival crowds.

**motor home:** a self-contained traveling home constructed on a large heavy-duty vehicle (truck or bus) chassis.

**motor scooter:** a low small 2- or 3-wheeled motorized vehicle resembling a child's scooter and having a bench seat so that the rider does not straddle the engine.

**Motor Method:** one of two methods used to determine the octane number (rating) of a vehicle fuel that compares the fuel being tested by direct comparison with a standard (usually 100 octane fuel) in a Cooperative Fuel Research (CFR) engine. The other, Research Method, is based more upon scientific analysis of a fuel. The two method results are averaged to give the Octane Number (Rating) used nationally to rate the anti-detonation characteristics of fuels. Motor Octane Number. Research Octane Number.

**mpg:** miles-per-gallon.

**mph:** miles-per-hour.

**mud flap:** a hinged deflector-panel behind the wheels of a large vehicle to block the spray of road debris downward and out of the path of following vehicle traffic.

**mud guard:** a fixed rigid deflector of road debris usually attached underneath or near the outer edge of a vehicle fender near the top-rear quadrant with a curved or angled surface oriented to direct liquid spray and small particulates outboard into the airstream around the vehicle. Protects the vehicle to which attached, often at the expense of vehicles in adjacent lanes.

**muffler:** a usually enlarged-section of a vehicle exhaust system that slows the gas velocity, cools and shrinks the exhaust volume, and uses baffles and acoustical absorbers to reduce the decibel level of the exiting gases, particularly of the peak pressure-pulse annoying pop or explosive blast.

**multi-disc clutch:** a power-transmitter disconnect device composed of a number (often 20 or more) of alternative drive/driven plates separated by matching friction-material plates. The design and engineering principle of multi-disc clutches allows smoother starts of heavy vehicles with high-horsepower fast-revving engines and significantly improves clutch effectiveness and useful life.

**multi-fuel engine:** a vehicle (or other) internal combustion engine capable of running satisfactorily on more than one fuel or type of fuel. The most common are "Dual Fuel" using either gasoline or natural gas, propane, butane, ethanol, methanol, et al., usually aimed at exhaust pollution reduction, usually heavily subsidized by direct federal grants or tax exemptions, and usually hyped as "alternatives" (to petroleum or fossil) which informs every literate scientist-to-shade-tree-mechanic that "their" fuel is inferior, as defined by Noah Webster meaning: "What we use when we can't get what's best, Ersatz, an inferior substitute. Always!" Face the scientific reality that any mechanical internal combustion engine can eat any fuel that any human/man one-liter internal combustion engine can metabolize.

**multi-grade oil:** a vehicle/engine oil that has been refined and compounded to react like a thin/low-viscosity (SAE #5, #10 or other) when it's cold outside and to act like a thick/heavy-viscosity (SAE #50, #100, or other) on a tropical summer day. Multi-viscosity.

**multi-leaf spring:** a vehicle suspension spring of long flat sections stacked sandwich-like to improve load-carrying, reduce metal fatigue and hysteresis heating, and assist in obtaining a desired spring rate. Buggy spring. Elliptical or semi-elliptical spring.

**multi-point injection:** a fuel injection system that discharges timed fuel-pulses directly into the combustion area of each individual cylinder or as near as practical to each individual intake-valve opening. Throttle-body injection.

**multi-stage turbine:** a turbine engine of any application that has more than one row or stage of working blades (buckets). Single-stage turbine (Pelton Wheel).

**multi-throw crankshaft:** an engine crankshaft with more than one off-set crank journal each of equal angles of less than 180° to adjacent cranks, excepting two-cylinder engines whose cranks are 180° apart. Common to in-line-cylinder engines.

**muscle car:** a vehicle with significantly more horsepower and performance than is ever required or can ever be used in normal vehicle operation by any rational driver. Such vehicles are designed for and advertised to that segment of the buying public that is motivated by excessive hedonism and irrational machismo.

**mushroom valve:** the conventional internal combustion engine exhaust and intake poppet valve configuration (or shape) having a relatively small diameter shaft (stem) topped by a disc-shaped head resembling a long-stemmed mushroom.

## LAGNIAPPE

**machinist's blue:** a spray color coat (usually blue) for metal to be scribed with lines for machining to shape and size. Dykem.

**Magnaflow:** similar to Magnaflux but using a liquid with suspended magnetic particles that concentrate along cracks/faults, emphasized by ultraviolet light and fluorescene dye.

**mallet:** soft hammer with plastic, rawhide, or rubber head faces.

**M-85:** vehicle fuel that is 85% methanol, 15% gasoline. E- Ethanol.

**micron:** one millionth of a meter. Micrometer.

**monel:** a very strong alloy used in high-stress, high-temperature areas in engines such as exhaust valves and long favored for boat propellor shafts because of its salt-corrosion resiatance.

**Mopar:** Chrysler's trademark for its Parts Division, a name that is often used by enthusiasts to apply to all Chrysler cars and parts.

**MTBE:** an emissions-reducing, octane-enhancing additive for gasoline. Methyl tertiary butyl ether.

**MVMA:** Motor Vehicle Manufacturers Association. A trade group.

## AUTOMOTIVE HALL OF FAME (SHAME?)
(A Good ol' <u>WHITE BOYS</u>' Club)

Know it? Believe it? Like it? Or not? It's a fact!

AHF was born AOT (Automobile Old Timers) October 18, 1939 in New York City, moved to Washington in 1960, and later moved to a used car lot in Warrenton, VA, because Miss Dorothy ("Dottie") Ross, administrative assistant (The Head Man) didn't like the 42-mile commute to work. Thus began Dottie Ross' 22 year reign, seeming to indicate that women deserved citizenship in the automotive world. Wrong!

In 1967 Walter P. Chrysler, Henry Ford, Charles F. Kettering, and Alfred P. Sloan, Jr. became the first "automotive famous" voted into the Hall of Fame--seeming to validate the AOT's original intent to honor "individuals associated with the design and manufacture of cars". Wrong again!

In 1971 AOT moved to the present site of its Hall of Fame Building on the Northwood Institute campus in Midland, MI, with a potential move (1995) of the administrative offices into downtown Motown (Detroit). October 29, 1976, when the ribbon was cut to the new home of history there were 45 "Old Timers" enshrined--all Caucasian males!

In 1981, AOT underwent a name-change operation, becoming Automotive Hall of Fame, Inc. Soichiro Honda penetrated the color barrier, becoming the first non-white in the "good ol' boy's club" (1989). Now there are two: since Eiji Toyoda marched through the crack in the white wall in 1994. So in 1995 the 130 "Famers" are still a good ol' _virtually_ white and _literally_ boys' club. Nary a single woman (or married) among 'em!

Strange statistics, indeed, considering that Miss Dottie Ross _literally_ ran and _headed_ the good ol' boys' club--for 22 years. Several years ago some simple mental gymnastics validated that many women had track records a lot faster than some of the "boy-Famers" enshrined in the Hall. Three stood above the crowd: Dr. Betsy Ancker-Johnson, Vice-President of General Motors Corporation; Madam Marlene Cotton, Vice-President and Director of Racing, Citroen Cars Corporation; and Dr. Roberta Nichols, Principal Research Engineer, Ford Motor Company (later becoming Ford's electric car maven). Since all were limited to those deceased or retired nothing could be done until one did it. Dr. Ancker-Johnson did retire in 1992.

Her nomination was submitted in 1994 for the '95 Hall of Fame reading: Vice-President (the first woman Vice-President of any major automobile manufacturer) General Motors 1979-1992; Associate Laboratory Director for Physical Research, Argonne National Laboratory (1977-1979); served under Presidents Nixon and Ford as Assistant Secretary, Department of Commerce (Science and Technology) 1973-1977; Boeing Company, Manager of Advanced Energy Systems and plasma electronics 1970-1973, and Research Specialist in Electronic Science at Boeing Scientific Laboratories 1961-1970; while at Boeing she was an affiliate professor in Electrical Engineering at the University of Washington 1961-1973; on the Technical Staff of the David Sarnoff Research Center, RCA, and a Visiting Scientist to the Bell Telephone Laboratories 1958-1961; (1956-1958) Senior Research Physicist, Microwave Physics Laboratory, Sylvania Electrical Products, Inc. She was a Junior Research Physicist and Lecturer in Physics at the University of California, Berkeley, and a staff member with the Inter-Varsity Christian Fellowship 1953-1956. This abbreviated abstract of Dr. Ancker-Johnson's employment only should give a hint of her stature as covered in a 61-page nomination to the Automotive Hall of Fame.

She wasn't selected. _Seven_ _men_ were. Some nondescript. _Many_ of the 130 men automobile "Famers" with tarnished halos suffer when compared with this _one_ outstanding "automobile woman". There are _many_ women who overshadow some of the "Famers".

The shades of the "first four" Walter P., Henry, The "Boss", and Charles P. would welcome Betsy at the "head table". The ghosts of the great would be aghast at how many of the already seated 130 don't resemble "individuals associated with the design and manufacture of cars"--their once lofty goal. No more!

Surely the "first four" would decry the seating of non-design, non-manufacturer--non-automobile--men and no women at their table. Now politically correct--"follow the dollar", select anyone who brings money (as long as it's spelled man)--the AHF has many published classifications that are eligible for "Fame". Would you believe: Auto advertiser; aftermarket; association; club; dealer (used car salesman?); educator; historian, journalist; race driver; service man; et al.? Add the unpublished--but documentable--classification of politician and even the myopic can see the polyglot pot of "good ol' white boys" enjoying FAME!

Jimmy-the-Greek will betcha' my nickel that a Helluva lot of the 130 "Famers" have never changed their oil, changed a tire, had grease under a fingernail, learned to spell stoichiometric, or driven a Model T Ford! And that few automobile aficionados would call 'em car men! Bring in the women. Selah!

If you've read this far and by now have begun to suspect that possibly I'm angry, discouraged, disgusted, disillusioned, unhappy, and upset--you're right!

I'm mad as Hell! At the "good ol' **white boys'** club". The Automotive Hall of Fame.

### SPEED TRAPS?

An illogical and ill-conceived phrase coined by a mega-buck-shyster to bamboozle a gullible hick-town Justice of the Peace into believing that his sports celebrity client had been somehow "trapped" into speeding 30-over in the posted School zone limit of 20 mph. WHOOPEE! For fairness, for human rights, and for blind justice.

Just as they hyped that illogical and ill-conceived cliche "Remember the Hindenburg" into the nemesis that has stymied development of Space Ship Earth's most benign, most plentiful, and safest fuel--HYDROGEN--our technically illiterate and morally flawed media have tied a millstone to law enforcement. No speeder has ever been, can ever be, or will ever be "trapped". Violators of posted speed limits are criminals who chose deliberately and willingly to speed.

There is no conceivable way that any police officer--even one who can "walk on water"--can cause any driver whose foot rests on an accelerator to speed on any roadway. No officer is equipped with a "zapper" to penetrate a vehicle and push that "footfeed".

Every officer should have a remote-controlled leg-iron trap as standard equipment in every highway vehicle. Then he could "trap" the guilty leg that pushed the foot that made the car speed. VOILA!

**N-Cars:** the 91 N-marques need the "N" words, nondescript and nonentity, as identifiers. Few will recognize other than Nash and Nissan. NSU will be historical for building the Spider, the world's first Wankel-engined automobile and for its landspeed record small engined motorcycles of the 1950's. Aficionados will drool over the 19teens massive 520 cubic inch Norwalk "underslung".

**NACA scoop:** a proboscis-like air inlet duct for engines or other inside-air needs. Sticks out into an area of smooth air flow away from exterior surfaces and streamlined to improve vehicle aerodynamics. Characteristic of large piston-engined aircraft. Developed by our National Advisory Commission for Aeronautics.

**nacelle:** a usually streamlined covering or enclosure for engines and sometimes crew of airplanes. Rarely seen in surface vehicles except a few very-high-speed landspeed race cars such as lakester class (belly-tank) machines.

**NADA:** abbreviation for National Automobile Dealers Association.

**NASA scoop:** a high-tech replacement for the NACA scoop providing an efficient air inlet duct that is virtually without air-drag. Effective and necessary on high-speed aircraft but generally non-functional on automobiles (except landspeed racers). Used for macho show and not for "go".

**naked:** slang term for a vehicle chassis. Synonym for "stripdown", the early-day homebuilt race car.

**narrow track:** applied to vehicles with less than the usual side-to-side distance between wheels.

**narrow whites:** a vehicle tire with a sidewall white strip significantly narrower (1 or 2 inches) than the total sidewall dimension.

**name brand:** a manufacturers name that becomes so associated with its product that the product description becomes unnecessary. Valvoline (oil); Goodyear (tires); Vise-grip (pliers); Snap-On (tools).

**name plate:** an identification plate (or stamping) affixed to a vehicle showing the manufacturer's name and vehicle serial number and usually specifications.

**nap:** the tufted surface of an upholstery fabric used in vehicle interiors.

**naphtha:** any of various volatile often flammable liquid hydrocarbon mixtures used chiefly as solvents and diluents.

**natural gas:** gas issuing from the earth's crust through natural openings or bored wells. A combustible mixture of methane and higher hydrocarbons used chiefly as a fuel now gaining acceptance for vehicle use.

**Naugahyde:** trademarked plastic used as a vinyl-coating for vehicles, upholstery fabrics, and as a top material.

**neat's-foot oil:** a fatty oil made from the bones of cattle and used as a leather dressing/preservative for vehicle interiors and seals.

**needle valve:** a valve with tapered seat and matching needle for accurate regulation and control of fluid flow.

**negative:** applied to the post of a vehicle battery, usually the "ground" side of the vehicle electrical distribution system, or to any portion of an electrical circuit having lower electric potential and constituting the post toward which the current (electrons) flows from the external circuit.

**neon:** a colorless, odorless, gaseous element used to enhance the colors of vehicle warning lights and reflective paints.

**neoprene:** a synthetic rubber made by the polymerization of chlorophene, extensively used for vehicle gaskets and seals because of its superior resistance to gasoline, oils, and other hydrocarbons.

**nested:** a group of objects designed and made to fit close together or within another. As vehicle parts or tools nested to save storage space.

**neutral:** a position of disengagement of all gears as in a transmission when the engine is totally disconnected from the driving wheels.

**nibbler:** a hand or machine tool designed to shear small increments of metal using a biting or nibbling action.

**nick:** a small scratch or dent usually in the exterior sheet metal of a vehicle but also in the surface of mechanical parts.

**nipple:** a fitting through which oil or grease is injected into lubricated wear surfaces. A short pipe coupling threaded at both ends.

**nitride:** a case-hardened surface finish on steel caused by forced nitrogen absorption. Frequently used to harden valves and valve seats against wear.

**nitro:** containing or being the univalent chemical group $NO_2$ united through nitrogen. Race car buff slang for nitromethane or nitrous oxide.

**nitrogen:** the colorless, odorless, tasteless, gaseous element that constitutes 78% of the Earth's atmosphere by volume and occurs in all living tissues. Used extensively in vehicle applications and chemicals.

**nitromethane:** a racers fuel/oxidizer additive that gives a significant boost in the power of an internal combustion engine. Usually mixed with methanol racing fuel.

**nitrous oxide:** a gaseous oxidizer usually injected into the intake manifold of racing internal combustion engines to provide a burst of extra power.

**nobby:** a slang descriptive name for deep-tread mud/snow tires usually those with cylindrical spike-like protrusions.

**noble gas:** any of a group of rare gases that include argon and helium that are used in welding to provide a gaseous shield around a welding flame to prevent oxidation and contamination. (heli-arc, MIG, TIG). Also called inert gas because they resist chemical activity with most common materials.

**no-fault:** of, relating to, or being a motor vehicle insurance plan under which an accident victim is compensated usually up to specified limit for actual losses by his own insurance company regardless of who is responsible for the accident.

**no-go:** a gauge or measuring tool that is slightly larger (or smaller) than the object to be measured. For example, a rod that is slightly larger (say 0.001 inches) in diameter than a hole size to be measured is used with a rod that is slightly smaller (say 0.001 inches) diameter to indicate that the hole size exists somewhere between these two limits (0.002 inches apart). The oversize dimension of the "no-go" gauge and the undersize dimensions of the "go" gauge dictate the accuracy limit of their ability to measure.

**noise pollution:** environmental pollution consisting of annoying or harmful noise levels as from excessive exhaust, horn, or on-board radio sounds. Regulated by most states by statute to a specified decibel maximum level.

**nonconducting:** any of a group of materials that insulate (resist the passage of) forms of energy as electricity, heat, light, sound, vibration, et. al.

**nonconforming:** a vehicle that fails to meet the statutory limits for size, weight, pollution, gas consumption, noise, et. al.

**nonrecurring:** a trouble, fault, or malfunction of a vehicle or component that is so rare that it is unlikely to happen again.

**nonrefundable:**  a down payment or deposit that is declared as not subject to being refunded.

**nonreturnable:**  a purchased item that the dealer will not accept back in return for a deposit.

**nonskid:**  a tire tread, highway surface, or floor with a usually rough surface designed to resist and prevent skidding.

**nonslip:**  a surface designed or of a material to resist slipping on the surface.  A fitting or fastener designed to remain tight, resisting slipping or loosening.

**nonstandard:**  a design or size of an item that is different from the norm for that unit. Usually of a deliberately different size or shape (from the original) part to allow proper fit when wear or damage has occurred.

**nonstick:**  a surface or a separator film or gasket allowing fastening securely to another item but allowing later easy removal from the mated part.

**nonunion:**  not belonging to or connected with a trade union. A shop or company that employs only nonunion workers.  A term used to identify a product as being made in a facility not recognizing unions.

**no-reserve:**  a sale classification used at a vehicle auction to indicate a for-sale item will be sold to the highest bidder without any minimum bid amount specified.

**normalize:**  to heat and cool in a controlled fashion welded or machined parts to relieve stresses associated with the manufacturing process.

**NOS:**  new old stock indicating a part for a vehicle that may be many years old but still new and undamaged and unused.  Such parts are highly prized by collectors of older cars and are usually found at estate auctions and the disposal of old-time vehicle dealer stocks.

**nosedive:**  the downward nose-first plunge as of a vehicle running off a cliff, overpass, or open bridge.  Applied to the action of some vehicles where, under hard braking, the front dips sharply downward.

**nosejob:**  body shop jargon for the refinishing or replacing the front sheet metal of a modern streamlined vehicle.

**nostalgist:**  a vehicle aficionado fond of objects and style of the past.  A car collector who remembers and tries to relive when grampa let him drive his 1913 Model "T" Ford, sitting on gramp's lap--or one who remembers seeing Jack Dempsey drive his Springfield Rolls-Royce down Broadway after the Firpo fight.

247

**notchback:** a back on a closed passenger automobile having a distinct deck as distinguished from a sloping fastback.

**NOX:** denotes any of the oxides of nitrogen now recognized as pollutants spawned by vehicle engine exhausts. An inevitable by-product whenever there is "burning" in the presence of air (about 78% nitrogen and 20% oxygen).

**noxious:** physically harmful or destructive to living beings. Descriptive of vehicle exhaust pollutants.

**nozzle:** a short tubular shape with an internal taper or constriction used to speed up or direct the flow of a fluid.

**NSRA:** National Street Rod Association, an automobile membership club devoted to the preservation and showing of the 1930s/40s home-built "Hot Rods" known for their "show" and "go".

**nuts-and-bolts:** the basic working parts or elements of the whole--the automobile. Implies a journeyman vehicle mechanic who knows it "from the ground up".

**Nut-Sert:** a trademarked sheet metal panel fastener that comes with tooling and parts for installing the fasteners. Extensively used for fastening cowling and sheet metal panels on race cars for quick, easy, and dependable removal and installation.

**nylon:** any of numerous strong tough elastic synthetic polyamide materials that are fashioned into sheets and solid shapes. Used in vehicles for insulation, for bearings, for containers, and for many machined and cast parts.


## LAGNIAPPE

**necking:** the reduction in diameter caused by excessive tension, high heat, and wear. Exhaust valve stems are subject to such necking/stretching, often leading to early failure when stressed beyond design parameters.

**NHTSA:** the National Highway Traffic and Safety Administration of the U.S. Department of Transportation that is responsible for establishing and enforcing all aspects of automotive safety regulations.

**Nomex:** tradenamed fire-resistant fabric used for race driver suits.

**normally aspirated:** using ambient air pressure as charge-air instead of supercharging or turbocharging.

**nut runner:** a hand-crank speed-wrench or air/electric-power wrench.

**Nylock:** tradenamed nut using a thread-locking ring insert of nylon.

248

**O-Cars:** Oldsmobile leads the parade of 81 marques with the first-letter O, with the followers being mostly obscure oddities. Ransom Eli Olds built his first automobile, a three-wheeled steam car, in 1891. Following the steamer he built a one-cylinder petrolfueled "dogcart" car and a number of electric cars before producing his famous Curved Dash Runabout in 1901, the world's first mass production automobile. Although at its best as a city runabout, Hammond and Whitman drove a "Curved Dash" from San Francisco to New York in 1903. Ransom Olds left his Olds Motor Works in 1904 to found his REO Company. General Motors absorbed the Olds in 1909 and a 1916 Oldsmobile became the 1,000,000 General Motors car. The "Merry Oldsmobile" seems destined to survive into its third century-- our 21st. Opel, General Motors since the late 1920's, was the first massproduced car (1935 Olympia) without a frame as the forerunner of the contemporary unibody cars. Opel was likely the world's first rocket-powered car, doing 125mph in 1927. In 1928 Opel was the leading automobile producer in Germany and the world-leading bicycle manufacturer.

**objet d'art:** an article of some artistic value. Another automobile synonym.

**obsolescence:** the condition of growing older and being out of use claimed by some to be a planned state by auto manufacturers to enhance sales of newer vehicles. Passe since the advent of the car collectors' craze.

**obstreperous:** another appropriate synonym for the Model "T" Ford car.

**ocher or ochre:** a reddish-yellow pigment used in vehicle paints.

**octane:** any of several isomeric liquid paraffin hydrocarbons used in vehicle fuels. $C_8H_{18}$. The name of the rating of a fuel designating its ability to resist "knocking".

**octane number:** a number that is used to represent the anti-knock properties of a liquid motor fuel and that represents the percentage by volume of isooctane in a reference fuel containing a mixture of isooctane and normal heptane and matching the knocking properties of the fuel being compared. Also called octane rating.

**OD:** abbreviation for outside diameter and for overdrive.

**OD grinder:** an abrasive tool/machine for finishing and sizing the outside of circular shapes and parts.

**odometer:** an instrument for measuring, displaying, and recording the distance traveled by a vehicle. Commonly associated as a standard component of vehicle speedometers.

**OEM:** abbreviation for original equipment manufacturer, applied to the maker of "name brands" and its products usually denoting higher quality as contrasted with after-market, clones, copycat imitations, or gypo--usually cheaper and of inferior quality.

**off:** to a state of discontinuance on suspension as: shut or turn off an engine, valve, or switch. As a function/action word to denote removed or distant from.

**off-center:** a rotating device that revolves around a point other than its geometrical or mass center. Eccentric, cam, or out-of-round.

**off-hour or off-peak:** a period of time other than a rush-hour as with freeway/roadway vehicle traffic density.

**off-road:** applied to vehicles designed for use or being used away from designated vehicle roadways. Usually denoting rough and difficult terrain.

**off-set:** an abrupt change in the profile or dimension of a part. To counterbalance or compensate by placing something off-center or off-axis.

**off-the-shelf:** available as a stock item from the retail seller. Not specially designed, custom-made, or ordered in.

**off-track:** racing other than on designated race courses. Betting or wagering on a race at a site away from the race track.

**ohc:** abbreviation for overhead cam. Includes single and double or twin overhead cam engines.

**ohm:** the practical meter-kilogram-second unit of electric resistance equal to the resistance of a circuit in which a potential difference of one volt produces a current on one ampere.

**ohmmeter:** an electrical instrument for indicating resistance in ohms directly.

**oil:** one of any of unctuous combustible substances that are liquid or at least easily liquefiable by warming, soluble in ether but not in water. Reduces sliding/rubbing friction when applied between two surfaces.

**oil analysis:** the testing of oil to determine the degree of contamination and to predict engine component failure from the quantity of detectable metals in the oil.

**oil can:** a can for/of oil, usually one quart. A spouted can designed to release oil drop by drop for lubricating machinery.

**oil filter:** a leak-proof container filled with filter media designed to trap all solid particulates and hold them from continuing with the circulating oil. Many contain acid and other combustion contaminant neutralizers. Most are full-flow, meaning that all oil must pass through the filter en route to the oil pump and lubricated engine parts.

**oil filter by-pass:** a pressure-sensitive valve that diverts oil around a full-flow filter when the filter becomes clogged thus preventing oil starvation of the essential engine components.

**oil hone:** a very fine grit abrasive device used with oil to impart a smooth finish to various friction surfaces.

**oil pan:** the lower section of the crankcase used as the lubricating-oil reservoir on an internal combustion engine.

**oil screen:** a fine-mesh wire screen that protects the engine oil-pump intake from stray metal particles in the oil from engine wear.

**oil seal:** an impervious to oil material used between mating, moving, rotating, or sliding surfaces to seal and retain the oil used for lubricating.

**oil separator:** a baffled tank through which air and gases that may contain small amounts of oil are diverted. The oil attaches to the baffles and is drained back into the oil pan or reservoir.

**oil spout:** a puncturing spout for penetrating and sealing a throwaway can of oil to facilitate pouring into an oil reservoir opening without using a funnel.

**oil tempered:** steel that is heated to a specified temperature and quenched in oil. Various degrees of hardness can be obtained by heating to the correct temperature prescribed for the desired hardness.

**Oklahoma credit card:** disparaging slang for a siphon hose reputedly used by the migrating "Okies" to steal gasoline en route to California.

**omnibus:** an automotive public vehicle (bus) designed to carry a comparatively large number of passengers.

**one-of:** limited to one single version. As an automobile that is different from all other automobiles.

**one-way:** that moves in or allows movement in only one direction. One-way traffic.

**on-the-bubble:** race track jargon indicating the current slowest speed car among those qualifying for a final race. Implies that another car can bump this car out of the starting line-up by going faster before qualifying attempts are ended.

**on-the-job:** of or relating to training or experience learned, gained, or done while working at a job such as vehicle mechanic or operator, often under supervision.

**opacity:** the relative capacity of vehicle exhaust emissions to obstruct the transmission of radiant energy (light). The degree of opacity of the smoke (soot) is measured with scientific exactness by electronic scanners and subjectively by human viewers using comparative gray-scale charts. Smoking beyond the legal limit may cause removal from service pending repairs.

**open-car:** an open-to-the-air vehicle with no side enclosure or glass and sometimes with no fixed top structure. Phaeton, roadster, topless, touring. May be supplied with removable side curtains or panels.

**open-end:** a type of vehicle lease with a variable final payment (balloon) subject to negotiable specified conditions. A mechanic's wrench that may be fitted onto the nut, bolt, or fixture from the side as well as from the top/end as with a box or socket wrench.

**open-loop:** a control system for an operation or process in which there is no self-correcting action as there is in a closed-loop.

**open-shop:** a vehicle establishment in which eligibility for employment or retention on the payroll are not determined by membership or nonmembership in a labor union although a specific union may be recognized as the sole bargaining agent.

**opera coupe:** usually an opulent often pretentious two-door, four passenger automobile. Frequently equipped with non-functional accessories such as landau irons (hinges), dual side- or post-mount spare tire/wheels, and cut-glass flower vases.

**opposed cylinder:** an engine with cylinders arranged end-to-end vertically or horizontally with the crankshaft between them. Though rare, opposed pistons operating in one long cylinder with a common centered-combustion area and two crankshafts resemble the opposed cylinder configuration.

**optical-fiber:** a single fiber-optic strand when bundled forms the "light-pipe" that conveys light or images to a more accessible viewing area.

**orange peel:** a rough bumpy painted surface resembling an orange. Usually unacceptable reflecting substandard workmanship, technique, or materials.

**orbital tool:** usually applied to grinder/polisher/sander devices using a generally circular though not necessarily concentric motion to prevent leaving a distinct surface pattern.

**order of magnitude:** a range of magnitude extending from some value to ten times that value. Multiplied by ten. Ten times as great.

**ordinate:** the Cartesian coordinate obtained by measuring parallel to the y-axis.

**organizer:** such as a display/storage device marked by the painted/shaped silhouette of the tool/part to be stored for ease in finding and replacement.

**orifice:** an opening usually sharp-edged designed to control/restrict/direct/shape/measure the flow of a fluid (liquid or gaseous).

**original:** applied to a vehicle that remains exactly as constructed by the manufacturer. Unchanged or modified since first assembled.

**o-ring:** a seal for preventing leaking of fluids or lubricating greases at joints or mating surfaces. Usually of a flexible, compressible material such as plastic or rubber but may be metallic as the copper o-ring used to seal the cylinder head joint against compression pressures. The "o" derives from the circular cross-section.

**ornate:** descriptive of some customized or personalized vehicles. Elaborately or excessively embellished in a florid manner.

**orphan:** a vehicle of questionable lineage or design which is often scorned by the aficionado elitist. Tucker, Edsel.

**oscillator:** an electronic device for converting the on-board direct current supply of a vehicle into alternating current in either the audio- or radio-frequency ranges.

**oscillograph:** a recorder for oscilloscope indications to provide a record and make available for future analysis and study.

**oscilloscope:** a cathode ray display tube (TV-screen type) for visually showing the condition and operation of many vehicle systems as detected by sensors connected to the system to be analyzed. A very accurate, versatile, and discriminatory diagnostic device.

**Otto, Nicholas August:** born in Germany in 1832, Otto formed the world's first company (1864) to manufacture internal combustion engines. His many inventions and patents were significant in the evolution of the IC engine into the automobile and aircraft era.

**ounce:** a measure of weight and/or capacity. One ounce is 1/16 pound or 1/32 quart.

**outboard:** a bearing, center, or support used in conjunction with but outside a main bearing. A position closer or closest to either of the sides of a vehicle.

**outgas:** to lose or to remove gases. Charging batteries outgas hydrogen. Heating a material sometimes outgases solvents.

**output:** power produced by a vehicle. Energy produced by an on-board component, generator/alternator, heater, air-conditioner, et. al.

**output shaft:** the shaft <u>from</u> a transmission that delivers "processed" torque/speed to the vehicle wheels.

**outrigger:** a projecting member run out from a vehicle to provide stability and prevent tilting as when an on-board crane is used to lift heavy loads.

**outsize:** a size larger than the standard. An unusually large or heavy vehicle.

**ovaltrack:** a race track in the shape of an oval or a rectangle having rounded corners. Traditional to vehicle races that are spectator-centered.

**oven-baked:** a vehicle paint job finished by drying inside a heated oven to accelerate the process and insure a smoother, harder exterior surface.

**overcharge:** to charge too much. To make an excessive charge. To overfill as putting too much pressure into a tank. Too rapid and excessive electricity applied to a battery.

**overcoat:** a final protective coat usually clear/transparent applied when painting a vehicle. Esthetic and utilitarian.

**overdrive:** a vehicle transmission gear that transmits to the drive shaft a speed greater than engine speed.

**overfill:** to fill to overflowing as with any vehicle fluid, gasoline, oil, water, air, transmission fluid, power steering fluid, windshield washer fluid, air conditioner refrigerant, brake fluid, grease.

**overflow:** the outlet or reservoir for excess radiator system coolant.

**overhaul:** to examine thoroughly, renovate, service, renew completely, and replace with new components. In vehicle parlance implies the return to the original manufacturer's specifications and tolerances.

**overhead cam:** a vehicle engine having the camshaft(s) over the cylinder head operating the valves by direct contact as contrasted to having the camshaft in the engine/cylinder block operating the valves through push rods and rocker arms.

**overhead valve:** a vehicle engine with exhaust and intake valves situated in the cylinder head as contrasted to being in the cylinder block.

**overheat:** to allow or to cause a vehicle engine to reach an operating temperature in excess of the manufacturer's specified limits. Prolonged overheating is likely to be disastrous and certain to be expensive.

**overpass:** a crossing of two highways or of a highway and pedestrian path or railroad at different levels where clearance to traffic on the lower level is obtained by elevating the higher level. Also denotes the upper level of such a crossing.

**overpower:** to provide a vehicle with more power than is needed or desirable. An overpowered vehicle becomes dangerous when operated by an inexperienced/incompetent driver.

**overpressure:** pressure significantly above what is usual or normal. Potentially dangerous.

**overrunning clutch:** a vehicle freewheeling device allowing power to be applied when the input exceeds the demand and disconnects the drive-line when inertia or a downslope causes power demand to decrease so that the vehicle continues at a steady speed or pushes (accelerates). The same freewheeling occurs when input power is decreased.

**oversize:** being dimensionally larger than original or standard.

**oversquare:** designated a vehicle engine whose cylinder diameter is dimensionally greater than its piston stroke. Characteristic of high rpm engines.

**oversteer:** the tendency of a vehicle to steer into a sharper turn than the driver intends sometimes with a thrusting of the vehicle rear to the outside.

**overweight:** a vehicle weighing in excess of the legally allowable weight.

**oxyacetylene:** utilizing a mixture of oxygen and acetylene to provide the heat source for welding.

**oxygen:** the element in air (21%) that makes possible the release of energy from fuels by rapid oxidation (combustion/ burning).

**oxygenate:** the adding of oxygen (as alcohol or MTBE) to vehicle fuels to improve combustion efficiency thus reducing exhaust pollutants.

**oxygen sensor:** an electronic oxygen-measuring device used in vehicle exhaust systems to indicate combustion efficiency and to send corrective signals to an on-board computer that adjusts fuel and ignition parameters to improve combustion and reduce exhaust pollutants.

**ozone:** a triatomic form $O_3$ of oxygen ($O_2$) formed naturally in the upper atmosphere by a photo-chemical reaction of many chemicals with solar ultraviolet radiation creating the ozono-sphere protective atmospheric layer that screens much of the sun's damaging ultraviolet from reaching the earth's surface. A number of vehicle exhaust pollutants are photochemically converted to ozone at low altitudes becoming a major component of smog.

## LAGNIAPPE

**Oakland:** a car first built in Pontiac, MI, in 1907, acquired later by General Motors who built a hot-selling model named Pontiac (1926), causing GM to phase out the Oakland name in 1932, forming its division, Pontiac Motor Co.

**off-highway:** referring to vehicles designed to be driven across rough terrain, or to driving a vehicle where no prepared roads exist.

**Offy:** slang for Offenhauser, the great racing engine, later built by Meyer-Drake as the "Indy 500" leader for so many years.

**ogee:** a piece with an S-shaped profile such as a landau-top hinge.

**OHV:** a valve-in-head arrangement with pushrod/rocker-arm operation of the valves from an in-block camshaft (usually high in the block).

**oil cooler:** an onboard heat exchanger/radiator to cool the engine oil or the differential/transmission lubricant.

**oil-fouled:** any component as a sparkplug whose air-gap has become bridged/fouled/shorted by excess oil or oil-based combustion residue.

**onboard computer:** the installed electronics using sensed operating data fed back to a programmed processor that uses these data to optimize engine operation. Some store operational data for use in diagnosing/locating malfunctions by a repair shop. Brain box.

**onboard fire-bottle:** a vehicle-installed extinguisher system (heat or manually actuated) with discharge nozzles under the hood, near the fuel tamk, and in the driver compartment.

**outer race:** the hardened outside round retainer and rolling track for ball or roller bearings rolling between it and an inner race.

**out-of-round:** interior or exterior of a part whose diameter varies.

**overlap:** that portion of the exhaust/intake cycles when both valves are open as measured in degrees of camshaft/crankshaft rotation. Typically, greater duration (overlap) is found in high-revving "full-race" engines.

**overspeed:** to operate an engine faster than its rpm (redline) limit specified by the manufacturer. Often causes disintegration failure.

**oxidation:** chemical combining of oxygen and another element (slow as with rusting iron--fast as when burning any fuel).

**oxides of nitrogen:** exhaust pollution inevitably caused by heating of air (78% nitrogen, 20% oxygen) by fire when there's pressure.

## SEND <u>ALL</u> ASH TRAYS TO THE ASH HEAP

Like Texan Eddie Chiles, I'm mad as Hell! Two new ash trays are parked in my garage--the umpteenth such "standard equipment" foisted upon me annually in about half-a-century of new cars. Why can we no longer choose a cut-glass flower vase for our doorpost, a buggy-whip holster for our side cowl, or a mohair lap robe? Give us a chance to select something useful and pleasing to our sensibilities instead of the customary cesspool-without-a-flush-valve (ash tray) that we are all <u>forced</u> to pay for in <u>every</u> new car. Why not?

With Environmental Impact Statements dictating man's very infrastructure, howcome the EPA allows that all-pervasive polluter, the automobile ash tray onboard <u>every</u> people-mover? With such a small percentage of us smoking, <u>why</u> should <u>every</u> <u>nonsmoker</u> be forced to pay for the ash trays in <u>every</u> new car (about $100 cost to replace)? Let <u>the</u> <u>smoker</u> <u>buy</u> his essential accessory. Selah!

Continental Airlines recently removed all ash trays from its 727 jet liners, saving the cost of hauling one passenger, every flight. forever! Why did it take so long? At this moment, more than 100,000,000 pounds of <u>never-used</u> ash trays are being hauled over our highways and through our skies--burning millions of barrels of OPEC oil annually.

Advocate the elimination of this <u>waste</u>! Don't genuflect to the Ash Tray God! Need I explain further?

**P-Cars:** Of 260 car names starting with a "P" some prominence should have emerged. Little did. The French Panhard (1889-1967), one of the greatest names in the history of motoring, and Peugeot (1889-to date), still controlled by the Peugeot family, that sold the first petrol-powered car in France led the P-pack. The American Packard (1889-1958) and Pierce-Arrow (1901-1938) became also-rans, and Plymouth (1928-to date) and Pontiac (1926-to date) got a late start along with the German Porsche (1948-to date).

**pace car:** an automobile (usually a new model sport machine) that leads the field of racing competitors through the pace (preliminary) lap but pulls off the track and does not participate in the race.

**pace lap:** the first lap of an auto racecourse by the entire complement of race cars before the start of the race to allow the engines to warm up, the racers to stabilize their assigned positions, and to permit an orderly flying start when the green flag drops.

**package deal:** the emerging practice of grouping and pricing a number of new car accessories as a package rather than as individual components.

**packing:** a sealing material designed and used to make no-leakage joints where there is relative movement between pieces. Valve, bearing.

**pad:** frictional material that presses against the discs of vehicle disc brakes.

**pad-wear indicator:** a device imbedded or attached to a brake pad during manufacture so that wear beyond design limits triggers a warning light or audible signal.

**paddock:** the area usually inside the oval racecourse where racing cars are parked, serviced, and repaired. Pits.

**pagoda:** a usually tiered tower near the starting line of an automobile racecourse that provides visible control of the track, speed timing equipment and public announcement/communications facilities. Control tower.

**paint booth:** a usually self-inclosed structure within a vehicle repair facility, lighted and ventilated, to provide a safe dust-free area for spray painting.

**paint chip:** a color display system using small painted samples (chips) of each paint color available for a customer to choose or for the painter to match to a vehicle's finish.

**paint gun:** a pressurized device with a paint reservoir for atomizing the liquid paint for smooth deposition on the desired surface.

**paint reducer:** a paint additive to improve the viscosity, adherence, drying, and sprayability of paint.

**paint stripper:** a chemical solvent/dissolver that softens paint surfaces allowing the brushing or rubbing away of the paint film. A heat source or vibrator/rotary mechanical tool designed to remove paint from a surface.

**paint thinner:** a paint additive to adjust a paint's thickness for brushing or spraying requirements.

**palladium:** a silver-white ductile malleable metallic element of the platinum group used in electrical contacts and as a catalyst.

**pallet:** a portable frame platform for handling, storing or moving materials and packages in a warehouse, shop, or large cargo vehicle.

**pallet truck:** an industrial vehicle equipped to lift and move freight on pallets. Fork-lift truck.

**pal nut:** a threaded or stamped spring nut that is tightened on a stud or bolt after the main nut is in place, thread-locking the two to prevent unwanted loosening as from vibration.

**pancake engine:** a vehicle engine usually with 4 or 6 cylinders arranged horizontally with half of them opposing on each side of the crankshaft.

**panel:** sheet metal component of a vehicle body, particularly when a part of the outer shell/exterior.

**panel truck:** a vehicle with a fully-enclosed cargo/van body, usually constructed using plastic, sheet metal, or wood panels and especially when windowless.

**Panhard rod:** a transverse stabilizer bar pivoted at one side of the chassis/frame and angling downward to a fitting on the opposite side of a beam axle to restrain lateral movement.

**pantograph:** a device designed to change the scale when copying drawings, to hold shop work lights, display instruments, and small power tools in easy adjustable work positions in a shop/bench/bay area.

**parabola:** something bowl-shaped as a vehicle headlight reflector. Technically defined as a plane curve generated by a point moving so that its distance from a fixed point is equal to its distance from a fixed line: the intersection of a right circular cone with a plane parallel to an element of the cone.

**parallel:** extending in the same direction, everywhere equidistant, and not meeting: something equal or similar in all essential particulars.

**park:** the position of an automatic transmission gearshift level/control that disengages the engine and locks the drive wheels. To place a vehicle and apply the parking (hand or foot) brake to restrain it from unwanted movement.

**parking brake:** a brake system that holds one or more wheel brakes or a driveshaft brake permanently "on" when a vehicle is parked. Handbrake. Emergency brake.

**parking lot:** a vehicle storage area marked and designed for orderly parking vehicles and providing occupants easy/nearby access to facilities as shopping, congregating, et al.

**parking torque:** the steering effort required when operating a vehicle at very low speed as when parking.

**park light:** lights usually of relatively low power (white at each front corner, red at each rear corner) to outline the presence of a parked vehicle.

**particulates:** various sizes (from visible to sub-microscopic) of solid materials supported and transported non-miscible by a fluid. Some are destructive to mechanical devices because of abrasive wear, some are pathogenic to humans. Emissions.

**particulate trap:** a device using filter media or labyrinths/ baffles/vortex to separate, restrain, and retain small particles such as dust, grit, or soot from a fluid such as incoming air, exhaust gases, fuel, or oil.

**passenger car:** a usually non-commercial self-powered vehicle designed for carrying a small number of occupants (generally 2-4).

**passing gear:** a vehicle transmission gear ratio designed to provide rapid acceleration for safer passing of an overtaken other vehicle. Usually automatically shifted when the driver presses suddenly harder on the fuel flow control.

**passing lane:** an extra roadway lane usually on up-hill or blind-curve segments to provide safer passing of slower moving vehicles.

**passive restraint:** a vehicle occupant restraint system that does not require occupants to fasten, operate, or secure. Automatic seat/shoulder belts. Air bags.

**patch:** the contact area of a vehicle tire upon the roadway surface. A repair piece usually cold adhesive or hot vulcanized for sealing a vehicle tire/tube puncture leak.

**pavement:** a generic term, once reserved for concrete/stone, now used to indicate a roadway/sidewalk surface of various wear materials. Asphalt. Blacktop.

**pawl:** a pivoted/hinged or sliding latch/lock on one part of a machine that is designed to fall (or be forced) into notches or interdental (teeth) spaces on another part (as a ratchet wheel) permitting motion in only one direction and locking reverse movement.

**payload:** the revenue-producing or useful load that a vehicle can carry. Excludes fuel and usually the weight of the driver/ operator.

**peak horsepower:** the highest power developed within the normal operating speed range of an engine.

**peak power engine speed:** the engine speed at which peak power is developed.

**peak torque speed:** the engine rpm at which peak torque is developed.

**peaky:** descriptive of an engine that develops useful/significant power over a narrow range of rpm. Most typical of highly-tuned two-stroke/cycle engines. Requires frequent shifting under varying vehicle loads (weight or roadway incline) to stay within the useful power range.

**pedal:** any foot operated control. Brake, clutch, fuel, et al.

**pedal car:** for children a miniature motor vehicle propelled by foot power.

**pedal effort:** the foot pressure required to operate a pedal control usually related to brake pedal effort.

**pedal pad:** the usually rubber-like form-fitting covering for a control pedal to provide a better friction surface and easy replacement as wear occurs.

**pedal travel:** the total movement of a control pedal, the effective movement of a control pedal, free-play travel is the movement before the pedal's functional action begins.

**pedicab:** a tricycle with a 2-seat passenger compartment usually covered by a folding top and a separate outside seat for the driver who pedals.

**peel rubber:** car jargon for an excessively fast acceleration causing wheel slippage that abrades the tire tread. Burn rubber.

**peen:** to bend, draw, flatten or shape by or as if by hammering with a peen (a hemispherical or wedge-shaped hammer-head).

**pendulum damper:** a balancing device used to attenuate crankshaft vibrations using oscillating weights in antiphase.

**penetrant:** a usually liquid (often colored or fluorescent) chemical that penetrates cracks in material surfaces making them visible to the mechanic/inspector.

**performance shop:** a vehicle maintenance/repair/parts facility specializing in vehicles that have been modified (hot-rodded) to improve handling, acceleration, and speed.

**permanent magnet:** a magnet that retains its magnetism after removal of the magnetizing force.

**petcock:** a small cock, faucet, or valve for letting out gases, releasing compression, draining fluids, or visually checking tank content levels.

**petrochemical:** a chemical isolated or derived from petroleum or natural gas.

**petrol:** British name for gasoline.

**petroleum:** an oily flammable bituminous liquid that may vary from almost colorless (sweet crude) to black (tar crude) occurring in many places in the upper strata of Spaceship Earth.

**phaeton:** an open usually four-door automobile with a folding or removable top covering. Touring car.

**phosphor bronze:** a bronze of great hardness, elasticity, and toughness containing a small amount of phosphorus.

**photo finish:** a race finish in which contestants are so close that a photograph of them as they cross the finish line has to be examined to determine the winner. A close contest.

**photovoltaic:** of, relating to, or utilizing the generation of a voltage when radiant energy (as light) falls on the boundary between dissimilar substances (as two different semiconductors). Used for sensing light, triggering other electrical/mechanical functions, charging batteries, powering lights in remote areas, et al. Photo cell, solar cell.

**physical science:** the natural sciences (as astronomy, chemistry, and physics) that deal primarily with nonliving materials.

**pi:** the ratio of the circumference of a circle to its diameter, a transcendental number that cannot be expressed by a finite number of algebraic operations.

**piano hinge:** a hinge that has a thin pin joint that extends the full length of the part to be moved.

**pickle fork:** car jargon for a two-claw prying/wedging tool used to remove tapered ground fittings such as ball-joints.

**pickup:** a light truck having a usually enclosed cab and an open cargo body with low sides and tailgate. Pickup truck.

**pickup coil:** a usually inductance coil used to sense a moving electrical/magnetic field to provide speed information and timing impulses for electronic ignition systems.

**pie chart:** a circular chart with sizes of wedges representing usually labeled amounts of the whole quantity as represented.

**pie wagon:** one of several street vending horse-drawn vehicles that evolved into early day motor vehicle counterparts. Bakery wagon, tank wagon, vegetable wagon, et al.

**piezoelectricity:** electricity generated by pressure/weight impressed upon certain crystalline materials (as quartz) and used to measure and display pressure/weight. A source of ignition spark in specialized applications as engines and fueled welding devices.

**pilot bearing:** an alignment bearing/bushing to maintain con-centricity of extended shafts such as the clutch/transmission/ flywheel bearing interface.

**pilot jet:** a carburetor jet that adds fuel usually downstream from the throttle for better acceleration/starting mixtures.

**pilot shaft:** a machine shaft designed for initial alignment and sometimes retention of fit relationship of assembly compo-nents involving interacting movements.

**pin boss:** an enlarged/strengthened area of material usually around a bolt, shaft, or stud hole/opening to improve align-ment, support, or wear.

**pinch bar:** a leverage device/tool similar in form and use to a crowbar sometimes having an end adapted for pulling nails/ spikes or inserting under a heavy wheel for hand-rolling. Pry bar.

**pinch bolt:** a usually locking bolt used to squeeze a split collar for retention of pieces of an assembly.

**ping:** fuel detonation or the sound thereof occurring in a spark-ignition internal combustion engine. Knock. Rattle.

**pinion:** a small gear wheel or the smaller of two mutually meshing gear wheels. Pinion gear.

**pin stripe:** a vehicle decorative stripe formerly hand-painted on early automobiles now usually appliqued as decals/transfers.

**pintle:** a usually upright/vertical pin/shaft on which another part turns. As a trailer articulated hitch.

**pip:** an inverted "V", spot, or line-trace on an oscilloscope screen displaying informational intelligence.

**pipe cutter:** a tool for cutting pipe using usually 1-3 sharp-edged wheels and pressure rollers forced inward by screw pressure to cut into the pipe workpiece as the tool is rotated around the pipe.

**pipe fitting:** a pipe shape as a "Y", a cross, a "T", an elbow, coupling, union, reducer, et al., used to connect pipes or pipes to other devices.

**pipe wrench:** a tool for gripping and turning a cylindrical shape (as a pipe) by use of two serrated jaws so designed as to grip the pipe when turning in one direction only.

**piston:** any reciprocating component shaped and fitted to its enclosing cylinder container where it operates creating or utilizing fluid pressure to do useful work.

**piston crown:** the closed end of a piston against which the working pressure acts usually configured flat, concave, or convex.

**piston pin:** the shaft that connects and articulates the piston and its connecting rod to a reciprocating engine crankshaft.

**piston pin hone:** an appropriate grit abrasive device that rotates inside a piston pin hole to create a desired size and surface finish.

**piston ring:** a sealing ring usually split and made of hard springy material set in a groove around a piston to contain the fluid working pressure within the cylinder enclosure.

**piston rod:** a connecting rod by which a piston is moved or by which that piston communicates reciprocating motion.

**piston skirt:** usually parallel-sided cylindrical walls of a piston, extending downward (toward the crankshaft of an engine).

**piston slap:**  the noise made by contact between an excessively loose or worn piston and the cylinder wall of an engine.

**piston speed:**  linear velocity of a piston in its reciprocating motion within a cylinder stated as mean (average) piston speed or instantaneous piston speed.

**pit:**  any of the areas alongside an automobile racecourse designated for refueling, repair, and servicing the race cars.  An excavation beneath a shop floor designed so that mechanics can stand and work underneath a vehicle placed over the pit.

**pit crew:**  a race car mechanic/service staff assigned to support a competing car during a race.

**Pitman arm:**  the lever that converts rotary output from a steering gear box to linear movement of a drag link.

**pit row:**  a row of race car service areas alongside an automobile racecourse.

**pit stop:**  an authorized stop by a racing vehicle during a race for fuel or repairs as the remaining field of competitors continues racing.  Car travel jargon for any place where food, fuel, and rest may be obtained and the act of stopping for such.

**pitting:**  chemical or mechanical surface damage to a metal usually undergoing friction contact evidenced by visible pits, depressions, or holes.  Scuffing.

**pivot:**  any shaft or pin on which something turns.  Pivot pin. King pin. Knuckle pin. Swivel pin. Wrist pin.

**plain bearing:**  any bearing whose moving contact is pure rubbing/sliding separated by a lubricating film.  An early car name usually for bearings that were cast from low-melting-point metals such as Babbitt/lead and scraped to the desired fit.

**planetary transmission:**  an epicyclic gear system consisting of an internally-toothed annulus/ring gear and a central externally-toothed sun gear with three or four planet gears/ wheels meshing with and between the inner sun gear and the outer ring gear.

**planet carrier:**  the disc or spider on which the orbiting planet gears of an epicyclic system are mounted.

**plasma torch:**  a device that heats a gas by electrical means to form a plasma for high temperature-operations (as welding/ melting metal).

**plastic:**  any of numerous organic synthetic or processed materials that are mostly thermoplastic or thermosetting polymers of high molecular weight and that can be cast, molded, extruded, drawn or laminated.

**Plastigage:** tradenamed system for accurate measurement of clearances as of bearings using appropriate sized plastic rods that are compressed/flattened when inserted between the bearing and journal and tightened to specifications. The width to which the plastic rod is flattened indicates the exact clearance.

**plate:** a smooth flat piece of material, cast, forged, or rolled metal in sheets usually thicker that $\frac{1}{4}$ inch, to cover with an adherent layer chemically, electrically, or mechanically, the usually flat or grid-formed anode of an electron tube at which electrons collect.

**platform scale:** a usually ground-level weighing surface onto which an entire motor vehicle can be driven and weighed.

**platform truck/trailer:** a truck/trailer with a load carrying cargo floor without sides. Flatbed. Lowboy.

**platinum:** a heavy precious noncorroding ductile malleable metallic element widely used as a contact surface for vehicle electrical devices.

**platinum catalyst:** baffles coated with metallic platinum in a vehicle exhaust catalytic converter that accelerates the conversion of carbon and hydrocarbon emissions and of nitrogen oxides into less harmful exhaust gases without the platinum itself being consumed.

**play:** free movement or looseness within a mechanism, as the movement that occurs in a steering wheel or clutch pedal before the steered wheels or clutch responds. Free play. Lash.

**Playboy:** the unforgettable 8-cylinder sport roadster built by Jordan in the late 1920s.

**plenum chamber:** any enclosure holding a gas at higher pressure than the ambient pressure.

**pliers:** any of various hinged small pincers for holding/tightening small objects or for bending, cutting, or twisting wire.

**Pliofilm:** trademarked glossy membrane made of rubber hydrochloride used chiefly for water resistant packaging of parts and devices.

**plug:** a usually removable closing device/element to prevent pressure loss or leakage. A removable electrical connector normally inserted into a female matching piece. Short for a spark plug.

**plug wire:** the high-voltage connection from the distributor to the spark plug.

**plumb:** exactly vertical or true. To make such.

**plumb-bob:** the metal bob/weight and suspension line used to establish or verify plumb.

**plunger:** a pumping piston usually as a solid rod ground-fit to its cylinder/sleeve and actuated by a cam/lever for delivering small-volume high-pressure liquids.

**ply:** one layer of woven material from which a vehicle tire carcass is made.

**ply rating:** the number of plies, once used as the index of strength of vehicle tire, no longer applies.

**pneumatic suspension:** a system using air or gas in compression to support and cushion a vehicle's weight. Air ride.

**pneumatic tire:** a flexible hollow toroid (doughnut) of rubber or synthetic that covers (attires) the outer rim of a vehicle wheel using air/gas pressure for support and cushioning.

**Pocher:** the brand name of a line of high-quality model automobile kits.

**point(s):** the electrical contacts of an ignition circuit interrupter usually located in the lower portion of the ignition distributor.

**point gap:** the distance between the fixed and movable contact points in a vehicle ignition electrical system when the cam lobe fully opens the circuit.

**poisoning:** the contamination, degradation, or destruction of a vehicle exhaust catalytic converter by fuel containing lead or other unauthorized ingredients.

**pole:** either extremity of an axis of a sphere. One of the two terminals/connections of a direct current (DC) electrical device. A region of a magnetized body/field at which the magnetic flux density is concentrated.

**pole position:** the inside front row position on the starting line of a multi-vehicle competitive racing event.

**pole sitter:** the race car driver with the fastest qualifying speed during the time trials used to eliminate slower non-competitive vehicles in selecting the starting field for a multi-car race.

**polishing compound:** grits of various coarseness usually mixed with a liquid carrier or in paste form and used to impart a smooth shiny finish to material or painted surfaces. Polishing rouge. Jeweler's rouge.

**polycarbonate:** any of various tough transparent thermoplastics characterized by high impact strength and high softening temperature.

**polytechnic:** a classification applied to most vehicle engineering/mechanical schools because of the many technical arts or applied sciences involved.

**polyurethane:** any of various polymers that are used especially in flexible and rigid foams, elastomers, and resins.

**poppet valve:** a valve with a disc-shaped sealing head attached to an alignment locating stem/shaft whose reciprocating movement causes the angle-ground edges of the disc head to open and close against its matching tapered seat. The most common exhaust and intake valving for internal combustion engines as valve-in-block or valve-in-head configurations.

**popping back:** premature ignition of the fuel/air mixture in the intake manifold. Back-fire.

**pop rivet:** a fastening device for use through wall areas inaccessible from one side prohibiting the use of a bucking bar or dolly to upset a rivet's locking end. A hardened rod is pulled through the hollow rivet expanding it to form a locking bulge.

**pop riveter:** a hand or hydropneumatic powered tool for seating and expanding pop rivets.

**pop-up:** an elevating/retracting roof structure for a trailer or vehicle allowing the interior vertical height to be varied. Usually lowered for driving and raised when stopped.

**porcelainize:** a vitreous coating fired onto metal components of vehicles such as exhaust manifolds/systems to provide protection against heat deterioration, improve insulation, and add to aesthetics.

**Porsche:** the German performance/prestige automobile and its name-source/designer/builder, Dr. Ing. Ferdinand Porsche, well-known designer of Lohner, Austro-Daimler, Steyer, and Mercedes cars as well as Auto Union racers and the venerable Volkswagen.

**port:** an aperture/opening shaped to facilitate the flow of a fluid from or into a chamber as the exhaust/intake openings into the combustion area of a vehicle engine.

**portapotty:** a portable latrine/toilet supplied for spectator convenience at large outdoor vehicle events such as racing or swap-meets.

**Portapower:** a tradenamed hydropneumatic push/pull cylinder tool used extensively especially in vehicle body/frame shops to apply tension/compression forces as needed during assembly/ disassembly, bending, shaping, and straightening of material.

**porte cochere:** a passageway through a building or screen wall designed to let vehicles pass from the street into an interior courtyard.

**port hole:** a usually round window as used in the wall areas of van-type vehicles. The circular openings through the fender body panels of period Buicks whose number 1 through 4 denoted size/price/prestige of the vehicle model.

**port match:** to grind or machine the port opening profile to fit exactly the opening of the mating manifold fittings to eliminate sharp edge turbulence.

**port of entry:** a designated stop usually at or near state lines where highway vehicles may be stopped for various inspections and taxation purposes.

**port polish:** to smooth and polish the interior wall surfaces of a port to reduce friction of the fluid flow with the wall.

**port relief:** to enlarge the interior area of a port to allow a greater volume of fluid to flow.

**positive camber:** vehicle wheel camber in which the wheel leans/slopes outward at its top.

**positive caster:** the arrangement of a vehicle's steering geometry in which the center of the tire contact (footprint) lies to the rear of the point where the steering axis intesects the road surface giving a positive or stable self-centering effect.

**positive crankcase ventilation:** the emission control system that draws crankcase gases (blow-by) into the engine induction system, allowing burning of most contaminants rather than venting them to the environment. PCV.

**positive displacement:** a pump that delivers a fixed or metered volume of fluid on each pumping stroke.

**positive offset steering:** steering/suspension geometry in which the intersection of the kingpin axis with the ground is inboard of the center of the tire contact (footprint),

**post:** a usually upright structural roof-supporting member for vehicles as a door post or windshield post. A usually metallic fitting attached to an electrical device (as a battery) for convenience in making connections.

**pot metal:** a low temperature melting-point metal with little strength formerly used in casting carburetor parts and ornamental handles.

**poured bearing:** a plain bearing that is cast by pouring molten bearing metal (usually Babbitt) into its working housing. The bearing surface is usually machined or hand-scraped to the desired fit with its mating shaft.

**power take-off:** a driven extension shaft usually extending from the casing of a vehicle transmission or an engine accessory section to provide auxiliary power to ancillary attachments to be operated from the vehicle engine.

**Power Wagon:** trade name for a series of Dodge utility work vehicles.

**power winch:** a rope or cable drum winch operated by power (electrical or mechanical) from a vehicle or outside power source.

**pre-heat:** to heat to a designated temperature before processing, as in heating two workpieces before welding to prevent distortion caused by the localized welding heat. Also to heat-expand a part that is to be heat-shrunk onto a pre-sized component part.

**press fit:** to dimensionally size internally or externally one part that is to be fitted onto or into another part by using a strong compression force as with a hydropneumatic cylinder (press) or a mechanical press.

**primary coil:** the coil through which the inducing current passes in an induction coil or transformer. Vehicle ignition coil.

**prime coat:** a preliminary coat of finishing material (as a paint) to provide an intermediate layer upon which the final exterior (finish) coating is applied. Primer.

**primer cup:** a small cup-like reservoir with a shut-off cock screwed into a cylinder head for priming the engine (before the days of the carburetor choke) with a measured amount of raw fuel directly into the combustion chamber for ease in starting.

**promotional model:** a miniature replica of a new year model provided to franchised dealers to use in advertising new production models prior to the delivery of the first full-size showroom cars.

**propane:** a heavy flammable gaseous paraffin hydrocarbon $C_3H_8$ found in crude petroleum and natural gas and used especially as a fuel.

**propeller shaft:** the shaft that transmits the vehicle engine's power from the transmission to the differential. Drive shaft.

**propylene glycol:** a sweet hygroscopic viscous liquid $C_3H_8O_2$ made from propylene and used as an antifreeze, brake fluid, and a solvent.

**proton:** an elementary particle that is identical with the nucleus of the hydrogen atom, that along with neutrons is a constituent of all other atomic nuclei, that carries a positive charge numerically equal to the charge of an electron and that has a mass (weight) of $1.673 \times 10^{-24}$ gram.

**prototype:** a first full-scale and usually functional form of a new type or design from which future production models (as of a motor vehicle) are essentially cloned.

**proving ground:** usually a conglomerate of test facilities where scientific experimentation or testing (as of motor vehicles) can be accomplished under operating conditions anticipated for the finished product before its sale to the buying public.

**prowl car:** a police vehicle used for patrol and surveillance in law enforcement and crime prevention. Squad car. Patrol car.

**Prussian blue:** a bluish green dye (usually ferric ferrocyanide) used as a sprayed or brushed coating on metallic workpieces to facilitate accurate fitting or the scribing of lines for cutting/machining guidelines.

**puffer:** mechanic's slang description/name of a vehicle supercharger/turbo charger whose pressurized air flow is pushed into and through the carburetor. As contrasted to a huffer that pulls the incoming charge-air through the carburetor before compressing the charge.

**puller:** any of many mechanical devices used to apply a pulling/stretching/tension force in order to remove, move, position, or tighten an object. Sometimes applied to front-wheel-drive vehicles as contrasted to rear-wheel-drive pushers. The tractor motive unit for a trailer(s).

**pulley:** a wheel used to transmit power by means of a band, belt, cord, cable, rope, or chain passing over its rim and linked with a suitable power-receiving device.

**Pullman:** sometimes used as descriptive of a very large and usually ostentatious automobile.

273

**pumice:** a very fine-grit abrasive/polishing powder of volcanic glass used for finishing and polishing.

**pump:** a device that raises, transfers, or compresses fluids or that attenuates gases especially by suction or pressure or both.

**punch:** a tool usually in the form of a short rod of steel that is variously shaped at the working end for performing different operations (as forming, perforating, embossing, or cutting).

**punch press:** a press equipped with cutting, shaping, or combination dies for working on material (as metal).

**puncture:** to make or a hole made by puncturing (forcing a pointed instrument or object) into material. As a tank or container.

**puncture proof:** a tank (as for fuel) or an inner tube (as for air in a pneumatic vehicle tire) that is made of or lined with a material that is relatively impervious to puncture damage or that automatically seals the puncture hole to minimize leakage.

**purr:** mechanic's descriptive sound of a finely-tuned vehicle engine's exhaust.

**purse:** the total amount of money offered in prizes to the contestants participating in a competitive event such as an automobile race.

**push bar:** a wooden or hard rubber-like material attached to the front bumper area of a race car support vehicle to make contact with a fitting on the rear of the race car to facilitate push-starting.

**push car:** the support vehicle used by a racing pit crew to push-start a race car when appropriate at the starting line of the racecourse.

**push fit:** descriptive of the tightness of the clearance between mating parts when they can be pushed into place by a mechanic's hand-strength.

**pyrometer:** an instrument for measuring high temperatures usually beyond the range of mercurial thermometers generally by measuring the change in electrical resistance in a metal, by the generation of an electric current as by a thermo-couple, or by the increase in intensity of light radiated by an incandescent body.

**P:** the position marker (usually the first or uppermost in the shift-order) on an automatic transmission shift indicator known as "Park", in which the gearing is disengaged from the engine and "locked" mechanically to prevent any rotation of the output shaft in either direction. See Park.

**parade lap:** in a closed-circuit race, the lap or laps prior to the pace lap (the last turn around the track before the green flag drops) allowing drivers to find their qualifying positions and warm up the cars.

**parallel circuit:** electrical circuits using a common ground (negative) and a common power source (positive), allowing individual circuits to operate independently and simultaneously without mutual interaction or interference. Series circuit.

**parasite loss:** energy (fuel) used for no productive purpose, such as for overcoming friction or drag (aerodynamic or road) caused by any device or part that does not contribute to the primary mission of a vehicle--transport.

**pH:** the standard scale of acidity/alkalinity with pH-0 being most acid, pH-7 being neutral, and pH-14 most alkaline. Several tests are used, the "litmus test" using a chemically-treated paper that changes color with pH change is most common.

**Pikes Peak:** the 14,110-foot Colorado Mountain that lends its name to the annual "Fourth of July Pikes Peak Hill Climb", a premier vehicle competition up one of our highest highways.

**pizza cutter:** a tall very narrow racing wheel (minimizing road and aerodynamic drag) that resembles the pizza knife/wheel. Evolution is toward smaller diameter but still skinny profiles.

**pony car:** so named because of its agility, possibly Freudian-tied to the Ford Mustang as the pony icon.

**powder puff:** a competitive vehicle event strictly for women.

**ppm:** parts per million, the accepted statement of quantitative measurement of exhaust pollutants compared to the total exhaust.

**prindle:** acronym for the automatic x-m shift sequence indicator PRNDL.

**psi:** abbreviation for pounds per square inch expression of fluid pressure or stress.

**Pyroil:** trademarked lubricating oil using various metallic elements such as copper, lead, molybdenum, and sulfur in suspension to improve its high-temperature lubricity.

**pyrolysis:** chemical reaction accomplished by or dependent upon heat (usually high).

## AUTOMOBILE ARTICULATION

### WHADDAYACALLIT?

| AMERICAN | ENGLISH | FRENCH | GERMAN |
|---|---|---|---|
| Displacement | Capacity | Capacite | Hub raum |
| Engine | Motor | Moteur | Motor |
| Exhaust | Exhaust | Debiliter | Aus puff |
| Fender | Wing<br>Mudguard | Amortisseur<br>Garde-boue | Kot fluegel |
| Gasoline | Petrol | Essence | Benzine |
| Hood | Bonnet | Capote | Haube |
| Kerosene | Paraffin | Petrole | Petroleum |
| Muffler | Silencer | Silencieux<br>Pot de eachapment | Aus puff<br>dampfer |
| Planetary | Epicyclic | | Planeten<br>radsatz |
| Rumble seat | Dickey | Siege de<br>derriere | Geotfened<br>hindern<br>sittze |
| Sedan | Saloon | Conduite inter-<br>ieure | Wagen |
| Station wagon | Shooting brake<br>Estate car | Wagon-salon | Combi wagen |
| Top | Hood | Capote | Dach |
| Town car | Coupe de ville | Sedanca de ville | Stadtwagen |
| Transmission | Gearbox | Boite de vitesse | Getribe |
| Tread | Track | Escartement des<br>roues | Wagen breite |
| Trunk | Boot | Tronc | Koffer raum |
| Two-cycle | Two-stroke | Deux temts | Zwei takt |
| Windshield | Windscreen | Glace | Windschutz |

NO PARKING!

OUTSTANDING TICKETS

**"Q" Cars:** there have been ten (10) automobiles with "Q" as the first letter in the name. Can you name even one?

**quadrant:** usually denoting an arc of 90° or less such as the scale on certain instruments (ammeter/voltmeter, temperature, fuel level, oil pressure, et al.). Sometimes as a metal arc with notched teeth for holding a throttle or ignition timing control at a desired angular position.

**Quadrajet:** a General Motors/Rochester high-flow-rate carburetor for large V-8 engines of the muscle-car era. Quadrajets are popular replacements for other carburetors by hot-rodders seeking better "breathing" capacity for high-performance engines.

**Quad-4:** a small-displacement 4-cylinder engine with double overhead cams intended by Oldsmobile to overshadow the performance of imported super race sports cars. It does, with traditional American reliability.

**quadrinial:** having four ways or roads converging at a point, not necessarily at right angles as a common "cross roads".

**quality control:** an integrated system of inspections and measurements used in manufacturing to insure the fit and functioning of the end product.

**quart:** one-fourth of a gallon liquid measure, the American standard measure of quantity of vehicle lubricating oils.

**quarter final:** the race immediately preceding a semifinal automobile elimination race (oval track, sports car, drag, et al.). Used to reduce the number of race cars to a safe and manageable group while selecting the final participants as the fastest competitors for the "main event".

**quartz-iodine lamp:** a head light with a quartz bulb and tungsten filament and filled with gaseous iodine giving a brighter light and preventing blackening of the bulb's inner surface.

**quench:** to cool (as heated metal) suddenly by immersion (as in water or oil) to control the "temper" (strength and hardness) of tools and vehicle parts to increase their strength, wearability, and longevity.

**quench area:** a portion of the combustion chamber of an internal combustion engine used to control the rate of flame-front propagation and combustion pressure distribution.

**quick-fix:** an expedient repair intended to temporarily prevent a machine's failure or to fix a breakage until permanent repair or replacement can be accomplished.

**quill:** a hollow shaft surrounding another shaft (which may also be hollow) to reduce surface rubbing velocity (as in high-rpm turbocharger sleeve bearings) or to control gaseous or liquid flow by the sliding or rotating alignment of flow passages (ports) in the shafts.

**Quonset:** a building (often prefabricated) with a semicircular arching roof using bolted steel trusses and corrugated metal covering often used for vehicle shops and storage by the military and large construction projects. Though originally intended to be portable and temporary many Quonset structures are permanent and adapted for universal usage.

## LAGNIAPPE

**Quattroporte:** the Maserati model so-named simply because it had four doors. The most irrational, while being logically descriptive.

**quenching:** rapid cooling of the leading edge of combustion flame front by contact with cooler combustion area surfaces, extinguishing the flame before all fuel is burned. See quench area.

**quick change:** an easily removable pair of gears in a race car gear system to facilitate quick ratio changes at the race track.

**quick charger:** a battery charger that supplies a high initial amperage to a discharged battery and automatically "tapers" (reduces) the charge rate, thus providing a faster turn-around time for disabled vehicles. Not as satisfactory as a slow-charge for many hours.

### Queer Cars

The one-wheeled car (gyro-stabilized) built and patented by Charles Taylor, a Denver engineer, in the mid-fifties. Ford's two two-wheeled (gyro-stabilized) experimental concept cars, a full-size Fairlane "500" (?) and the 1961 Gyron model.

The eight-wheeled 1911 Octo-Auto by American M.O. Reeves steered all four front wheels and the two rearmost. The first front-and-rear steering automobile and the first powered by a V-8 engine.

"Bucky" Fuller's 1933-1934 incomparable Dymaxion was rear-engined (Ford flat-head V-8), front-wheel-drive, and rear steered.

Herman P. Anderson's 1958 clear plastic six-foot diameter Ball Car was driven the thirty miles from his Brentwood home to the Nashville Tennessee State Fair, followed by a seven-mile-long queue of traffic, afraid to pass a ball rolling along the highway. Dubbed the "Marsmobile" by a Nashville newspaper because a following elderly driver suffered a heart attack and when revived was yelling "the Martians are coming"--Orson Wells' radio program inspired.

**R-Cars:** In between the Raba automobile built in Hungary (1912-1925) and the Rytecraft Scootacar built in Great Britain (1934-1940) there are 266 other cars in the family whose names start with the letter "R". There are two Rolls-Royces among the "in-betweens" that some of us "red, white, and blue Yankee Doodles" will always see differently than the rest of the world views <u>the</u> Rolls-Royce--the only one they know, the "Limey" Rolls-Royce. Few will believe--because too few know--about that Great American Rolls-Royce built by the Rolls-Royce of America, Inc., Springfield, Massachusetts, USA from 1919 until our "Depression of 1929" killed the incomparable "Springfield Rolls" in 1931. In a factory purchased from the American Wire Wheel Company, the American Rolls-Royce Company American Craftsmen built 2,944 "Springfield Rolls". Although the automobiles were clones (identical twins), unlike the British parent, R-R of America always featured and advertised complete coachwork and delivered completed turn-key-cars to their customers. Most bodies were by Brewster, a firm that was taken over by R-R of America, making the entire car "in-house". The British Rolls-Royce--the one everyone knows--covered England, starting in Manchester in 1904, moving to Derby in 1906, and to Cheshire after World War II in 1946 after surviving the German bombings in World War I and the "Battle of Britain". The Rolls-Royce continues as "The Best Car in the World" throughout the world despite the fervor of those who genuflect to Henry Ford's "Tin Lizzie" and whose Model "Ts" wear the bumper sticker "Recycled from Old Rolls-Royce Parts". The R-R marque that adorned the rooftop radiator underneath the "Flying Lady" changed from red letters to black letters supposedly to honor and mourn Sir Henry Royce who died in 1933. Beginning in 1953, the "Best" became better when Rolls began buying General Motors' Hydromatic transmissions. Is there only one marque beginning with the letter "R" that is worthy of mention? Some think "yes"!

**Raba:** unquestionably the first "automobile word", or possibly any word, in an alphabetical listing of words beginning with the letter "R". See R-cars.

**rabbet:** a technique used for joining wood as the frame members and panels in early automobiles that involves the fitting of matched grooves or channels in adjoining pieces of wood.

**rabbit:** race car slang for the car in a two-or-more-car racing team that is assigned to go as fast as possible in the early stages of a long race to entice other competitors to abuse or break their race cars so that the designated driver of the team can drive conservatively and safely during the early laps with the intention of a strong winning finish at the end.

**rabbit ears:** a usually roof-mounted vehicle-version of the in-home dipole television antenna with two rods connected at the front to form a horizontal-Vee used for TV or other radio-frequency signal reception. Or just for ego polishing.

**race:** (1) A competitive speed event for vehicles, or to compete in such competition. (2) To speed (as a vehicle engine) without a working load or with the vehicle transmission disengaged (out-of-gear). (3) A channel, groove, or track in which something rolls or slides (as for the balls or rollers in bearings).

**racecourse:** a course for racing, usually implying over a significant distance with many directional changes (curves). Raceway.

**race driver:** one who is skilled and usually specifically trained and experienced in driving motor vehicles at high speeds in competitive events. Racer.

**racehorse start:** the beginning of a competitive speed event for vehicles with all contestants starting abreast from a standstill and sometimes with added requirements such as drivers being required to sprint to their vehicles and start the engines.

**racer:** a driver who drives race cars/motorcycles and/or a car/motorcycle that is designed, configured, and intended to go fast in competition with others. Race driver.

**race track:** a usually oval course of relatively short distance designed for highspeed vehicle racing over a designated number of complete circuits of the oval (laps). Oval track.

**raceway:** See race course.

**RAC horsepower:** a horsepower rating system originally calculated from engine displacement and instigated in England by the Royal Automobile Club and designed to establish tax rates rather than as a true measure of a vehicle engine's power. Now obsolete and discredited.

**rack:** a bar with teeth machined into one flat (face) for meshing (gearing) with a pinion or worm gear to transform rotary motion to linear motion or vice versa (as in a vehicle steering mechanism). See rack and pinion.

**rack and pinion:** a vehicle steering system in which a pinion (gear) on the lower end of the steering shaft engages (meshes) with a transverse rack whose left-right-left linear movement is relayed to the steerable wheels by tie rods and steering arms.

**rack railway:** a railway having between its rails a rack whose teeth mesh with a gear wheel or pinion of the locomotive for better traction on steep grades. One of the better known is the Pikes Peak "Cog" Railway whose locomotive does not use the rack solely for steep segments of its railway but is cogged (geared) from base-to-peak-to-base because it's too steep all the way there and back for wheel traction to do the job. Cog railway.

**racy:** having a body fitted for high-speed driving and looking like it--long-bodied, lean, and streamlined.

**RADAR:** as applied to vehicles, a radio-frequency (RF) device or system for locating, identifying, and accurately measuring the speed of a vehicle (as one suspected of breaking a posted speed limit) by means of ultrahigh-frequency radio waves reflected from the speeding vehicle and converted to a visible miles-per-hour read-out by a police officer's radar "gun".

**radar detector:** a usually portable radio frequency receiver that is designed, manufactured, sold, purchased, and used for just one purpose--to warn a vehicle driver that a police officer is monitoring vehicle speeds in his vicinity and therefore to aid in the driver's premeditated and deliberate intention to violate legal statutes establishing speed limits. Patently an accessory to the commission of a crime and therefore illegal under common law. Radar detectors are illegal and prohibited by statute in many countries and in one of Uncle Sugar's states. Fuzz Buster.

**radar patrolled:** as when a section of highway is being scanned by a police officer with a radar gun to detect and apprehend vehicles that are exceeding the posted speed limits.

**radial engine:** a multi-cylinder internal combustion engine using one or more rows of cylinders that radiate outward like the spokes of a wheel from the crankshaft which has only one throw (crank journal) for each row of cylinders. Each row has at least 3 (up to 9) cylinders (odd numbers to insure running balance) with one being the "master cylinder" whose connecting rod is bearinged to the crankshaft with all other rods being link rods "pinned" around the "big end" bearing boss of the master rod. Rare in typical land vehicles but commonly used in airplanes, helicopters and military combat tracked-vehicles (tanks).

**radial ply tire:** a vehicle tire in which the reinforcing plies are arranged radially (at right angles to the bead, the nominal direction of travel of the vehicle). Radial tire.

**radiation:** the combined processes of emission, transmission, and absorption of radiant (heat) energy.

**radiator:** an essential function of every internal combustion engine, the elimination of excess heat from combustion by cooling the engine to its design temperature parameters, the use of cooling fins for air-cooled engines, and the use of a liquid coolant heat exchanger (radiator) for transferring waste heat from the engine to the ambient air. The engine coolant radiator is often complemented by oil cooling devices (radiators). Most vehicle radiators are actually forced heat convection devices (not primarily pure radiation) using coolant pumps, and air blowers or fans.

**radiator cap:** the sealing cover (usually screwed on) that closes the filler pipe or opening to a vehicle radiator header tank or reserve reservoir (overflow or expansion tank).

**radiator core:** the radiating surface, usually finned tubes or a honeycomb labyrinth, filled with coolant liquid supplied from upper and lower header tanks.

**radiator flush:** a chemical additive for radiator coolant that loosens scale and water contaminants so that they can be drained. To treat a radiator with chemicals and drain and add new coolant.

**radiator grill:** a decorative and protective guard to conceal a vehicle radiator and protect it from impact by road debris while allowing free passage of cooling air. Grill.

**radiator sealant:** a chemical additive compounded to remain liquid while in a coolant solution but that hardens when exposed to air so that any radiator/coolant system leakage will harden at the leak site and seal the leak.

**radiator shell:** a metal covering or shroud around a vehicle front radiator that protects it from side damage and sometimes forms an extension of the adjacent sheet metal (as of an engine hood).

**radiator shutter:** a Venetian blind-like arrangement of overlapping thin flat narrow strips (slats) that turn to open or restrict the flow of cooling air through a vehicle radiator to maintain engine temperature when driving in very cold weather.

**radiotracer:** a radioactive material incorporated in a vehicle component so that its condition or wear can be determined by the amount of the tracer found by oil analysis or direct-reading detectors.

**radius rod:** a suspension structural member that establishes and maintains the exact fore-and-aft location of a front or rear vehicle axle.

**rag top:** mechanic's or automobile buff's lingo for a convertible or roadster top because of its usual cloth fabric material.

**rail:** race car lingo for a dragster ($\frac{1}{4}$-mile drag racer) identifiable by its large rear engine and tires and its very long low and narrow nose with usually small front wheels/tires. Rail derives from the long nearly parallel tubing frame (rails).

**rain check:** originally, an admission ticket stub good for a later (future) automobile race when the currently scheduled race is canceled because of rain.

**rain date:** a date, usually scheduled and announced in advance, when an automobile race will be run/completed/re-run should the currently scheduled race be canceled due to rain before or during the race.

**raised letters:** the very large and wide tires with machismo names in big white or garishly-colored raised (molded) letters on the tire sidewalls of some show-off four-wheel-drive off-road vehicles.

**rake:** sometimes applied to describe a sloping windshield or the slant-back sloping top and trunk top of a passenger vehicle.

**rally:** a competitive automobile "run" conducted on public roads and under ordinary traffic rules with the object of main-training specified average speed between checkpoints over a route unknown to the participants until the start of the race.

**ram air:** charge air forced into a vehicle radiator for cool-ing or into a carburetor intake duct by the forward motion of a vehicle through the air with the amount of air "rammed" into the cooling or induction air passages determined by the speed of the vehicle.

**ram air induction:** raising the carburetor air intake pressure by using the momentum of the incoming air enhanced by a tuned-length air-passage. Tuned intake.

**ramp:** (1) a sloping floor or sometimes two wheel-width tracks from ground-level to vehicle-floor height to facilitate loading of cargo or other vehicles. (2) The entry/exit access road to a freeway from the secondary road system.

**Ranchero:** a popular Ford stylized pickup truck often used in lieu of a more formal passenger car.

**R and D:** abbreviation for Research and Development whose ef-forts are usually first seen by the public as a manufacturer's "concept car" when featured at "auto shows".

**range change:** a gear-ratio range multiplier usually for long-haul cargo trucks incorporated as a two-speed differential (extra set of selectable gears) that doubles the number of speed changes (gear ratios) incorporated in the main trans-mission (gearbox).

**Rankine cycle:** the theoretical "ideal" thermodynamic cycle (heat/energy balance) that defines the entropy of steam used as the working fluid in converting heat into useful work (power). Rankine propounded a modification of the Carnot Cycle with both illustrating the Second Law of Thermodynamics and applying to either reciprocating or turbine engines using steam as their working fluid. "Steam" is available with a wide range of work-ing temperatures from the low-boiling-point Freons through the more common "water steam" to the very-high-boiling-point liquid-metal, mercury--all "obeying" the laws of Carnot, Rankine, and Thermodynamics.

**Rankine Temperature:** a temperature scale that corresponds to the Kelvin Scale, but is based on the absolute zero of the Fahrenheit system, so that 0° Rankine equals -459.69° Fahrenheit, thus making the freezing-point of water 491.69° Rankine and its boiling-point 671.69° Rankine.

**rapid transit:** the use of faster-than-normal passenger-carrying vehicles for mass transportation (elevated, subway, or surface) in urban or suburban areas.

**rash:** mechanic's lingo to describe minor damage/defects in a vehicle's exterior surfaces comparable to a human skin-rash, such as scratches, scrapes, or abrasions that "barely scratch the surface" not causing major material deformation/dents. Superficial cosmetic degradation. Parking lot dings.

**rasp:** a coarse file with cutting points instead of lines and used for rapid removal of soft materials as of some aluminums or wood.

**raster:** the scanning lines projected on the viewing screen by a cathode ray "gun" that use dots to form a picture image or the graphics output of a computer. CAD/CAM.

**rat-a-tat-tat:** a vocal description often used by vehicle drivers/mechanics to illustrate an engine's tapping sounds. Clicking sound. Vibration.

**ratchet:** a mechanism consisting of a bar or wheel having in-clined teeth, into which a pawl drops, so that motion can be imparted to the bar or wheel to allow effective motion in one direction only, in small self-locking steps, that are repeat-able using small angular movements of the operating handle/lever.

**ratchet wheel:** a toothed wheel held in a locked position or rotated by an engaging pawl (a usually spring-loaded pivoting latch/tongue).

**ratchet wrench:** a mechanic's tool available in many configura-tions allowing small but repeatable increments of rotary motion selectively in either direction for tightening or loosening.

Most common is the ratchet handle with interchangeable sockets and other adaptors.

**rated horsepower:** exact meaning is dependent upon which "horsepower" is intended, but the most meaningful, useful, and scientifically accurate "horsepower" is "brake horsepower" as measured by a prony brake or engine dynamometer from the actual horsepower produced at the output shaft of the engine. See rated power.

**rated load:** the maximum weight for which a vehicle is designed and authorized to carry. Maximum load. Maximum gross weight.

**rated power:** the horsepower (maximum) of a vehicle engine so measured and stated in accordance with a recognized standard. See rated horsepower.

**rated speed:** the engine speed at which rated power (maximum horsepower) is developed, a speed usually somewhat slower than the maximum allowable rpm (red line), and obtainable from a power curve for the engine. Horsepower is the product of two primary variables: speed (rpm) and torque (foot-pounds), and modified by a number of small variables. The speed (rated speed) at which peak horsepower is developed by a specific engine can be shifted up (faster) or down (slower) by changing the cam's timing relationship to the crankshaft speed.

**rattletrap:** a mechanic's pejorative slang expression for a usually older automobile that is rattly or rickety and in a state of disrepair or gross neglect.

**rattle wrench:** an electric or pneumatic powered-tool that converts hammering force into turning torque force for loosening/tightening of threaded fastening, deriving the mechanic's slang name from the sound of its operation.

**ray gun:** a disparaging term that is used especially by those who would flaunt or disregard our posted speed limits to describe a police radar scanner device.

**reach:** (1) most commonly, the length (depth) of threads on a spark plug or (2) a bearing shaft or coupling pole.

**reaction engine:** a jet engine or rocket motor that develops thrust by expelling a jet/stream of fluid or particles from a rearward-pointing nozzle.

**reaction member:** any suspension arm, bar, or strut that reacts (supports) a load or force and provides a fixed locus for another member (as an axle).

**reactive suspension:** a package of two or more close-spaced axles linked between the axles or their suspension systems to provide interactive response to braking or power forces or to road-bump/bounce.

**reactor:** static reaction section of fixed vanes or deflectors in a torque converter.

**rear axle:** a vehicle's back axle.

**rear-end roll-steer:** the steering effect on a cornering vehicle caused by the rear suspension roll-deflection.

**rear engine:** a vehicle engine located aft of the rear axle/wheels.

**rear fender:** the body panel or formed shape covering the rear wheel of a vehicle.

**rear spoiler:** a transverse air foil, body panel, or flat plate at or near the rear of a vehicle, ostensibly to reduce drag and lift.

**rear-view mirror:** an inside, usually center-mounted at the windshield top, mirror to provide the driver a rearward view through the back and side windows.

**rear-wheel drive:** a vehicle using the rear wheels for traction, whether powered by a front, mid, or rear engine.

**re-babbitt:** to renew a damaged, defective, or worn plain/sleeve bearing by melting out the old bearing metal, pouring new molten metal as a replacement, and, after cooling, machining the new metal to proper dimensional size and surface finish.

**rebore:** machine boring of a damaged or worn cylinder to an oversize dimension proper for a new or replacement piston.

**rebound:** return movement of suspension travel beyond its static position after extreme compression from the bounce of a severe road bump.

**rebound clip:** a restrainer to prevent space separation between leaves of a multileaf spring on rebound from a bump.

**rebound stop:** a device that increases spring rate towards the limit of rebound travel and that stops spring travel at a preset limit.

**rebuilder:** a usually collision-damaged vehicle that is considered to be repairable by a competent mechanic/shop and that is expected to be represented as such (as a rebuilt vehicle) by any subsequent seller, but often isn't. "Builder".

**recall:** a directive/order by a government agency, or a manufacturer of vehicles, notifying of a correctable defect that if the current vehicle owner will present it to an authorized repair facility the defect will be corrected at the sellers expense. Some restrictions usually apply.

**recapped tire:** a worn or damaged tire whose original tread is totally or partially removed and rebuilt with new rubber/ synthetic to the original tread design and thickness using heat-molding and vulcanizing processes.

**recessed piston head:** a piston with a concave depression to reduce compression ratio and or to generate a swirl pattern for better mixing of the fuel and air.

**recessed spark plug:** placement of a spark plug down in a hole, e.g., between the cam chambers of a dual-overhead-cam engine, in an access hole in a tall valve cover, in a cylinder head with a large-capacity coolant jacket, et al.

**rechrome:** a process of straightening, smoothing, and electro-plating damaged vehicle bumpers and other chrome-plated parts to as-good-as-new condition and appearance.

**reciprocating balls:** possibly the simplest application is a tube filled end-to-end with hardened balls with no space be-tween them so that a force or movement imparted against the ball at either end is transmitted to the ball at the other end relatively undiminished in force or movement. The effect is reversible. Some early overhead valve systems operated without push rods or rocker arms. A vertical tube was filled with balls with the bottom ball in contact with the cam lobe through a cam-follower rod at the lowest point of the tube, which-- still filled with balls--had a smooth 180° bend down to the upper end of the valve stem where a short push-rod completed the contact from the top ball to the valve-stem end. Simple. Effective. Efficient. No clearance/free-play/lash.

**reciprocating engine:** an engine in which a piston attached to a crankshaft by a connecting rod moves back-and-forth in a cylinder with a closed end and coordinated inlet and exhaust valves that facilitate the thermodynamic cycle (intake stroke, compression stroke, combustion/power stroke, and exhaust stroke, if a four-stroke/cycle engine). Turbine engine. Jet thrust engine. Rocket thrust motor. Electric motor. Steam engine.

**reciprocating forces:** in a vehicle engine, in addition to friction forces to be overcome from sliding/scraping/hammering acting on the bearings/piston/rings/valves, the acceleration/ deceleration and mass/momentum forces creep into the big picture.

**recirculating ball gear:** used where smooth low-friction gear drive is essential as in a worm-and-nut steering gear in which ball bearings that recirculate occupy space between the nut and worm teeth, eliminating rubbing contact and substituting rolling contact (ball bearing teeth).

**reclaimed oil:**  oil that has been used in vehicle engines and drained at prescribed intervals is stored, filtered, and refined and recompounded for reuse in vehicles.

**recliner seat:**  a vehicle seat whose back is hinged at the base to allow it to lean backward to accommodate occupant preference as to seat-back angle with a positive lock in the desired position.  Some seat-backs may be lowered to a horizontal position, forming a bed.

**recoil starter:**  a small-engine (as a lawnmower or chain saw) starter using either coil-spring-stored energy that, when released, turns the engine for starting or a hand-pulled cord that is rewound by a coil-spring-reel for successive cranking pulls, to turn the engine until it starts.

**recon car:**  a lightly-armored military vehicle designed for all-terrain travel and equipped with mobile communications to relay findings from its reconnaissance.

**reconditioned engine:**  a used or damaged vehicle engine that is rebuilt/remanufactured usually to equal or higher standards than when new with all substandard components and parts refurbished or replaced.  A "short-block" implies that the cylinder head and bolt-on accessories were not overhauled.

**record run:**  at a vehicle race approved to certify records (of whatever type, e.g., a world landspeed record in a particular sanctioned/recognized class) or the official run, observed and timed by certified judges, by any vehicle that has met all qualifying requirements.

**Red Crown:**  an early day trademark for a gasoline that used a lighted crown-like globe atop its fuel dispensers and that gave free miniature "red crowns" for vehicle inner tube/tire valve-stem caps as an advertising gimmick.

**redesign:**  when a vehicle component/device proves to be substandard in service it is customary for the manufacturer to improve the piece for future models and often to offer the improvement at no-cost to existing vehicle owners.

**red flag:**  an internationally-honored signal used at automobile races to signal all racing to stop immediately with all competitors holding positions.

**red-green blindness:**  an individual eye affliction involving dichomatism in which the color spectrum is seen in tones of yellow and blue.  A legal disqualification for licensing for certain occupations requiring red-green perception.  Color blindness.

**red heat:**  the temperature at which a substance is considered to be red hot, the red glow visible to the eye.  Red hot.

**red hot:**  a material's state of heating that causes it to assume a distinct red color.  Red heat.

**red lead:**  an orange-red to brick-red lead oxide ($Pb_3O_4$) used in storage batteries, in glass and ceramics, and as a paint pigment, usually in corrosion-resistant coatings.

**red light:**  an internationally-recognized warning of danger as a highway traffic stop signal, a vehicle tail light, or braking stop light, et al.  In a drag race or other competitive speed events, to cross the starting line early.

**red line:**  a recommended safety limit, as on a vehicle instrument, the fastest, farthest, or highest point in degree considered safe and marked by a red line on the instrument face (meaning to never exceed this reading).

**Red Seal:**  trademarked vehicle engine by Continental Motors used in many "assembled" (as contrasted to "manufactured") automobiles of the 1920s-1930s and including the Kaiser-Frazer marques into the 1950s.  Many aircraft manufacturers use(d) the aircooled Continentals for power.

**reed valve:**  a one-way (check) valve with overlapping spring plates that open by pressure differential to admit a working fluid as in the intakes of two-stroke engines and some air compressors.  Not leakproof but suitable in many applications.

**Reid Vapor Pressure:**  a standard measure of fuel volatility used to indicate its volatility that affects its mixability with charge air and also its likelihood of creating a vapor lock in a vehicle fuel-delivery system.

**replicar:**  a car manufactured or sold as a kit for purchaser-assembly that purports to replicate one of the great automobiles of yesteryear but usually fails to be a reasonably accurate replica and fails the test of the marketplace.

**repo:**  vehicle lingo for a vehicle that has been repossessed and is now again being offered for sale, or the act of repossessing a vehicle, usually legally.

**repro:**  mechanic's slang for a component/part for a vehicle that is a reproduction (often illegally) of an original equipment manufacturer's (OEM) part and usually of inferior quality.

**Research Octane Number:**  one of the standard rating scales used to indicate the octane (resistance to detonation) of a vehicle fuel and usually averaged with Motor Octane Number (obtained by testing in a laboratory engine) to provide a more realistic rating of a fuel.

**reserve:** (1) A value assigned to a vehicle offered for sale at auction by the owner, representing the minimum bid that will be accepted on the vehicle. (2) A small quantity of fuel that is retained in a vehicle tank and available only by operating a special control/valve for its release to the engine, the purpose being the prevention against inadvertently exhausting the fuel supply and being stranded.

**resilver:** to remove and replace the silver reflective backing that forms the working surface of a vehicle mirror reflector.

**resonate:** to enrich or intensify sound(s).

**resonator:** a device as a vehicle exhaust system chamber designed to intensify and often to impart a throaty roar to an ordinary engine's muffled exhaust to satisfy the driver's/owner's machismo.

**restart:** to initiate another beginning of a vehicle race that has been interrupted for whatever reason (rain or accident, usually) with the competitors resuming their positions occupied at the time of interruption of racing.

**restoration:** as a vehicle of historical, monetary, or sentimental value that is returned to its original state (with degrees of perfection), or to accomplish such an endeavor.

**restraint:** (1) An act of or equipment for restraining, as a passenger or child restraint (safety belts, infant seats) to provide increased safety in the event of a crash. (2) A limit strap, snubber, stop block, et al., to restrain or restrict motion of movable parts.

**restriction plate:** an under-carburetor plate with sized-opening to limit engine power/speed by restricting charge gas flow (sometimes imposed by automobile race officials as a handicap or speed control on certain cars).

**retaining ring:** annular ring used to hold another usually circular part securely in place, e.g., the outside framing ring around an instrument cover glass or the large trim ring around a headlight cover glass.

**retard stop:** a mechanical block that restricts the amount of ignition retard by a centrifugal advance unit on a distributor shaft.

**retarded ignition:** an ignition spark that occurs after the optimum spark timing point for a particular engine, fuel, and operating condition of rpm and load.

**retarder:** a usually heavy vehicle (truck) braking aid that dissipates momentum as by electrical, hydraulic, or compression ("Jake Brake") loading.

**retractable top:** a hard-top coupe whose articulated top allows hydraulic cylinders to fold the top to a manageable size and retract it into a storage compartment behind the rear seat.

**retread:** See retreaded tire.

**retreaded tire:** a tire whose tread has been damaged or worn out that has a new tread of rubber or synthetic material vulcanized to the original carcass.

**rev:** abbreviation for revolution but often used alone or with "up" as rev up, meaning to increase the speed (revolutions-per-minute) of an engine. Revved. Revving.

**rev counter:** mechanic's lingo for a tachometer which is sometimes a true revolution counter recording as a totalizer or more commonly a revolution count per unit of time and presented as such, usually as revolutions-per-minute (RPM).

**reverse gear:** the gear in a vehicle transmission that changes the direction of rotation of the output shaft counter to the direction of rotation of the input shaft (engine), thus reversing the rotation direction of the drive wheels.

**reverse rod:** the rod from the in-car-gear-selector lever that effects the reverse selection in an automatic transmission.

**reversing alarm:** on large commercial vehicles, an acoustic warning that is automatically sounded whenever the reverse gear is selected. Back-up alarm.

**reversing light:** a usually clear light facing rearward at the rear of a vehicle to illuminate to the rear for backing safety. Back-up light.

**rheostat:** an arrangement of windings of resistance wire in a circle or straight form with a wiper contact for engaging (making electrical contact with) varying numbers of turns of wire to change the circuit resistance thus regulating current flow.

**rhombic:** in some Stirling engines having two pistons operating out of phase on a common axis, the arrangement of connecting rods and geared wheels for converting the piston push-rod's reciprocating motion into rotary motion.

**rib:** (1) the raised circumferential bands of tire tread material between parallel grooves. (2) A narrow raised section of sheet metal (often welded or riveted to a large flat sheet) used to stiffen sheet metal panels or to hold an outer panel's contour.

**Ricardo engine:** with Sir Harry Ricardo's name a research engine with variable compression ratios making it ideal for scientific laboratory testing.

**Ricardo head:** a cylinder head for side-valve (in the block) engines having high-squish and a high-turbulence combustion chamber design.

**rich mixture:** a fuel/air mixture having more fuel than the stoichiometric proportion for chemically complete combustion.

**Rickenbacker:** American automobile (1922-1927) built by Captain Eddie Rickenbacker, World War I ace and famous race driver who built and ran Eastern Airlines, and that used his fighter squadron "Hat-in-the-Ring" insignia for the car marque. The car used a V-6 engine with two flywheels for smoothness and many other engineering innovations, with its design sold to Audi who used it in two models for several years.

**right-hand drive:** a vehicle usually manufactured for countries that drive on the left side of the road and that has the steering wheel and all controls located on the right side of the vehicle.

**rim:** the part of a vehicle wheel on which the tire is mounted.

**rim flange:** the outer formed stiffener around both edges of a vehicle wheel that supports, retains, and seals the tire at the bead.

**rim width:** the width across a wheel as measured between the flanges.

**ring and pinion:** any matched pair of gears, with the "ring" being the large-diameter (usually-driven gear) and the "pinion" being the small diameter "driver" gear.

**ring expander:** a thin-section annular spring placed in a piston ring groove under a piston ring to improve the ring's sealing pressure.

**ring gap:** gap in the ring that makes it possible to spring it open slightly for installing over the ring land and into its recessed groove.

**ring gear:** a descriptive term most usually applied to the hardened steel ring with peripheral spur gear teeth that is heat-shrunk onto an engine's flywheel and driven by the starter Bendix/pinion to start the engine, but also applied to any large-diameter gear-wheel with whatever tooth design.

**ring groove:** the annular machined slot in a piston circumference into which the sealing ring is fitted.

**riser:** a vertical pipe in a tank outlet that retains a small amount of liquid (as fuel) as a reserve, available only when the reserve valve is opened.

**rivet:** a headed pin or rod of metal used to unite two or more pieces (usually plate/ sheet metal) by passing the rivet shank through matching holes in all pieces and then enlarging (up-setting) or flattening the exposed shank by hammering or pressing until a second head is forged.

**rivet gun:** a usually pneumatic hand tool that produces a repetitive hammering force to accomplish riveting.

**roadability:** the qualities of balance, "sure-footedness", stability, and steadiness that make a highway vehicle "driver friendly". Road holding.

**Road Atlanta:** a world-famous automobile racecourse, designed and built for road racing as a premier track to challenge the best contemporary race drivers.

**roadbed:** the aggregate/earth foundation and the surface layers of a highway or roadway.

**roadblock:** a road barricade usually set up by law enforcement officers when a dangerous road condition (as a bridge washout) exists ahead or to apprehend a fleeing criminal.

**roadeo:** a vehicle driver skill contest as a bus or truck roadeo (word borrowed from the western rodeo) with a variety of events such as parking at a curb (parallel) between two parked vehicles, stopping distance, acceleration, backing an eighteen-wheeler through an obstacle course into a warehouse loading door, et al.

**road feel:** sensory feedback of front suspension and steering bounce/force/vibration impact to the steering wheel and through it to the vehicle driver.

**road hog:** an inept or irresponsible vehicle driver who obstructs others especially by occupying part of another's traffic lane.

**road holding:** the qualities of a vehicle that tend to make it "hold the road".

**road map:** a map tailored to the needs of highway/road users (for pleasure or profit) showing the road network of the in-cluded area with mileages and topographic information, major construction areas, licensing and operating laws/regulations, tourist attractions, and large-scale supplements of urban population centers.

**road "metal":** automobile slang for aggregate, broken stone, gravel or other strengtheners used in building or repairing highways/roads.

**road racing:** racing over public roads specifically sports car racing over roads or over a closed course designed to simulate roads (as with chicanes, left- and righthand turns, sharp corners, and hills).

**road roller:** a machine with large-diameter heavy smooth wide rollers (often heated) used for compacting, flattening, and smoothing compactable roadway surfaces. Steam roller. Compactor.

**roadside:** the strip of land along a road and also used as a prefix word-modifier, e.g., roadside diner or roadside farmer's market.

**roadster:** a two-passenger open automobile (without windows) with a folding or removable fabric top followed by a luggage compartment (trunk) or rumble seat in the rear.

**roadster pickup:** whether you look first at the front or the rear of a vehicle, a roadster with a pickup truck cargo body, or a pickup truck with a roadster passenger compartment.

**road tanker:** a commercial vehicle with large-capacity/volume tank(s) for hauling fluids (gaseous or liquid), or bulk particulates/powder. Tanker. Tank truck.

**road test:** a test of a vehicle under practical operating conditions on an active highway, road, or street.

**road train:** a heavy commercial cargo-hauling vehicle consisting of a tractor coupled to/with multiple trailers (resembling a railroad train).

**road washer:** a usually large water-tank vehicle with high-pressure spray nozzles for flushing road debris off the surface, sometimes assisted by squeegees and heavy rotary-power scrub brushes.

**rock deflector:** a flat plate of clear plastic about 5 inches wide (high) extending across the upper front of a vehicle hood/radiator to which it is attached in a rearward-leaning attitude to deflect the on-coming air stream (and any small gravel or road debris) up and over the top preventing rock/sand-pitting of the hood/windshield. Bug deflector.

**rocker:** any of various mechanical devices that work with a rocking motion. Walking beam. Horsehead oil-well pump. Valve rocker arm.

**rocker arm:** a center-pivoted lever to push a vehicle-engine exhaust or intake valve open using force applied to the other end of the lever by a cam lobe action.

**rocker arm cover:** a protective cover and grease/oil splash container over the rocker arms and associated valve gear of a valve-in-head engine. Valve cover.

**rocker arm shaft:** a hardened shaft about which a valve rocker pivots, usually in bushings or needle bearings See rocker shaft.

**rocker panel:** in most instances the bottom 4 to 6 inches of the outside body panels of an automobile, usually from the rear of the front wheel opening beneath the door(s) lower edge(s) and ending at the front of the rear wheel opening (usually painted the same body color as adjacent panels).

**rock guard:** usually applied to a heavy plate between the front wheels sometimes extending back underneath the engine and transmission oil pans and called a skid plate to protect against large rocks.

**rock shield:** in many shapes and forms, stainless steel plates behind the front and rear wheels to shield nearby body panels from small rocks/pebbles tossed back by the tires.

**rod:** automobile jargon for: (1) hotrod, (2) engine connecting rod, (3) to ream a clogged radiator cooling tube.

**rod bearing:** the piston rod bearing for attaching it to the crankshaft throw.

**rod run:** a fun tour by a hot-rodder's club, usually as a caravan of hotrods to a car show site.

**Roesch rocker:** a pressed-steel rocker arm with a vertical pivot stud-hole with a rounded bottom where a concave-headed hardened nut retains, spaces, and serves as the rubbing/wear contact-fulcrum for the rocker arm.

**roll:** the angular displacement of a vehicle body/chassis about its longitudinal axis caused by various roll-over forces.

**roll axis:** a calculable imaginary longitudinal line through a vehicle's "roll centers", the most influential being the center-of-mass (gravity center).

**roll bar:** (1) An overhead structural beam or tube that loops over the passenger seat and has aft angular bracing designed to protect occupants in case of a turn-/rollover. (2) The anti-roll or anti-sway bars incorporated into a vehicle suspension system.

**roll cage:** a structural framework of beams or tubes attached to, or built-in, a vehicle that offers full-surround protection to all operator/passengers in the event of a collision or roll-over.

**roll center:** a moveable center determined by suspension geometry, load distribution and other variables that are constantly changing vehicle characteristics and about which it tends to roll.

**roller bearing:** a bearing in which the journal rotates in peripheral contact with a number of caged and hardened rollers.

**roller clutch:** a freewheeling or one-way rotation clutch using hardened steel balls in tapered detents.

**roller lifter:** a cam follower, lifter, or tappet with a small usually needle-bearinged roller or wheel making rolling contact with the cam lobe.

**rolling radius:** the distance from the axle center of a vehicle wheel to the roadway.

**rolling resistance:** the vehicle's resistance to rolling on a flat roadway consisting of tire friction and mechanical drive-train friction but excluding aerodynamic drag.

**rolling road:** mechanic's slang for a chassis (whole vehicle) dynamometer.

**roll pin:** a retaining pin device, usually pressed in through matching holes in a collar on a shaft and usually configured as a split-walled tube-section of spring steel.

**roll rate:** the angular velocity of a vehicle's rolling motion as initially affected by suspension stiffness (until one side loses contact with the roadway).

**roof bow:** a metal or steam-bent wood frame with a rounded top extending from side-to-side of a vehicle to form and support a flexible (usually fabric) top covering as for a convertible, phaeton, or roadster automobile or a cargo-carrying flat-bed or stake-bodied truck. Top bow.

**roof console:** a housing as for supplementary accessories, controls, or instruments mounted inside a vehicle roof or a housing as for air conditioning or ventilating equipment mounted outside, atop the roof. Ceiling console.

**roof rack:** a usually open rack or platform with side rails for carrying extra luggage or out-sized light cargo as bicycles, light canoes, or skis atop a passenger vehicle.

**roof rail:** a usually low rail around the periphery of a vehicle roof for securing/ tying items hauled on the top.

**roof scoop:** a small controllable air inlet or exit in a passenger car top.

**roof spoiler:** an aerodynamic roof device used on passenger cars to reduce rear-end turbulence and prevent rear window splash obscuration and on trucks to streamline airflow at the truck-to-trailer gap and around the following trailer(s).

**roof vent:** a usually hinged opening in a larger vehicle (van or truck) to force air in or out for ventilation.

**roof window:** a transparent panel (usually openable or removable) in a vehicle top to provide extra ventilation or visibility. Moon roof. Sun roof.

**rooster tail:** a high arching cloud of dust, salt, or track debris thrown up behind a fast-moving race car--a common sight and expression at the Bonneville Utah Salt Flats "flying mile" racecourse.

**ropeway:** (1) A powered endless aerial cable used to transport freight (as logs and ore). (2) A fixed or multiple cable(s) between supporting towers that serve as an overhead track for suspended passenger- or freight-carrying gondolas.

**Roots supercharger:** a belt-, chain-, or gear-driven engine supercharger in which intake air (charge air) is pressurized by the contiguous rotation of two or three meshing-lobed rotors.

**rose coupler:** an eye (looped-end) or ball-and-socket connector (as for a trailer) that uses a spherical bearing.

**rotameter:** a fluid flow-rate meter consisting of a usually tapered vertical graduated glass tube containing a loose-fitting, free-floating marker whose height indicates the volume of fluid flowing upward through the tube.

**rotary engine:** any engine that converts fuel's expansion energy directly to rotating mechanical power as: (1) a turbine using gas flow reacting upon blades, buckets or vanes; (2) a Wankel using a tri-lobed cam-rotor; or (3) early aircraft engines whose crankshaft was fixed/stationary with the cylinders rotating and fixed to the load receiver (as a propeller). Not a true rotary, just a reciprocating engine that looks like a rotary to the uninitiated.

**rotary valve:** any valve that matches ports in a rotatable disc or sleeve with a matching fixed disc or sleeve port when the movable element is turned.

**rotating valve:** a rotary valve whose movable element is continuously driven and that delivers intermittent or timed pulses of fluid whose duration and frequency results from design choice of port location, shape, and size. Distributor valve.

**rotating beacon:** any light used for warning or as a marker that projects a beam that rotates as the light source turns continuously.

**rotational balance:** the correction of out-of-balance or off-center weight distribution in a rotating device that reduces unwanted vibration and potentially destructive forces.

**Rotoflex joint:** trademarked universal joint using a hexagonal rubber (donut-like) ring as the flexing member that is similar to U-joints using flexible material selectively bolted between flanges or yokes.

**rotor:** any of various components or parts that rotates about its own axis usually within or attached to a stationary (as related to the rotor) part, e.g., brake rotor, distributor rotor, alternator rotor, water-pump impeller, et al.

**rouge:** any of various very fine grit abrasives usually in paste form for polishing metal.

**Royal Enfield:** marque of a famous British motorcycle.

**rpm:** abbreviation used for revolutions per minute.

**rubbing strip:** the molding strip usually at the widest bulge along a vehicle's body side panels that prevents minor dents and scratches from irresponsible opening of doors of closely-parked vehicles. Door molding. Side molding.

**Rudge nuts:** quick release wheel-retaining nuts as on racing cars used to speed tire/ wheel changes during pit stops. Instead of multiple "lug" nuts the Rudge (originally a "knock-off" with hammer "ears") was one large hex-head nut screwed onto the center axle threads using a splined wheel-hub and ground taper-seating cones for a strong retaining system.

**rumble seat:** a folding seat built into the trunk compartment of coupe- or roadsterbodied automobiles without top or window protection and usually seating two passengers who had to climb in over the rear fenders and body side.

**runaway ramp:** an exit ramp from a steep downhill roadway designed exclusively for vehicles which have had brake failure and cannot slow their downhill acceleration to make a high speed exit onto a side road with an uphill grade and high-drag surface therefore slowing the runaway vehicle to a safe stop.

**running board:** a long step extending from the front fender to the rear fender beneath the door sills along both sides of early day automobiles to facilitate entry/egress to/from the high-floors.

**running gear:** usually defined as the unsprung components of a motor vehicle: the axles, wheels, suspension, and steering parts.

**running-in:** the process of driving or operating a new or re-built engine or vehicle at reduced power and speed to condition the new operating parts to the movement and vibrations of high-power-speed.

**runout:** eccentricity, out-of-roundness or wobble of a shaft, wheel, or other rotating part of concern only when design or manufacturing parameters/tolerances are exceeded.

**rust:** the reddish brittle coating formed on iron or other ferrous alloys when exposed to air and moisture by oxidation resulting in the hydrated ferric oxide film.

**rust bucket:** mechanic's slang for a badly rusted vehicle or component usually as a result of neglect or unprotected expo-sure to known rusting hazards.

**rust inhibitor:** a dipped or painted coating or film that shields the metal from contact with air or moisture.

**rust proof:** a metal or alloy that is impervious to rusting.

**Rzeppa joint:** a constant velocity universal joint in which driving power is transmitted through caged balls to the driven shaft.


### LAGNIAPPE

**radix point:** the index which separates the digits associated with negative powers from those associated with the zero and positive powers of the base of the number system in which a quantity is repre-sented. Binary point. Decimal point.


### WILLY T. RIBBS, JR.
(automobile race-driver <u>nonpareil</u>)

The first African-American to drive the famed Indianapolis "500" Memorial Day automobile race, in 1991, Willy T. Ribbs topped his meteoric rise as a world-class race driver on the Indy Car cir-cuit that year. Denver race fans cheered Willy to a 6th-place finish in Schlenker's 1991 Denver Grand Prix, advancing from his 13th-place starting position.

Willy's U.S. race tracks were plagued with pot-holes and speed-bumps until he paid his own way to England in 1977 and rented a run-of-the-mill Formula Ford. His prowess took him to a third-place finish in his first race. He won his second race, ran second in his fourth start ahead of the great Nigel Mansell, and went on to win six of eleven races and the series championship.

Back home in 1978-1981, Ribbs' sole ride was in the Long Beach Formula Atlantic Grand Prix, performing well against Bobby Rahal, Kevin Cogan, and Keke Rosberg. In 1982 he drove the Red Roof Inns' Ralt racer, winning the pole in the Long Beach Formula Atlantic Grand Prix, outdistancing Michael Andretti, Al Unser, Jr., and Geoff Brabham.

Stepping up to the Trans-Am Circuit in 1983, Willy drove a Camaro to five first-place wins in the 12-race season and was named SCCA Rookie-of-the-Year. Impressed by this showing, Edsel Ford signed Ribbs to drive the Ford Trans-Am entry, winning more races (17) than any other Trans-Am driver 1984-1986. He failed to qualify at Indy "500" in 1985 in a deal with boxing promoter Don King because the car was too slow. Willy boxed regularly with King's stable of heavyweights to keep in driving shape.

Joining family friend, Dan Gurney, to drive the Toyota GTO, Willy won four races and International Motorsports Racing Association (IMSA) Driver-of-the-Year in 1987, repeating with three wins and IMSA Driver-of-the-Year again in 1988. In 1989 he drove Dan Gurney's new GTP-Eagle prototype on the IMSA Circuit before going with the Raynor Door-Cosby (Bill, the TV entertainer) Motorsports. Their debut was in the Pittsburg Plate Glass Cup race in Long Beach.

Shifting to Walker Motorsports in 1991, Willy finished 17th in points in 9 starts on the PPG Cup Circuit. Under MacDonald's ("Big Mac") sponsorship he qualified and drove the Indy "500" and finished in the points in 5 other Indy Car races including the Denver Grand Prix. He also drove Dan Gurney's Toyota GTP IMSA car in the Daytona "24-Hours" and in the Sebring "12-Hours"--earning $424,779 for the year's driving.

Willy started only one race, Laguna Seca, in 1992, driving for Walker Motorsports. In 1993 (1944 results not yet available) he started 13 races for Walker Motorsports with full-time sponsorship by Pepsi and Service Merchandise, scoring 5 points-paying finishes earning $281,653.

His full name is William Theodore Ribbs, Jr. His first job, at age nine, was as a ranch hand on his grandfather's ranch. His hero and Idol--Mario Andretti. Actor/producer Michael Douglas and Columbia Pictures have purchased the rights to Ribbs' life story for a future movie.

Not bad for a nine-year-old San Jose California ranch hand who shares my birthday--forty years late.

**S-Cars:** Four hundred forty-six (446) cars have/had names starting with the "crooked letter". With so many to choose from, why can't we find at least one "Duesy"? Studebaker takes the staying power award, metamorphosing from wagons to electrics to Loewy-lovely gas-buggies. Saab swooped down from an airplane drawing-board as a two-cylinder two-stroke car, soon adding another cylinder and then two more strokes when it gained yet another cylinder, becoming a four-cylinder four-stroke that retained a lot of its aeronautical heritage. The yuppies who yearned to fly adopted the Saab to satisfy their fantasy-ego. Harry Stutz left us few of his great Bearcats, the American sports car <u>nonpareil</u>, to satisfy the dreams of car collectors of owning a <u>man's</u> car.


**S:** the nineteenth letter of the English alphabet without which no car could start, we would have few plurals, fewer possessions, and no satisfaction--or <u>S</u>tudebaker Driver<u>s</u>.

**saber saw:** a hand saw with a distinctly tapered blade, a light portable electric with a pointed reciprocating blade.

**Sabra:** Israel's indigenous automobile.

**sac:** a reservoir or cavity immediately before the discharge orifice of a diesel fuel injector.

**sac volume:** volume or capacity of the sac of a diesel fuel injector.

**sacrificial metal:** of or relating to the glob/hunk/piece of metal immersed in the liquid of a cooling system to serve as an anode to be electrolytically consumed thus substituting for the chemical destruction of radiator/water-jacket surfaces.

**sacrificial plug:** a threaded plug insert with attached sacrificial metal that can be removed for ease in inspection or replacement.

**S-cam brake:** a brake assembly using an S-shaped cam designed to compensate for brake lining wear.

**saddle:** the molded seat for the rider of straddle riding of a bicycle or motorcycle. The flat or concave attachment/support plate on an axle or vehicle frame on which a leaf or coil spring is mounted usually with a cushion or wear-pad separating the spring and the saddle surface.

**saddle soap:** a mild soap used for cleansing and conditioning upholstery leather.

**saddle tank:** a container tank usually for fuel that hangs over and outboard of a vehicle frame, often serving as a step surface for access to a vehicle cab. Common to pick-up trucks and over-the-road tractor trucks.

**SAE:** Society of Automotive Engineers, a professional group of automotive and aerospace workers who have demonstrated their dedication and contribution to the various related engineering disciplines. Since 1905 the SAE has grown to 62,922 members (January, 1993) representing every major country--with 240 student chapters in engineering colleges and universities.

**SAE number:** the American standard of engine horsepower measurement assigned to a "bare" engine, excluding all parasitic losses such as generator, pumps, fans, and other ancillaries. Also called "SAE horsepower". See DIN rating.

**safari:** often used to ascribe the capability, function, or use of various off-road vehicles.

**safety:** to attach in a manner that prevents loosening as by shaking or vibration. To safety a nut on a threaded bolt, safety wire through drilled holes, castellated nuts and cotter pins, lock washers, and self-locking nuts are used.

**safety belt:** a belt fastening a person to an object to prevent falling or injury. A belt or system as lap and shoulder straps to restrain vehicle occupants from inadvertent ejection.

**safety clip:** a spring steel pin with a tension locking shape designed to retain various types of fasteners.

**safety glass:** glass for vehicle windshields and windows likely to be subjected to shock or impact. Usually two sheets of glass with a separating lamination of flexible adhesive plastic to prevent shattering. Sometimes containing a wire mesh reinforcement. Sometimes compounded for great strength and to resist penetration and shattering as "bullet-proof" glass.

**safety island:** a pedestrian waiting area or vehicle separation area within a roadway from which vehicular traffic is excluded (as by pavement markings, curbing, or barriers).

**safety lamp:** a lamp constructed to avoid explosion in an atmosphere containing flammable gas (by enclosing the flame in a fine wire gauge and by protecting the outer bulb from breakage with suitable metal guards).

**safety pin:** a pin in the form of a clasp with a backing guard covering its point when fastened.

**safety valve:** an automatic escape or relief valve as for any pressurized gas or liquid containment system.

**salvage yard:** a storage area for used vehicles/parts. Junk yard.

**sand:** a loose granular material resulting from the disintegration of rocks, consisting of particles smaller than gravel but coarser than silt. Used in building materials, road surfaces, and as abrasives. Spread on icy surfaces to provide traction for vehicles and animals.

**sand blast:** a stream of sand forcibly projected by steam or air pressure (for cleaning vehicles/parts).

**sand blaster:** a machine to produce the stream of sand in a controllable and useful manner, usually in an enclosure/cabinet for capturing and re-using the sand.

**sand box:** a sand supply in a receptacle along roadways to provide motorists the abrasive material to sprinkle on icy surfaces to provide vehicle traction.

**sand cast:** to make vehicle parts by pouring molten metal into an appropriately-shaped sand mold.

**sand casting:** a casting that was made by pouring molten metal into a sand mold. The surface smoothness of the casting is determined by the grain size of the sand used to form the mold.

**sander:** one that sands; a device for spreading sand as on icy roads; the truck that hauls the sanding device; a machine that smoothes, polishes, or grinds by means of sand impregnated belts or discs. Sanding machine.

**sanding block:** a block or pad around which sandpaper is attached or wrapped for hand-finishing/polishing.

**sanding disc:** a sand impregnated disc that is rotated/spun by a sander.

**sanding belt:** a sand impregnated belt that runs on a sander.

**sandpaper:** paper with a sand coating glued on one side and used for smoothing and polishing. To rub with sandpaper.

**sandsoap:** a gritty soap used by vehicle mechanics for cleaning hands/skin of grease. LAVA soap.

**sandshoe:** the weight-distributing pad used at outrigger ends to stabilize vehicular cranes used in sandy areas.

**satin black:** a paint that dries with a finish between flat and glossy.

**scale model:** an accurate larger, or usually smaller, representation of a vehicle designed for more economical evaluation/testing--as in a wind tunnel.

**scam:** descriptive of the fraudulent claims for vehicle gadgets, gimcracks, or gimmicks that purport to decrease pollution, enhance performance, or increase fuel mileage--but don't.

**scanner:** a diagnostic device for evaluating vehicle testing data. A device that searches through the spectrum of radio frequencies without the manual turning of a dial control.

**scarify:** to break up and loosen the surface as of an asphalt roadway in preparation for resurfacing. To roughen a surface before painting or glue application.

**scatter shield:** a protective cover for any vehicle moving part subject to explosive stress failure such as the flywheel, clutch, transmission, or chain drives of high-performance vehicles.

**scavenger pump:** an oil return pump that removes oil back to the reservoir of a dry sump lubrication system. Any pump that removes unwanted fluids.

**scavenging:** the removal of exhaust gases from an engine using induced flow as with a "tuned exhaust" path.

**scavenging efficiency:** the ratio of the amount of exhaust gas remaining in an engine cylinder at the completion of the exhaust cycle as compared to the total charge air/fuel mass inducted into the engine.

**schematic:** a drawing or diagram depicting a schematic flow as of a vehicle electrical or pneumatic/hydraulic system.

**Schnuerrle scavenging:** loop or reverse loop scavenging in two-stroke/cycle engines in which the flow of gases enters and exits valve-ports on the same side of the cylinder forming a loop pattern around the combustion chamber.

**Schrader valve:** the one-way non-return filler valve for pneumatic tires/tubes with a spring-loaded release that allows inflation and tire pressure measurement.

**scoop:** an aperture opening through the outer skin/surface of a vehicle to gather and direct impact air flow for cooling and engine breathing. The NACA scoop extends outside the body contour creating some air drag. The NASA scoop is a flush opening that does not enlarge frontal area, creating little air drag.

**scouring:** a form of tire wear caused by dragging the tire sideways from inaccurate tracking alignment.

**scout car:** a small military vehicle (Jeep) designed for reconnaissance and scouting missions.

**scrape:** to remove metal using a hardened tool, usually triangular in cross-section.

**scraper ring:** the bottom piston ring that scrapes excess oil from the cylinder walls and returns the oil to the engine crankcase.

**screen:** a barrier to or control of passage. A solid material such as a windshield that stops and/or deflects wind and rain/snow, allows vision, but selectively passes light frequencies. A mesh or perforated surface that passes smaller particles while stopping larger ones. A surface for display of information as a translucent rearprojection (TV/CRT tube) or an opaque reflective (movie screen). To guard, protect, or separate.

**screw:** a simple machine for transferring motion and/or securely fastening using the inclined plane principle. Most common is the rod with spiral groves and a recessed or shaped head matched to a torque delivering tool. Infinite applications.

**scribe:** a hardened sharp-pointed cutting/scratching tool used for marking lines. To use such a tool.

**scuffing:** the abrasive or adhesive damage to friction surfaces. Abrasion results from lack of lubrication or foreign particles. Heating causes metal from one surface to weld/adhere to the other increasing the roughness-heating and building the thickness of the adhered metal, usually leaving pits/depressions where it was melted and scuffed from.

**seal:** the material, shape, process, or device used to slow or to stop fluid leakage at mating or sliding/rubbing contact by two or more components. May be contact sealing or gaskets, lip seals, or liquid/paste compounds (hardening or pliable). Shape-sealing uses labyrinths, threads, or lands and grooves.

**sealant::** a chemical agent usually adhesive for sealing mating surfaces or leaks. May be liquid, paste, or solid and hardening or pliable.

**sealed beam:** vehicle lights, usually forward-facing in which the light source is hermetically sealed within the lense/reflector enclosure.

**sealed bearing:** a bearing, of whatever type, that has sealing devices at the moving junctures to seal lubricants in and/or to seal contaminants out.

**seat belt:** a vehicle occupant restraint system consisting of appropriate anchors, harness, and latches.

**seat cover:** a permanent/removable/temporary protective covering for vehicle seats.

**secondary road:** a road not of primary importance. A feeder road.

**secondary safety brake:** a vehicle braking system that automatically applies brakes when the hydraulic/pneumatic actuation mechanism fails.

**secondary shoe:** the trailing shoe of a vehicle drum brake.

**secondary venturi:** a small venturi mounted concentrically within a carburetor main venturi to boost the pressure differential for increased accuracy of the fuel/air ratio.

**sector gear:** a gear segment of less than 360° as used in steering or the operation of damper-like valves.

**sector shaft:** the output shaft of a gearbox to which a pitman arm or bell-crank is affixed to transform rotary motion to push-pull motion.

**sedan delivery:** a van-like or enclosed station wagon type body usually on a passenger car chassis for commercial light-cargo.

**sediment bowl:** a separator reservoir for removing and retaining undesirable contaminants such as water and particulates from vehicle fuels.

**seize:** a sudden locking-up of parts normally in lubricated sliding/rubbing contact due to surface welding resulting from lack of lubrication or insufficient clearance. As a piston/rings in a cylinder or a crankshaft and its main or rod bearings.

**self-adjusting brakes:** brakes with a ratcheting mechanism that maintains the desirable clearance as friction material wear progresses.

**self-adjusting tappet:** a valve tappet that automatically compensates for variations in valve clearance usually using an oil-filled valve-controlled cushion chamber to maintain zero-lash operation.

**self-aligning bearing:** usually using a gimbal mounting mechanism to accommodate small dimensional variations.

**self-hardening:** the internal chemical hardening that occurs without the application of external influence as with heat or evaporation. Epoxy adhesives, paints, and sealants.

**self-leveling suspensions:** as the Citroen Hydropneumatic leveling of all four wheels to maintain a constant ground

clearance or the rear-only leveling that compensates for varying rear-end loading preventing tail-low trim of a vehicle.

**self-parking windshield wiper:**  the automatic positioning of
wiper blades (parking) out of vehicle occupants' line-of-sight
when wipers are turned "off".

**self-sealing:**  pneumatic/hydraulic components as tires/tubes/
hoses that automatically stop leaking from minor damage/wear.

**sellabration:**  the buzz-word of the used car lot hyping a
simple sale event.

**selsyn:**  an electrically-paired motor-generator system in
which the angular rotation of the generator is mimicked and
reproduced instantaneously by the motor.  Used to provide
remote-indicating accurate information (instrument readings)
and to remotely-position vehicle controls.

**semaphore:**  the simulated-arm turn-signal used by earlier cars
before the flasher-switch invention.

**semi:**  half, partial, or incomplete.  Vehicle vernacular for
tractor-trailer combinations.

**semi-automatic transmission:**  a vehicle gear-box that shifts
automatically after the operator/driver selects, pre-selects,
or directs the desired action.  Historically, many push-button
solenoid-actuated, shifter/clutchers proliferated.  Citroen
Citromatic, Chrysler push-button, Packard Ultramatic.

**semi-conductor:**  any of a class of solids (as germanium or
silicon) whose electrical conductivity is between that of a
conductor and that of an insulator.  Essential to modern
vehicle electronic systems.

**semi-diesel:**  an internal combustion engine working on other
than the ideal diesel cycle as for example with an externally
heated continuous <u>hot</u> <u>spot</u> to insure combustion.

**semi-elliptical spring:**  half of a full-leaf spring operating
as a pin-ended beam to support a beam axle.

**semi-final:**  the next-to-the-last heat race in an automobile
elimination speed competition.

**semi-floating axle:**  a live axle assembly in which the vehicle
weight is transferred from the fixed outer axle housing to the
rotating axle shaft through axle bearings within the housing.

**semifluid:**  having the properties of both a liquid and a solid.
Viscous.  As oil and grease lubricants.

**semigloss:** a surface coating, as a paint, that produces a finish midway between gloss and flat. Semi-matte is similar but with rougher feel.

**semi-tracked vehicle:** a vehicle with front-wheeled support/steering and with the rear cargo-carrying traction supported by a continuous-tracked surface contact. A half-track.

**semitrailer:** a cargo trailer attached to and supported by a tractor vehicle using a fifth-wheel, ball-and-cup, or pintle-and-pin, forming an articulated combination with the tractor.

**semi-trailing arm:** a type of trailing rear suspension with the pivot arm inclined backwards in its horizontal plane thus imparting an increase in trail as load increases.

**sender:** an electrical, hydraulic, or pneumatic device that transmits a sensor signal to a remote indicator or recorder.

**sensor:** a device that responds to a physical stimulus (as heat, light, magnetism, or motion) and transmits a resulting impulse for display, recording, or operating a control or warning.

**separator:** a device for removing suspended particles from a fluid or separating non-miscible fluids air/fuel, air/oil, air/water, or fuel/water.

**sequencer:** an event-timing device that when activated automatically triggers a series of actions. Automatic windshield washer's on-squirt-wipe-park-off.

**serial number:** a number indicating order of manufacture and used as a means of identification of vehicles, engines, and major components.

**serrated:** a part or object marked by a notched or toothed edge.

**service brake:** the primary system for slowing and stopping a vehicle.

**service road:** a supplementary roadway paralleling a freeway. Frontage road.

**service station:** a retail station for servicing motor vehicles with gas, oil, and limited mechanical repairs.

**servomechanism:** a device or system for controlling and/or magnifying small amounts of power or motion into larger amounts. Power brakes, steering, windows. Power-assisted or remote-controlled.

**servo-motor:** a power-driver (electrical, hydraulic, or pneumatic) mechanism that supplements a primary control operated by a comparatively weak force.

**setscrew:** a screw screwed through one part tightly upon or into another part to prevent relative movement. A screw to regulate or restrict a control movement as of a valve or throttle or a spring tension. Stopscrew.

**setup:** the manner in which the elements or components of electrical, hydraulic, or mechanical mechanisms are arranged, assembled, or designed. The arrangement of the workpiece, the tools, and the apparatus for performing machining operations.

**shackle:** the pivoting link between a leaf spring and its mounting composed of two coupled parallel bars through-bolted through the eye of the spring leaf end and a mounting spring bracket.

**shade-tree mechanic:** a sometimes derisive term applied to the lone mechanic working in a makeshift shop with limited equipment who often belies the derision with long experience and a wealth of innate logic. The singular individualist who nurtured our early-day automobiles through their growing-up era.

**shaft:** a commonly cylindrical bar used to support rotating pieces or to transmit power or motion by rotation.

**shaft horsepower:** horsepower transmitted by an engine shaft.

**shaft runout:** a non-concentric rotation in certain linear positions indicating a bent shaft.

**shaft whip:** to thrash about flexibly in the manner of a whiplash as from out of balance.

**shaft wobble:** an irregular or rocking unequal motion as from excessive bearing wear.

**shag boy:** slang for the chauffeur or hostler or parts pick-up messenger at a vehicle dealership or shop who does various jobs involving errand driving and the parking and shifting the positions of vehicles.

**shake-down:** testing under operating conditions of a new vehicle or a new overhaul for possible faults and defects or to familiarize operators with it.

**shank:** the end as of a drill bit that is gripped in a chuck. The straight part of a bolt, nail, pin, or screw.

**shatterproof:** a material as glass or metal that is compounded or tempered to resist breakage from impact forces.

**shear:** a cutting instrument similar or identical to a pair of scissors but typically larger. Any of various cutting tools or machines employing opposed cutting edges of metal.

**shear pin:** an easily replaceable pin inserted at a critical point in a machine and designed to break when subjected to excess stress, protecting other machine components from breakage.

**shear strength:** a measure of the ability of a material to resist damage or failure from shearing forces.

**sheepskins:** genuine or synthetic skin of a sheep used to cover and protect vehicle seats providing warmth in winter and cooling in summer.

**sheet metal:** a thin flat section (usually rolled) of metal used for vehicle outer surfaces and various container enclosures.

**sheet metal brake:** a clamping and bending machine for forming sheet metal into shapes involving angles.

**shelf life:** the period of time during which parts or supplies may be stored and remain suitable for use.

**shell:** a walled enclosure made chiefly of sheets or panels without major framing. Body shell. Camper shell. Monocoque. Stressed skin.

**shell bearing:** a plain bearing formed from two interlocking and abutting thin walled semi-circular cusps.

**shift boot:** a flexible sealing sheath around a shift lever and its clearance opening in a floor or panel.

**shifter:** the arm, lever, or arm connected to the shift fork to effect its desired movement.

**shift fork:** a forked member for moving a sliding pinion gear into and out of mesh (engagement) in a system of gears (as a transmission).

**shift gate:** the slotted guiding pattern that directs and precisely limits the movement of a transmission shift lever.

**shift pattern:** the shift gate shape that insures the accurate and ordered selection of transmission gear pairs (ratios).

**shift valve:** valve that actuates the automatic gear change in an automatic transmission following the signal from the throttle and governor.

**shim:** a thin often tapered piece of material used to fill space in between things (as for support, leveling, alignment, or fit).

**shim stock:** thin sheets of appropriate material that can be cut to size and shape for use as shims.

**shimmy:** low amplitude/frequency mechanical vibration, usually as an imbalance in front wheels or a looseness in the steering mechanism frequently initiated by imperfections in the road surface.

**shock absorber:** any of several devices for absorbing the energy of sudden impulses or shocks in machinery or structures. Vehicle suspensions, engine, body, and component mountings. Shock, shocker.

**shock mount:** the integral or bolt-on bracket for attaching or anchoring a shock absorber.

**shoe:** the arcuate internally expanding element of a vehicle drum brake to which the friction lining is attached.

**shooting brake:** British designation of a station wagon, estate car, or depot hack.

**shop jack:** a vehicle lifting/raising device usually wheeled for positioning vehicles for repair/service.

**shop manual:** an instruction/specification book prepared by the manufacturer or specialty publisher for reference and guidance in vehicle maintenance, repair, and service.

**shop rate:** the hourly charge for vehicle repair/service, usually publicly posted. The pre-computed charge based upon actuarial experience for frequently occurring services. Essential for pre-performance estimates of costs.

**shop steward:** in unionized vehicle shops a union member elected to effect go-between dealings with the management.

**short block:** an incomplete vehicle engine, usually lacking cylinder head(s) and ancillary accessories, used to replace a damaged, defective, or worn-out engine. May be new or rebuilt to "like-new" specifications.

**short circuit:** an electrical connection of comparative low resistance accidentally or intentionally made between points on a circuit between which the resistance is normally much greater. A common cause of vehicle electrical failure, fires, and blown fuses.

**short gears:** vehicle transmission/differential gears with a low speed ratio, enhancing power rather than speed.

**short stroke:** a reciprocating engine whose piston stroke is numerically shorter than its cylinder bore (diameter). Oversquare.

**short track:** designation of automobile race tracks usually of less than one-half mile and to the racing vehicles designed for such tracks.

**shot blast:** to spray with a high-speed stream of metal pellets to clean metal or to impart surface hardness or expansion through the peening or forging impact force. Shot peen. Koetherize.

**shoulder harness:** vehicle occupant restraint system with anchored belts passing over one or both shoulders and usually fastened at waist height with a seat belt.

**showroom fresh:** a new vehicle that has never been driven--only displayed in a showroom. Sometimes used to describe an exceptionally clean and maintained vehicle with low driving mileage.

**shrink fit :** the fitting of parts by utilizing the coefficient of temperature expansion as by heating a bored part such as a gear or pulley to enlarge its inner diameter to fit over a cooler shaft and allowing it to cool and shrink tightly onto the shaft.

**shrink wrap:** to wrap as a vehicle part in tough plastic film that is then shrunk by heating to form a tightly fitting hermetically sealed package.

**shunpike:** a side road used to avoid the toll on or the speed and traffic of a superhighway.

**shunt winding:** the electrical winding of an alternator, generator, or motor so arranged as to divide the armature current and lead a portion of it around the field magnet coils.

**shut-off:** to close a fluid conduit/duct as with a valve. To stop a vehicle engine with the ignition switch or by closing the fuel supply valve. Shut-down. Kill.

**shutter:** a mechanical arrangement of movable vanes to control, direct, or close off the flow of air or the passage of light. As a radiator blind the rapid flow of impact air can be blocked partially or completely to facilitate proper engine temperature during cold weather driving.

**siamesed:** of cylinder bores, joined metal-to-metal to the full length of the cylinder with no inter-cylinder coolant passages. Of exhaust pipes, parallel pipes joined along part or all of their length. Of valve ports, arranged so that two adjacent valves share one port.

**side car:** a single-seat single-wheeled appurtenance attached to the side of a motorcycle to carry a passenger or cargo.

**side-draft:** a carburetor whose incoming charge air flows horizontally through its venturi en route to the engine cylinder.

**side intrusion bar:** reinforcing beam, usually set within a vehicle door structure to reduce intrusion injury from side impacts.

**side lamp:** low intensity lights mounted near each forward corner of a vehicle to indicate vehicle clearance width. Parking light.

**side-marker light:** lights mounted along the sides of a long vehicle or vehicle combination to indicate its presence and length to other vehicles.

**side pipes:** vehicle pipes that extend outside the body shell usually exiting the engine hood side panels as individual cylinder stocks with graceful downward chrome curves as they head rearward into a common tailpipe. Usually functional but sometimes purely ornamental and ego-inspired.

**side stand:** a retractable side support that maintains a motorcycle in a slightly slanted upright position when parked. Kick-stand.

**side swipe:** to strike another vehicle or object a glancing blow along the side or with the side of your vehicle.

**side valve:** designation of a vehicle engine with valves made into the cylinder block alongside the cylinder bore. "L"-head, "T"-head, overhead.

**side vent:** a ventilation opening through the side body panels of a vehicle for incoming or exhaust air.

**sidewall:** the side of a vehicle pneumatic tire between the tread shoulder and the rim bead.

**signal seeker:** a vehicle radio with automatic tuning that seeks the transmitted signal of broadcast stations and "locks on" such signals.

**sign post:** a post alongside roadways with signs that advise, direct, inform, or warn traveling motorists.

**silencer:** a baffled or expansion box, chamber, or enclosure within a vehicle engine exhaust system for reducing the inherent noise. Muffler.

**Silenbloc bearing:** a Trade named rubber/metal anti-vibration mounting to reduce audible bearing noise.

**silicon carbide:** a very hard (approaching diamond) abrasive extensively used in vehicle manufacture, maintenance, and repair.

**silicone:** any of various polymeric organic silicone compounds used for water-resistant and heat-resistant lubricants, sealers, protective coatings, and electrical insulators.

**silicone rubber:** rubber made from silicone elastomers and noted for its retention of flexibility, resilience, and tensile strength over a wide temperature range.

**silver plate:** the plating of choice for finishing the exterior ornamental metal work of early prestige vehicles before the perfection of modern chrome plating.

**simple machine:** any of various elementary mechanisms formerly considered as the elements of which all machines are composed and including the lever, the wheel and axle, the pulley, the inclined plane, the wedge, and the screw. Our magnificent machines all evolved from these simple devices into today's modern motor vehicles.

**single acting engine:** an engine in which the combustion acts on one side of the piston only, always pushing toward the crankshaft direction. The prevalent practice.

**single anchor brake:** vehicle drum brakes with the leading and trailing shoes pivoting around one fixed point (anchor).

**single axle weight:** the legislated definition of the total weight transmitted to the road by wheels whose axes are 40 inches or less apart.

**single beam headlight:** a headlight whose light source is a single filament that can provide either an upper or lower beam (as focused) but not both.

**single disc clutch:** a mechanical clutch with one driving unit (flywheel), one friction unit (disc), and one driven unit (pressure plate).

**single overhead cam:** designation of an engine type whose single camshaft is located above the cylinder head and has cam lobes that operate both the intake and exhaust valves from one rotating shaft.

**single pivot steering:** with a beam axle pivoted at its midpoint. Rare except on small farm vehicles and horse-drawn ones.

**single plane crankshaft:** crankshaft whose cranks (rod journals) are all in line or half at 180° to the other half.

317

**single-row bearing:** a ball bearing with just one row of balls between the inner and outer races.

**sintered:** to agglomerate or mix into a coherent mass dissimilar materials by heating to a temperature just below their melting point. A sintered brass bushing has a higher strength or better lubricating material added.

**sipe:** a knife-cut shallow slice across the tread of a vehicle tire that may reduce noise, dissipate heat, increase flexibility, and improve road surface contact.

**six-banger:** slang for a six-cylinder engine, stemming back to the straight-six inline type.

**six-pack:** hot rod slang for six-carburetors on one engine.

**six point:** a wrench (box or socket) that has six flat engagement/gripping surfaces. Hexagonal, hex.

**six-way seat:** a manual or power-operated movable vehicle seat with six directional adjustments as up/down, back/forward, front/rear tilt-angle.

**skid:** a sideways sliding motion or a forward slide with the wheels not rotating. The loss of friction between a vehicle tires and the roadway.

**skid pan:** a protective plate under a vehicle to allow sliding contact over road debris or when traversing deep ruts or adverse terrain to prevent damage to vulnerable underside components.

**skins:** vehicle tires whose friction tread pattern is worn smooth--or manufactured smooth as racing tires (to reduce air drag). Slicks.

**skip:** a missing power impulse--regular or erratic--in an operating engine. Usually an ignition-related problem.

**skipshift:** deliberate or unintentional failure to utilize all transmission ratios (gears) in numerical progression as going from second gear directly into fourth gear without using third gear. In automatic transmissions a skipped shift indicates a mechanical malfunction.

**skirt:** the side-wall of an engine piston below the rings that spreads side-load thrust forces and maintains alignment within the cylinder bore. Also a downward extending body panel, fixed or removable, to deflect and control road soil and air flow.

**skylight:** a transparent panel in a vehicle top, sometimes openable for ventilation. Moonroof, sunroof.

**slalom:** an individually timed automobile race over a winding or zigzag course past a series of flags or markers.

**slant six:** a six cylinder engine (as the Chrysler Plymouth) with the engine leaned/slanted/angled distinctly to one side to reduce the height of the hood enclosure.

**slap:** a smacking noise caused by badly worn piston sidewalls or piston pin wear.

**slave cylinder:** a cylinder and piston actuated by hydraulic or pneumatic pressure from a master cylinder to operate mechanical devices (brake shoes/pads, clutch pressure plate).

**sledge hammer:** a large heavy hammer that is wielded with both hands.

**sleeper cab:** a commercial long-haul vehicle cab providing sleeping accommodations for a driver.

**sleeve:** a tubular part that fits inside or outside another tubular or solid part usually long compared to its diameter. A bush or bushing is short. A hard lining usually replaceable within an engine cylinder.

**sleeve bearing:** a cylindrical shape that is slipped over a shaft from the end. Often several concentric sleeves for very high rpm machines as a turbocharger shaft.

**sleeve control:** a diesel engine metering control system using a coaxial sleeve around the pump piston to control the opening and closing of the spill port. Common to distributor-type pumps.

**sleeve valve:** reciprocating and/or rotating sleeve with aperture ports located concentrically between piston and cylinder wall that serves as both intake and exhaust valve by aligning its openings with ports through the cylinder wall. Willys-Knight.

**slide hammer:** a weight that slides along a shaft imparting a pounding force when forcibly stopped. Uses gravity in a vertical application.

**slide puller:** a weight that slides along a shaft with puller attachments on one end and a positive anvil stop on the other end. The sliding weight's inertia imparts a hammering impact in the pulling direction when it hits the end stop.

**slide valve:** a pair of contact plates or shapes with matching openings that are opened/closed by sliding one or both plates.

**sliding dog:** internally splined collar that the selection fork slides along the mainshaft of a manual transmission to

positively engage the mainshaft gear to the mainshaft.
Synchronizer.

**sliding door:** van or cargo door that slides horizontally or vertically to open/close eliminating interference from hinged closures.

**sliding gear:** a movable gear in a multi-ratio manual transmission.

**sliding gear transmission:** manual transmission with sliding gears on the mainshaft that are moved into engagement with fixed gears on a countershaft by a selector fork.

**slim jim:** a thin flexible metal strip used by car thieves (and mechanics, locksmiths, and police officers) to jimmy car-door locks when no keys are available.

**slingshot:** a dragster race car with the driver seat located at the extreme rear of the car, behind the rear engine and the rear wheels. In a multi-car race a passing maneuver in which the following car gains acceleration advantage by drafting to start the burst of speed to pull out and pass.

**slinger:** a rotating disc or ring that can be used to sling coolant or lubricant outward into a collector or toward areas needing cooling or lubricating.

**slip angle:** angle between the plane of wheel and the direction of movement of the center of a vehicle tire surface contact. Normally zero in straightaway driving with a perfectly aligned vehicle. At a maximum at the beginning and ending of a steered turn (or with extreme cross winds).

**slip fit:** a fit of two mating parts that allows them to be assembled/disassembled easily without them being forced apart.

**slip joint:** a joint as where a driveshaft is joined by a male/female splined connection to keep the shaft at a fixed length as the axle moves with the differential.

**slipper skirt piston:** a piston with skirt cut away beneath the piston pin axis to provide crankshaft clearance.

**slipping clutch:** a maladjusted or excessively worn friction contact surface(s) that lacks sufficient adherence to transmit the applied power through either a manual or automatic vehicle transmission.

**slipstreaming:** using the air wake of a preceding vehicle to reduce the air resistance of the closely-following vehicle. Drafting.

**slotted skirt piston:** a piston whose skirt has been slotted to allow for the coefficient of thermal expansion in the piston material.

**slow-running jet:** a jet that supplies extra fuel for the richer mixture required when idling. Idle jet.

**sludge:** the mud-like suspension in engine crankcase oil or other lubricant supplies of ingested dust and the miscible particulates and chemical combustion contaminants.

**small end:** the piston pin end of an engine connecting rod. Big end is the crankshaft end.

**smitty:** hot rod slang for a vehicle exhaust muffler that has been gutted of baffles and sound-deadening to produce a louder tail-pipe noise. Newly manufactured mufflers deliberately designed to emphasize exhaust sound volume.

**smoke:** visible emission from a vehicle exhaust consisting of combustion particulates (carbon) or vapor (water).

**smokemeter:** measuring device for measuring smoke in vehicle exhausts: Opacimeter.

**smoke tunnel:** a wind tunnel using smoke streams to visually display air flow patterns over a test vehicle or component.

**snow blade:** a windshield wiper blade that has its pressure springs encased in a thin rubber sheath to prevent snow accumulation from blocking the spring action.

**snow chain:** a removable tire chain assembly with cross-links across the tread with lugs to dig into mud, ice, and snow for better wheel traction.

**snow tire:** a vehicle tire manufactured with a deep tread of lugs or cross-bars for better traction in mud or snow. Sometimes with embedded abrasive material or hardened metal pins. Snow tread is an after-market retreading for the same effect. Tires are usually marked "M & S" for mud and snow.

**snubber:** compressible rubber or spring to prevent excessive suspension travel. Before the invention of hydropneumatic shock absorbers various friction devices, leather straps, chains, and mechanical stops were used to limit suspension travel.

**soak time:** the interval of time required an engine and all components and surroundings to attain a stable high or low temperature. Hot soak. Cold soak.

**soapbox:** a miniature race car without an engine for juveniles to race against the clock (individually timed runs) on downhill inclined tracks. An American Legion annual sponsored national competition.

**socket:** a tubular total-surround wrench whose interior is configured to fit the bolthead, nut, or other shape and that is fitted to an appropriate handle that provides torque.

**sodium-cooled valve:** an engine exhaust valve with a hollow stem filled with sodium that becomes liquid when heated. A good heat conductor, the sodium sloshes along the inner stem carrying the intense heat from the valve head to the stem area for transfer through the valve guide into the engine cooling system.

**sodium-vapor light:** a high-efficiency high-intensity large-area light commonly used for roadway and large vehicle parking area lighting.

**soft babbitt:** a bearing metal usually used for poured bearings in slow-turning applications.

**soft plug:** a removable/replaceable plug used to close openings in castings resulting from the manufacturing process or to provide access to assembly fittings.

**SOHC:** single overhead cam.

**solar cell:** a photovoltaic cell capable of converting light energy directly into electrical energy. Used to charge vehicle batteries in remote areas and to provide electrical power when there is no surface power grid.

**solder:** a metal or metallic alloy used when melted to join metallic surfaces of compatible materials.

**solenoid switch:** electro-magnetically activated electrical switch.

**solid-axle suspension:** vehicle suspension in which wheels are mounted at either side of a solid beam axle so that any vertical movement of one wheel is transmitted directly to the opposite wheel. A non-independent suspension.

**solid drive clutch:** a simple disc clutch in which the contacting elements have no cushioning friction material. Metal-to-metal.

**solid injection:** a fuel system that sprays a pulse of high pressure liquid fuel directly with no conversion to fuel vapor for mixing with the combustion charge air.

**solid-state ignition:** a vehicle ignition system employing non-moving electronic devices to create the ignition spark and to insure its proper timing.

**soluble:** susceptible of being dissolved in or as if in a fluid.

**solvent:** a usually liquid substance capable of dissolving or dispersing one or more other substances. Petroleum liquids are extensively used to clean vehicle parts of dirt, grease, or grime.

**"Somewhere West of Laramie":** visualize an impressive-appearing westerner peering out the window of a speeding train at a Jordan Playboy roadster racing the Iron Horse across the Wyoming plains. Ned Jordan's advertising genius was never better showcased than in this poignant caption to his full-page magazine ad for his straight-eight Playboy (about 1930).

**sonic:** relating to sound having a frequency within the audibility range of the human ear. Relating to the speed at which sound travels at standard atmospheric conditions (741 miles per hour).

**soundproofing:** materials and techniques used in vehicles to control and reduce sound levels and transmission within and outside the vehicle.

**space frame:** a three dimensional vehicle structural framework usually of welded tubing or extrusions that serves in lieu of the conventional underbody frame and as an alternative to the pure monocoque frameless stressed-skin design. Typical of race cars. Birdcage.

**spacer:** usually a thick washer or flat plate of appropriate shape/thickness/ material used to establish or control dimensions of assemblies of machined components.

**Spackle:** trade name for a powder/particle filler used in paint to fill surface defects and to leave a roughened finish for anti-glare, esthetics, and limited sound control.

**spade connector:** an electrical connection using a blade section that is inserted into a matching female spring clamp.

**spark advance:** the angular distance in crankshaft degrees that an ignition spark occurs before the top dead center between the compression stroke and the power (combustion) stroke of an internal combustion engine.

**spark ignition:** a vehicle system that creates an electrical spark and delivers it at the proper place and time to ignite the fuel/air mixture.

**spark ignition engine:** Otto cycle. Any form of internal combustion engine in which the fuel/air mixture is ignited by a spark. Often designated as an SI (spark ignition) engine in contrast to the CI (compression ignition) or Diesel engine.

**spark knock:** detonation within a vehicle engine caused by excessively advanced spark timing.

**spark plug:** an insulated device usually screwed into the cylinder head/combustion chamber of a vehicle engine that delivers the electrical spark energy to ignite the fuel/air charge.

**spark plug gap:** the distance/space between the insulated (usually center) electrode and the ground electrode of the plug across which the arc of the ignition spark is generated.

**spark plug heat range:** a rating from "Cold" to "Hot" of spark plugs determined and controlled by construction and materials used. A longer heat transmission path from the combustion flame to the engine block coolant causes a plug rating that is "hotter".

**spark plug wire:** an electrical wire of very high voltage insulating ability that delivers the spark energy to the spark plug and prevents arcing danger under the vehicle hood and shock danger to people.

**spark timing:** the process of causing the ignition spark to occur at exactly the best time to insure optimum engine performance. Most commonly accomplished by breaking the low voltage circuit inducing the very high voltage to the spark plug. The moment of firing is first established by the static timing of the distributor whose internal mechanism then modifies (advance or retard) the timing by centrifugal or vacuum forces.

**specialty shop:** applied to vehicle maintenance, repair, and parts shops serving only one segment of vehicle needs such as alignment, electrical, carburetion, muffler, upholstery, brakes, glass, grease and oil change, and tune-ups.

**specific fuel consumption:** vehicle engine fuel consumed as an amount per unit of power per unit of time usually as pounds per brake horsepower per hour. SFC.

**specific gravity:** the ratio of the density of a substance to the density of some substance (as pure water or hydrogen) taken as a standard when both densities are obtained by weighing in air.

**specific heat:** the quantity of heat required to impart a unit increase in temperature to a unit mass of a substance: commonly expressed in calories per centigrade degree per gram of the substance, thus defining the specific heat of a substance as its thermal capacity per unit mass. Hydrogen is considered to have the highest specific heat at 2.418, with water second at 1.0, and gold and lead the lowest at 0.031.

**speed:** the magnitude of the vector <u>velocity</u>. Speed is a scalar quantity and is expressed in units of length divided by time. To drive at excessive or illegal speed.

**speed bump:** a crosswise raised section in a road surface designed to impart a severe jolt to a vehicle driving faster than allowed for that location.

**speed limit:** the maximum or minimum speed permitted by law in a specified area under given circumstances. Rarely enforced and seldom obeyed: the scourge of a depraved society.

**speedometer:** a vehicle instrument that measures its speed and contains an odometer that measures, totalizes, and records distance traveled. Speedo.

**speedometer roll-back:** an illegal act of changing the recorded distance on a vehicle odometer to show fewer miles than the vehicle has actually been driven.

**speedometer tampering:** any illegal modification to a vehicle speedometer that causes it to show faster or slower speeds or lesser or greater distances than the vehicle actually travels.

**speed shop:** a vehicle parts store or repair shop that caters to owner/drivers of racing vehicles of any type including the wannabe amateurs and the ego-exhibitionists.

**speed trap:** a misnomer. The mythomaniacal alibi or complaint from the willful speeder when caught. Every vehicle driver has sole and complete control of the accelerator so he/she can never be coerced or trapped into speeding in excess of any speed limit.

**speedway:** a public road on which fast driving is permitted. A racecourse (race track) for automobile or motorcycle speed competitions.

**sphere:** a ball or globe-shaped container or tank usually for very high pressures as a vehicle hydraulic pressure device. Often made with a separator diaphragm for containment of two dissimilar fluids in one unit. Used with evacuated double outer-walls for cryogenic storage (thermos bottle).

**spider:** any component with any number of legs or shafts radiating from a central hub. A cruciform wheel lug wrench with different sized sockets on each leg.

**spill port:** hole through which excess fuel is returned to the fuel system in a diesel or gasoline injector pump at the end of injection.

**spine-back:** or backbone narrow central chassis frame found mainly on heavy-duty vehicles. Used by several older vehicles. Notably by Mercedes.

**spin-out:** a rotational skid by a vehicle usually causing it to leave the roadway.

**spiral bevel gear:** a crown wheel with teeth that radiate as part of a geometric spiral. Common to differential "ring gears".

**splash guard:** a flexible hanging deflector shield behind road wheels to prevent spray of water/road soil onto following vehicles.

**spline:** a multiple-toothed key/keyway machining on the outer diameter and inner diameter of solid/hollow shafts that mate to form a strong load-carrying junction.

**split skirt piston:** piston with skirt slotted to accommodate thermal expansion.

**spoiler:** a transverse aerodynamic shape attached to or a component part of a vehicle that changes or controls air flow patterns.

**spoke:** a radiating member between the hub and rim of a wheel. Thin spokes as a wire transfer the axle-load from hub to rim through tension. Thick spokes as of wood transfer the load through compression.

**spoke tuning:** with wire spokes tension and length must be equalized among all spokes. Old time craftsmen usually verified the final adjustment by striking or plucking each spoke and matching their audible tones.

**sportscar:** generically, a low comparatively small usually 2-passenger automobile designed for quick response, easy maneuverability, and high-speed driving.

**spot:** a small area visibly different as in color, finish, or material from the surrounding area. An area marred or marked by dirt or a material foreign to the major surface. To locate accurately. To indicate or designate an exact location with a spot or a mark.

**spot light:** a front-mounted bright narrow beam light that can be aimed by the vehicle driver. Aimable lights are illegal in many countries.

**spot brake:** a conventional caliper disc brake often with circular pad contact areas.

**spot polish:** using a drill-press or milling machine to spin a small polishing pad or abrasive wheel to create a circular design on a metal surface. The pattern prominence is determined by abrasive grit size. Pattern may be individual full-circles or overlapping circles of infinite variability. Engine turning.

**spring:** an elastic material or device that recovers its original shape or position when released after being distorted or displaced.

**spring brake:** an auxiliary vehicle brake held in the released position by brake system pressure whose removal causes a compression spring to apply the brake. For parking or safety.

**spring compression:** the shortening of a spring by a weight/force pushing inward toward the spring.

**spring hanger:** bracket on a vehicle chassis member to which a leaf spring end is attached.

**spring rate:** the ratio of weight to distance of spring lengthening/shortening under tension or compression usually expressed in pounds per inch.

**spring tension:** the lengthening of a spring by a weight/force pulling outward from a spring.

**spring washer:** a lock washer that exerts force against the assembled pieces to resist movement or vibratory loosening.

**spring-over shock:** a shock absorber inside a coil spring designed to assist in load carrying and bounce absorption.

**sprint car:** a race car designed to run at maximum speed for short distances.

**spur gear:** a gear wheel with radial teeth parallel to its axis.

**squad car:** a police automobile usually connected by a two-way radio with a dispatcher or headquarters. Cruiser. Prowl car.

**square engine:** an engine whose cylinder bore diameter is dimensionally equal to the piston stroke.

**square four:** a V-4 cylinder engine in which each cylinder axis forms one corner of a square, the engine being essentially two parallel vertical twin engines operating one crankshaft. Aeriel Square Four.

**square nut:** a threaded nut with a square-shaped head. Typical of the horse-drawn wagon era and of early automobiles.

**square wheel:** slang for a vehicle wheel whose circumference has been so damage-distorted that its rotation imparts a jolting bounce as if it were square.

**squeeze tester:** slang for compression tester that measures the amount that the incoming charge is squeezed (compressed) by the engine's compression stroke.

**squawk-sheet:** a vehicle test driver's report sheet listing defects and deficiencies (squawks) to be repaired/corrected by the vehicle mechanic.

**squeal:** noise of high frequency vibration, slipping, or skidding as from brake application, a loose accessory belt, or a tire losing friction contact with a road.

**squish:** the area of minimal clearance in a engine combustion chamber between the cylinder head and the piston head at top dead center.

**stability:** the tendency of a vehicle to remain in a steady state when influenced by disturbing forces or to return to that steady state when momentarily diverted from it.

**stabilizer bar:** a torsion bar coupling near side and off side wheel suspensions of an independent suspension system to minimize body roll. Anti roll-bar.

**staggered-V engine:** in an engine with cylinders arranged in two banks with their banks forming a V angle the axes of the individual cylinders in each bank are staggered with respect to the opposite side to prevent interference of the bores.

**stainless steel:** a steel alloy with chromium and sometimes nickel or molybdenum that is nearly impervious to rust or corrosion.

**stake body:** a vehicle truck body with a platform floor with stakes along the outside edges to retain a load. Stake truck.

**stall:** to cause a vehicle engine to stop because of overload, use of improper gear, abuse of controls, too steep a grade or engine failure.

**stand-off:** a fitting or a device used for holding something at a distance from a surface as an insulator.

**standpipe:** an outlet pipe whose opening is above the bottom of a tank to retain a reserve as of fuel that requires the opening of another valve to access.

**Stanley Steamer:** well-known early American steam automobile (1897-1927) known for its quiet dependability, outstanding acceleration, and high speed (127.66 mph at Daytona Beach in 1906).

**starter:** a high-torque electric motor for starting a vehicle engine usually by a high ratio geared drive to the flywheel ring gear. Starter motor. Cranking motor.

**starting handle:** a crank handle that engages a dog at the crankshaft front end for manually starting the engine.

**starting tap:** a threading tool with a tapered starting end to facilitate straight alignment and ease of starting. Bottoming tap.

**static toe:** the difference in distance between corresponding points at the front and rear of paired wheels with the vehicle stationary. As toe-in if the front is narrower or toe-out if the front is wider.

**station wagon:** an automobile with an interior longer than a sedan's with one or more rear seats readily lifted out or folded to enable light cargo hauling. Usually with an adjustable rear window and opening tailgate. Estate car. Shooting brake.

**stator:** a stationary part of a machine in or about which a rotor revolves as the static blades in a torque converter or the static windings in an alternator.

**stealth shield:** a device sold with false advertising claims that it will make a vehicle invisible (non-detectable) to police speed-detecting radar/laser equipment.

**steam bent:** the wooden, usually oak, top bows for early American automobiles were steam soaked/softened to make the oak pliable enough to be bent to shape where it was clamped until fully dry.

**steam car:** a motor vehicle propelled by a steam external combustion engine instead of the conventional internal combustion engine.

**steam roller:** a highway surfacing machine for compacting and smoothing asphaltic road topping using a steam-heated very heavy surface roller and propelled in earlier days by a steam engine.

**steam tractor:** early American farm/ranch tractors powered by steam engines that pulled plows and powered harvesting machines.

**steerable headlight:** a vehicle headlight steered by linkage from the wheel steering system so that the headlight beam always pointed in the direction of travel, lighting the way around sharp curves in our early American roads. The Tucker's Cyclops headlight was the only known American post World War II automobile with this feature.

**steering:** mechanism or means whereby the direction of a vehicle's movement is controlled.

**steering angle:** the angle between the longitudinal axis of a vehicle and the plane of the steered wheel.

**steering arm:** a lever attached to the wheel spindle or stub axle assembly that imparts the steering action/force from a tie rod or track rod.

**steering box:** gear box in which the rotary motion of the steering column in converted to the angular movement of the Pitman arm.

**steering column:** the shaft that transmits the steering wheel rotation to a gear box or rack and pinion.

**steering column shifter:** a transmission shift lever mounted on the steering column, operating the selector forks through a system of interconnecting rods and levers.

**steering damper:** device for damping vibrations or shock loads in the steering system to the steering wheel, usually a hydro-pneumatic shock absorber.

**steering feel:** a highly-subjective biased driver opinion contaminated by many imponderables making a scientific rating essentially impossible.

**steering gear:** the total package of components comprising the system by which a vehicle is steered.

**steering knuckle:** the combination of the spindle (stub axle) and the Pitman (steering) arm.

**steering lock:** a security/anti-theft device that locks or disables a vehicle's steering.

**steering ratio:** ratio of angular turning of the steering wheel to the corresponding angular turning of the steered wheels.

**steering stability:** the degree to which a vehicle maintains a direction of travel without driver corrections and returns to the desired direction after being misdirected.

**steering wheel:** the wheel used by the driver to control the vehicle's direction of travel.

**stellite:** a very hard metal alloy noted for hardness and wear resistance at high temperature. Used for coating exhaust valves and exhaust valve seats as well as the cutting edge of high-speed machining tools.

**step-down:** to lower a voltage as by a transformer or voltage-dropping resistor. To lower rotational speed by smaller-to-larger belted pulleys or gears. A designation for passenger cars with floor levels below that of the chassis frames.

**step-frame trailer:** a vehicle trailer or semi-trailer with its forward section raised to clear its tractor chassis while leaving the main cargo platform lower for ease of loading and a lower center-of-gravity.

**step-plate:** usually an add-on plate to prevent wear to vehicle components as running boards, fenders, or door sills.

**step-up:** a designation for a pick-up truck using a running board-like step for easy access to the cargo-carrying area.

**stick-shift:** a manually-operated gearshift control (stick, lever) mounted on the steering column or through the floor of a vehicle.

**stiffener:** a structural member (brace) usually at an angle used to strengthen a vehicle frame or structure.

**Stillson:** a flexible adjustable-head wrench designed for gripping various shapes (particularly rounded) without slipping. Pipe wrench.

**Stirling engine:** an external-combustion engine having an enclosed working fluid (as helium) that is alternately compressed to operate a piston(s) to produce useful work. The practical Stirling engine, using two co-axial pistons, does not work on the idealized Stirling cycle.

**stirrup-pump:** a portable hand-pump held in position by a foot bracket (stirrup) and used to supply tire inflation air pressure usually for roadside emergencies.

**stock:** a vehicle that remains configured as originally manufactured. Stock car a racing vehicle/class that must be delivered for sale to the general public.

**stoichiometric mixture:** the ratio by weight of fuel-to-air as supplied to an internal combustion engine that is chemically correct thus insuring complete combustion with no residual unburned fuel or excess air. This idealistic perfection is difficult or impossible of attainment in a practical workaday environment.

**stop:** an adjustable or fixed barrier, device, or control that can end movement or activity in a positive manner. Throttle stop, door stop, limit switch, check valve.

**stop cock:** a fluid valve with a half-turn from on-to-off. Useful for sampling fluid availability and as a quick and positive shut-off of fluid flow.

**stopleak:** a sealant that when added to the air in a pneumatic tire coats the interior surface penetrating small openings and stops air from leaking. When added to engine coolant stopleak seeps through small leaks then air-hardens and seals the leak.

**stop light:** a rear warning light that illuminates whenever a vehicle is slowing or stopping. Brake light.

**stop light switch:** an electrical switch to the stop light that is actuated by brake system pressure or linkage as brakes are applied.

**storage battery:** the on-board vehicle electric battery that stabilizes the electrical system voltage when the vehicle is operating and supplies stored electrical energy for starting and for lighting when parked.

**straightaway:** the straight segments of a closed race course for vehicles as of an oval track.

**straight engine:** a multi-cylinder in-line vehicle engine (when more than four) often called a "straight six" or "straight eight".

**straight through:** a vehicle exhaust system with minimum restrictions to exhaust gas flow as no muffler, no resonance chamber, no catalytic converter. Straight pipes. Loud pipes.

**strainer:** a coarse filter as a metallic or synthetic screen or mesh that is usually full-flow sometimes with a by-pass in the event of clogging.

**strain gauge:** a measuring device that measures and records the strain (force or weight) experienced by a vehicle component during use.

**stratified charge:** vehicle engine combustion system utilizing a relatively fuel-rich mixture to initiate combustion which then spreads throughout the remaining fuel-lean charge. Lean burn is thus practical in increasing fuel economy and reducing pollution.

**street machine:** a post-1948 American automobile that has been modified, often extensively and expensively, to accelerate and to handle better and to go much faster than the original stock vehicle. The old time hot rodders disdainfully claim that there's more show than go under all of their glitz.

**street rod:** a pre-1948 American automobile modified to make it a true racing machine, usually representing the ingenuity and expertise of the automobile aficionado who pridefully does his own work in his backyard garage. Most have redesigned exteriors that reflect the owner's dream cars.

**stress relief:** the elimination of localized abnormal stresses in metal caused by welding, forming, and shaping, usually by heating/cooling in a temperature regulated oven.

**stretch limo:** slang for a limousine that has been lengthened and ostentatiously outfitted to an absurd extent.

**strobe light:** as an ignition timing device the bright very short flashes are triggered by each spark plug impulse thus providing a visual look at the moving crankshaft timing marks as if they were standing still. As a warning light the bright repetitive flashes from a strobe light can effectively warn of obstacles (day or night).

**stroke:** the total axial reciprocating movement of a piston (up-or-down) in its cylinder bore equaling the diameter of the circle formed by the crankshaft's crankpin axis rotation.

**stroke-to-bore ratio:** ratio of the dimensional distance of piston travel (stroke) to the measured diameter of the cylinder (bore). "Long-stroke" when the stroke exceeds the bore, "square" when the two are equal, and "short-stroke" when the stroke is less than the bore.

**stroking:** increasing the length of an engine's stroke by installing a crankshaft with a longer "throw" or by regrinding the existing crankshaft. Increases engine displacement.

**stub axle:** a short cantilevered axle on which a vehicle wheel is mounted.

**studded tire:** a vehicle tire with hardened metal or ceramic nail-like studs imbedded into the tread surface to give better traction on icy roads.

**stump poller:** slang for a very low ratio gear or low-geared vehicle that provides tremendous pulling power at very slow speeds.

**subcompact:** a car smaller than a compact, using the DOT vehicle size classification.

**submerged pump:** a fluid pump that is inmersed in its fluid supply. In-tank fuel pump.

**subsonic:** a speed below the speed of sound. A frequency below the normal audibility range of the human ear.

**suburban:** a vehicle type designed for suburbanites with a usually heavier chassis and combined features of a passenger car/station wagon/light cargo carrier.

**suction manifold:** intake or induction manifold.

**suction stroke:** the intake or induction stroke of an engine. The first stroke of an internal combustion engine cycle.

**suicide doors:** vehicle side doors opening from the front with rear hinges creating the potential for violent opening by slip-stream air.

**sulfated plates:** storage battery plates that have become coated with lead sulfate reducing battery strength and life.

**sulfur oxides:** generic term for various oxides as exhaust pollution from the sulfur in petroleum fuels. Tend to form sulfuric acid in combination with the water from the combustion of the hydrogen.

**sump:** a fluid reservoir as the crankcase oil pan.

**sump pump:** a pump that scavenges the oil from the crankcase of a dry-sump engine, returning it to an exterior oil sump/tank/reservoir.

**sun gear:** the central spur gear wheel of an epicyclic gear train. Sun wheel.

**sun roof:** a fixed or adjustable (for ventilation) transparent panel in a vehicle roof.

**sun shade:** a fixed porch-like overhang for sun protection. An interior Venetian, tinted, or roll-up curtain to exclude the direct sun. Sun screen.

**Sun Tester:** trade named electronic diagnostic trouble-shooter system widely used in vehicle shops for rapid identification and isolation of malfunctions.

**sun visor:** hinged screen or panel to shield the driver or occupant's eyes from direct sunlight or glare.

**supercharge:** to increase the pressure and therefore the mass of the charge air and fuel mixture in the intake induction system of an internal combustion engine.

**supercharger:** a mechanical pump or compressor for increasing the pressure of the charge air and fuel entering a vehicle engine. A turbocharger is a supercharger that uses the recovered heat (power) from the engine exhaust instead of direct mechanical energy from the engine.

**superhighway:** a high-speed roadway with limited access to cross-traffic and usually free from traffic stops or slow areas.

**supersonic:** a speed faster than the speed of sound. A frequency higher than the upper auditory limit of the human ear usually above 20,000 cycles per second.

**suppressor:** an electrical device for minimizing radio frequency interference emitted by a vehicle's high voltage ignition system. Usually by using very high resistance and/or RF shielding.

**surface embrittlement:** a reaction by certain metal surfaces when exposed to certain elements in the presence of extreme heat. A steel/iron surface heated by combustion or welding and exposed to carbon or hydrogen. Carbon/hydrogen embrittlement.

**surface grinder:** any of several types of abrasive grinders used to remove metal from mating surfaces or to smooth those surfaces for a more precise fit.

**surface harden:** to impart a harder layer or modification to the surface of a metal by chemical treatment, heating and quenching, coating, plating, or peening to increase wear or strength.

**surface ignition:** ignition in a vehicle engine caused prematurely by hot spots on the surface of the combustion chamber (cylinder head/walls and piston head) that are carbon clumpings or metal projections that glow red from the previous combustion cycle.

**surface-to-volume ratio:** the numerical ratio of the exposed combustion chamber surface area to the contained volume at the top dead center position.

**surface tension:** a condition that exists at the free surface of a body (as a liquid) by reason of intermolecular forces about the individual surface molecules and is manifested by properties resembling those of an elastic skin under tension. Related to vapor pressure and evaporation characteristics of a liquid.

**surfactant:** a surface-active agent as a detergent, soap, or wetting agent.

**suspension:** the total of the components needed to support the vehicle body and its load on the ground-contact under-carriage such as springs, fittings, shock absorbers, linkages.

**suspension roll:** the side-to-side or roll of the sprung mass of a vehicle with respect to its undercarriage.

**swage:** to bond two metals by extreme pressure sometimes from highly-levered squeezing, hydropneumatic pressing, or forge-hammering.

**swaging tool:** a tool, usually operation-individualized, such as for cable fittings where the cable end is inserted into a hollow end-piece (clevis, rod) and surrounding metal forcibly compressed onto the cable.

**swapmeet:** a usually outdoor gathering of automobile aficionados to buy, sell, exchange, or swap automobile-related items. A practical way to find or to dispose of rare components for antique vehicles.

**swash plate:** a disc or plate obliquely mounted on a shaft (as the crankshaft) with connecting rod attachments that convert reciprocating motion from pistons/cylinders located parallel to the shaft to shaft rotation.

**swash plate engine:** an engine, external (steam) or internal combustion using a swash plate instead of a crankshaft to produce a rotating power output from reciprocating pistons.

**sway bar:** a bar that torsionally couples the right and left independent suspension of a vehicle to reduce roll and sway.

**swept volume:** the measured displacement of a reciprocating engine found by multiplying the cylinder area and the stroke of the piston times the number of cylinders. Cubic capacity.

**swing axle:** a driven half-axle, pivoted at a central differential case, resulting in wheel camber angle change as vehicle height changes from change in either static or dynamic load.

**swirl:** the induced rotation of combustion gases in an engine cylinder to improve mixing, heat transfer, and scavenging.

**swirl chamber:** a cavity formed into a cylinder head or piston in a shape to promote a swirling motion in the combustion gases.

**switchback:** a sharply curved zigzag mountainous road involving 180°+ turns that cause a vehicle to do a complete reversal of direction of travel. Required to maintain a negotiable angle of climb up the face of a steep slope.

**synchromesh gearbox:** a vehicle transmission in which the speed of rotation of a selected gear is automatically synchronized (speed-matched) with that of the mainshaft immediately prior to engagement.

**sync ring:** the sliding clutch by which gear engagement is synchronized in a synchromesh transmission.

**SCR:** silicon controlled rectifier, a solid-state device that converts alternating current into direct current. Thyristor.

**serpentine belt:** usually an accessory-drive micro-Vee or toothed belt driving several units, often in opposite directions and following a complex circuitous path around their pulleys.

**SI:** (1) Spark ignition (engine). (2) An international system of metric and scientific units of measurement.

**skin effect:** drag resulting from fluid friction with a surface(skin) as liquid in a conduit or air flow around a vehicle surface. Air Drag. Reynolds Number.

**sonic test:** measurement of metal thickness (where mechanical micrometers or calipers cannot reach) using sound frequencies.

**SM:** the 1971-1973 Maserati V-6 powered Citroen coupe, called "Super Machine"--because it was!

## "SEVEN-SEVENTY-SEVEN"

The first American-built automobile to go over 200 mph was built by Bill Kenz and Roy Leslie at Denver, Colorado, in 1950 after they first competed in the first Bonneville Speed Week in 1949 with a two-engined (flat-head Ford V-8s, with one behind the cab) pickup truck. Bill and Roy learned from their truck that speed was spelled a-e-r-o-d-y-n-a-m-i-c-s when their "777" streamliner went 210.648 miles-per-hour on the same two engines.

Streamlining had prevailed before when Frank Lockhart drove his 3-litre V-16 Stutz Blackhawk 203.45 mph in 1928 (but was killed at Daytona Beach Florida on the return run--thus failing to establish the two-way average speed required for an official world record). On March 29, 1927 Sir Henry Segrave (an Englishman) set the first official two-way World Landspeed Record over 200 (203.75 mph) with two V-12 aircraft engines of 2,746 cubic inch displacement powering his 8,000 pound automobile.

"777" continued to reign as "King of Speed" through 1957 when it was clocked at 270.470 mph (and retired) running three flat-head Ford V-8 engines of 304 cubic inches each. Five times this Denver-built "hot rod" was named "National Champion" because of its advanced automotive design, its innovative technologies and because it proved to be the fastest participant at each of those United States National Speed Trials.

"777" ran well--and fast--on one. two, and three engines. 178 mph in 1955 on one engine. 255.045 mph in 1953 on two engines. 270.470 mph in 1957 on three engines. Bill Kenz, Roy Leslie, and "777" could count as well as they spelled--aerodynamics!

**T-Cars:** Of 175 T-Marques, the Thomas Flyer that won the 1908 New York to Paris Race (did it swim?), with a 781 cubic inch engine is considered the most memorable. This car sold at auction in 1913 for $200 but later became a priceless showpiece of the Harrah's Automobile Collection at Reno, Nevada. The British Triumph was likely the most hardy of the lot. The Tatra, the Toyota, and the Tucker emulated the aerodynamics of the mid-thirties Chrysler and DeSoto Airflow models. Al seemed to borrow a little from "Bucky" Fuller's 1933/34 Dymaxion tear-drop design but none ever matched the very low coefficient of aerodynamic drag attained by the Dymaxion.

**T-trivia:** Toyota's home, Toyota City, arose from the ashes of Koromo, Japan, a suburb of Nagasaki, that was destroyed by a 10,000 pound "pumpkin" high-explosive bomb dropped from the B-29 "Bockscar" by USAF Captain Fred Bock on August 14, 1945. The "Bockscar" had dropped the "Fat Man" atomic bomb that devastated Nagasaki on August 9, 1945. Did the "Bockscar" spawn the Toyota? Eiji Toyoda, Chairman of Toyota Motor Corporation, the second Japanese (the other, Mr. Honda) inducted into the American Automotive Hall of Fame, wrote in his autobiography that several USAF B-29s dropped several bombs on his factory. Actually only one B-29 dropped only one 10,000-pound "pumpkin".

**tab:** a small handle-like protrusion used for grasping to install/remove small mechanical parts or for precise location.

**table:** a working surface as for a machine such as a drill press, milling machine, welding, et al.

**tach:** mechanic's abbreviation for tachometer.

**tachograph:** an instrument, usually electrical, for recording vehicle operational data against a time base, normally by a stylus on a moving paper disc or strip.

**tachometer:** an instrument for measuring, displaying, and/or recording speed of rotation as of an engine crankshaft or a wheel. Usually expressed as revolutions per minute.

**tack:** a short small nail usually with a larger head used extensively in vehicle upholstery when wood was widely used for body/seat framing.

**tack claw:** a small hand tool shaped for removal of tacks.

**tack hammer:** a small upholster's hammer, usually magnetized, for ease in starting and driving tacks.

**tack rag:** a chemically treated wiping rag designed for efficient dust removal from a surface prior to painting.

**tacky:** the consistency of many adhesives used in vehicle repair/maintenance for attachment and for gasket/seam sealants.

**tag:** vehicle colloquialism for a vehicle license plate, an attached identification plate, or a parts identification card or label.

**tag axle:** a trailer dead axle.

**tail fin:** a vertical appurtenance resembling an airplane or shark fin usually along the top rear of rear fenders. Rarely functional. Usually ostentatious for visual effect.

**tail gate:** a closure panel at the rear of a vehicle (as a pickup) that can be removed or hinged downward for ease in loading cargo. To drive dangerously close behind another vehicle. To hold a tail gate picnic as at outdoor sporting events. Tail board.

**tail light:** a red warning lamp usually at both corners of the rear of a vehicle usually incorporating a brighter red brake warning light. Tail lamp.

**tail pipe:** the rearmost pipe of a vehicle exhaust system, downstream of the rear muffler.

**tailshaft:** an output or drive shaft from an engine, gearbox, or other device of rotating machinery.

**tailshaft governor:** a speed-sensitive device that monitors torque converter tailshaft speed and governs engine speed accordingly.

**take-off:** a mechanism for transmission of the power of an engine or vehicle to operate some other mechanism not an integral part of the vehicle. Power take-off.

**take up:** to make tighter or shorter (as take up the slack).

**Talladega:** internationally recognized automobile racecourse in Alabama where some of the fastest closed-course competition speeds are recorded. Auto manufacturers frequently use this track for high-speed vehicle testing (usually endurance runs).

**tall gears:** high numerical-ratio vehicle gears used to obtain higher road speeds while using lower engine speeds (lower revolutions per minute of crankshaft rotation).

**tamper:** to make illicit changes or modifications to a vehicle to weaken, to interfere with or change for the worse the functioning of legally required components. Tampering with odometers or emissions equipment is a federal offense.

**tandem axle:** vehicle undercarriage arrangement where two or more axles are close-coupled one behind the other to spread the load over the vehicle structure and upon the roadway surface.

**tandem brake master cylinder:** two brake master cylinders in one housing for operating divided system brakes for safety redundancy in the event of a hydraulic system leak.

**tandem plunger pump:** a distributor-type diesel fuel injection pump in which a second pair of pumping plungers provides excess fuel for engine starting.

**tank:** a receptacle, container, or reservoir usually closed or capable of being sealed designed to hold, transport, or store fluids or a granulated or pelletized solid material. An enclosed heavily armed and armored combat vehicle that usually moves on appropriate endless belt-like tracks.

**tanker:** a large tank mounted on a suitable vehicle for transporting fluids.

**tank farm:** a collection of adjacent tanks for storing fluids.

**tank slush:** a liquid coating used to seal the inside of vehicle fuel tanks to prevent small leaks. Tank sealer.

**tank trailer:** a truck-drawn trailer equipped as a tanker for transporting fluids.

**tap:** a tool, hand or machine operated, designed to cut female threads inside a drilled hole or to cut female threads into a soft material that has not been pre-drilled.

**taper:** gradual diminution of thickness, diameter, or width in an elongated object. Progressively narrowed toward one end.

**taper leaf spring:** a single leaf spring of tapering section usually of high capacity for weight carrying.

**taper pin:** a pin designed to be driven or pressed into a corresponding tapered hole through two objects (as a shaft and a pulley hub) to effectively lock/join them together to function as a single unit.

**taper roller bearing:** a rolling element bearing employing conical rollers between inner and outer races and able to carry thrust (axial) loads as well as journal (radial) loads.

**tappet:** a cylindrical reciprocating cam-follower (valve lifter) that converts cam lift into linear reciprocating movement which it transmits directly to a valve through a rocker arm or indirectly through a push-rod to a rocker arm to the valve.

**tare weight:** the weight of an empty vehicle (including fuel) that must be deducted from the gross weight as obtained on drive-on scales to obtain the weight of the on-board cargo load.

**targa top:** a removable rigid roof panel, particularly of a sports car.

**tarp:** tarpaulin, a canvas or synthetic fabric-like flexible sheet for covering a vehicle or its cargo.

**tarp hook:** cleats, rings, or hooks firmly attached to structural members of a truck body for use in tying down flexible coverings (tarps) to protect cargo and equipment.

**tax-exempt:** a typical government ruse used to subsidize the products of powerful special interests. Favored fuels are given fuel tax exemptions as are propulsion choices without consideration of the financial/scientific impact upon the automotive industry and the vehicle-using public. Selective taxing is never fair nor equitable, denying sensible comparison of the real cost of the choices.

**taxicab:** a passenger-carrying automobile that is licensed and carries patrons for a fare usually determined by the distance traveled. Taxi. Air-taxi. Water-taxi. Cab. Hackney.

**TCP:** tri-cresyl phosphate. A fuel additive.

**TEL:** tetra-ethyl lead. An anti-knock fuel additive (anti-detonant). Ethyl.

**teamster:** one who drives a team or a motor truck as an occupation. A member of the Teamster's Union.

**teardown:** the disassembly of a machine for diagnosis, repair, or replacement of damaged/worn components (as of a vehicle engine/transmission).

**teardrop:** something shaped like a falling tear or raindrop. Descriptive of vehicle (especially small trailers) shapes. Streamlined.

**technetronic:** technological + electronic. Shaped or influenced by the changes wrought by advances in technology and in electronic communications.

**technician:** a specialist in the technical details of a subject or occupation.

**Teflon:** trademarked synthetic resin used widely to reduce friction as bushings, et al., where lubricants are difficult to apply/retain.

**telemetry:** the science or process of telemetering data. To transmit quantitative measurements from the data-generating source to the point-of-use or display.

**telescopic:** having parts that slide or pass one within another like the cylindrical sections of a hand telescope.

**telescopic fork:** steering/suspension arrangement as for motorcycles in which the steered wheel is straddled by two telescopic struts linked below the steering head.

**telescopic shock absorber:** a coaxial tubular hydropneumatic damping device.

**telescopic steering column:** a steering column designed to progressively collapse upon impact from collision forces that would drive the column upward/backward into the driver's torso or the driver's impact upon the steering wheel as caused by strong sudden deceleration forces upon his unrestrained upper body.

**telltale:** the extra indicator hand (pointer) on a recording instrument that moves with the regular hands but remains at the maximum or minimum reading for future reference before the hand is manually reset in readiness for the next reading.

**temperature:** the degree of hotness or coldness measured on a definite scale. For scientific acceptability any temperature measurement must be by calibrated instruments.

**temperature diagram:** an isothermic plot of points of equal temperature measured by sensors throughout an operating component or device to provide guidelines for redesign of thermal dissipation of the tested item.

**temperature sensor:** a sensor incorporating a bi-metallic spring to generate mechanical movement, a thermocouple to generate an electrical voltage, or a fluid capsule (either gas or liquid filled) to generate a pressure change in consonance with temperature variations that can be detected and displayed on an appropriate instrument.

**temperature tape:** a selection of tapes that indicate the degree of hotness or coldness of a material to which they are attached by the color change of the tape. Temperature-sensitive paints and crayons are available with a similar capability.

**template:** a gauge, pattern, or mold used as a guide for laying out a workpiece for machining to specifications and after machining for checking the shapes and dimensions of the finished piece.

**ten penny nail:**  a nail that is three inches in length with compatible diameter.

**tensile strength:**  the greatest longitudinal stress a substance can bear without tearing apart.

**tensiometer:**  a device for measuring tension as in structural material, the tension of a cable, or the tension of a belt or chain.

**tension:**  the act or action of stretching or the condition or degree of being stretched to stiffness.

**tension rod:**  a vehicle steering-tracking rod or tie rod.

**terminal:**  a device attached to the end of a wire or cable or to an electrical apparatus for convenience in making connections.

**terminal post:**  a usually tapered circular stub or a lug-shaped fitting on a battery to which battery cable connections are attached by clamping or threaded devices.

**terneplate:**  sheet iron or steel coated with an alloy consisting of about four parts of lead and one part of tin to provide surface protection against corrosion.

**Terraplane:**  the lower-priced Hudson marque that replaced the Essex Six (1932-37) and that became the basis for the British Railton automobile.

**test cycle:**  a laboratory or highway test procedure that follows a strictly controlled sequence of operating parameters simulating real-life driving conditions to measure vehicle performance involving emissions and fuel economy.

**test drive:**  to drive a motor vehicle (usually prior to purchase) to evaluate its performance, comfort, and suitability or by a mechanic to verify a repair.

**test track:**  a vehicle driving area including a high-speed track and various obstacle courses suitable for testing to insure performance, durability, and safety as promised by the manufacturer.

**tete-a-tete:**  face-to-face, the seating arrangement in some early automobiles.  The opposite of do-si-do.

**tetraethyl lead:**  a heavy oily poisonous liquid $Pb(C_3H_5)_4$ now being phased out as an antiknock additive to motor vehicle gasoline.  As is tetramethyl lead.

**THC:** total hydrocarbon contained in motor vehicle exhausts that significantly affects and contributes to atmospheric pollution. NOT the tetrahydrocannabinol, marijuana.

**therm:** a unit of quantity of heat (energy), 100,000 BTUs (British Thermal Units). The therm is a logical quantification of fuel energy (about 83% of a gallon of gasoline) and must be adopted as a standard to ensure fair and equitable pricing of all motor vehicle fuels. Without such a standard, fuels cannot be compared as to price or ability to power a motor vehicle. The lying misrepresentations about fuels by political pimps and special interests will continue until such a standard is adopted.

**thermal:** of, relating to, or marked by the presence of heat or caused by heat.

**thermal efficiency:** the ratio of useful work performed by an engine to the total energy content of the fuel consumed as a measure of combustion efficiency. BTU output divided by BTU input.

**thermistor:** an electrical resistor coupled with a semi-conductor whose resistance varies sharply and predictably with temperature changes making it ideal as a sensor/detector of temperature capable of sending reliable information to a temperature indicator or for operating temperature regulating devices.

**thermocouple:** a pair of wires of dissimilar metals joined at their ends (as at a spark or oil plug gasket) and used to measure temperature by the amount of change in the electric current developed by a difference in temperature at the junction.

**thermodynamics:** the branch of physics that deals with the mechanical action or relations of heat.

**thermostat:** an automatic device for regulating temperature as by controlling the supply of fuel (gas, electricity, et al.) or the supply of coolant (air, water, et al.). Thermostatic switches also operate fire alarms, automatic sprinklers, or machinery shut-off devices.

**t-head:** descriptive of a cylinder head for an internal combustion engine that has the two valves (intake and exhaust) on opposite sides of the cylinder bore.

**thickness:** the smallest of three dimensions: length, width, and thickness. Thickness gauge, a package of varying thickness flat strips for determining many vehicle clearances defining clearance and thickness as equal opposites.

**thing-a-ma-bob:**  something that is hard to classify or the name of a part that is unknown or forgotten by the mechanic. Thing-a-ma-jig.

**throttle:**  a valve for controlling and regulating the amount of fuel and/or air delivered to a vehicle's engine to regulate its power/speed.  The lever or foot-pedal controlling this valve. To reduce fluid flow.

**throttle-body:**  the housing containing the throttle valve and its ancillary equipment (as a carburetor).

**throttle-body injection:**  the injection of fuel by one nozzle (injector at/or near the valve that controls the intake charge-air) in lieu of carburetion spray devices and in contrast to port injection at/or near the individual cylinder intake valves or direct injection into the closed combustion chamber of each cylinder.

**throw:**  the movement imparted to a pivoted or reciprocating piece (as a piston rod) by the length of the radius of a crank (as of a crankshaft) or the virtual radius of a cam or an eccentric.  Twice the radius (diameter) of a crank movement equals the stroke of an internal combustion engine piston (the distance from top-dead-center to bottom-dead-center).

**throwaway:**  a device designed to be thrown away at the end of its useful life.  Most typical is the modern oil filter. Disposable.  Some throwaways are repairable, most are recyclable, but not efficiently as individual items but in mass numbers.

**throw out:**  to disengage a clutch or a pair of meshed gears.

**throwout bearing:**  a bearing installed on the transmission power input shaft and within a clutch/disk/pressure plate mechanism that transmits force to compress the clutch springs to disengage the engine from the transmission.

**thrust:**  a force acting lengthwise along a shaft.

**thrust bearing:**  a bearing configured to control or absorb a force acting lengthwise along a shaft in one or both directions.

**thrust washer:**  a washer designed to accept linear force along a shaft.

**Throne Car:**  a ceremonial limousine with an ornate throne-like seat behind the driver used for parades.  Usually associated with religious leader "Father Divine".

**thumb-screw:**  a screw with a knurled or flattened head that can be turned by the thumb and forefinger.

**thyristor:** any of several semiconductor devices that act as rectifiers, switchers, or voltage regulators.

**tick over:** the running of an engine at the slowest practical speed. Slow idle.

**tie bar:** a structural member used for connecting or bracing. Strut.

**tie-down:** a cable, chain, or strap usually with a tightening and locking attachment used to secure cargo or coverings on a vehicle.

**tie-rod:** a rod used for attaching, bracing, or actuating usually as a tension link. Any nominally transverse rod member that directly or indirectly actuates steered wheels.

**TIG:** a welding process/system using an inert gas (as argon or helium) to surround and shield the welding flame and "puddle" from the oxidizing effects of the surrounding air.

**Tiger-in-the-tank:** an advertising catch-phrase used to promote various fuels and additives used with simulated tiger tails to be hung near the vehicle tank filler-pipe making it appear that a tiger is in the tank with tail hanging out.

**tiller:** an operating lever direct-mounted to a vertical steering shaft in lieu of a steering wheel. Not used since the very earliest land vehicles. A holdover from boats.

**tilt-bed:** a trailer or vehicle with a load-carrying floor designed for tilting to allow loading and unloading from a ramp or for matching its height with a loading dock.

**tilt-cab:** a forward-control truck driver's cab hinged so that it can tilt forward to provide access to the vehicle's engine and running gear for service and maintenance.

**tilt-trailer:** a cargo trailer whose floor tilts upward at the front to form a sloping ramp that allows ground-level loading/unloading of cargo. Beaver tail.

**tilt wheel:** a vehicle steering wheel whose steering-shaft angle may be changed and locked to provide driving comfort and preference for different sized drivers.

**timed fuel injection:** an engine fuel system that provides accurately measured fuel quantity in correctly timed pulses to each individual cylinder in contrast to the continuous discharge into a central point in the inlet air system (intake manifold). Injection directly into the combustion chamber is preferable to the central-point (throttle-body) or port-discharge systems.

**time trial:** a competitive event as in automobile racing in which individual entrants are timed over a set course or fixed distance often to establish eligibility to compete against others.

**timing:** the scheduling and actuation of events necessary for the optimum functioning of a vehicle's internal combustion engine such as valve operation (intake, exhaust, and fuel) and ignition operation (spark production and discharge).

**timing belt:** a toothed (flat or shaped) flexible belt for insuring synchronization of timed operations (spark, fuel pulses, charge air) with the rotation of the vehicle engine's crankshaft position locked to the rotation ratio of the timed function.

**timing chain:** a continuous roller or toothed metal chain that drives a vehicle's timed events/functions.

**timing gear:** either of two meshing (or interconnecting through an idler gear) toothed gears used to insure a fixed rotational ratio between an engine's crankshaft and any synchronized (timed) mechanism. Most usually applied to driving the camshaft.

**timing hole:** an opening or window providing visual access to a timing mark operating within a mechanism and frequently with the fixed reference mark inscribed on an opening edge. Most timing holes are covered by removable protective dust covers or plugs.

**timing light:** a pulsed test or depiction light whose flashes are initiated (triggered) by a rotating or repetitive moving device. When the flash duration is sufficiently short any lighted moving object appears to be stationary allowing the viewer's eye to see and evaluate events that are not normally seen clearly. When triggered by a vehicle's ignition system the light causes the rotating crankshaft to appear to stand still, allowing a rotating mark to be seen in relation to a fixed reference mark nearby, verifying the exact instant of spark occurrence with relation to crankshaft (and piston) position. Used for diagnosing and setting engine spark timing.

**timing mark:** an easily identifiable mark (usually permanently machined into a surface) on a camshaft, crankshaft, flywheel or other rotating or reciprocating part to serve as a reference to another similar mark or a stationary mark as on a block or casting surface for timing one or more components to another.

**tin:** a soft bluish white lustrous low-melting-point metallic element that is ductile and malleable at ordinary temperatures and that is used as a protective coating, in soft solders, and many alloys.

**tin can:** the deformation of a thin sheet metal surface evidenced by an inward or outward bulge caused by stress or vibration and often accompanied by a percussive sound.

**tinsmith:** a worker skilled in the shaping, fabrication, and repair of thin sheetmetal components as ducts, et al.

**tire:** the circumferential covering of a wheel that supports a vehicle by contact with the roadway surface providing wear resistance, traction, and shock absorption/ damping. Most vehicle tires are air-filled under controlled pressures

**tire balance:** the state of mass distribution throughout a tire that insures static balance at rest and dynamic balance when rotating giving a more comfortable ride and eliminating material failure and wear from the vibration caused by out-of-balance centrifugal forces. Correction for minor imperfections in balance is accomplished by adding appropriately sized and located weights around the wheel rim.

**tire bead:** the reinforced ring around the inner diameter of a vehicle tire intended and shaped to seal and retain the tire in place on the wheel rim.

**tire casing:** the tread, shoulder, and sidewall of a tire composed of rubber-bonded cord and fabric and molded rubber.

**tire chain:** a chain assembly of loops with lateral cross links (often welded lugs) and fastening/tightening latches that form an exterior shroud around the tire to provide added traction on ice/snow and through mud.

**tire changer:** a mechanical or hydropneumatic device for installing and removing a vehicle tire onto/from its wheel rim.

**tire guage:** a pressure-indicating device designed to check the air pressure in vehicle tires and to allow changing the pressure to optimize tire performance.

**tire oxidation:** damage to weather-exposed tires that are not compounded to resist the deleterious effect of ozone ($O_3$), a highly reactive form of oxygen and a common component of atmospheric smog.

**tire pressure:** the pressure of the air in an inflated tire usually measured and stated as "pounds"--meaning the differential pressure in pounds-per-square-inch above the adjacent surrounding outside air pressure (existing atmospheric pressure).

**tire profile:** the dimensional ratio of the cross-sectional height to width of a tire usually expressed as a Series #70 meaning that the height is 70% of the width. Relatively wide tires are called "low profile" and narrow tires "high profile".

**tire screech:** the shrill sound caused by loss of traction and spinning or sideslip of a tire tread against the road surface. Tire squeal.

**tire scrub:** sideways sliding motion of a tire contact with the road surface caused by misalignment or the inevitable slip angle during vehicle directional changes.

**tire tool:** a hand-operated pry-lever shaped to facilitate stretching a tire bead over the retaining rim of a vehicle wheel.

**tire tread:** the thick contact section of a vehicle tire's outer circumference that usually has a molded surface to improve traction and wear while reducing tire noise.

**tire wear:** normal with repeated rolling contact with road surfaces. Abnormal when influenced by excessive braking, abusive driving, imbalance, and wheel misalignment.

**tire well:** a usually rounded receptacle in a fender or trunk lid for carrying the spare tire/wheel. Fender well. Continental mount.

**titanium:** a silvery gray relatively light but very strong metallic element used in alloys usually with steel and to form protective coatings and in its pure form.

**titanium white:** a brilliant white lead-free pigment consisting primarily of titanium dioxide with barium sulfate and zinc oxide.

**Tite-Bond:** a trade-named adhesive used to cement weather stripping around enclosure openings.

**toe-in:** adjustment of the oppositely-paired wheels (usually the steered front wheels) of an automotive vehicle so that they are closer together at the front than the back.

**toe-out:** adjustment of oppositely paired wheels (usually the steered front wheels of an automotive vehicle) so that they are wider apart at the front than the back.

**toggle switch:** an electrical switch actuated to open or close the circuit when the projecting lever of a toggle joint with a spring is pushed through a small arc.

**tolerance:** the allowable deviation from a standard especially the range of variation permitted in maintaining a specified dimension in machining a piece or in selecting and fitting a new piece.

**tollbooth:** an attended or unattended booth as alongside a highway or bridge entrance where tolls are paid. Toll gate.

**toll bridge:** a bridge where a toll is charged for crossing. Toll road.

**toluene:** a liquid aromatic hydrocarbon ($C_7H_8$) used as a solvent, in organic synthesis, and formerly as an anti-knock agent for gasoline (before tetraethyl lead).

**Tom Boy:** the lower-priced, 6-cylinder version of Ned Jordan's great Play Boy 8-cylinder sports roadster of the late 1920s.

**tongs:** any of numerous grasping/lifting devices usually consisting of two pieces joined at one end by a pivot or hinged like scissors.

**tongue:** the projecting section of a structural member (beam, extrusion, or pole) at the front of a towed vehicle (trailer) that serves to connect it to the towing vehicle (tractor).

**ton-mile:** a unit of freight transportation measurement equivalent to the movement of a weight of one ton over a distance of one mile.

**tonneau:** the usually uncovered rear section or compartment of an automobile having seats for passengers.

**tonneau cover:** a usually flexible fabric covering for an automobile tonneau during inclement weather.

**tool:** something (as an instrument or apparatus) used in performing an operation or necessary in the practice of a vocation or profession.

**tool belt:** a waist or shoulder strap with loops or hooks for holding tools frequently or repetitively used by mechanics, thus eliminating or reducing trips to the tool repository.

**tool box:** a container chest for tools that may be fixed in place, hand-carried, or a roll-around.

**tool caddy:** a usually open tray for carrying a small number of tools to a mechanic's work site. Tool pouch.

**tool maker:** a highly specialized machinist who builds, maintains, repairs, and calibrates the tools used in machine shops.

**tool steel:** a special steel formulated to be hard enough and durable enough to cut, machine, and shape other steels used for vehicle components. Usually amenable to tempering by controlled heating and/or immersion cooling to change its metallurgical make-up to fit the exact requirements of a particular machining operation.

**tooth:** one of the regular notch-like projections along the outer edge of a flat piece or on the circumferential edge of a

351

circular piece of material designed to remove a softer material as with a saw or to engage with matched projections on another meshing piece (wheel or bar) in order to transmit force or motion (as a gear).

**toothed belt:** a continuous flexible belt with parallel surface striations (projections) that mesh with compatible grooves in the circumferential edge surface of a driving wheel (gear) and a similar driven wheel. Sometimes called a cogged belt. Used in applications where no slippage can be tolerated and where a roller chain with matching sprockets may also be used. Timing belt

**top:** the uppermost limit of a thing or object as of movement or speed or height.

**top bow:** a wooden support cross-member for a flexible fabric top as for a phaeton or roadster. The bow is usually steam-bent oak with a slightly curved top center section that bends downward at about a 90° angle for fastening to the sides of the vehicle body.

**top dead center:** the uppermost movement of a piston in a cylinder, or the point farthest from the crankshaft axis. TDC.

**top speed:** the maximum attainable steady speed of a vehicle (full power "wide open") measured with a flat level roadway from start to finish, with no wind. True top speed is likely to be somewhat slower than that attained for short level distances after a downhill run.

**torque:** a turning or twisting force as from a vehicle engine that applies rotation to the drive shaft for transmission to the traction wheels. Torque measurement is quantified as the effect of the force multiplied by the perpendicular distance from the line of action of the force to the axis of rotation. Usually stated (U.S.) as foot-pounds of torque.

**torque arm:** any arm, beam, or lever used to resist or transmit torque as the linkage that transmits the driving or braking wind-up to/from the axle of a vehicle.

**torque converter:** the heart of most automatic transmissions that transmits and converts torque from a vehicle engine to its traction wheels using hydraulic forces to adapt the engine's output most efficiently to the requirements of varying vehicle speed, acceleration, or pulling modes.

**torque ratio:** the ratio of the output torque to the input torque of a torque converter usually expressed as a percentage.

**torque rod:** a suspension component as a radius rod.

**torque tube:**  the tube that encloses and protects the drive shaft from a vehicle transmission to its differential/rear axle and acts as a structural member to transmit the drive power and braking forces to/from the vehicle structure and the driving wheels allowing the suspension to support the weight force only and not the propulsion and stopping forces.  Eliminates one of the drive shaft's universal joints.

**torque wrench:**  a mechanic's tool handle/holder that accepts various sockets for tightening holding devices to an exact degree of tightness usually stated in foot-pounds or inch-pounds units.

**torsion:**  the twisting or wrenching of an object by the application of forces tending to turn one end or part about a longitudinal axis while the other end is held fast or turned in the opposite direction.

**torsion bar:**  a long bar, rod, or tube in a vehicle suspension that has one end held rigidly to the frame and the other twisted and fastened to an axle or wheel support, acting as a spring in lieu of the usual coil or leaf springs.

**torsional vibration damper:**  any mechanical or hydraulic device that reduces torsional vibrations as in a vehicle engine crankshaft or transmission shaft.

**torus:**  a circular-section ring commonly used in torque converters to contain the spinning fluid.  A flexible coupling of toroidal shape as a rubber donut and extensively used as a universal joint where small angular changes in drive-line alignment are experienced.

**totalizer:**  a gauge or meter that indicates the remaining total amount as of fuel in a vehicle tank or series of interconnecting tanks.  Fuel gage.

**tour:**  a journey or trip for whatever reason in which one returns to the starting point as the completion.

**touring car:**  from the early 1900s, an automobile suitable for long-distance driving usually with two cross seats, four doors, and a folding top.  Tourer.  Phaeton.

**tow:**  to drag or pull a trailer or other vehicle behind the towing vehicle or tractor unit.

**tow bar:**  the rigid bar or tube by which a trailer or towable vehicle is towed over relatively long distances.  Drawbar.

**tow chain:**  with appropriate attachments on both ends, a chain intended for towing other vehicles over relatively short distance where braking of the towed vehicle is not critical and must be accomplished by an additional driver/operator.  Tow cable. For lighter tows: tow ropes or tow straps (webbing belt) are used.

**town car:** a four-door automobile with a permanently enclosed passenger compartment in the rear separated from the driver's compartment by a sliding glass window.

**towing fork:** British for trailer hitch, applied to the mechanical attachment (ball and cup) and supporting structures with which a trailer is coupled to its tractor.

**towing hook:** a vertically oriented hook or pin (pintle) attached to a tractor chassis or other rigid structural member over which the towing eye of the trailer/towed vehicle is dropped and usually safety-restrained by positive locking devices or clamping jaws.

**tow truck:** a heavy-duty pick-up or heavier truck equipped with a crane, power winch, and sometimes stabilizer outriggers and booms for lifting and towing disabled or wrecked vehicles. Wrecker. The contemporary trend in vehicle rescue is the tilt-flat-bed car-hauler that reduces damage to the rescued vehicle.

**track:** the transverse measured distance between the center-lines of the left- and right-side wheels on a common axle. Tread width. A continuous linked or flexible belt assembly upon which small wheels (bogies) roll while supporting a vehicle's progress across soft or uneven surfaces. Crawler.

**track arm:** a pivoted transverse member constraining a vehicle wheel against forces/ movement (essential for wheels mounted on Chapman or MacPherson struts or non-rigid axles).

**track chain:** the continuous linked track of a tracked or track-laying vehicle as a military tank or a crawler tractor.

**track-laying vehicle:** a vehicle whose wheels run within a continuous chain or track. As a half-track the traction wheels lay a track while the steering wheels roll on the supporting surface traversed.

**track pin:** the metal shaft (hinge pin) that forms the pivot and coupling between two track elements of a track chain.

**track pitch:** the distance between the track pin centers of adjacent pins of a track chain.

**track rod:** the transverse rod (tie rod) that connects the steering arms of steered wheels maintaining the geometric relationship between them at all times. With independent suspension each wheel must have its own track rod (tie rod) to accommodate up-and-down movement of wheels which are connected by the rack in rack-and-pinion steering or by a single intermediate rod or relay rod from a steering gearbox.

**track rod end:**  the ball joint forming the pivot between track rod (tie rod) or rack and steering arm.  Tie rod end.

**track rod lever:**  a steering arm, Pitman arm, or other lever actuating a track rod.

**track thrash:**  periodic whipping motion of the upper (return) portion of the moving track of a track-laying vehicle.

**tracking:**  the telltale visible track left on any insulating surface by electrical voltage leaking through surface contaminants.  The relative directional orientation (following) of wheels of a vehicle.  The alignment of a vehicle steering and suspension system.

**tracking error:**  misalignment of road wheels indicated by steering feel, tire wear, or alignment tools.

**Tracta joint:**  a proprietary constant velocity (CV) joint using forked jaws in sliding engagement with two slotted knuckles.

**traction:**  a pulling force, the motive power that moves a vehicle, or the adhesive force between two surfaces such as a vehicle tire and a roadway.

**traction avant:**  front-wheel-drive.  Commonly associated with the Citroen front-wheel-drive automobile.

**traction bar:**  a rod or beam strut from a live axle to the chassis of a vehicle to transmit torque loads and prevent or minimize wind-up wheel hop.

**traction engine:**  the road locomotive of yesteryear, normally steam-powered and used especially for heavy cargo and to move or operate farm machinery.

**tractive effort:**  the measure of a vehicle's ability to haul or pull.  Horsepower or draw-bar pull.

**tractive unit:**  the towing vehicle of an articulated commercial vehicle.

**tractor:**  a steerable vehicle for towing as a farm tractor or highway vehicle with a fifth-wheel weight-carrying attachment for a semi-trailer.

**trade discount:**  a deduction from the list price of goods allowed by a manufacturer or wholesaler to a retailer.

**trade-in:**  an item of merchandise (as an automobile) taken as payment or part payment for the purchase of another automobile. The common practice in automobile purchases because of the initial cost, the relatively long life, and the desirability and necessity of automobiles throughout our society's economic strata.

**traffic:** the conglomerate mass of movement of all things mobile: animals, man, and machines over/through air, land, and water.

**trafficator:** a replica of a man's arm, illuminated at night, attached to the driver's side of a vehicle and mechanized to indicate the driver's intention to turn, slow, or stop. Obsolete today with our modern signal devices.

**traffic circle:** a highway crossing with circular connector segments allowing vehicles to enter the traffic flow in the right lane and then exit the flow pattern to the right without crossing the path of another vehicle.

**traffic cone:** a conical marker of resilient material used for temporary marking of road hazards, repair activities, temporary driving lanes, et al. Cone zones.

**traffic court:** a minor court for prosecution of minor violations of statutes, ordinances, and local regulations governing the use of highways and motor vehicles, et al.

**traffic engineering:** engineering dealing with the design of highways/streets and the control of traffic thereon.

**traffic island:** a paved or planted segment in a roadway designed to guide, and separate the flow of traffic.

**traffic manager:** a supervisor of the traffic functions in a commercial or industrial organization.

**trail:** the horizontal distance between a vertical line through a front wheel centerline and the projection of the kingpin axis measured at roadway level. Trail angle.

**trail bike:** a small motorcycle designed for uses other than on highways and for ease in transport as on an automobile bumper, roof, or trunk rack.

**trailer:** a non-powered vehicle designed to be towed by any motorized vehicle capable of serving as its tractor.

**trailer sway:** excessive swerving or weaving of a trailer from the desired direction of tow caused by side-slip of the trailer wheels or improper design of the tow hitch.

**trailing arm:** suspension linkage supporting a chassis from a wheel/axle assembly that is located aft of the suspension's transverse pivot axis.

**trailing axle:** the rear axle of a tandem-axle pair.

**trailing shoe:** the secondary shoe of a drum brake system in which the actuated end trails, facing the normal (forward) direction of rotation.

**tram:** any of various vehicles traveling on rails as a street-car, on overhead rails or suspended from a cable as a gondola. Lightrail.

**tramway:** usually the rails of a municipal transit system em-bedded in the streets, but also overhead rails or monorail and cable suspensions.

**transaxle:** contraction of transmission and axle implying the inclusion of the differential gearing that changes the power-flow direction to the wheels and allows efficient turning. Though most usually confined to front-wheel-drive applications the rear-wheel-drive becomes a true transaxle when the gear-change functions are accomplished at that location by being attached to the differential.

**transceiver:** a radio transmitter-receiver that uses essen-tially the same electronic components to both receive and send radio signals. Police/fire radios, taxicab radios, mobile telephones, C-B radios, and Walkie-Talkie radios are among the many surface vehicle applications.

**transducer:** a device that is actuated by power from one system and supplies power to or control of another system. Various vehicle systems such as the "senders" that activate circuits to provide visual instrumentation of pressures, motion, quantity, weight, or temperatures may utilize this principle. Piezo crystals can convert weight directly into usable electrical signals.

**transfer case:** the system of gears usually incorporated in or attached to a vehicle's main transmission that apportions the driving force to the front and rear axles of four-wheel-drive vehicles.

**transfer drive:** a bevel gearbox usually 1:1 with an output shaft at an acute angle to the input shaft and mainly used as the drive from the engine-mounted gearbox to the propeller shaft in transverse rear-engined buses. Commonly called a vee-drive or angle-drive in rear-engined boats.

**transfer port:** the aperture slot or valve opening in the cylinder wall of a two-stroke/cycle internal combustion engine through which the compressed combustible fuel/air incoming charge passes from the crankcase to the combustion chamber.

**transfer pump:** an auxiliary fuel pump, usually electric, used to move fuel between tanks or compartments on multiple-tanked vehicles or in storage tank-farms.

**transformer:** a device employing the principle of mutual induction to convert (transform) variations of current in a primary electrical circuit into variations of voltage and current in a secondary circuit. The basis for the vehicle's high-voltage ignition coil operation.

**transistor:** an electronic device that is similar to the electron tube in amplification and rectification of voltage and current but is smaller, simpler and cheaper to manufacture, and requires less power, creates less unwanted waste heat, and withstands vehicle vibrations better.

**transistorized ignition:** a conventional breaker-point/coil spark producing circuit that has been enhanced by add-on (usually aftermarket) components (transistors) that permit longer dwell-time, higher spark plug voltages and thus higher engine speeds.

**transition system:** the fuel flow and metering system in a carburetor that insures smoother engine operation/response during transient conditions as varying throttle openings from idle-to-acceleration-to-full-throttle or any combination of such changes in either direction.

**transmission:** a generic term for the collection of components such as clutch, torque converter, gear box, gear selector, and driveshaft that facilitate and control the transference of the vehicle engine's power to the driven wheels. A manual or automatic change speed gear system and its ancillary equipment.

**transmission brake:** a vehicle brake operating on a transmission component (usually within the transmission housing casting as on a planetary gear outer drum) in addition to and separate from the wheel brakes. Other ancillary brake systems: inboard brakes near the center of the axle thus reducing un-sprung weight, or the drive shaft brake (primarily for parking or emergency braking).

**transmission loss:** that portion of a vehicle engine's horsepower that is absorbed by the transmission components' less-than-perfect efficiency. A usually small though not insignificant loss.

**transmission shaft:** the drive shaft that transmits the vehicle's power from the gearbox output shaft to the rear-axle differential.

**transmission tunnel:** the raised section (hump) in the floorpan that covers the transmission shaft along the vehicle's center-line through the passenger compartment of contemporary cars.

**transporter:** a specialty vehicle designed as a tractor-trailer or as a usually open flat-bed truck with the angled-bed extending upward and even forward of the cab roof and windshield and configured for hauling multiple automobiles.

**transverse:** acting, lying, or being across: set or affixed crosswise.

**transverse engine:** an engine placed with the crankshaft axis athwart the vehicle, at a right angle to the axis of motion.

**transverse springs:** semi-elliptical leaf springs located across the vehicle chassis/frame. In mechanic's lingo a "buggy spring".

**trapped fuel:** the small amount of residual fuel in a vehicle tank that is unavailable for use due to fuel-outlet design or location, or because of adverse angularity or deformation of the tank bottom.

**travel trailer:** a relatively light trailer towable by a passenger car that provides limited liveability to travelers.

**tread:** the outer-circumference portion of a vehicle tire that comes in contact with the roadway and is usually grooved or patterned for better wear or traction. The transverse distance between the center lines of the left and right tires on a common axle of a vehicle.

**tread contact area:** the footprint size in square inches of a tire tread's contact with the roadway surface largely determined by the weight in pounds on the wheel divided by the tire's inflation pressure in pounds-per-square-inch. This simple arithmetic validates the self-delusion of the hot rodder who is convinced that ultra-wide tires "put more rubber on the ground".

**tread contact length:** the footprint length in the wheel plane of a tire tread's contact with the roadway surface.

**tread contact width:** the transverse distance across the footprint of a tire tread's contact with the roadway surface.

**tread depth:** the distance from the bottom of a tire tread groove and the top of adjacent tire tread ribs, usually measured in thirty-seconds of an inch.

**tread noise:** the sound produced by the interaction of the tread pattern and the variations in a roadway surface.

**tri-axle:** three closely spaced axles designed to better distribute concentrated vehicle weight to the road.

**triboelectricity:** an electrical charge generated by friction involving susceptible materials. A source of considerable concern when transporting, transferring, storing, or servicing volatile vehicle fuels. Static electricity. Air flow over/ around a moving vehicle or an occupant rubbing against certain upholstery materials can generate sufficient voltage (electro- motive force) to create an explosion-causing spark or discon- certing shock to occupants.

**tribology:** the branch of engineering dealing with the design, friction, wear, and lubrication of interacting surfaces in relative motion, as in bearings and gears.

**tricar:** a three-wheeled automobile common in less affluent societies.

**Trico:** tradenamed product line of windshield wiper components and accessories.

**trigger rod:** the hand-lever-squeeze/turn, or finger-pull rod that disengages the locking pawl/ratchet on a vehicle hand- brake.

**trimmer:** auto mechanic's lingo for an upholsterer.

**trimotor:** having three motors (engines) as an airplane. A number of world landspeed record automobiles have used three engines.

**Triplex:** tradenamed safety glass used as windshield/window glass.

**tripod:** a three-element universal joint capable of acting as a constant velocity power transmitter for front-wheel-drive/ steering vehicles. Tri-pot plunging joint.

**trip odometer:** an extra distance-recording segment of a vehi- cle speedometer that can be set manually to zero and reset at any time to record a trip distance or portion thereof, inde- pendently of the primary cumulative-total-only odometer.

**Trippe Light:** an aftermarket headlight of yesteryear used to supplement or replace factory-stock lights.

**triptane:** a liquid hydrocarbon ($C_7H_{16}$) with high antiknock properties used especially in aviation and racing gasolines.

**Triumph:** the British car manufacturer that started building three-wheeler cycle cars and motorcycles in 1903 and played a dominant role in evolving our contemporary automobiles.

**trochoidal rotor:** a triangular form rotating in a similarly- shaped sealed enclosure that effectively duplicates the four- stroke cycles of a cylinder-and-piston internal combustion engine without utilizing reciprocating components. Wankel. Rotary.

**trolley bus:** a people carrying conveyance with or without track rails that draws electrical power from overhead wires via a trolley and that operates generally in urban areas.

**truck:** a cargo-carrying vehicle usually heavier than a light delivery unit although some jurisdictions consider, license, and tax all pick-ups and light delivery/passenger vans as full-blown trucks.

**truck cab:** the enclosed driver's compartment of a commercial vehicle.

**trunk:** the rear enclosed luggage compartment of an automobile partitioned from the passenger area with a lifting cover to provide access from the exterior.

**T-slot piston:** an internal combustion engine piston with a slotted skirt to improve heat dissipation and coefficient of expansion cylinder-fit.

**tubeless tire:** a vehicle tire impervious to air linkage with airtight sealing to the wheel rim thus eliminating the need for an inner tube. Tube-type tire.

**Tucker:** Preston Tucker's innovative design and fancy financing 1946-48 could produce only 49 of his and Alex Tremulis' innovative car that was powered by a helicopter engine and equipped with three headlights.

**tudor:** possibly first misspoken but then accepted as the name for the two-door sedan.

**tune:** to adjust the operating variables of an engine (ignition timing, fuel/air mixture, et al.) to give peak performance. Tune up.

**tune buggy:** descriptive name for various special-built vehicles (to resemble or simulate the musical instrument associated with the owner), as a guitar-shaped exterior for a string-picker.

**tuned pipes/manifold:** configuring the interior passages of engine intake/exhaust by matching the acoustic resonance of the manifold system to the velocity, frequency, and mass flow of the intake/exhaust pulses. Contemporary flow-bench technology can measure and validate tuning efficacy.

**tune-up in-a-can:** a vehicle mechanic's derisive description of the snake-oil scams that Barnumesque con artists claim can cause an engine to run better, faster, stronger, longer, using less fuel and polluting less—simply by adding a little of their elixir to the engine.

**tungsten:** a gray-white heavy high-melting-point ductile hard polyvalent metallic element that resembles chromium and molybdenum in many of its properties and is used for electrical filaments and in hardening alloys as of steel. Wolfram.

**tungsten halogen lamp:** a light bulb of sealed-beam type that is filled with halogen iodine which combines with the evaporated tungsten of the heated filament to form tungsten iodide which does not deposit an opaque film within the bulb envelope but ionizes and redeposits the tungsten on the filament. The bulb envelope is normally made of quartz, hence the terms quartz halogen or quartz iodide also being used.

**turbine:** an engine that derives its energy of rotation from the impulse/reaction of the flow of a fluid impinging upon the curved vanes (buckets) around the periphery of a wheel turning its output shaft. The working fluid for vehicle engines is most often the expanding hot gases from combustion of hydrocarbon fuels and less frequently from steam.

**turbocharger:** an energy recovery device (turbine) that drives a compressor (charger) utilizing a piston engine's exhaust to pressurize and pump intake air into the same engine. A significant amount of the waste heat (energy) inherent to the IC engine is thus returned to the engine by improving its volumetric efficiency with the added mass flow to its intake charge-air.

**turn signal light:** the visible element of a turn signal system that indicates the intention of the driver to turn. Flasher.

**turning circle:** the minimum diameter of the circle within which a vehicle turns when steered at the full lock position of the steering wheel.

**turntable:** the flat bearing surface of a fifth wheel that supports a trailer-tongue load.

**turret top:** the all-steel vehicle roof that superseded the earlier tops with fabric center panels, often without center-posts at the door openings. Hard top.

**TVR:** a British sports car popular with sports/racing aficionados, marketed as a finished unit or in kit form since 1954 using various British and American engines and components.

**twelve-point:** a box-end or socket wrench with twelve locking serrations instead of the traditional six-flats (six-point) mechanic's tools; allowing the installation and removal of hex-head bolts, nuts, and fittings in locations having restricted access for the turning arcs of a tool with fewer points/flats/serrations.

**twin camshaft:**  the arrangement of two parallel camshafts per bank of cylinders, normally with one operating the intake valves and the other the exhaust valves, alike only in the length and journal diameter but very un-twinlike in the profile and orientation of the cam lobes.

**twin carburetor:**  having two carburetors, usually connected by a balance tube.

**twin cowl:**  a phaeton with a hinged cowl and usually a second windshield covering the area between the front and rear seats. Dual cowl.

**twin pipes:**  a right and left exhaust pipe running parallel from the engine to the rear bumper area of a vehicle ostensibly to reduce exhaust back pressure.

**twin screw:**  a vehicle with both tandem axles being driven, with the rearmost differential driven by a short drive shaft from the front one.

**twist drill:**  a drill bit having deep helical grooves extending from the point to the smooth portion of the shank.

**twist grip:**  a hand control utilizing twisting force/movement to impart a push-pull length change to a usually-shrouded flexible cable as a motorcycle handle-bar handgrip that operates the throttle.  Fuel mixture adjustment, shut-off valves, clutches, and electrical switches in hard-to-access locations are similarly operated.

**two-banger:**  vehicle mechanic's slang for a two-cylinder engine, derived from its distinctive exhaust sound when running at slow speed.

**two-speed axle:**  a vehicle drive axle with two gear ratios that may be shifted automatically (as with overdrive), or manually, to suit driving requirements, thus doubling the number of gear ratios available from the main transmission alone.

**two stroke:**  the thermodynamic operating cycle of a spark or compression ignition (Diesel) engine in which the induction, compression, power, and exhaust strokes take place within one revolution of the engine's crankshaft.

**two-way converter:**  a vehicle emissions catalytic converter utilizing conversion beds of both palladium and platinum to extend the range of exhaust contaminants that can be reduced to harmless gases.  Three-way converter.

**type homologation:**  approved by a sanctioning organization for specific model and marque automobile to compete in sanctioned class events limited to that particular type of competition vehicle.

# LAGNIAPPE

**"T":** that American Icon, the 1909-1927 Model T Ford. 'Nuff said!

**tang:** a tab or lip-lock on a plain bearing insert for alignment.

**TDC:** see top dead center. Bottom dead center (BDC).

**thermal reactor:** emissions elimination device using very high temperature to oxidize (burn) unburned fuel and burnable pollutants.

**Thermoflow piston:** tradenamed design using an unobstructed heat-flow path from the crown/head of the piston to the skirt for better heat transfer to the cylinder wall coolant.

**thermosyphon:** the cooling of an engine without a coolant circulating pump, utilizing the natural law "Heat Rises" to induce liquid flow. Typical of all early automobiles before invention of the water pump.

**thrash:** the often severe transverse oscillation or whip of the return/slack side of a belt or chain drive with a pulsating load.

**throat:** the cylindrical induction-charge passage through a carburetor (often containing discharge jets, throttle plate, and venturi).

**throttle valve:** butterfly/damper/disk that controls the flow of charge-air into/through an injector manifold or carburetor.

**thrust flange:** a machined-face flanged surface around the crankshaft center to accept longitudinal force (thrust) against a matching block surface.

**top eliminator:** overall winner of a series of dragster eliminations.

**top loader:** a manual-shift transmission with the access panel on top of the gear case, making in-car repairs easier.

**two tone:** a vehicle painted with two different colors, either complementary or in contrast. To paint a vehicle in such fashion.


## EXCUSES, EXCUSES
(From Traffic Court Records)

I told the police that I was not injured, but upon standing up, I found a broken leg.

The indirect cause of this accident was a little guy in a small car with a big mouth.

I think that the scenery was just so beautiful outside that I must have failed to pay close enough attention to the speedometer inside.

## The Model T Ford's Nemeses
(Altitude; non-gasoline fuels; Hills, UP and DOWN; & Winds, head or cross)
\* \* \* \* \* \*

Few have ever really known the topography of their own neighborhood, their state, or their country. Because they never drove a Model T Ford. There are myriad hills all around us, even in your driveway, at both ends of your city block, between your house and the barber shop, church, grocery store, gas station, school, and work--and each is UPhill in both directions. Even if you live in Mississippi--where every hill is also two-feet deep in crawly sand. If you drive a T Model!

If you live in Colorado, with 54 of Uncle Sugar's 64 mountain peaks over 14,000 feet high (in the "contiguous-48"), one of them always rises between you and your destination. If you drive a Model T! If you don't have "Rocky Mountain Brakes" you don't dare start DOWNhill on the rare occasions when one of them suddenly inverts and inserts a ski-slope into your tour route. Few have the temerity to venture out of the driveway to go UP to the corner unless he's got a Ruxtell under the rear and a "Fronty" or a "Rajo" under the hood.

No Colorado "Tall Model T" driver dares head UP any canyon when there's a "Chinook" headed DOWN. Speedsters with all the goodies have been known to poke their way into a "Chinook's" blast by tail-gating a wide-bodied pack burro. Every prudent Model T pilot always verifies wind velocities at all altitudes along a planned crosscountry route through the "high country". A "Blue Norther" or an ordinary prevailing Westerly whistling across a prairie that can overturn an eighteen-wheeler will turn a "Tall T" into a tumbleweed, end-over-end.

In 1921, my friend Marty Keller, already a Model T aficionado and experienced mechanic, together with his older brother driving while he rode "shotgun", embarked on a 28-mile junket over 12,095 feet high Independence Pass from Aspen, CO, to Granite equipped with beef jerky rations, a cold-patch tire repair kit, extra transmission bands, and snowshoes. Their "mountain goat" was a 1918 "runabout" (a roadster with a wooden box behind the seat).

The low-gear and reverse bands had to be replaced before topping the highpoint of the pass and the reverse and brake bands failed before level ground was reached on the DOWNhill side. Those bands weren't quick-change, either. After a few challenges by sharp rocks, all four inner tubes were spotted like Dalmatians with many cold-patches and the beef jerky was all consumed before reaching Granite--but the snowshoes were never tied on. Two days and one night to go less than 30 miles? A successful and enjoyable trip--for masochistic and macho man's T Model.

Everybody knows the stories about having to "back-up" Lookout Mountain or Floyd Hill, because of great-Grampa's reminiscing about the "good old days"--meaning the "Model T Days". But no one knows the real reason "why" unless he's driven a Model T UPhill. With the gas tank under the driver's seat (until the '26/'27 models when the "T" was metamorphosing into the "A" and the tank went upstairs behind the dash), less than a full tank of gas and more than a 14° UPhill grade starved the carburetor. Those in the know knew also that even through the 1927 model the planetary "low gear" (10 to 1) wasn't low enough to climb a prairie-dog-hill but that the "reverse gear" was low enough (15.56 to 1) to climb a pinion pine--even with a 17-horsepower Denver engine (due to the mile-high altitude). You won't go anywhere fast in any gear. You can't climb Pike's Peak or cruise in the fast lane of Interstate 80 or Colorado Boulevard with that kind of horsepower and those gear ratios, even when wide-open or in reverse.

Since Colorado University's Orange Bowl heyday, alumni who drive Model T's have learned how to win against hills. They haul four 300-pound football linemen who are trained to jump out and push whenever the T's front-end inclines upward toward our mountain peaks or the sky.

As a CU alumnus, I aim my fun-poking at the football fanatics. Fellow-alumni, my wife, co-owner of our Model T, and her brother jump out and the neighborhood 90-pound kids footballers come a-running to boost our hydrogen-fueled turbocharged 1924 Depot Hack UPhill (our driveway hill) into its home garage. It's a 14-horsepower Model T when burning natural gas, an 11-horsepower H-bomb when burning hydrogen, and a 2-horsepower buggy when it's fed a diet of buffalo chips, corn cobs, or sawdust. To get across Denver to its Winter storage garage, a sea-level route has been surveyed that's three times as far as the direct route, which has a steep overpass with a traffic signal on the UPhill side in both directions. The drive-time must be 3 AM to avoid the speeding race drivers who shout obscenities and "finger" a slow-moving Depot Hack during rush hour traffic.

Any naturally-aspirated internal combustion engine loses about 15% of its horsepower (compared to gasoline) when burning natural gas and as much as 30% when fueled with hydrogen. These losses accrue because of reduced volumetric (breathing) efficiency when a low energy-dense fuel is mixed in the intake, thus displacing a significant volume of charge air in the induction system. That's like one of Henry's $5-a-day assemblers leaving one or two cylinders lying on the factory floor when your "T" rolled by his station. Take any stock-engined Model T a mile high, and add a heavy white oak Depot Hack body and you've got **BIG TROUBLE** just trying to keep abreast of every Model T's scientific and technological nemeses.

Modern man will never experience the thrill of combat with the Model T's nemeses because he's now got 200-horsepower under one foot, POWER brakes under the same foot, and only needs two fingers resting lightly on his POWER-steering wheel. Man's evolution into our AUTOMATIC and POWER era has even robbed him of the third foot and the third hand once needed to cope with the Model T's idiosyncrasies and its confusing array of foot and hand controls. Without any POWER assist. He'll never know the satisfaction of resting his right arm in a sling for about a month out of every year (after being kicked while hand-cranking his Model T with the spark too-advanced.

Happy motoring! In America's Icon, The Model T Ford.

MODEL T, DRAFTING into a CHINOOK
behind a
WIDE-BODIED PACK BURRO

MODEL T POWER-PLAY, PUSH-UP, BACK UP

MODEL T, ALTERNATIVE-POWERED
by
FIVE 4-FOOT 90-POUND FOOTBALLERS
burning
"BIG MAC" and PIZZA ALTERNATIVE-FUEL

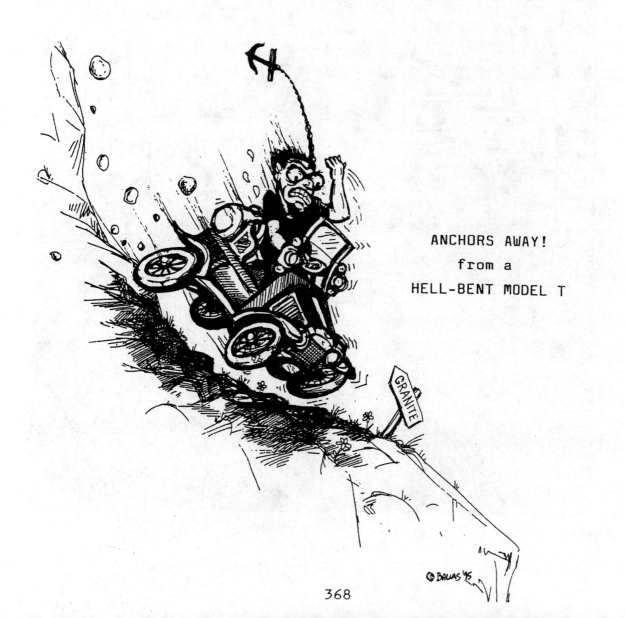

ANCHORS AWAY!
from a
HELL-BENT MODEL T

**"U"-Cars:** of 34 makes the U shares the distinction with the Z of being the only cars having a single-letter name.

**u-bolt:** a holding device in the shape of a U used extensively in vehicles for fastening axles to springs and for other assemblies involving the joining of round and flat shapes while retaining replacement and disassembly capabilities.

**u-clamp:** a u-shaped device for joining tubes or pipes where one end is slipped concentrically over a slightly smaller diameter other end. Also used for attaching tubular shapes to flat shapes.

**uglify:** what results when a "customizer" (even a Barris) reconfigures an original automobile designed by a Darrin or a Loewy. Analogous to a housepainter with a 6" whitewash brush "improving" Mona Lisa's smile or a Christo gift-wrapping a Duesenberg.

**u-joint:** an articulated mechanism designed to transmit force or motion through an angular direction. Used throughout vehicle power trains to accommodate relative motion such as drive-shaft angularity changes as load or road bounce vary wheel position.

**ullage:** the empty space above the fluid in a tank. Sometimes sealed and pressurized or evacuated, sometimes vented to the outside atmosphere, and sometimes filled with a non-miscible gas or liquid.

**Ultramatic:** a Packard high-efficiency planetary-geared automatic transmission featuring a speed-sensitive lock-up to eliminate engine/wheel slippage.

**ultrasonic:** a movement/vibration having a frequency above the human ear's audibility limit of about 20,000 cycles per second. Can cause wear and even structural failure by metal fatigue of vehicle components or can be used to detect pending failure of such.

**ultraviolet:** that part of the light spectrum situated beyond the eye's visible violet limit having a wavelength shorter than the wavelengths of visible light and longer than those of x-rays. Useful for reflective luminescence of instruments and controls and in the non-destructive testing of vehicle components (Zyglo).

**undercarriage:** the supporting framework beneath a vehicle.

**undercoat:** the base coat of paint in a multi-layered finish. The asphalt (or other) based paint used to waterproof and soundproof the underside of a vehicle.

**undercut:** a machining operation to reduce the outer diameter or increase the inner diameter of mating parts to provide touch-free movement or ease of assembly.

**underdrive:** a gearing unit (usually accessory to the transmission or differential) offered to provide a "lower" gearing than the standard/stock ratios to give more moving power by increasing engine speed while reducing wheel speed (rpm). See overdrive.

**undersize:** dimensionally less than standard or stock design size.

**underslung:** from the days of the high-wheel (large diameter) cars when vehicle frames were suspended beneath the axles to lower the overall center of gravity.

**underpass:** the lower level of the crossing of two highways or of a highway and a railroad or pedestrian path where clearance for the upper level is obtained by depressing the lower level.

**undulant:** rising and falling in waves as a road surface remembered as "washboard" from the days of dirt roads and vehicle suspensions without shock absorbers.

**up-draft:** a carburetor that draws the engine intake air upwards through the carburetor into the intake manifold.

**up-shift:** the act of shifting the gearing ratio higher in a manual or automatic transmission or a multi-ratio differential to lower the engine rpm while retaining vehicle velocity.

**unibody:** see unitized.

**unitized:** a generic term applied to vehicle construction where no separate frame is used. Monocoque, unibody. Using the body as the frame can increase strength and crashworthiness while reducing weight.

**unsprung:** a vehicle with the axles/wheels fastened directly to the frame/body. Characteristic of some early models and some world landspeed race cars. Reduction of unsprung weight (axles/wheels/ tires) on modern cars adds to the smoothness and stability.

**upset:** to enlarge a metal shape by hammering or forging (cold or hot).

**upstroke:** either the compression or the exhaust stroke of a 4-cycle internal combustion engine. The compression stroke of a shock absorber.

**utility vehicle:** one designed for a specific utilitarian use: tank truck, tow truck, ambulance, hearse, et al.

**U-turn:** a vehicle turn resembling the letter U especially a 180° reversal of direction by a vehicle in a road. Usually illegal.

**u-v:** see ultraviolet.

**u-v filter:** a substance that "blocks" ultraviolet light frequencies while letting other portions of the light spectrum pass through. Used in window glass and human eyeglasses to prevent the fading and deteriorating of interiors and to reduce the formation of cataracts. Also used in paints to reduce the harmful effects of ultraviolet rays on the painted surface and upon the paint itself.

## LAGNIAPPE

**unburned hydrocarbons:** vehicle fuel because of too-rich mixtures, failure to ignite, or other malfunctions, is blown out the exhaust as raw fuel (HC) becoming a major atmospheric pollutant unless reduced to an innocuous gas by a catalytic converter.

**understeer:** a cornering mode (usually design related) involving loss of traction by the front wheels causing a slide/slip toward the outside of a turn.

**unleaded gas:** gasoline that contains no lead or lead compounds (as tetraethyl lead) as lubricant or octane enhancer. Use mandated by law for most vehicles to reduce atmospheric pollution.

**USAC:** United States Auto Club, the sanctioning authority for the Indianapolis "500" annual automobile race on Memorial Day.

## CAR COMEDY

An elderly motorist, plagued with failing memory, entered his car with his wife to begin a cross-country junket. He complained "I can't even find the steering wheel". The wife quavered: "Why don't we get in the _front_ seat?"

## EXCUSES, EXCUSES
(From Traffic Court Records)

Coming home late on a dark night, I drove into the yard and collided with a large tree that I don't have.

My car was legally parked when I backed into the other car.

The telephone pole was approaching at a high rate of speed. I was just attempting to swerve out of its way when it struck my left-ront fender.

## THE "POINT-NINE (0.9) SYNDROME"

Back when automobiles were still horseless carriages, car owners usually tanked up at livery stables and later at competing apothecary shops (pharmacies) and grocery stores. The fuel was often alcohol (grain), benzene, and various combinations with the crude petroleum distillates. Filling stations, as fuel dispensers, did not appear until the mid-teens of the Twentieth Century. The original "filling stations" were air-dispensing facilities provided primarily in urban areas by the French Michelin Tire Company.

There were about 14,000 cars registered in Denver, CO, when the first gasoline filling station opened for business at Broadway and Speer Boulevard in 1915. The early fuel dispensers had hand-pumped cylindrical glass reservoirs that gravity-fed gas through a hose into the vehicle tank. Few could measure less than a whole gallon which was usually priced in "even money"--like 10¢ per gallon, becoming 20¢ per gallon or "5 gallons, one Buck" until World War II arrived.

During the 1930's, our urban areas sprouted filling stations on every street corner. Competition spurred the Madison Avenue hype (disparagingly called "Jewish Engineering") of pricing things to make them appear attractively cheaper to the mathematically illiterate. Huge signs shouted "gasoline 19$^{9}$ cents per gallon" with a Helluva big "19" and a minuscule "point-nine (0.9)". 'Twas the same old 20 cents per gallon. But the "come on" worked. Now the practice is universal and modern eyes are blind to the "point-nine" and no mouth is shaped right to say it. They wishfully say nineteen.

An actuarial survey revealed that purchase patterns created a computational pertubation that favored the seller--admittedly slight, until multiplied by millions. VOILA!

But is the practice illegal? Hell yes it is! Although no Federal, State, or Local Statutes address the dilemma, English Common Law, which rules in such absences, "prohibits the pricing of any article in an amount for which there is no legal tender-- exact coinage denomination--meaning that it is impossible to return to the purchaser his exact change as due."

### NO KIDDIN'!

A story in the magazine YOUTH'S COMPANION in 1896 first used the name "Auto-Mobile".

In 1904, the YMCA (Young Men's Christian Association) established one of our country's first automobile mechanic's schools.

In 1902, automobile manufacturers gave a 60-day warranty.

The ten leading builders of automobiles organized the first professional group aimed at policing and standardizing the building of cars (1903), the Association of Licensed Automobile Manufacturers.

**V-Cars:** Fourteen of the 112 V-marques were manufactured in the United States. Only a few may remember the Velie, built in Moline, IL, 1909-1928, probably not even the residents of Velie, LA, that was so-named because so many Velies were bought there. You could guess that the Vapomobile was a steam car but nothing else. You do know the Swedish Volvo, the choice of the elite and the German Volkswagen, the car of the proletariat, simply because VW surpassed Henry Ford's Model "T" production record of 15,007,003 units of an individual model on 17 February 1972 when the Beetle took the checkered flag in that race and has since "kept going, and going, and going". Every hungry race driver knows the Formula Vee--since 1963. Only the one remaining member of the Ancient Order of Automobile Aficionados will know how the VEERAC automobile, built in Anoka, MN, got its name, "**V**alveless, **e**xplosion **e**very **r**evolution, **a**ir-**c**ooled" describing the 2-cycle (2 stroke) 1.6 liter engine with planetary transmission. Thanks to General Motors, English "Limey's" have the Vauxhall and the Nobility have VANDEN PLAS. Readers of Clive Cussler's bestseller novel <u>Sahara</u> can spell Voisin, the French marque featured in his book. The Voisin in the book is also in Clives's great car collection in Golden, CO. The shades of the remaining 104 V-marques are orbiting somewhere in outer space. Forgotten.

**vacationland:** Colorado, an area with recreational attractions and facilities for vacationists.

**vacuum:** a space absolutely devoid of matter. Unattainable. A degree of rarefaction below atmospheric pressure. Any negative pressure.

**vacuum bottle:** a cylindrical container with a vacuum between an inner and an outer wall to keep material, especially liquids, either hot or cold for considerable periods. See Dewar flask.

**vacuum brakes:** a power-braking system for vehicles using vacuum power to assist the foot-power or hand-power of the vehicle operator.

**vacuum formed:** a shape formed by laying a sheet material over a die that has holes arranged to suck the sheet tightly around the conforming die and hold it until thermosetting or chemical-setting makes the formed material permanently rigid to the desired configuration.

**vacuum gauge:** a gauge indicating the degree of negative pressure at the test point.

**vacuum packed:** having much of the air removed before hermetically sealing the enclosed area.

**vacuum pan:** a tank designed for rapid evaporation and condensation in industrial processing of a substance by boiling at a low temperature.

**vacuum pump:** a pump for exhausting air from an enclosed space. Used in vehicles to provide the pressure differential to power windshield wipers, power brakes, and duct valves.

**vacuum tank:** a storage tank that is evacuated below atmospheric pressure to provide sufficient operating power for vacuum-operated devices. Early vehicles used vacuum tanks in lieu of fuel pumps to supplement gravity to provide fuel flow from the vehicle tank to the engine.

**vacuum shift:** a transmission gear shifting system using vacuum cylinders or diaphragms to power the shifting mechanism.

**vacuum switch:** usually a piston, diaphragm or valve used to physically operate another mechanism thus using a small force to effect and control a much larger reaction. As a solenoid electric switch.

**vacuum tube:** an electron tube evacuated to a high degree of vacuum. Incandescent and other lighting bulbs are similarly evacuated but to a lesser degree.

**vacuum washer:** for the windshield a vacuum/fluid reservoir designed to spray the windshield of a vehicle for better driving vision. Connected to the windshield wiper system to enhance the cleaning process.

**'Vair:** car buff jargon for the Chevrolet Corvair automobile.

**valence:** the degree of combining power of an element or chemical group as shown by the number of atomic weights of a univalent element (as hydrogen) with which the atomic weight of the element or the partial molecular weight of the chemical group will combine or for which it can be substituted or with which it can be compared.

**valet:** an employee (as of a hotel or other public facility) who parks and returns vehicles from and to the facility for patrons.

**value-added tax:** an incremental excise that is leveled on the value added at each stage of the processing of a raw material or the production and distribution of a commodity and that has the impact of a sales tax on the ultimate consumer

**value judgment:** a judgmental evaluation of the value (as being good or bad or a monetary amount) of a part or service.

**valve:** any of numerous mechanical devices by which the flow of liquid, gas, or loose material in bulk may be started, stopped, or regulated by a movable part that opens, shuts, or partially constricts one or more passageways or ports.  The moving part of such a device.

**valve clearance:**  the space (distance) between the valve stem and its operating mechanism such as a rocker arm, push rod, tappet/lifter or cam lobe.  Necessary in a pure mechanical operating train to insure tight closing of the valve with its seat surface.

**valve cover:**  an oil-tight cast or stamped sheet metal covering protecting the valves and/or cams of an overhead valve/cam vehicle engine.

**valve cover gasket:**  the sealing material that leak proofs the joint between the cylinder lead and the valve cover of a vehicle engine.

**valve face:**  the variously-angled flat surface circumferentially around the head of an engine valve that mates with and seals  against a matching internal surface around the internal circumference of the valve seat in the cylinder block/head.

**valve grinder:**  a lathe-like machine that holds and spins an engine valve (intake or exhaust) while an abrasive spinning wheel grinds and finishes to size the angled face of the outer circumference of the valve head for a perfect sealing fit against the valve seat.

**valve grinding/lapping compound:**  a paste or oil carrier containing abrasive dust with various grits for final finish polishing and fitting of the seat face of a valve head to the seat face of the valve entry opening into an engine block/cylinder head.

**valve guide:**  a machined shape that is pressed into an engine block/cylinder head to guide the alignment of the valve head with its seat in the block/cylinder head and to provide an accurately sized cylindrical hole in which the valve stem reciprocates effecting the opening and closing of the valve.

**valve head:**  the formed disk-like shape made integrally with the valve stem that forms the moving sealing portion of the engine's valves.

**valve-in-head engine:**  an internal combustion engine in which both inlet and exhaust valves are located in the cylinder head rather than in the cylinder block as a side-valve engine.

**valve keeper:**  a usually tapered split locking device that fits within the internally tapered hole of the valve spring retainer-washer and locks into a machined matching grove near the end of the valve stems thus mechanically restraining the valve spring force that closes the valve while allowing the opposing cam force that opens the valve to move the valve.

**valve lapper:** a tool for hand or machine spinning a valve head against its valve seat alternating the clockwise/counterclockwise/counterclockwise directions as desired with valve grinding/ lapping compound applied between the valve and valve seat surfaces to fit/polish the mating surfaces.

**valve seat grinder:** an electric drill-like tool that spins small abrasive wheels on a mandrel shaft that will turn inside the valve guide allowing the abrasive wheel to grind the seat surface in the cylinder block/head.

**valve seat insert:** because most cylinder block/heads are composed of relatively soft metals a ring-like hardened metal seat is routinely fastened into the cylinder block/head valve opening to provide protection from combustion heat and valve pounding thus extending the time between valve overhauls.

**valve stem:** the shaft-like section that is integrally machined/formed with the valve head that reciprocates within the valve guide to open and close the valve.

**valve timing:** for a four-cycle/stroke vehicle engine each valve opens and closes once for each two revolutions of the crankshaft. This exact two-to-one revolution reduction is insured by a camshaft gear, sprocket, or toothed-pulley having twice the number of teeth of the crankshaft gear, sprocket, or toothed-pulley. Distinctive timing marks on the matching gears, sprockets, or toothed-pulley when assembled as specified for the engine insure the correct valve opening and closing sequence at the exact proper time for each appropriate piston stroke.

**van:** a multipurpose enclosed motor vehicle usually having a box-like shape and rear or side doors and side panels with or without windows and having seats for passengers that can be removed for added cargo.

**vanadium:** a grayish malleable ductile metallic element used especially to form alloys (as vanadium steel) used in vehicles.

**vandalism:** willful or malicious destruction or defacement of public or private property. Vehicle vandalism is usually, but not exclusively, limited to broken window glass, scarred/ dented/scratched metal body and fender panels, broken lights, slashed tires/upholstery/tops, and broken outside mirrors/ antennas/windshield wipers.

**vane:** a thin flat or curved plate that is rotated about an exit by a flow of fluid or that rotates to cause a fluid to flow or that redirects the flow of a fluid. A vane pump such as some engine water pumps, vacuum pumps, or "smog" air pumps.

**vanity plate:** a vehicle license plate bearing letters, numbers, symbols, or words selected by the vehicle owner.

**vanpool:** an arrangement by which a group of people commute to and from their workplace in a van.

**vapor:** a substance in the gaseous state as distinguished from the liquid or solid state. A mixture (as the explosive mixture in an internal combustion engine) of such a vapor of gasoline (or other fuel) and air.

**vaporize:** to convert a fluid (as by application of heat or by spraying) into a vapor. A simple carburetor is designed to vaporize liquid fuels for more efficient combustion in vehicles as are the injection nozzles' spray directly into the combustion chamber.

**vapor barrier:** a layer of sheet material or film used to retard or prevent moisture absorption usually through wall areas of a vehicle.

**vapor lock:** partial or complete interruption of flow of a fluid (as fuel or brake fluid in a vehicle) caused by the formation of vapor bubbles in the fluid feeding system usually at high altitudes with high temperature or high vapor pressure of the fluid.

**vapor pressure:** the pressure exerted by a vapor that is in equilibrium with its solid or liquid form. A vehicle fuel is nominally rated in relationship to its vapor pressure indicating its tendency to vapor lock.

**variable venturi:** a carburetor venturi that is movable or controllable in a manner that changes its venturi effect of speeding up the rate of flow of the intake charge thus assisting in controlling the fuel/air ratio.

**varnish:** a liquid preparation that when spread and allowed to dry on a surface forms a hard lustrous typically transparent coating. Also an undesirable coating inside of an internal combustion engine that results from the products of fuel combustion and hardens in a manner similar to a painted varnish.

**Vaseline:** a petroleum jelly normally therapeutic but used for specialized lubrication needs in vehicles.

**V-belt:** a power-transmission device (belt) with a cross-section shape like the letter "V" often with the point of the "V" cut-off (flattened) to various degrees or rounded. The sides of the "V" provide the friction contact-area with the inner walls of the "V" of the pulley. The V-belt requires less

379

belt tension than the flat belt resulting in less side force/ wear on associated bearings. V-belts are used singly or in multiples.

**V-blocks:** matched pairs of metal blocks usually of hardened steel but sometimes of soft metals with a matching "V" in each block permitting their use in a vise or other clamping device to hold a round or cylindrical-shaped workpiece. Also used on a level area with the "V" on the upside to hold a shaft while checking its straightness

**"vee":** something shaped like the letter "V".

**veer:** to change direction or course or a change in direction or course.

**vehicle:** a means of carrying or transporting something. A piece of mechanized equipment

**V-8:** an internal combustion engine having two banks (rows) of four cylinders each with the banks at an angle to each other. An automobile having such an engine.

**Velcro:** trademark name for a nylon fabric that attaches or clings to itself.

**velocipede:** a lightweight wheeled vehicle propelled by the rider. Also a 3-wheeled railroad handcar.

**velocity:** time rate of linear motion in a given direction. The scientific unit of velocity in the cgs system is the centimeter per second. For practical vehicle usage it is the mile per hour or kilometer per hour.

**velocity stack:** an entry duct section with a smoothly curved bell-shaped profile that directs air into carburetor inlets insuring a smooth non-turbulent flow.

**velodrome:** a track usually circular with near-vertical banked turns designed for cycling. As a motordrome for powered vehicles.

**velour:** any of various fabrics with a pile or napped surface resembling velvet used in heavier weights on vehicle upholstery.

**velvet:** clothing and upholstery fabric characterized by a short soft dense warp pile.

**vend:** to dispose of something by sale.

**vendee:** one to whom something is sold. Buyer.

**vendor:** one that vends. Seller.

**vendor space:** an area at a vehicle/parts sale/swapmeet leased to a seller for the duration of the sale.

**veneer:** a thin sheet of material as a layer of wood of superior or excellent grain to be glued to an inferior wood. The dash/instrument panels of early automobiles made extensive use of wood veneer as did window and door trim sections.

**venetian blind:** a blind (as for window) having numerous horizontal slats that may be set simultaneously at any of several angles so as to vary the amount of light admitted.

**V-engine:** an internal-combustion engine whose cylinders are arranged in two banks forming an acute angle or a 90-degree angle.

**vent:** an opening for the escape of a gas or liquid or for the relief of pressure.

**venturi:** a short tube with a tapering constriction in the middle that causes an increase in the velocity of flow of a fluid and a corresponding decrease in fluid pressure and that is used especially in measuring fluid flow and for creating a suction (as for drawing fuel into the flow stream of a carburetor).

**vernier:** a short scale made to slide along the divisions of a graduated instrument for indicating parts of divisions to improve the accuracy of measurements using the instrument.

**vernier caliper:** a measuring device that consists of a main scale with a fixed jaw and a sliding jaw with an attached vernier scale.

**'Vette:** car jargon for Chevrolet Corvette.

**VHT paint:** a paint (enamel) formulated to withstand and resist very high temperatures such as encountered with exhaust manifolds, turbochargers, exhaust pipes and mufflers.

**viaduct:** a bridge, especially when resting on a series of narrow reinforced concrete or masonry arches, having high supporting towers or piers, and carrying a road or railroad over an obstruction (as a valley or another railroad or highway).

**vibrate:** to shake, to swing, or to move to and fro. To set in vibration.

**vibration:** the action of vibrating. A quivering or trembling motion. The state of being vibrated.

**vibrator coil:** an electrical device that converts direct current into pulsating direct current. The electrical pulsations can generate mechanical pulsations or can be used

**vinyl:**  a polymer of a vinyl compound or a product (as a resin or a textile fiber) made from one.

**vinyl covers:**  weather protective sheet materials usually vinyl-coated fabrics for covering vehicle cargo and accessories such as exposed spare wheel/tires.

**vinyl roof:**  a vehicle roof-covering material of vinylcoated fabric used for convertible tops and for overlays that may be both functional and decorative with metal roofs.

**virtual memory:**  external memory (as magnetic disks or tapes) for a computer that can be used as if it were an extension of the computer's internal memory--called also virtual storage. Many race cars now store all race performance data for playback on their pit area computer.  Most contemporary passenger vehicles have on-board recorders that record all driving malfunctions that can be retrieved by service point computers for ease in trouble-shooting and repairs--frequently before the vehicle owner/driver becomes aware of a problem.

**vis-a-vis:**  face-to-face.  Some early automobiles with two seats had the front seat facing to the rear and the rear seat facing to the front.

**viscosimeter:**  a device used to measure the viscosity of a fluid (as of an engine lubricating oil.).  Also viscometer.

**viscosity:**  the quality or state of being viscous.  The property of a fluid or semifluid that enables it to develop and maintain an amount of shearing stress dependent upon the velocity of flow and then to offer continued resistance to flow.

**viscosity index:**  an arbitrary number assigned as a measure of the constancy of the viscosity of a lubricating oil with change of temperature with higher numbers indicating viscosities that change little with temperature.

**vise:**  any of various tools with two jaws for holding work that close usually by a screw, lever, or cam.

**Vise Grips:**  a trademarked name for a type of locking pliers used extensively in repairing vehicles for tightening, loosening, mechanical attaching devices and for temporary clamping and holding workpieces.

**visor:**  a usually movable flat sunshade attached to the top of a vehicle windshield.  Also a fixed contoured sunshade attached to the outside top area of a windshield providing shade and deflecting rain/snow from the windshield.

**vitreous enamel:** a fired-on opaque glossy coating on metal (as steel). Used in early vehicles to protect and beautify engine parts.

**vocational:** of, relating to, or being in training in a skill or trade to be pursued as a career as in vehicle mechanic training.

**volatile:** readily vaporizable at a relatively low temperature.

**volatilize:** to make volatile. To pass off in vapor.

**volt:** the practical meter-kilogram-second unit of electrical potential difference and electromotive force equal to the difference of potential between two points in a conducting wire carrying a constant current of one ampere when the power dissipated between these two points is equal to one watt and equivalent to the potential difference across a resistance of one ohm when one ampere is flowing through it.

**voltage:** electric potential or potential difference expressed in volts.

**voltage divider:** a resistor or series of resistors with taps at certain points and used to provide potential differences from a single power source.

**voltage regulator:** a device for controlling and maintaining the proper voltage value of the vehicle alternator/generator output to insure proper functioning of the vehicle electrical system. The interdependence of voltage and current requires that both be regulated usually using one integrated mechanism. Too high a voltage can reduce lightbulb life and also cause total failure from burn-out. Other voltage-sensitive components react similarly. Too much current causes overcharging, boiling, and early failure of the vehicle storage battery and can damage other circuitry by overheating.

**voltaic:** of, relating to, or producing direct electric current by chemical action (as in a vehicle battery).

**voltammeter:** an instrument for indicating one or more ranges of values of volts and amperes by changing terminal connections.

**volt-ampere:** a unit of electrical measurement equal to the product of a volt and an ampere that for direct current constitutes a measure of power equal to a watt.

**voltmeter:** an instrument (as a galvanometer) for measuring in volts the differences in potential between different points in an electrical circuit.

**volume:** the amount of space occupied by a three-dimensional figure as measured in cubic units (as inches, quarts, or pecks). Cubic capacity.

**volumetric:** of, relating to, or involving the measurement of volume.

**vortex:** a mass of fluid and especially of a liquid with a whirling or circular motion that tends to form a cavity or vacuum in the center of the circle and to draw toward this cavity or vacuum bodies subject to its action.

**vroom:** imitation of the noise of an engine. To operate a motor vehicle at high speed or so as to create a great deal of engine noise.

**vulcanization:** the process of treating crude or synthetic rubber or similar plastic material chemically to give it useful properties/elasticity, strength, and stability.

**vulcanize:** to subject to vulcanization. In the early days to patch a tire or tube air leak using a hot patch.

## LAGNIAPPE

**vacuum advance:** the control of ignition spark advance using manifold pressure (vacuum) to operate a push-pull diaphragm.

**vacuum motor:** (1) Vacuum actuated diaphragm used to operate push-pull mechanisms. (2) A true motor using atmosphere/vacuum differential pressure to impart rotary or oscillatory motion.

**valve-angle:** the machined matching angles of a valve/valve-seat.

**valve rotator:** a machined interface that imparts a small angular turn each time the valve closes/opens to minimize seat/valve wear.

**variable resistor:** an electrical control allowing resistance to be changed from its minimum to maximum ohm-ratings in progressive increments.

**vicky:** car jargon shortening of a carriage called victoria (Queen Victoria's pleasure carriage with a calash top) popularized by the Model A Ford close-coupled two-door sedan with the model designation "Victoria" (since copied in many variations because of its enthusiastic reception).

**voltage drop:** the inevitable decrease in voltage in any operating circuit caused by resistance in the wire and components/connections. Faulty or loose connection losses are undesirable but correctable/preventable by/with good maintenance. Resistance loss must be tolerated but can be minimized with low-resistance materials.

# DIRTY LINEN
## (Unlikely ever to be White again)

Maybe akin to Ross Perot's oft-repeated quote "that's like a "Crazy Aunt" that should be kept chained in the basement", our automobile community has a lot of skeletons in its closet that too few car buffs have ever seen. Over sixty years ago, as a pre-engineering school apprentice (helping build "Bucky" Fuller's Dymaxion), the author became a self-appointed nemesis committed to a vengeful vendetta against all who would sell "snake oil" and gimcracks guaranteed to "burn" air or water, or equally implausible claims of faster acceleration, better mileage, or less pollution. Conning the usually trusting, but often naive and technically unsophisticated, car owner. The dollar sign representing losses to the automobile community from these pandemic frauds has many zeroes following its digits.

The following examples, all inarguably documented, from my files are mentioned to enlighten, to tweak the reader's curiosity, and hopefully to pique anger and arouse effective opposition against the crooks. Indictments were requested against many. Few were punished. Too many who got "took" are too apathetic, embarrassed, or gutless to complain.

President Gerald Ford, major stockholder in the Webster-Heise Valve, abetted by top GOP "brass" (President George Bush, and his counsel C. Boyden Gray, DOT Secretary Drew Lewis, DOD Secretary Melvin Laird, Army Secretary John Marsh, VA Senator John Warner, Congressmen James Broyhill, NC, and Edward Madigan, IL, sold us a gimcrack that READER'S DIGEST (June 1983) said would "eliminate the need for high-octane gasoline and improve mileage 20%....cost less than $100....save $300 per car in pollution-control equipment... save at least 600,000 barrels of oil a day....Congressional Research Services verified....even removed salt from sea water at half the traditional cost." The "Valve" is still being sold today, claiming the same the same lies! Albert Papay, President of Environmental

Testing Corporation, who was given 10,000 shares of Webster-Heise stock and who falsified government-funded test results had his hands slapped by the SEC and returned the stock. (WALL STREET JOURNAL, 28 February 1984). Who quashed the WSJ front-page expose (naming the GOP "names" and their involvement) after one day's run and who kept Albert Papay out of the "pokey"? Wanna' bet?

Colorado's "Born Again" Senator Bill Armstrong in a full-page bylined feature (DENVER POST, 20 June 1982) guaranteed that "SERI'S new invention, a hydrogen-fueled car (it wasn't) would give twice the mileage of gasoline, be zero-polluting, fueled with farm wastes, available for sale to the public--cheaply--in 2 years". That mega-buck DOE boondoggle is rusting away today at Colorado School of Mines as a monument to "Born Again" lies, stupidity, and waste of our taxes by the U.S. Department of Energy.

"Born Again Bill" again joined hands with DOE in pushing Nutronics Corporation's "AlterBreak", a gimmick claimed to "increase gas mileage over 30%, reduce pollution over 50%, and eliminate our $15 Billion monthly foreign trade deficit". Senator Armstrong's Office "tested, verified, and endorsed the scam". DOE gave Nutronics a $55,000 grant to promote the lies. Luckily a Federal Judge disagreed. The U.S. Patented "AlterBreak" is still around but Nutronics and our 55,000 tax dollars disappeared. Since published DOE/EPA CAFE-fuel-use-tests showed conclusively that a vehicle's alternator or generator uses less than 5% of its fuel (when operating full-time), shouldn't Bill Armstrong/DOE/Nutronics have been required to reimburse our 55,000 tax dollars for aggrandizing, subsidizing, endorsing, and selling a part-time cut-out of the alternator which they all guaranteed would save 30% of a vehicle's fuel? The Judge, the jury, the GAO, and the crooks who signed a Consent Agreement after signing a nolo contendere plea ignored my insistence.

Astronaut Gordon Cooper "took" us for a few million bucks with his U.S. Patented "G-R Valve" that claimed to "improve gas mileage 50% and reduce pollution to zilch". Gordo's nolo contendere plea and a Consent Agreement to "cease and desist" was justice?

USA TODAY (that's where Gerald Ford's "Webster-Heise Valve" was first launched) headlined George Miller of Johnstown, PA, whose Buick not only burned pure air but made its own air (19 June 1984).

BUSINESS WEEK (full page #47, 8 August 1994) aggrandized Rudolph Gunnerman's U.S. Patented 55% Water Fuel (half-owned with Caterpillar, Inc.) supported by Pena's U.S. DOT's Mark Richards, the U.S. Air Force, Reno city buses, Minnesota Transportation Department, University of Minnesota, the Governors of Minnesota and Nevada, et al. The U.S. Patent shows that Gunnerman's "gunk" will work with from 20% to 80% of water in the mix. So why the Hell weren't they running 80% water?

The author offered to pay for testing of the "Water Fuel" at a competent facility (recommending the Federally Approved Colorado Institute for Fuels and Engine Research [CIFER] in Denver or the Southwest Research Institute in San Antonio) and to donate thirty thousand dollars to a charity of their choice (BUSINESS WEEK, Caterpillar, Gunnerman, and any of the believers--or guarantors--of the "Water Fuel") if it improved fuel mileage 40%, as claimed. Provided they'd reciprocate. No takers, to date! Not even a reply. A gas chromatograph will name every atom in Gunnerman's "secret" catalyst and "emulsifier"--even spell their names correctly. A chassis or engine dyno will yell out loud (with my favorite cuss words) when there's a 40% improvement in mpg as the vested interests claim.

The Smithsonian's AIR & SPACE magazine (page 32, October/November 1991) giggled at Stanley Meyer's (Grove City, OH) guarantee to fly my friend (ex?) Bill Brooks' twin-engined corporate airplane around the world on one tank of water--twice, non-stop! Stan has a gaggle of U.S. Patents on his "water burners" that "the Lord told him how to build". But can Stan walk on water? He can and has sold $50,000 limited partnerships in his patented "water burners". He also promised Bill Brooks that his gimcracks would get the "energy equivalent of 2½ millions barrels of crude oil" from each gallon of water and promised to make Bill's world landspeed record-holding Corvette (271 mph) go faster than anyone ever had--anywhere. It didn't! Bill's money did! Bill Brooks called me from Paris assuring me that he and his partner, Roger Lessman, were going to win the trophy that my wife and I had offered to the fastest hydrogen-fueled car to run at the Bonneville Nationals 1991 "Speed Week", converting water to hydrogen on-board his Corvette. A student racing team from Middle Tennessee State University won the trophy--burning fuel that they made from "Tennessee Sunshine" (hydrogen electrolyzed from water by electricity from photovoltaics). Those agricultural students also burned "Tennessee Moonshine" in their home-built race cars (ethanol made by distilling beer from farm wastes into 200-proof fuel-grade alcohol).

At the "1991 EKO EXPO" in Denver's Convention Center, John Denver, Congresswoman Pat Schroeder, and Dennis Weaver exhorted thousands of attendees to buy from the 500 exhibitors. Many bought 27¢ "cow magnets" (the price at veterinary suppliers) for $89.00 as the "Energy Saver" from Orbit Sales of Wentzville, MO, and as the "Gas Booster" for $29.95 from Saveco of Philadelphia, PA--both claiming 23.6% increase in mileage and 97% reduction in pollution. It is particularly reprehensible that the public figures sponsoring the ecological exposition would give their support to the sale of these two fraudulent devices and at least 200 others. Where was the Federal Trade Commission? Just two blocks away! My complaints to all concerned were unheeded--not even answered.

As there's little new in automobiles, the bewhiskered "cow magnets" have "been realigning the molecules in your gasoline" since before the electric starter. Possibly the first car "guaranteed to go 1,000 miles at 55 mph on one tank of air" was the 1902 Hahan, from a factory in Pueblo, CO, according to the PUEBLO CHIEFTAIN, similar to so many of the Barnumesque bamboozles still being sold. All patented, tested and approved by U.S. Government Laboratories, and advertised in our "Motherhood-and-apple-pie" publications.

389

**W-Cars:** Whither went the 173 w-marques? Maybe "down yonder" where all bad cars are said to go--where the hot fires melt 'em down to be recycled as Rolls-Royce "flying lady" radiator ornaments. Starting as a treadle sewing machine, the White evolved into a pretty good steam car. What other "W" or any other letter-marque could go 100 miles at 75 miles-per-hour on one tank of water? There's no record of how much coal oil the White's flash boiler burned. Mutating genes changed the steamer into a gasoline "stinker" with a 16 valve 4-cylinder engine in 1916. That's the year the car metamorphosed into a truck. The Waltham started as a steam car in a bicycle factory (not built by watchmakers), soon became an electric, before turning into a gas buggy and disappearing in 1908. Maybe Willys became a Jeep because it couldn't decide whether to be a Willys-Overland or a Willys-Knight. Winton built some really BIG cars with engines of over 1,000 cubic inches displacement before becoming a marine engine Division of General Motors in 1924.

**wabble:** a variation of wobble.

**wad:** a soft mass of usually fibrous material used to stop a leak or to hold grease around an axle.

**wafer:** a thin disk or ring resembling a wafer and used variously as a valve or diaphragm.

**wafflestomper:** a vehicle tire with a deep bar mud/snow tread pattern that leaves a wafflelike pattern in soft road surfaces.

**wagon:** a vehicle used for specialized hauling usually with a descriptive prefix: station wagon, milk wagon, patrol wagon, paddy wagon.

**wagonette:** a light vehicle with a transverse front seat and with two facing seats along the sides in the rear.

**wainwright:** a term for the maker and repairer of horse-drawn wagons that carried over to the mechanics of early powered vehicles.

**waiting lounge:** an area usually provided by large vehicle dealer shops for the convenience of patrons who wait while minor repairs and service are being accomplished.

**walking beam:** a pivoted lever/beam used to direct and control the motion of push-pull rods/cables.

**walnut-shell tire:** a vehicle tire with a tread having imbedded walnut shells as an abrasive material to improve traction on snow and ice.

**wander:** the tendency of a vehicle with directional instability to deviate from a fixed path.

**Wankel-engine:** an internal combustion rotary engine with a rounded triangular rotor functioning as its piston and rotating in a chamber within the engine.

**want list:** an informal listing sheet used by vehicle mechanics to note repair parts and supplies needed to accomplish vehicle repairs.

**warmed over:** used to describe a new model vehicle that has only superficial changes made to the previous models.

**warm up:** to let a vehicle engine run slowly until its lubrication system and temperaturesensitive clearances have reached the manufacturer's recommended values.

**warning strip:** a strip in a vehicle roadway designed to create a distinctive sound to alert the driver aurally to his exact position.

**warp:** a twist or curve that has developed in something that was originally flat or straight. To twist or bend out of a plane.

**warrantor:** one that warrants or gives a warranty.

**warranty:** a usually written guarantee of the integrity of a product or service and of the warrantor's responsibility for repair or replacement for a stated period of time.

**washboard:** a road or pavement so worn by traffic as to become corrugated or ridged  transversely.

**washing soda:** sal soda.

**washout:** the result of erosion by running water destroying a section of roadway making it impassable. Usually caused by heavier than normal rain or by a cloudburst.

**washrack:** a specially designed facility for washing vehicles usually partially open-sided and well-drained.

**water:** the bane of the existence of every vehicle mechanic proving Murphy's Law "where there is water there are leaks". The common constituent of all living matter, lurking somewhere in most machines, and the scientific basis for man becoming man and Space Ship Earth becoming his home. The evil genie behind potholes, mud, ice, snow, hail, slick roads, poor visibility, spin-outs, wet seats, shorted ignitions, busted blocks, roof, trunk, window, windshield, window, door, radiator, hose, gasket, water pump, pet and people (little people) leaks. When pure it's virtually non-conductive--always contaminated it shows electricity how, when, and where to leak. Ban the bane of water and eliminate all car problems--and cars. Or break water into hydrogen and oxygen cleanly, efficiently, and economically (using clean photovoltaic or fusion electricity) and ban OPEC and pollution forever with the vehicle fuel of the future--hydrogen.  There is no other choice.

**water bag:**  essential to vehicle travel through the arid West. Hanging out in the breeze the evaporation from a canvas bag keeps the water cool to keep man and machine alive to reach the next oasis.

**water can:**  once the spouted can common to every filling station for replenishing vehicle radiator coolant before the modern sealed and pressurized systems eliminated evaporation. Contemporary car aficionados know only grampa water can's grand kid--jerry can.

**water-cooled:**  to denote a vehicle engine cooled by a circulating liquid coolant as contrasted to an engine cooled by air.

**water-cooled manifold:**  an engine manifold usually the exhaust surrounded by coolant circulated by the engine cooling system or as in boats by a separate water supply from the outside and usually dumped into the exhaust pipe downstream from the manifold and discharged overboard with the exhaust gases.

**waterflood:**  the process of waterflooding the area around an oil well to cool and to minimize the possibility of a fire or to assist in the control and extinguishment of an existing fire.  Also the technique of pumping water into the ground around an oil well nearing depletion in order to loosen and force the remaining oil out of the ground.

**water gas:**  the descriptive name for an early industrial/city gaseous fuel made by blowing air and steam over red-hot beds of coke or coal resulting in a combustible fuel consisting mostly of carbon monoxide (CO) and hydrogen ($H_2$) with small amounts of other gases.  Water gas (known also as city gas, producer gas, and manufacturer gas) was used for street, home, and industrial illumination as well as heating long before the discovery of crude oil and natural gas.

**water heater:**  the universal vehicle interior heater using circulating engine coolant through a forced air radiator to maintain a comfortable environment for passengers.

**water jacket:**  the enclosure surrounding a vehicle's internal combustion engine and components requiring cooling for dependable efficient functioning.  The circulating water absorbs excess heat from the hot areas and transports it to appropriate radiators for dissipation back to the atmosphere.

**water pipe:**  a pipe for conveying water.  Usually rigid, the plumbing systems of early vehicle cooling have given way to flexible hoses lacking the automobile ambience of yore.

**water proof:** impervious to water. To make impervious to water.

**water pump:** a vehicle mechanical pump that circulates the engine coolant. Likely to become extinct as an energy-robbing parasite. Long overdue.

**water repellent:** treated with a finish that is resistant but not impervious to water. Water resistant.

**water spot:** a visible vehicle surface spot that remains when other than pure water forms a spot and then evaporates leaving the contaminants coating the surface.

**watertight:** impermeable to water except when there is sufficient pressure to cause structural failure.

**water vapor:** water in vaporous state especially when below boiling temperature and diffused (as in the atmosphere).

**water wagon:** name for the vehicle (tank truck) with a perforated spreader manifold (pipe) that sprays water during costruction projects to allay dust and to provide optimum moisture content for surface stabilization prior to surface overlayment as with concrete or asphalt.

**watt:** the absolute meter-kilogram-second unit of power equal to the work done at the rate of one absolute joule per second or to the rate of work represented by an electric current of one ampere under the pressure of one volt and taken as the standard in the U.S. Equal to 1/746 horsepower.

**watt-hour:** a unit of work or energy equivalent to the power of one watt operating for one hour.

**wattmeter:** an instrument for measuring electric power in watts.

**wave:** to swing something back and forth or up and down. The undulating trace or path created when a linear dimension is added to the wave motion.

**waveband:** a band of electrical/electronic/electomagnetic frequencies.

**wave equation:** a partial differential equation of the second order whose solutions describe wave phenomena.

**waveform:** a graphic representation of the shape of a wave that indicates its characteristics (as frequency and amplitude)-- also called "waveshape".

**wave guide:** a device (pipe, duct, coaxial cable, or glass fiber) designed to confine and direct the propagation of electromagnetic waves including visible light waves.

**wavelength:** the distance in the line of advance of a wave from any one point to the next corresponding point on an adjacent wave form.

**wave number:** the reciprocal of the wave length.

**wave washer:** a thin spring-steel lock washer characterized by its wave shape that provides positive tension against a threaded nut to prevent loosening.

**wax:** a natural substance as beeswax secreted by bees or numerous substances of plant and animal origin that differ from fats (being less greasy, harder, and more brittle) in containing esters of higher fatty acids and higher alcohols and saturated hydrocarbons. Chemically-compounded synthetic wax-like polishes are rapidly replacing the natural waxes. Used variously to create a durable lustrous finish on metal or painted surfaces of vehicles. To apply wax.

**wax buffer:** a device usually electric or air-powered designed to impart a circular, orbital, or reciprocating motion to polish pads for spreading or "rubbing-out" waxes on vehicle surfaces.

**way:** the guiding surfaces or track on the bed of a machine along which a table or carriage moves.

**weak-kneed:** a common description of early cars whose "knee-action" suspension units became worn or weak allowing the vehicle to sag and the wheels appear to spread and lean.

**wear:** to diminish, decay, or fail with use or age. Inevitable with vehicles.

**wear and tear:** considered normal attrition/depreciation when a vehicle is operated within its design parameters.

**wear out:** to become useless from long or excessive wear or use.

**weather:** state of the atmosphere with respect to heat or cold, wetness or dryness, calm or storm, clearness or cloudiness.

**weather-beaten:** worn or damaged by exposure to the weather.

**weather-checked:** descriptive of a vehicle finish that is cracked and peeling from sun and weather exposure.

**weather-front:** the name for a fabric covering over the front of a vehicle radiator to limit exposure to cold winter air and precipitation. Usually with adjustable openings to control air flow through the radiator.

**weatherize:** to prepare a vehicle against winter weather use by checking and adding proper fluids (antifreeze, winter-weight lubricants, windshield de-icer, fuel) installing snow tires/chains, and tuning engines for expected temperatures.

**weatherproof:** able to withstand exposure to weather without damage or loss of function.

**weather seal:** sealing material used at any joint or opening to keep out the weather elements.

**weather strip:** a strip of material to cover the joint or fill excess space at the opening edges of doors, windows or vents to exclude rain, snow, and cold air while allowing functional operation.

**web:** a thin metal plate sheet or strip. The plate connecting the upper and lower flanges of a girder or rail.

**webbing:** a strong narrow closely woven tape used in vehicle upholstery and for straps for towing vehicles and tying down cargo.

**weber:** the practical meter-kilogram-second unit of magnetic flux equal to that flux which in linking a circuit of one turn produces in it an electromotive force of one volt as the flux is reduced to zero at a uniform rate of one ampere per second.

**web member:** one of the several members joining the top and bottom chords of a truss or lattice girder.

**wedge:** a tool that tapers to a thin edge and is used for splitting or separating material, raising heavy bodies, or for tightening by being driven into something that expands within an internal shape. To fasten or tighten by driving a wedge. To force or press something into a narrow space. To become wedged.

**weep:** to leak fluid slowly, usually in drops.

**weep hole:** a hole deliberately designed into a machine to drain off accumulated fluids.

**weigh:** to ascertain the heaviness of something using a scale or balance. To make heavy.

**weigh down:** overburden with excessive weight.

**weigh-in:** the act or instance of weighing a vehicle to determine compliance with specified weight limits for entry as a competitor in a contest.

**weight:** the amount that a thing weighs. A heavy object. The force with which an object is attracted toward the earth by gravity. Equal to the product of the mass and the local gravitational acceleration.

**weight and balance:** calculations to determine the center-of-gravity of a vehicle to evaluate performance and handling characteristics.

**weirdie:** a vehicle of such extraordinarily strange appearance, design, or construction as to offend one's normal sensibilities. Queer, weirdo.

**weld:** to unite metallic parts and some plastics by heating and allowing the materials to flow together and to harden, becoming as one homogeneous mass. A welded joint. The state or condition of being welded.

**welder:** a mechanic who is a proficient welder. A machine used in welding.

**wellhead:** the top of or a structure built over an oil well. Derrick.

**wellhead price:** the price less transportation costs charged by the producer for petroleum or natural gas.

**welt:** a separating strip used to insure the filling of open space forming a leakproof joint between mating body parts of a vehicle (such as the fender attachment to a vehicle side panel). Also used in the seams of vehicle upholstery. Usually rolled edge of the welt is left exposed on the finished side to exclude small particulates from entering the seam.

**wet clutch:** a friction clutch that operates immersed in liquid usually a specially compounded oil. Provides smoother engagement, cooler running, and extended wear.

**wet-or-dry:** a very fine-grit abrasive paper or cloth that can be used for finishing vehicle painted surfaces either dry or using an appropriate liquid as a lubricant.

**wet-sand:** to use a fine-grit sandpaper for smoothing a vehicle surface while keeping the work surface wet with a gentle stream of water or by repeated dipping of the sanding pad in a container of water.

**wheel:** the genesis from which all vehicles evolved. An essential appendage. To drive a vehicle at high speed. To make or perform a fast turn or circle.

**wheelbase:** the distance in inches between the centers of the front and rear axles of an automotive vehicle.

**wheeler-dealer:** a derisive but descriptive characterization of a used car salesman.

**wheelwright:** a maker and repairer of vehicle wheels. Still in demand for the wood and wire-spoked wheels of car collectors. Rapidly becoming a forgotten art/skill.

**wheeze:** descriptive of the hissing whistling sound made by an engine breathing with intake system leaks.

**whet:** to sharpen or make keen the cutting edge of a tool by rubbing with an appropriate abrasive.

**whetstone:** a stone for whetting tool cutting edges.

**whine:** a prolonged high-pitched sound typical of a high-speed rotating axle turning in a bearing that is improperly lubricated.

**whiplash:** injury usually to the cervical vertebrae resulting from a sudden sharp whipping movement of the neck and head (as to a person in a vehicle that is struck head-on or from the rear by another vehicle).

**white flag:** one of the standardized automobile racing informational flags whose meaning has varied throughout racing history and among the race sanctioning bodies. Best known as the "final lap" flag, white also is selectively used to indicate a spectator danger, a disabled or too slow race car, or a rescue vehicle on the track.

**white elephant:** a vehicle requiring much care, expense, and repair and yielding little profit or use. Something of little or no value and difficult to sell.

**white gasoline:** vehicle gasoline containing no tetraethyllead with a low octane rating and also called "white gas" and "regular".

**white heat:** a temperature (as for copper and iron from $1500^{\circ}$ to $1600^{\circ}$ C.) which is higher than red heat and at which a body becomes brightly incandescent. White-hot.

**white lead:** any of several white lead-containing pigments used in early vehicles as gasket/thread sealer and locks.

**white line:** a stripe painted on a road to delimit driving lanes making traffic separation more precise by providing better driver references.

**white metal:** any of several lead-base and tin-base alloys (as Babbitt metal) widely used in vehicle bearings.

**whiteout:** a blizzard that severely reduces visibility creating a condition where there are no shadows and only dark objects are discernible.

**whitewall:** a vehicle tire having a white band on the sidewall, primarily decorative.

**whitewing:** passe with the passing of horsedrawn vehicles. Stemming from the street sweeper, traditionally clothed in white uniforms, who cleaned up after horses.

**wholesaler:** a middleman buyer/seller of used vehicles who sells (by law in many states) only to licensed retail dealers. The vehicle "dealers' auction" is the most structured wholesaler.

**wicker:** a woven or interlaced covering of wood, usually willow, used in early vehicles as a seat covering and on exteriors for decorative effect. Wicker trunks and fitted picnic baskets were common.

**wick oiler:** usually for slow-turning large axle bearings consisting of an oil container with twisted, braided, or woven cord of soft-spun cotton threads whose capillary action delivered small amounts of oil to be wiped from the wick onto the turning shaft. Crude but effective.

**widdershins:** in a left-handed, wrong, or contrary direction. Since most vehicle engines rotate in a clockwise direction (when viewed from the front) early mechanics used this ancient term to denote an engine that rotated in the counterclockwise direction.

**wide white:** a vehicle tire with a wide band of white around the sidewall.

**wide track:** a vehicle with wider than typical side-to-side spacing of the wheels.

**widget:** a usually meaningless name applied by a vehicle owner to a component or part when he doesn't know the correct nomenclature and similarly by a vehicle mechanic when he has forgotten the name. Makes for difficult and confusing communication between owner and mechanic.

**width:** the maximum dimension of a vehicle between extremities taken at right angles to the vehicle length.

**wildcatter:** one that drills wells in the hope of finding oil/gas in territory not know to be a productive oil field. A worker who goes out on an unauthorized strike.

**winch:** any of various machines for lifting or pulling and marked by one or more drums on which the rope, cable, or chain is wound. Turning the drum through gears multiplies the mechanical advantage of the system.

**wind:** a natural movement of air in a generally horizontal direction. An artificial apparent motion of air relative to the motion of a body through the air (as a moving vehicle with movement through still air resulting in a wind relative to the vehicle at approximately the vehicle speed).

**wind deflector:** an aerodynamic device usually attached near the front upper edge of a vehicle hood to deflect the air/wind upward over the windshield to reduce windshield moisture and/or scum.

**winding:** the coiled wire around the magnetic pole cores of armatures for electric motors, alternators or generators and transformer coils (ignition coil). One turn of a wire in such a coil. A curved or sinuous roadway.

**window:** a wall opening to provide light, ventilation, or visibility through a wall area.

**window channel:** a window frame/guide to allow the freedom for vertical or horizontal sliding motion while providing tight closing.

**window shade:** a fabric closure usually roller-retractable used in early automobiles for privacy or shade for the passengers.

**window seat:** a vehicle seat adjacent to a window as in a passenger bus.

**window sticker:** an adhesive attachment usually intended to indicate special legal authorization/compliance as parking/ pollution. Many stickers especially ego statements, advertisements, or slogans are illegal but tacitly condoned.

**window vent:** before vehicle air conditioning became so universal, uniform cooling and heating a vehicle was a real challenge. Using a vertically-pivoted (vent) segment of about $\frac{1}{4}$ the area of each side window could serve to draw air from the interior or force air into the interior depending upon the angular position of the vent pane with respect to the on-coming air.

**windscreen:** the British name for the front window of a vehicle providing the driver forward visibility while shielding the front seat occupants from the elements and the on-rushing wind when in motion. See windshield.

**windshield:** a transparent screen in front of the occupants of a vehicle. See windscreen. The finer early open cars used dual windshields for the front and back seats.

**windshield washer:** an electrical (formerly manual or vacuum) pump designed to squirt a stream of water or cleaner onto a windshield to assist the wiper in removing road grime (as dust and mud).

**windshield wiper:** an electrical (formerly manual or vacuum) device designed to wipe a squeegee-like blade or a pad repeatedly across a windshield front surface, removing any obstruction (rain, snow, and other) to the occupants' vision.

**wind tufts:** light flexible pieces of yarn cemented to a vehicle outside surface so that the effect of air flowing past the vehicle can be observed and evaluated during actual road driving or wind tunnel testing.

**wind tunnel:** a tunnellike passage through which air is blown at varying known velocities to determine the effects of wind pressure upon efficiency, handling, and performance of a vehicle. Scale models and full-sized vehicles can be so tested and a simulated movement of the roadway (moving belt) can be added to insure realism and accuracy of test results.

**wind wing:** see window vent.

**wing:** an aerodynamic shape attached to a race car with adjustments so that up or down or lateral forces can be generated by the wing to improve the handling of the car during high speed races.

**wing nut:** a nut with wing-like surfaces that allow tightening and loosening using the thumb and a finger.

**winner's lap:** an extra lap or turn around a race track by the winning car/driver to allow for crowd applause for the victor. The victory lap.

**winter front:** a fabric blanket-like covering for the front of a vehicle radiator with a variable opening to control in-coming air flow to keep the engine warmer than possible with the full flow of cold winter air.

**winterize:** to prepare a vehicle for winter operation by checking/changing fluids and lubricants to the manufacturer's specifications for cold weather use and by tuning the vehicle engine for proper starting and operation at the expected temperatures.

**winter wiper blade:** a windshield wiper blade designed to prevent snow or ice accumulation on the blade that would reduce its wiping efficiency.

**wiper arm:** a usually flexible arm of a windshield wiper assembly that sweeps the wiper blade back-and-forth across the windshield.

**wire cloth:**  a fabric of woven metallic wire used for vehicle oil and air strainers.

**wire draw:**  to draw or stretch forcibly through a die.

**wire-feed welder:**  a welding machine that feeds welding wire at the proper rate into the molten metal at the weld site relieving the mechanic from having to feed welding rod by hand. Common to automatic production welding.

**wire gauge:**  a gauge especially designed with accurately sized openings for measuring wire diameters.

**wire glass:**  window glass reinforced with wire mesh and often used in heavy construction vehicles to prevent shattered windows.

**wire rope:**  a rope (cable) formed wholly or chiefly of metallic wires and used as vehicle control cables as well as for heavy pulling and lifting.

**wiring diagram:**  a schematic hard-copy representation of the complete electrical circuitry of a vehicle essential for diagnosing, troubleshooting, finding, and repairing electrical system failures.

**wiring harness:**  interconnecting wires usually bundled together that allow for unit circuit replacement rather than the cumbersome time consuming replacement of individual wires in a complex electrical circuit. Consolidation of wires and prefabrication insure standardization and neatness rather than a random tangle of individual wires in a vehicle.

**wiring loom:**  an outer protective covering for a grouping of wires preventing tangling and insulation damage. Looms are usually somewhat flexible coverings, rigid conduits, serving the same purpose, are inflexible.

**wobble:**  a hobbing or rocking irregular motion of a vehicle wheel indicating a bent or deformed wheel, improper assembly/ installation or looseness.

**wobble pump:**  a hand-operated fluid pump named so because of the back-and-forth motion of the pump handle and used for draining vehicle fuel tanks or on-site servicing of vehicle fluids from portable drums/tanks.

**wood grained:**  real wood, wood veneers, and simulated wood used for dash/instrument panel, functional and decorative trim and emphasizing the natural wood grain appearance.

**wood graining:**  the art/technique of emphasizing natural wood grain appearance or simulating the effect.

**Wood lights:** a tradenamed headlight popular with early cars because of its unusual design usually with a vertical configured lens (sometimes quite narrow and not too effective a light source).

**woody:** a wood-paneled station wagon.

**work:** scientifically, the conversion of energy into something useful and quantified as force multiplied by distance. Adding time as a multiplier provides a measure of power as: one horsepower equals 33,000 foot-pounds per minute.

**work bench:** in vehicle shops a bench usually equipped with a vise and bench grinder where vehicle components can be repaired/assembled more efficiently than in the vehicle.

**work hardened:** a condition of increased hardness of a metal attained by peening or hammering. The condition becomes undesirable as in operating machines when repeated pounding/hammering/impact can over-harden to the point of brittleness and failure from stress-cracking.

**workpiece:** material being machined or shaped as with manufacture or assembly of a vehicle part.

**work stand:** any of various stands for facilitating vehicle maintenance/repairs: engine stand, elevated work platform.

**work station:** an area with equipment for a single worker and usually a single operation/purpose as in production-line assembly or maintenance.

**worm gear:** a gear or worm (resembling threads) on a shaft mating/meshing with a toothedgear on a wheel providing great mechanical advantage (multiplication of force/torque) when worm-driven but becoming self-locking and incapable of being reversed or wheel-driven.

**wraparound:** made to curve from the front around to the sides or to conform to the enclosed shape. Vehicle windshields and vehicle sheet metal for the contemporary streamlined vehicles.

**wrecker:** a specialized truck vehicle equipped with hoisting apparatus and with towing/ hauling equipment for rescuing wrecked or disabled vehicles.

**wrecking ball:** a heavy iron or steel ball dropped or swung by a crane or derrick to smash damaged vehicles into smaller pieces to facilitate moving, shipping, storage, or incinerating/melting.

**wrecking bar:** a crowbar with a curved claw on one end for pulling things apart and a chisel end on the other end for prying and separating.

**wrecking yard:** a storage yard for disabled or worn-out vehicles awaiting further disposal as used components/parts or for recycling/salvage.

**wrench:** a hand or power tool for holding, turning, or twisting an object such as a bolt or nut.

**wrinkle finish:** a paint coating compounded to develop surface ridges and furrows as it dries to resemble a textured leather.

**wrist pin:** a stud, shaft, or pin that connects a vehicle piston to the piston rod, allowing reciprocating/rotational movement.

**wrought iron:** a commercial grade of iron that is relatively soft and therefore rarely used in contemporary vehicles.

**W-shaped:** an expansion spacer of spring steel in the shape of the letter "w".


## LAGNIAPPE

**water brake:** a load absorption unit for dynamometers that pumps against a head or uses fluid friction to dissipate the energy/heat/horsepower of the engine/vehicle being tested.

**water injection:** liquid or vapor injected/added directly into engine combustion chambers or indirectly into induction charges to control detonation and cool combustion. Water <u>never</u> burns, <u>always</u> reduces power (available fuel energy) and/or volumetric efficiency, but <u>does</u> cool, and <u>allow</u> burning of <u>more</u> fuel, giving more power.

**weight transfer:** the forward-shift (to the front wheels) when braking and the rearward-shift (to the rear wheels) when accelerating, inherent, but aggravated by center-of-gravity height and suspension design and stiffness.

**welch plug:** a slightly dished/domed disk that is hammer-expanded to seal access/clean-out apertures/holes in castings. Freeze-plug.

**wets:** race slang for tires designed for use on wet track surfaces.

**wet sleeve:** literally <u>not</u> a cylinder <u>liner</u>, but the actual wear-resistant cylinder wall itself, inserted into an engine block casting and wetted by physical contact with the coolant. Dry sleeve.


## EXCUSES, EXCUSES
(From Traffic Court Records)

After the accident the driver and his passengers departed immediately for an extended ocean voyage with injuries.

# THE FIRST AUTOMOBILE
### (Who Says?)

Use "Bucky" Fuller's spelling--egomobile--and country logic
can view the contraption as what it does--move the ego to the size
of a Charles Atlas biceps and grow a Durante/Pinocchio nose on the
98-pound weakling owner.  Change the word to "powerwagon" and it
fits my four-wheeled cart that has engine power that I must feed,
crank, point it where it's to go and constantly correct its direction
to avoid others that would devour it, tell it to stop and then insist
upon it--while it does nothing automatically to get me to my old
fishing hole, catch a fish, and hurry home for a hamburger.  Betcha'
your car never took any wholly involuntary, spontaneous, or uncon-
scious action, and that it's not self-acting, self-starting, or
self-regulating.  Maybe you and I ain't got an automobile!

Every reasonable mind is likely to agree that there is proof
positive that Karl Benz did not build, drive, or invent the world's
first internal combustion-powered automobile.  (If one can spell
Issac de Rivaz!).  Benz's rather crude tricycle weighing 580 pounds
with a two-thirds horsepower engine first ran on a public road in
July 1986.  His first four-wheeled "Vicktoria" ran in 1893.

Documented records in French and Swiss archives cause Benz's
trike of 1886 to pale by comparison with Swiss engineer Issac de
Rivaz's 2100 pound grand char mechanique (truly an automobile),
a mechanical grand chariot, when viewed from any direction.

On 18 October 1813 (Isn't that about 73 years before Benz?),
Rivaz's automobile, 17 feet long and 7 feet wide, running on four
wheels, attained a speed of about three miles per hour and climbed
a hill with about a 12% incline, powered by an internal combustion,
gas-fueled, electric spark ignition-engine.  The 1813 "grand chariot"
was a virtual clone of Rivaz's several such vehicles, first built
in 1805.  A French patent was awarded to Issac de Rivaz for his
grand char mechanique engine 30 January 1807.  Wasn't he the first?

**X-cars:** China, Great Britain, and the United States have each produced a car named "X___": Xian-Jin, Xenia, and Xtra, respectively.

**x-___:** as a prefix, x not only represents the Christ in Xmas, marking the "spot", or the unknown in mathematics, but also denotes <u>trans</u> or <u>cross</u>.

**xanthippe:** sometimes used to describe a contrary, cantankerous automobile like the Ford "T" Model. From: an ill-tempered woman.

**x-axis:** the axis in a plane Cartesian coordinate system parallel to which abscissas are measured.

**xenophile:** one attracted to foreign cars (imported).

**xenophobe:** dyed-in-the-wool Americans who dislike, distrust, and would never buy any car built outside our great country.

**x-frame:** a cross frame in the shape of an x between parallel frame members that imparts great strength and rigidity.

**x-member:** a cross frame usually at right angles to and between parallel frame members. Separates and positions the parallel side frames but requires additional angle braces for strength and rigidity.

**x-m:** the universal abbreviation for transmission.

**x-mission:** transmission or gear box.

**x-ray:** to inspect or photograph using X rays in nondestructive testing of a substance.

**X ray:** invisible electromagnetic radiation similar to visible light but of an extremely short wave length of less than 100 angstroms.

**X-section:** a cross-sectional view as in a working drawing to provide detail for the builder or assembler to work from.


### LAGNIAPPE

**x-drilled crankshaft:** a vehicle crankshaft using two oil passages drilled at right angles through the main-bearing journals of the crankshaft to insure better oil flow to the main bearings.

**xylene:** any of three toxic flammable oily isometric aromatic hydrocarbons that are di-methyl homologues of benzene and that are used as a mixture with ethyl-benzene to remove grease and paint.

## A DISQUISITION TOWARD
## A FAIR AND EQUITABLE FUEL TAX
(Non-existent in America Today)

Every vehicle fuel (air, land, and sea) must be taxed at a rate that will support initial infrastructure cost and maintenance, environmental cleanliness, amortize depletion of finite feedstock, and fund administrative expenses. No fuel is so taxed today. That's not equitable when some fuels are heavily taxed and some are taxfree. It's not fair when a little old lady on your block who never drove a car, never took an ocean cruise, and never jet-setted anywhere has contributed so much to the General Tax Fund that built our Interstate Highway System, any major airport, or any seaport.

That's why Uncle Sugar's fuel has hovered around a buck-a-gallon (often fictitiously lower) while the rest of the world fights to keep their fuel price under $5-a-gallon. That's why we use an inordinate share of Space Ship Earth's finite energy supply (it's so cheap) and why it's imperative that we purge our peccadillos or become unhappy pedestrians. Likely sooner than you think.

The fix? Tax every fuel fairly and equitably. How? By the Therm (100,000 BTUs)--by the pound--at the actuarial rate that will fund its keep. Any fuel's energy production is accurately calculable only by weight--never directly by volume (impossible), and so must be so taxed. Volumetric imponderables thus become meaningful and quantifiable. Pricing by the Therm is as necessary as is taxing by the Therm.

The distance that a vehicle is propelled by its fuel is directly BTU-dependent and so is vehicle distance, when modified by vehicle weight, coupled to roadway wear-and-tear. To properly equate various fuels' wear-and-tear a surtax must be added to the mileage/Therm tax for fuels requiring heavier on-board tank weight.

Pollution potential of a fuel demands a second surtax varying from 0% for non-polluting fuels to appropriate percentages as their pollution increases. Our fallacious and irrational assessment of fuel pollution, only "from the filler-pipe to the tail-pipe", must be expanded to include the pollution produced beginning with the feedstock acquisition, processing/refining into a usable state, storing, and transporting to the vehicle where the "filler-pipe to the tail-pipe" exhaust pollutants must be added. Some fuels pollute more getting to the filler-pipe than when exiting the tail-pipe as exhaust.

Clarifying the above paragraph with real-life examples: my electric car is zero-polluting at the tail-pipe--doesn't even have one! I drink the exhaust from my hydrogen-fueled Model T Ford Depot Hack, demonstrating that it's nothing but the purest of water (before the engine warms up enough to make the water of combustion exit as vaporous steam). Nary a tummy-ache from hundreds of swigs.

But "Truth in Advertising" elicits the fact that my--and your, and all battery-powered electric vehicles--are inarguably the most polluting of all cars. And my Model T--you don't have one--is the second most polluting (maybe a photo-finisher for the most polluting honor[?]). Neither pollutes my front yard.

The electric pollutes the Indian hunting grounds where their cheap dirty coal heats the steam generators before spilling pollution into our Grand Canyon. My T's hydrogen is made at a distant site using natural gas--polluting there and all the way to my quick-fill tank fitting.

Wherever the polluting occurs, its cost must be assessed against the vehicle/owner that ultimately burns the fuel, but fairly and equitably. No subsidies allowed under my pricing/taxing program. Let the "Better Mousetrap" survive. "Alternatives" bedamned!

The Scriptures of Science and our Natural Laws are terribly unforgiving of those who propose the many simple political solutions to complex scientific problems. They're always WRONG!

**Y-Cars:** of 17 "Y's" the Yugo is unquestionably the best known and is likely the most maligned.

**yagi:** a highly selective and directional shortwave radio antenna frequently used on the cars of avid amateur radio buffs. More ostentatious than functional.

**yahoo:** a derisive term often applied to driver/owners of "off-road" vehicles who flaunt their macho-ego on public roadways.

**yank:** a strong sudden pull.

**yard sale:** also called garage sale usually involving the sale of cast-off or un-wanted auto-related items.

**yaw:** a rotating movement of a vehicle in motion causing it to turn around its vertical axis. Spin. Spin-out.

**y-axis:** the axis of a plane Cartesian coordinate system parallel to which ordinates are measured.

**year model:** the numbered year closely corresponding to the calendar year indicating the manufacturers designation for identification of vehicle age. Major body, engine, and design changes are usually incorporated at the beginning of this period with minor superficial changes occurring throughout the ensuing 12-months. Manufacturers usually introduce the next year's model three to four months before the beginning of the calendar year.

**yecch:** the appropriate expletive to use when you see a purple automobile.

**yellow ocher:** a common pigment used in tinting paint to obtain a desired shade of color.

**yoke:** a branching lever or control segment usually used to equalize operating force or movement to multiple units.


### LAGNIAPPE

**Y block:** a Vee engine block whose casting extends below the bottom of the "V" increasing the depth of the crankcase, looking like "Y".

**Y pipe:** a pipe fitting that merges two passages into one passage, or splits one passage into two passages.

**yellow flag:** a signal to drivers in a closed-course race warning of a hazerd ahead and for them to slow the pace until a green flag is given to resume full-speed racing.

# THE SOCIETY OF AUTOMOTIVE ENGINEERS

In 1905, when the SAE was formed, the pioneers who powered automobile manufacturing to industrial greatness were all engineers (whether degreed, with diploma, or dirty-handed from hands-on labor). Many industrial icons presided over our Society as its Presidents: Charles F. ("Boss") Kettering (1918); Vincent Bendix (1931); and Howard Marmon (1913). They bellwethered SAE into its current prestigious position of world leadership in engineering excellence--with 65,000 members (1995).

The distaff side of our automotive engineering family grew from two women in 1920 to over 5,000 in 1995. Dr. Shirley Schwartz, an SAE Member since 1982, is Staff Research Scientist (Tribology) with the General Motors Research Laboratories and author of LOVE Letters to the Lubrication Engineers. Dr. Betsy Ancker-Johnson, Vice-President of General Motors from 5 February 1979 until her retirement 1 May 1992, an SAE Member since 1979 and on the SAE Board of Directors for 3 years, was the first woman Vice-President of any major automobile manufacturer and was nominated for the American Automobile Hall of Fame in 1994. Dr. Roberta Nichols, the first woman Fellow-Grade SAE Member (1989), was retired at the end of 1994 as Manager, Electric Vehicle External Affairs, Ford Motor Company, serving many years as Ford's Principal Fuels Research Engineer.

Since 1989, SAE has provided funding, curricula, and advisers to promote science/technical education through its, A World in Motion program for grades 4-through-6 in over 12% of the school districts in the United States. SAE was presented the President's Summit Award for volunteerism in introducing young students to the excitement of math, engineering, and science.

Over 250 SAE Student Branches and Clubs at most major engineering colleges and universities are similarly supported and encouraged to compete in SAE inter-school competitive events each year. These competitions include: Super Mileage Competition (with winners exceeding 2,000 miles-per-gallon); Formula SAE Race cars and races; Mini-Baja Off-Road Racing; Walking Machine Decathlon; hybrid (internal combustion engine--alternator/generator--electric motor) powered vehicles; Sunraycer (photovoltaic) electric vehicles; and Aeronautical Design involving radio-controlled aircraft competing in weight-carrying competitions.

The Society of Aeronautical Engineers merged with the SAE in 1917 and now comprise over 5,000 members. SAE publishes, monthly, a newspaper, UPdate, and the magazines Automotive Engineering and Aerospace Engineering, while selling over 60,000 technical and scientific books annually (1994).

The annual SAE International Congress and Exposition, held in the Cobo Center, Detroit, MI, is the world's largest and most prestigious automotive engineering event. The "Granddaddy" of 'em all. Long live the Society of Automotive Engineers!

412

**"Z" Cars:** of the 28 z-marqued cars the names of two started with "z" and ended with "z" and with nothing in-between. Just plain z's.

**Zagato:** a model designation of a named marque used by a number of manufacturers, notably by Carlo Abarth, the Austrian performance car aficionado, who modified stock Fiat, Porsche, and Simca models into true racing machines. The Abarth Zagato "Double-Bubble" coupe is the most widely known because of its many racing records.

**z-axis:** the third (with x and y) axis in a three-dimensional rectangular coordinate system. Widely used and essential in the design of vehicular stability and handling systems.

**zebra crossing:** the standard roadway surface marking of broad white or yellow stripes to indicate a crossing point at which pedestrians have the right-of-way over vehicles.

**zeolite:** any of various hydrous silicates used in cooling system liquids for anti-corrosion agents and as ion-exchangers and catalysts.

**zero-lash lifter:** a mechanical/hydraulic device that replaces a solid lifter ("tappet") between the valve-actuating push-rod and the rotating cam lobe on the camshaft insuring zero-clearance ("lash") in the valve system. Increased efficiency, lack of the typical "tapping" noise, longer life, and decreased maintenance are insured.

**Ziebart:** an aftermarket sealant, sound-proofing, anti-corrosion coating developed by a Chicaco entrepreneur to counteract the salt used for winter street-deicing.

**zig-zag:** an erratic travel pattern used deliberately to test the stability and handling of a vehicle and the skill of a driver. Sometimes indicative of a drinking or incompetent driver.

**zinc:** a bluish-white crystalline metal extensively used as a protective coating for iron and steel. Galvanize.

**zinc chromate:** a corrosion resistant yellowish-green coating (paint) used on metal particularly where salt is a hazard. Commonly found on highway bridges, vehicles exposed to salt air or road salt, and seaplanes operating on or near salt water.

**zipper:** a toothed closure mechanism used to provide access into air ducts, dust covers, and grease "boots" on vehicles.

**zirconium oxide:** a white crystalline compound ($CrO_2$) used in thermal and electrical insulation, in abrasives, and as pigment in enamels and glazes.

**Zyglo:** a non-destructive method of inspecting metal parts using a fluorescein dye penetrant illuminated by black light (ultraviolet) to reveal cracks or defects invisible to the unaided eye.


## LAGNIAPPE

**zerk fitting:** a pressure-ball quick-release attachment where lubricant is injected into vehicle moving joints as of steering linkage.

**ZF box:** a German-built transmission/transaxle favored by many top high-performance race car drivers throughout the world of racing.


## AUTOMOBILE ENGINES
### (BIG 'uns and little 'uns)

The biggest of the BIG--the 6,840 cubic inch show car with four 1710 cubic inch V-12 Allison aircraft engines that powered the P-38, P-39, P-40, P-63, B-39, and YFM-1 in World War II, built by Californian "Tex" Collins in the mid-fifties. The smallest, the <u>one</u> cubic inch streamliner that ran at Bonneville (62 mph)?

The in-betweens: Sir Henry Segrave, on 29 March 1927, drove a 2,746 cubic inch Sunbeam with two V-12 Napier Lion aircraft engines to 203.790 mph, becoming the first to go over 200 mph (two-way-run) at Daytona Beach, FL. Another Englishman, George Eyston's Thunderbolt with two Rolls-Royce aircraft engines displacing 4,392 cubic inches set world landspeed records at Daytona Beach in 1937-1938.

Several 28 liter V-1710 12-cylinder aircraft engines were driven in single-engined streamliners at Bonneville Salt Flats and at many dragstrips during the 1960s. The Arfons brothers, Art and Walt, were among the fastest.

In 1965 the American Summers Brothers established the wheel-driven landspeed record of 409.270 mph using four 7-liter Chrysler engines with about 2,400 horsepower. This record stood until 1991 when Al Teague drove his single-engine Dodge V-8 7-liter at 409.986 mph (The current piston-engine wheel-driven World Landspeed Record). At Bonneville Speed Week 1964, Alan Richards drove his streamliner 56 mph using a Garelli 2.8 cubic inch two-stroke engine.


## EXCUSES, EXCUSES
### (From Traffic Court Records)

The elderly pedestrian was unsure which direction to run, so I ran over him.

While entering the freeway, I glanced at my Mother-in-law, and headed over the embankment.

**COMMENTS**
(From those whose opinions the author values)


BEN, IT IS GREAT TO BE A "FAST WOMAN" AMONG YOUR <u>AUTOMOBILE</u>
<u>DICTIONARY'S</u> "FAST WOMEN".
         . . . . Janet Guthrie, the first woman to drive the
           "Indy 500", and still driving fast cars.


A DICTIONARY IN WHICH <u>AIN'T</u> IS "POLITICALLY CORRECT".
             . . . . Noah Webster's Ghost


READING THE DRAFT OF THE <u>AUTOMOBILE DICTIONARY</u> WAS A LOTTA
FUN AND WE LEARNED MANY THINGS ABOUT OUR CARS, INTERESTING
TRIVIA ABOUT AUTOMOBILES, AND HISTORY THAT WE NEVER KNEW
BEFORE. (WE GOT OUR TIPS). WANNA' KNOW THE "STRAIGHT SKINNY"?
WE LEARNED NOTHING FROM THE BOOK. DIDN"T READ IT! WE'D HEARD
IT ALL BEFORE--FIRST-HAND FROM THE AUTHOR. HE TALKS A LOT!
    . . . . The author's barber and his newspaper delivery boy.


WHEN ASKED, CLIVE CUSSLER AGREED: THIS DICTIONARY'S <u>TRUTHS</u>
(LIKE THE ONE-WHEELED AUTOMOBILE AND THE ONE WITH THE 6,840
CUBIC INCH ENGINES) VERIFY LORD BYRON'S CONTENTION IN <u>DON JUAN</u>,
CANTO XIV, STANZA 3, THAT "TRUTH <u>IS</u> STRANGER THAN <u>FICTION</u>".
   . . . . Clive Cussler, whose over 60,000,000 volumes of high-
      adventure novels involving automobiles, and still writing
      <u>fiction</u>, give him a photo-finish in any race with <u>truth</u>.


A BOOK THAT LEGITIMIZES ONE HENRY'S (CAVENDISH) HYDROGEN USED
IN ANOTHER HENRY'S (FORD) TIN LIZZIE.
         . . . . The shades of "999" and Phlogiston


THERE'S THAT SMELL IN THIS DICTIONARY, OF CASTOR OIL AND DISKS
IN A BURNED CLUTCH -- REMINISCENT OF MY V-12 PACKARD'S AROMAS.
           . . . . Merle Norman's Memories
        (Who created such pleasant perfumes and
         collected so many great automobiles.)


ONE CAN HEAR THE MELDING OF MELODIES FROM THE TAIL-PIPE OF
ANY MODEL T FORD WITH RETARDED SPARK, FROM A B-29'S TURBO-
WASTE-GATE AT TAKE-OFF POWER, AND FROM AN OFFY ON THE "INDY"
BACK-CHUTE--WHEN YOU OPEN THIS BOOK. LISTEN!
       . . . . Channeled down from our "Iron Eagle",
    General Curtis E. LeMay, on whose TWENTIETH AIR FORCE
    WORLD WAR II B-29 staff the author served.


WISH THIS BOOK BORE THE CLYMER BY-LINE . . . . Floyd's ghost.